Lucifer

A Dalliance with the Damned

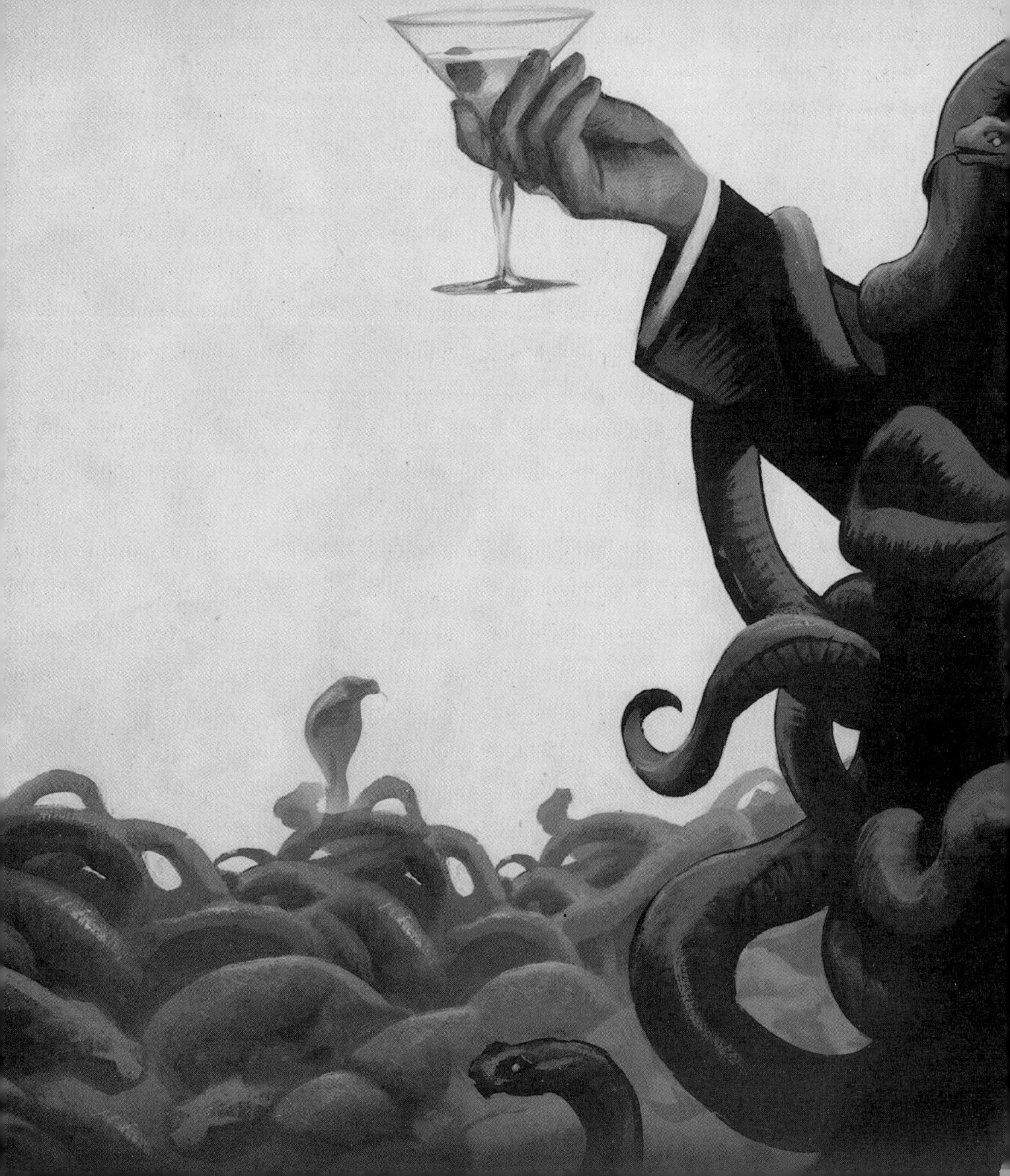

LUCIFER: A DALLIANCE WITH THE DAMNED

DC Comics, 1700 Broadway, New York, NY 10019
A division of Warner Bros. - An AOL Time Warner Company
Printed in Canada. Second Printing.
ISBN: 1-56389-892-6
Cover illustrations by Christopher Moeller

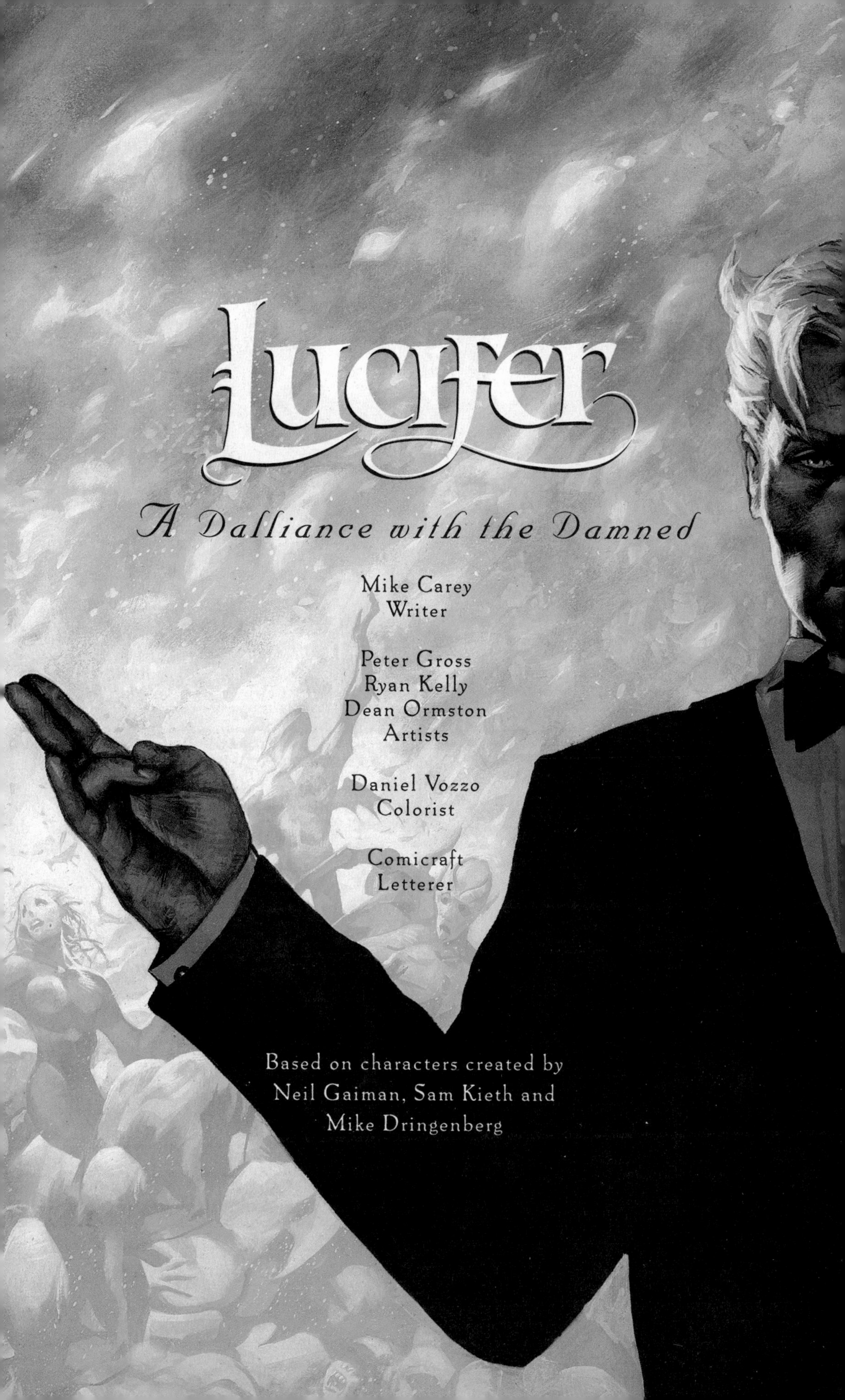

Lucifer

A Dalliance with the Damned

Mike Carey
Writer

Peter Gross
Ryan Kelly
Dean Ormston
Artists

Daniel Vozzo
Colorist

Comicraft
Letterer

Based on characters created by
Neil Gaiman, Sam Kieth and
Mike Dringenberg

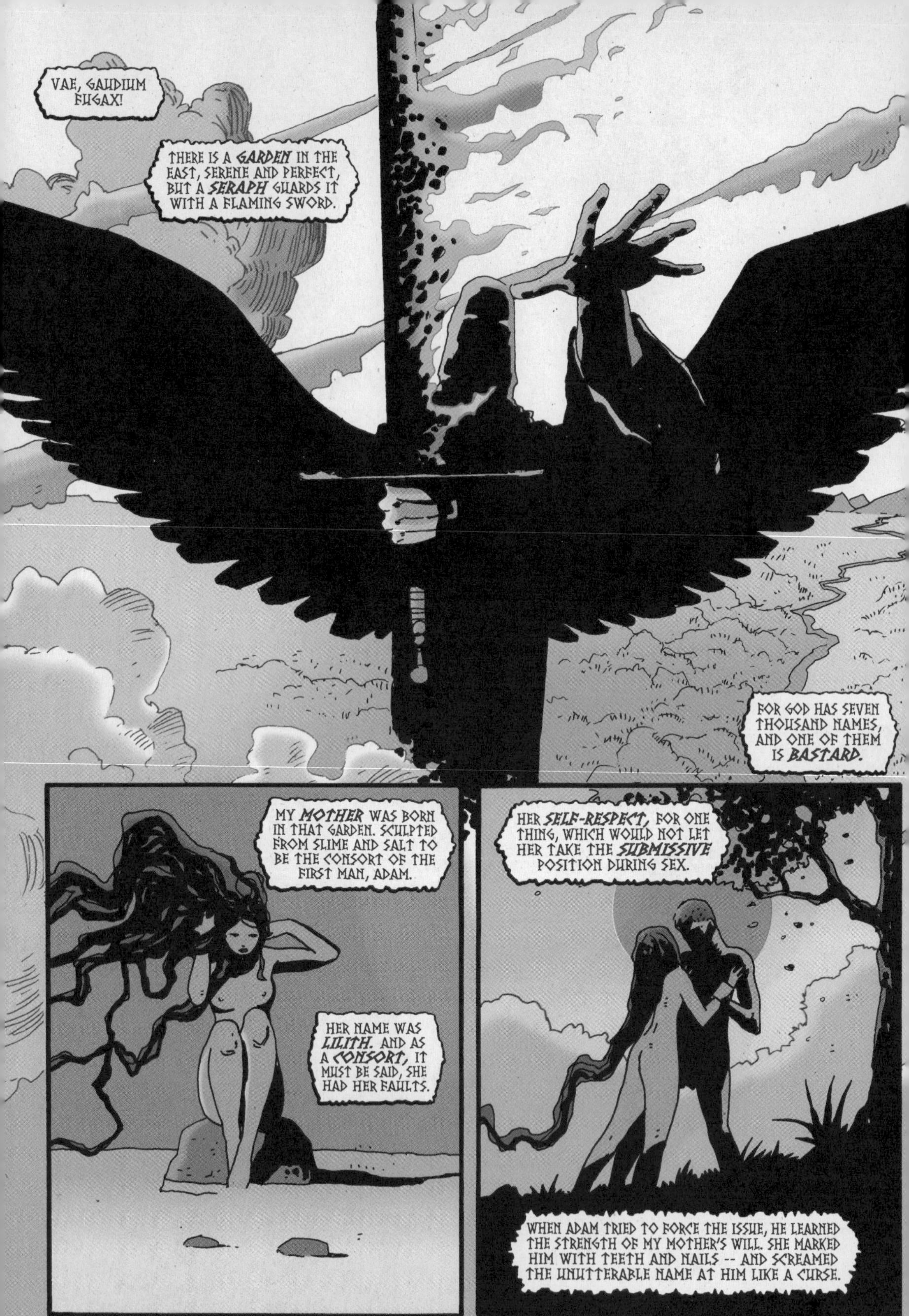
VAE, GAUDIUM FUGAX!
THERE IS A GARDEN IN THE EAST, SERENE AND PERFECT, BUT A SERAPH GUARDS IT WITH A FLAMING SWORD.
FOR GOD HAS SEVEN THOUSAND NAMES, AND ONE OF THEM IS BASTARD.
MY MOTHER WAS BORN IN THAT GARDEN. SCULPTED FROM SLIME AND SALT TO BE THE CONSORT OF THE FIRST MAN, ADAM.
HER NAME WAS LILITH. AND AS A CONSORT, IT MUST BE SAID, SHE HAD HER FAULTS.
HER SELF-RESPECT, FOR ONE THING, WHICH WOULD NOT LET HER TAKE THE SUBMISSIVE POSITION DURING SEX.
WHEN ADAM TRIED TO FORCE THE ISSUE, HE LEARNED THE STRENGTH OF MY MOTHER'S WILL. SHE MARKED HIM WITH TEETH AND NAILS -- AND SCREAMED THE UNUTTERABLE NAME AT HIM LIKE A CURSE.

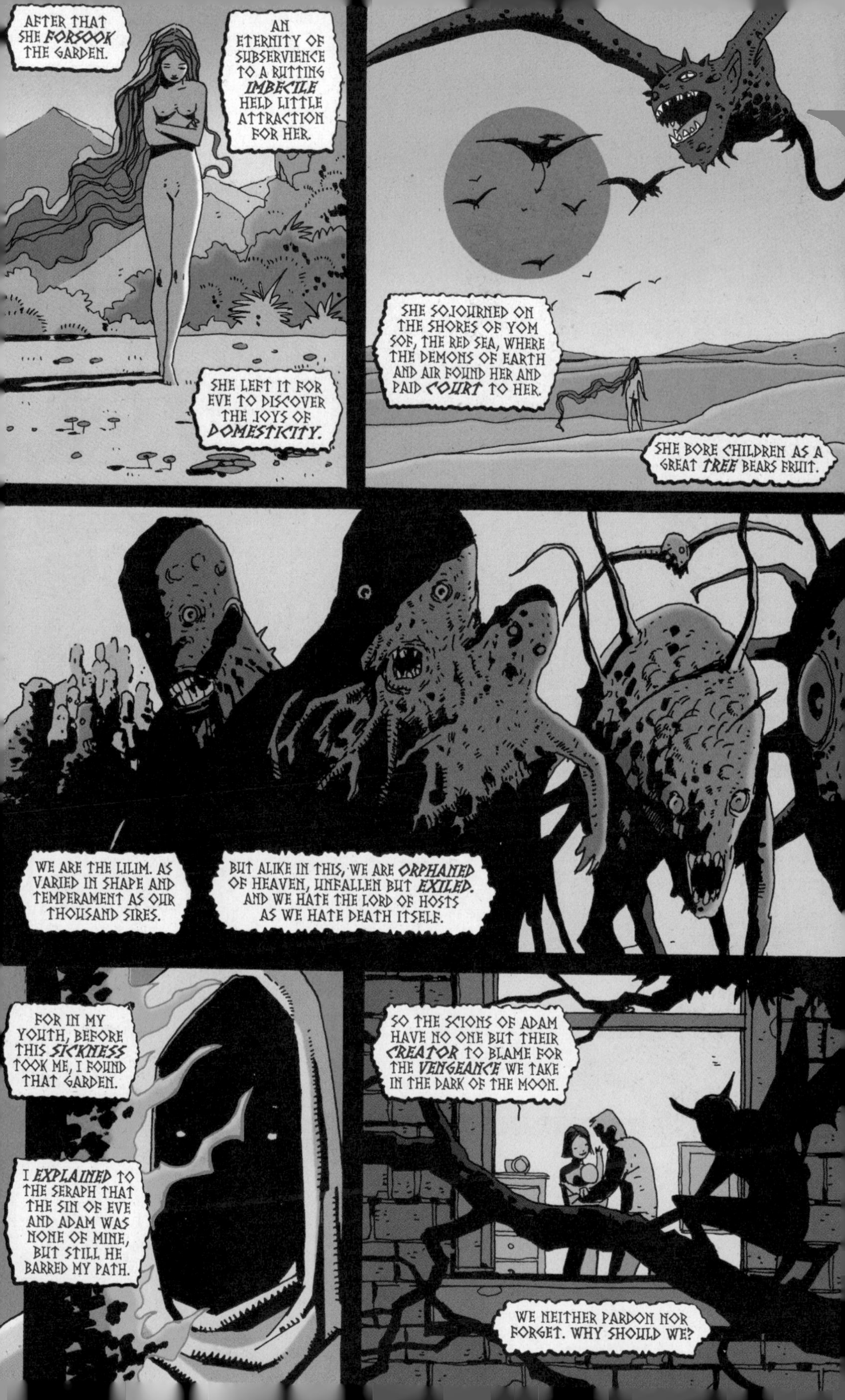
AFTER THAT SHE FORSOOK THE GARDEN.
AN ETERNITY OF SUBSERVIENCE TO A RUTTING IMBECILE HELD LITTLE ATTRACTION FOR HER.
SHE LEFT IT FOR EVE TO DISCOVER THE JOYS OF DOMESTICITY.
SHE SOJOURNED ON THE SHORES OF YOM SOF, THE RED SEA, WHERE THE DEMONS OF EARTH AND AIR FOUND HER AND PAID COURT TO HER.
SHE BORE CHILDREN AS A GREAT TREE BEARS FRUIT.
WE ARE THE LILIM. AS VARIED IN SHAPE AND TEMPERAMENT AS OUR THOUSAND SIRES.
BUT ALIKE IN THIS, WE ARE ORPHANED OF HEAVEN, UNFALLEN BUT EXILED. AND WE HATE THE LORD OF HOSTS AS WE HATE DEATH ITSELF.
FOR IN MY YOUTH, BEFORE THIS SICKNESS TOOK ME, I FOUND THAT GARDEN.
I EXPLAINED TO THE SERAPH THAT THE SIN OF EVE AND ADAM WAS NONE OF MINE, BUT STILL HE BARRED MY PATH.
SO THE SCIONS OF ADAM HAVE NO ONE BUT THEIR CREATOR TO BLAME FOR THE VENGEANCE WE TAKE IN THE DARK OF THE MOON.
WE NEITHER PARDON NOR FORGET. WHY SHOULD WE?

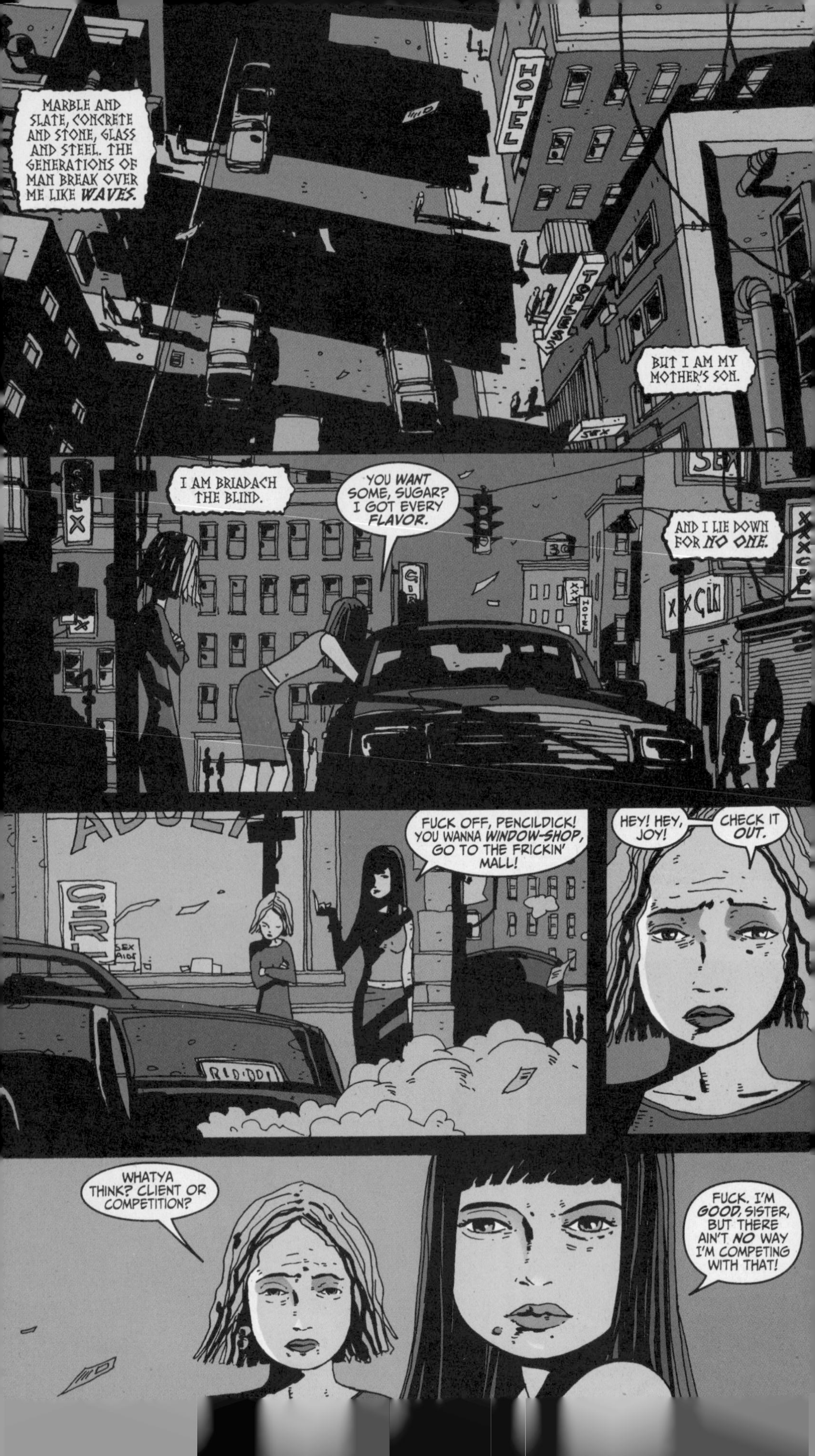
MARBLE AND SLATE, CONCRETE AND STONE, GLASS AND STEEL. THE GENERATIONS OF MAN BREAK OVER ME LIKE WAVES.
HOTEL
TOPLESS
BUT I AM MY MOTHER'S SON.
SEX
I AM BRIADACH THE BLIND.
YOU WANT SOME, SUGAR? I GOT EVERY FLAVOR.
AND I LIE DOWN FOR NO ONE.
HOTEL
FUCK OFF, PENCILDICK! YOU WANNA WINDOW-SHOP, GO TO THE FRICKIN' MALL!
HEY! HEY, JOY!
CHECK IT OUT.
WHATYA THINK? CLIENT OR COMPETITION?
FUCK. I'M GOOD, SISTER, BUT THERE AIN'T NO WAY I'M COMPETING WITH THAT!

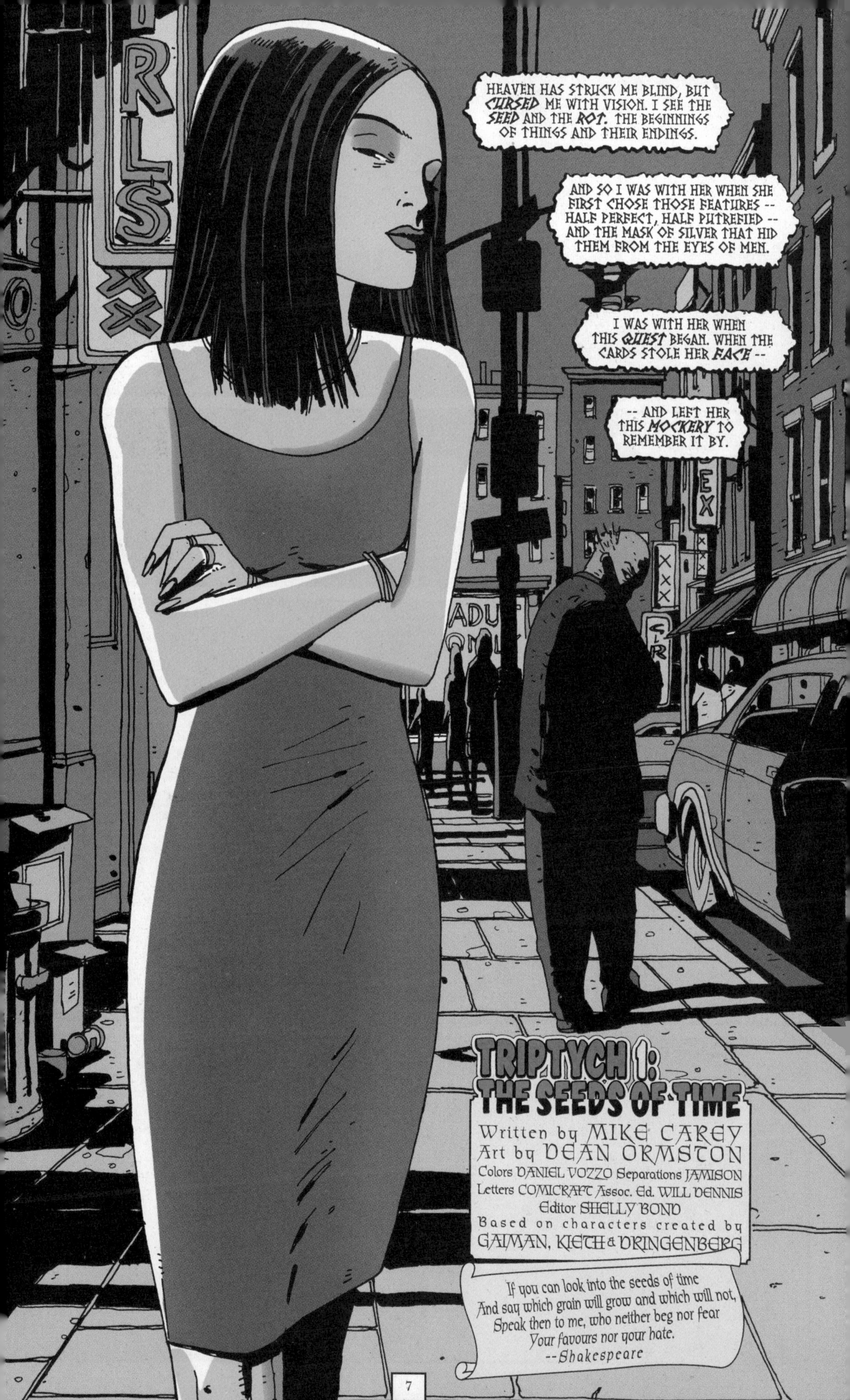

HEAVEN HAS STRUCK ME BLIND, BUT CURSED ME WITH VISION. I SEE THE SEED AND THE ROT. THE BEGINNINGS OF THINGS AND THEIR ENDINGS.
AND SO I WAS WITH HER WHEN SHE FIRST CHOSE THOSE FEATURES -- HALF PERFECT, HALF PUTREFIED -- AND THE MASK OF SILVER THAT HID THEM FROM THE EYES OF MEN.
I WAS WITH HER WHEN THIS QUEST BEGAN. WHEN THE CARDS STOLE HER FACE --
-- AND LEFT HER THIS MOCKERY TO REMEMBER IT BY.
TRIPTYCH 1: THE SEEDS OF TIME
Written by MIKE CAREY
Art by DEAN ORMSTON
Colors DANIEL VOZZO Separations JAMISON
Letters COMICRAFT Assoc. Ed. WILL DENNIS
Editor SHELLY BOND
Based on characters created by
GAIMAN, KIETH & DRINGENBERG
If you can look into the seeds of time
And say which grain will grow and which will not,
Speak then to me, who neither beg nor fear
Your favours nor your hate.
--Shakespeare

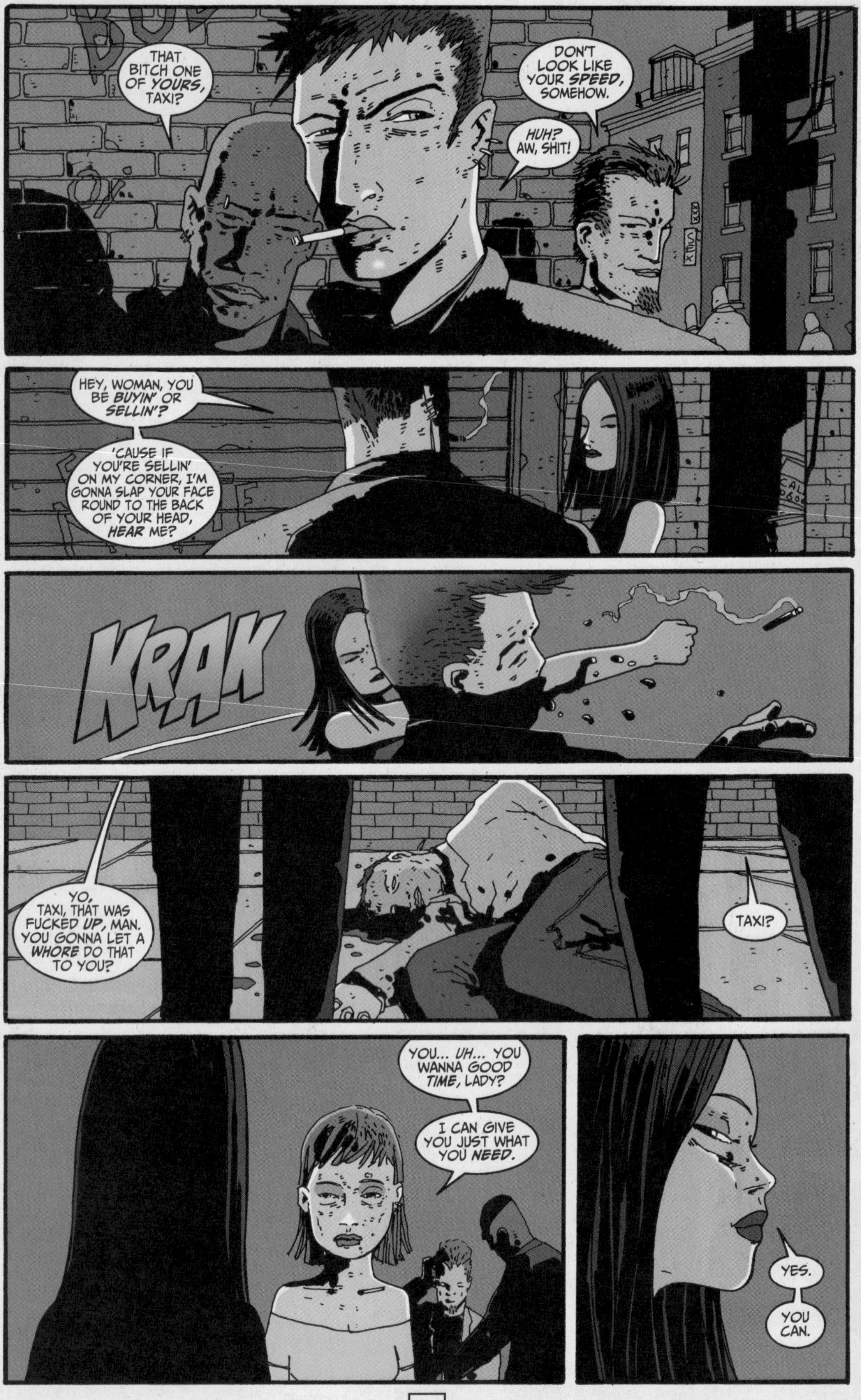
THAT BITCH ONE OF YOURS, TAXI?
DON'T LOOK LIKE YOUR SPEED, SOMEHOW.
HUH? AW, SHIT!
HEY, WOMAN, YOU BE BUYIN' OR SELLIN'?
'CAUSE IF YOU'RE SELLIN' ON MY CORNER, I'M GONNA SLAP YOUR FACE ROUND TO THE BACK OF YOUR HEAD, HEAR ME?
KRAK
YO, TAXI, THAT WAS FUCKED UP, MAN. YOU GONNA LET A WHORE DO THAT TO YOU?
TAXI?
YOU... UH... YOU WANNA GOOD TIME, LADY?
I CAN GIVE YOU JUST WHAT YOU NEED.
YES.
YOU CAN.

-- ONE OF SEVERAL FREEWAY ACCIDENTS APPARENTLY CAUSED BY DRIVERS LITERALLY FALLING ASLEEP AT THE WHEEL.

NOW FOR MORE ON THOSE UFO SIGHTINGS IN L.A., LET'S --

SO WHAT WAY DO YOU LIKE IT? YOU WANNA DO A SIXTY-NINE, OR WHAT?

I WANT YOU TO BE *QUIET*. VERY QUIET.

OR ELSE I WILL HOOK OUT YOUR *EYEBALLS* WITH MY FINGERS.

OH JESUS. OH PLEASE, LADY, DON'T *KILL* ME.

I GOT A KID. I SWEAR, YOU CAN DO WHATEVER YOU WANT AND NOT EVEN PAY.

I'M NOT GOING TO KILL YOU.

HER MAGIC IS LIKE *MINE* -- LIKE ALL OUR KIN'S. BLOOD AND PISS. SEMEN AND TEARS. MUCUS AND MENSTRUM.

THE *KISS* IS TO MIX THEIR JUICES.

THEN SHE SPITS ON THE FLOOR, AND DRAWS A *CIRCLE*.

NO PENTAGRAM. NO WORDS OF BINDING. JUST A CIRCLE.

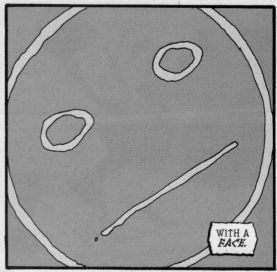

WITH A *FACE*.

WH... WHAT ARE YOU --?
OH GOD! OH PLEASE!
GAAAAHH!
IT WON'T *TAKE.*
SHE TRIES THREE MORE TIMES BUT THE RESULT IS THE SAME.
THE *WHORE'S* FACE IS AS MALLEABLE AS PLASTIC, BUT HER *OWN* REFUSES TO SWAP PLACES WITH IT.
AH! AH! AH!
HER OPTIONS HAVE NARROWED TO *ONE.* THE RISK IS GREAT, AND THE CHANCE OF SUCCESS VERY SLIM...
BUT SHE'S GOING TO HAVE TO FALL BACK ON HER *FAMILY.*

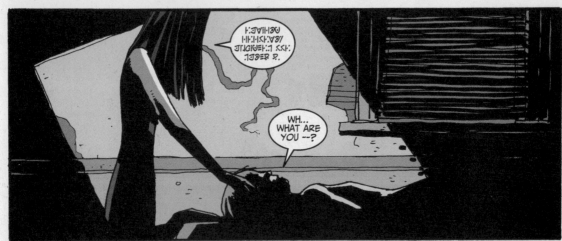

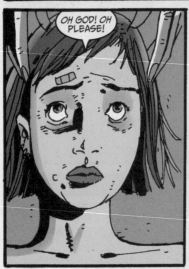

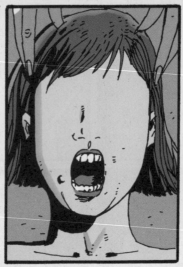

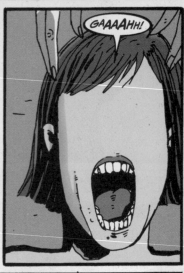

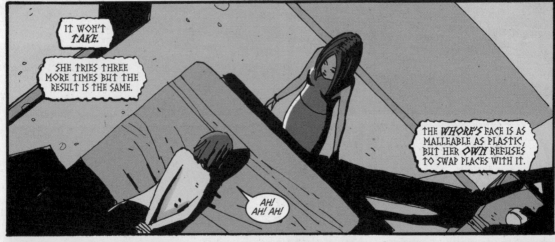

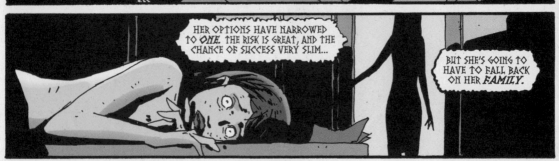

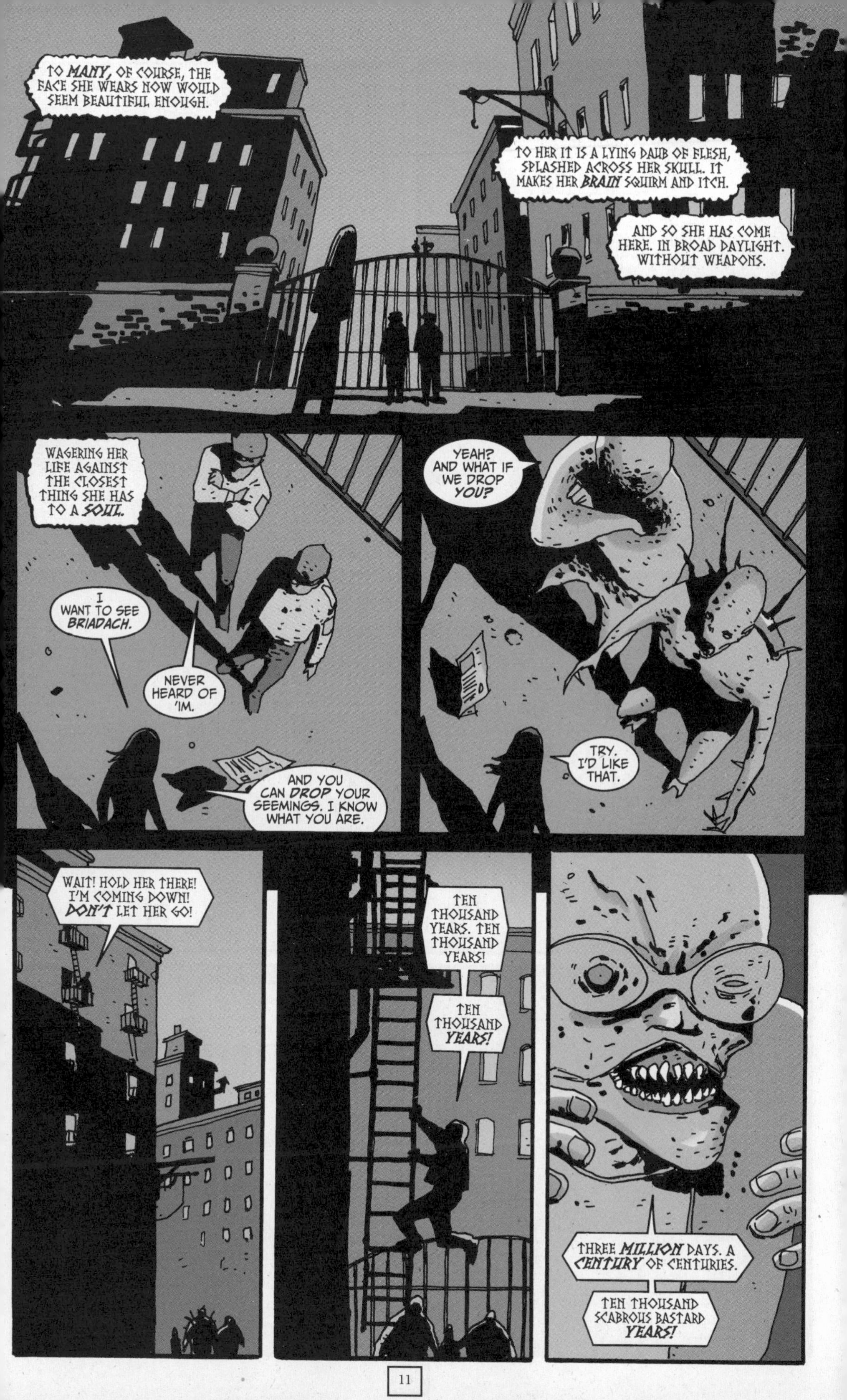
TO MANY, OF COURSE, THE FACE SHE WEARS NOW WOULD SEEM BEAUTIFUL ENOUGH.
TO HER IT IS A LYING DAUB OF FLESH, SPLASHED ACROSS HER SKULL. IT MAKES HER BRAIN SQUIRM AND ITCH.
AND SO SHE HAS COME HERE. IN BROAD DAYLIGHT. WITHOUT WEAPONS.
WAGERING HER LIFE AGAINST THE CLOSEST THING SHE HAS TO A SOUL.
I WANT TO SEE BRIADACH.
NEVER HEARD OF 'IM.
AND YOU CAN DROP YOUR SEEMINGS. I KNOW WHAT YOU ARE.
YEAH? AND WHAT IF WE DROP YOU?
TRY. I'D LIKE THAT.
WAIT! HOLD HER THERE! I'M COMING DOWN! DON'T LET HER GO!
TEN THOUSAND YEARS. TEN THOUSAND YEARS!
TEN THOUSAND YEARS!
THREE MILLION DAYS. A CENTURY OF CENTURIES.
TEN THOUSAND SCABROUS BASTARD YEARS!

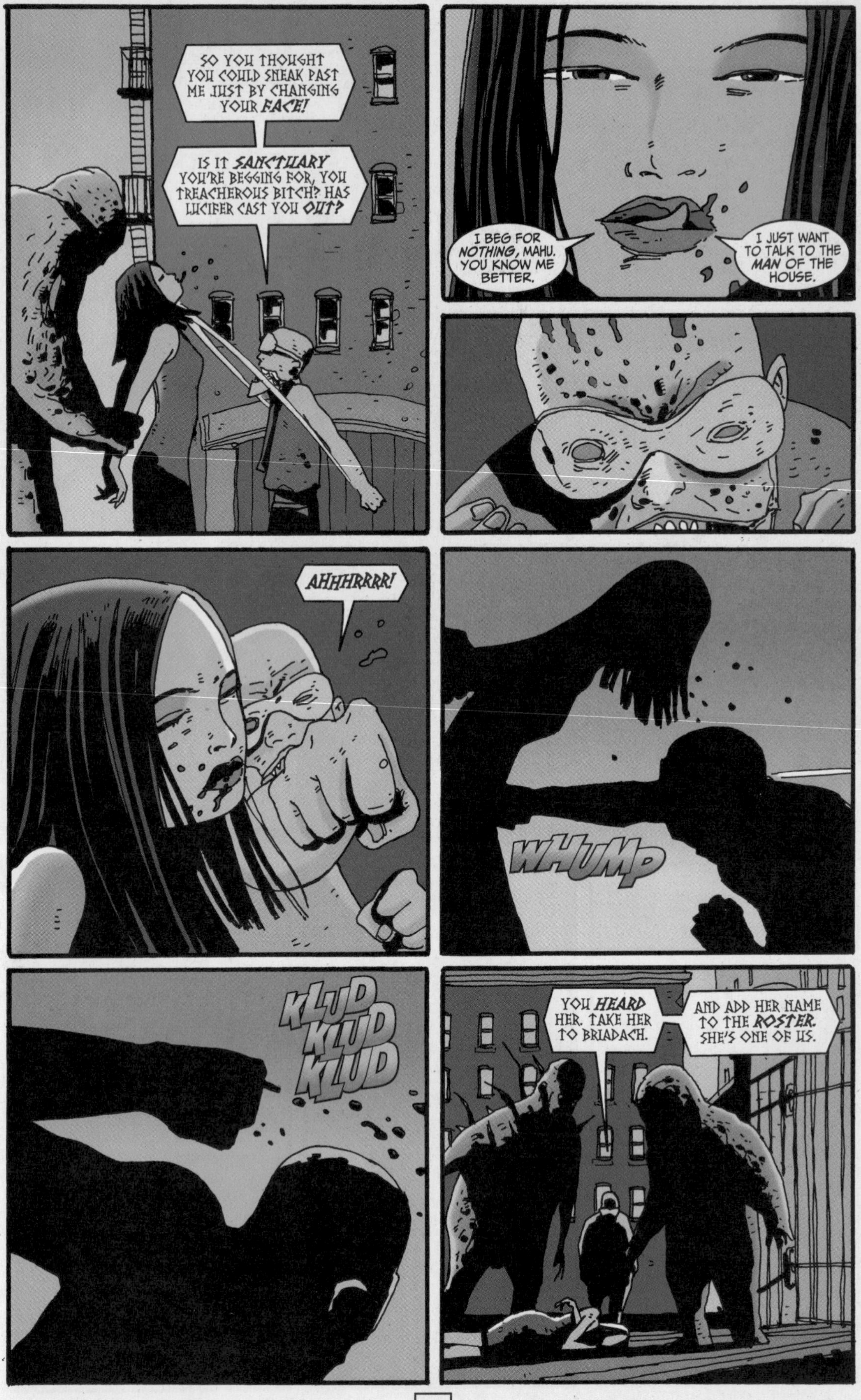
SO YOU THOUGHT YOU COULD SNEAK PAST ME JUST BY CHANGING YOUR FACE!
IS IT SANCTUARY YOU'RE BEGGING FOR, YOU TREACHEROUS BITCH? HAS LUCIFER CAST YOU OUT?
I BEG FOR NOTHING, MAHU. YOU KNOW ME BETTER.
I JUST WANT TO TALK TO THE MAN OF THE HOUSE.
AHHHRRRR!
WHUMP
KLUD KLUD KLUD
YOU HEARD HER. TAKE HER TO BRIADACH.
AND ADD HER NAME TO THE ROSTER. SHE'S ONE OF US.

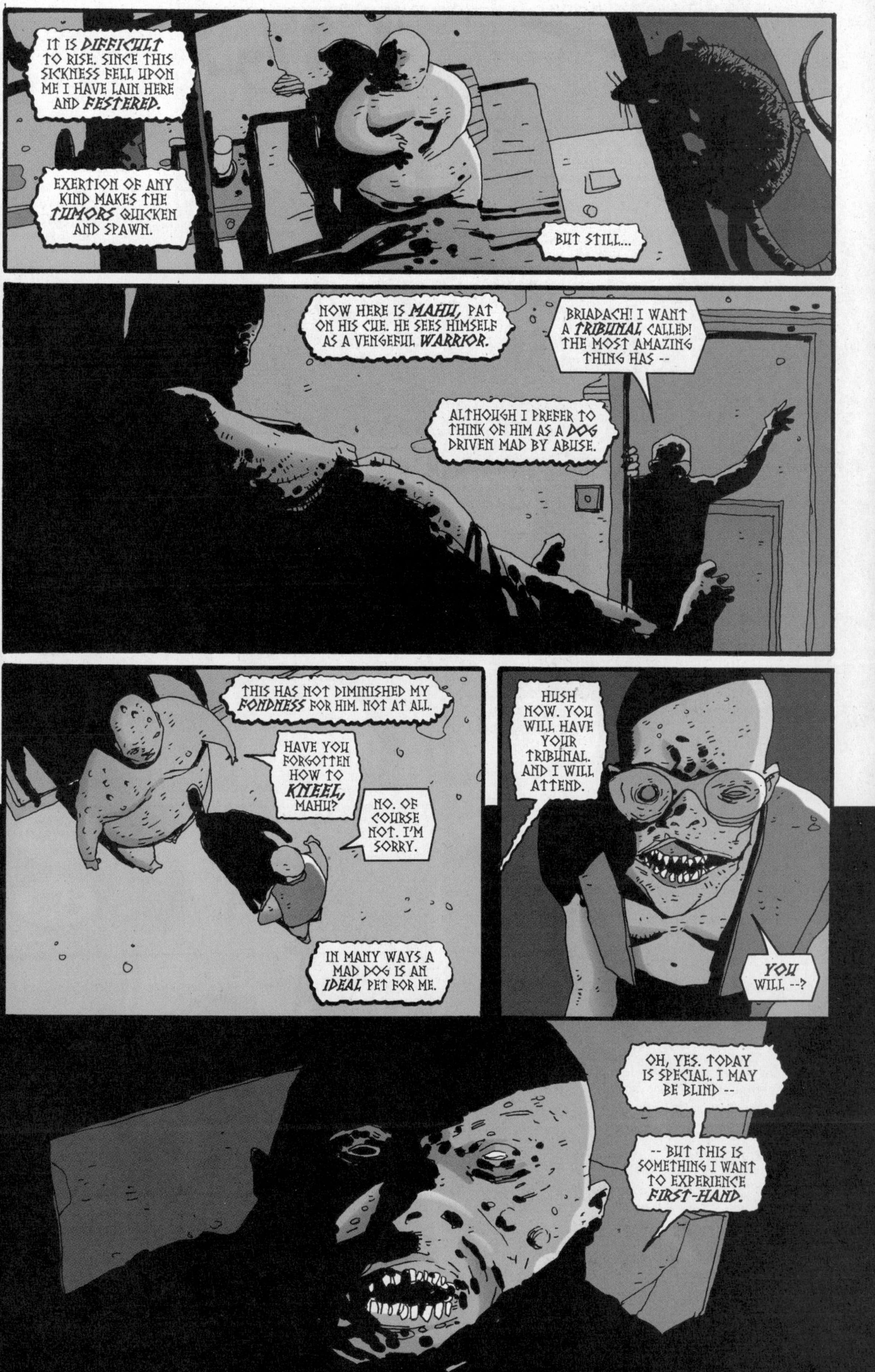
IT IS DIFFICULT TO RISE. SINCE THIS SICKNESS FELL UPON ME I HAVE LAIN HERE AND FESTERED.
EXERTION OF ANY KIND MAKES THE TUMORS QUICKEN AND SPAWN.
BUT STILL...
NOW HERE IS MAHU, PAT ON HIS CUE. HE SEES HIMSELF AS A VENGEFUL WARRIOR.
BRIADACH! I WANT A TRIBUNAL CALLED! THE MOST AMAZING THING HAS --
ALTHOUGH I PREFER TO THINK OF HIM AS A DOG DRIVEN MAD BY ABUSE.
THIS HAS NOT DIMINISHED MY FONDNESS FOR HIM. NOT AT ALL.
HAVE YOU FORGOTTEN HOW TO KNEEL, MAHU?
NO. OF COURSE NOT. I'M SORRY.
IN MANY WAYS A MAD DOG IS AN IDEAL PET FOR ME.
HUSH NOW. YOU WILL HAVE YOUR TRIBUNAL. AND I WILL ATTEND.
YOU WILL --?
OH, YES. TODAY IS SPECIAL. I MAY BE BLIND --
-- BUT THIS IS SOMETHING I WANT TO EXPERIENCE FIRST-HAND.

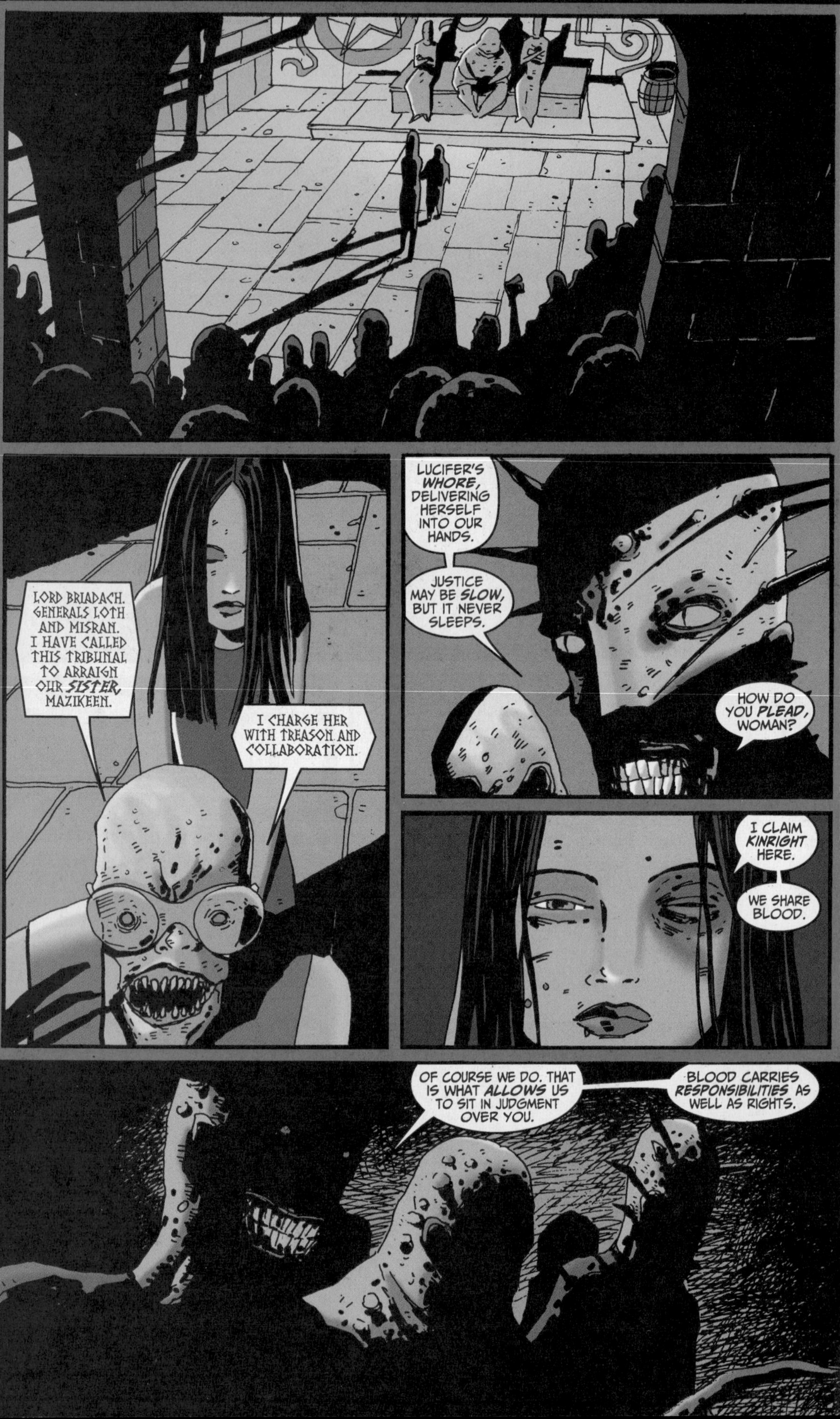
LORD BRIADACH. GENERALS LOTH AND MISRAN. I HAVE CALLED THIS TRIBUNAL TO ARRAIGN OUR SISTER, MAZIKEEN.
I CHARGE HER WITH TREASON. AND COLLABORATION.
LUCIFER'S WHORE, DELIVERING HERSELF INTO OUR HANDS.
JUSTICE MAY BE SLOW, BUT IT NEVER SLEEPS.
HOW DO YOU PLEAD, WOMAN?
I CLAIM KINRIGHT HERE.
WE SHARE BLOOD.
OF COURSE WE DO. THAT IS WHAT ALLOWS US TO SIT IN JUDGMENT OVER YOU.
BLOOD CARRIES RESPONSIBILITIES AS WELL AS RIGHTS.

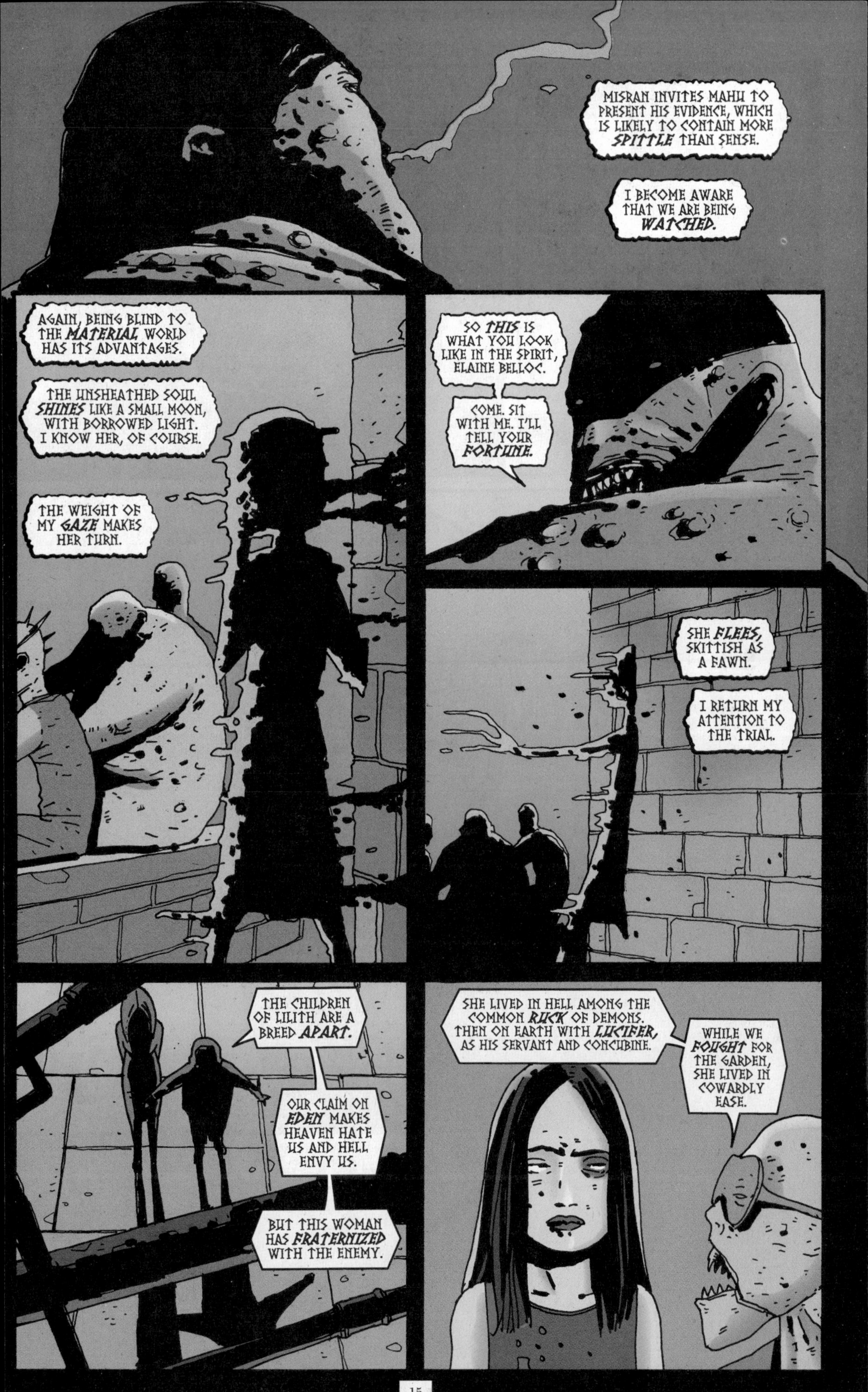
MISRAN INVITES MAHU TO PRESENT HIS EVIDENCE, WHICH IS LIKELY TO CONTAIN MORE SPITTLE THAN SENSE.
I BECOME AWARE THAT WE ARE BEING WATCHED.
AGAIN, BEING BLIND TO THE MATERIAL WORLD HAS ITS ADVANTAGES.
THE UNSHEATHED SOUL SHINES LIKE A SMALL MOON, WITH BORROWED LIGHT. I KNOW HER, OF COURSE.
THE WEIGHT OF MY GAZE MAKES HER TURN.
SO THIS IS WHAT YOU LOOK LIKE IN THE SPIRIT, ELAINE BELLOC.
COME. SIT WITH ME. I'LL TELL YOUR FORTUNE.
SHE FLEES, SKITTISH AS A FAWN.
I RETURN MY ATTENTION TO THE TRIAL.
THE CHILDREN OF LILITH ARE A BREED APART.
OUR CLAIM ON EDEN MAKES HEAVEN HATE US AND HELL ENVY US.
BUT THIS WOMAN HAS FRATERNIZED WITH THE ENEMY.
SHE LIVED IN HELL AMONG THE COMMON RUCK OF DEMONS. THEN ON EARTH WITH LUCIFER, AS HIS SERVANT AND CONCUBINE.
WHILE WE FOUGHT FOR THE GARDEN, SHE LIVED IN COWARDLY EASE.

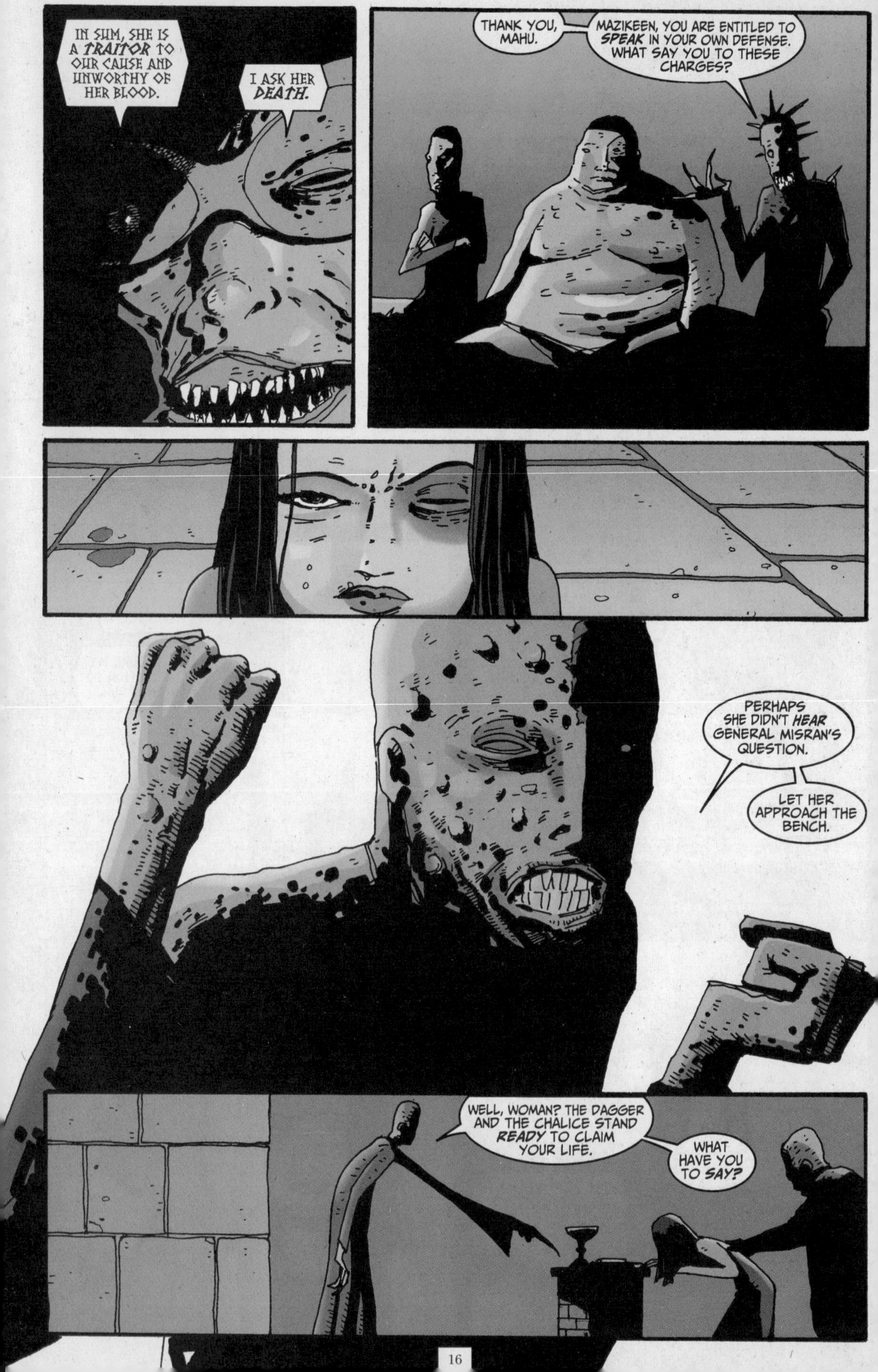
IN SUM, SHE IS A TRAITOR TO OUR CAUSE AND UNWORTHY OF HER BLOOD.
I ASK HER DEATH.
THANK YOU, MAHU.
MAZIKEEN, YOU ARE ENTITLED TO SPEAK IN YOUR OWN DEFENSE. WHAT SAY YOU TO THESE CHARGES?
PERHAPS SHE DIDN'T HEAR GENERAL MISRAN'S QUESTION.
LET HER APPROACH THE BENCH.
WELL, WOMAN? THE DAGGER AND THE CHALICE STAND READY TO CLAIM YOUR LIFE.
WHAT HAVE YOU TO SAY?

THE BITCH IS MOCKING US.
LOTH. SHE THINKS TO OUTMANEUVER US. SHE KNOWS WE CAN'T GIVE A VERDICT WITHOUT HEARING HER DEFENSE.
BUT THERE IS ALWAYS TRIAL BY COMBAT.
NO, NO. MAHU WILL LOSE. YOU KNOW HER REPUTATION.
I SAY AS LITTLE AS POSSIBLE.
IT IS PERMISSIBLE TO HANDICAP HER.
DESTINY NEEDS A PUSH. BUT A VERY SMALL PUSH WILL DO.
BRING CHAINS. AND A BLINDFOLD.
IF SHE WON'T SPEAK, THEN LET HER FIGHT.

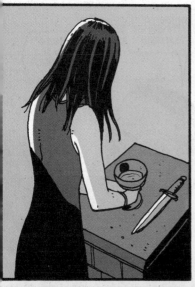

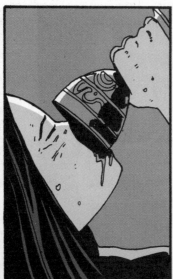

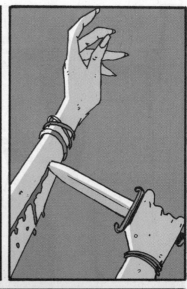

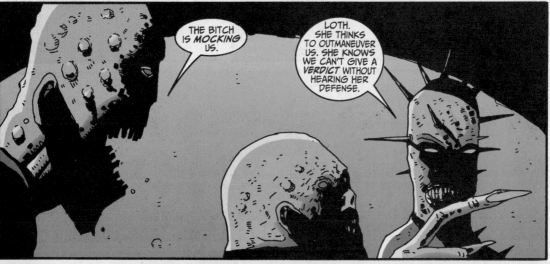

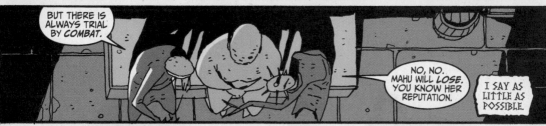

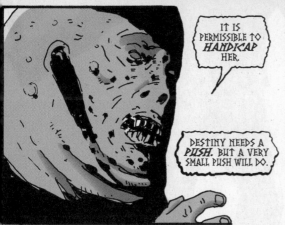

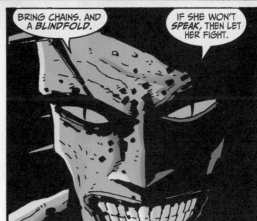

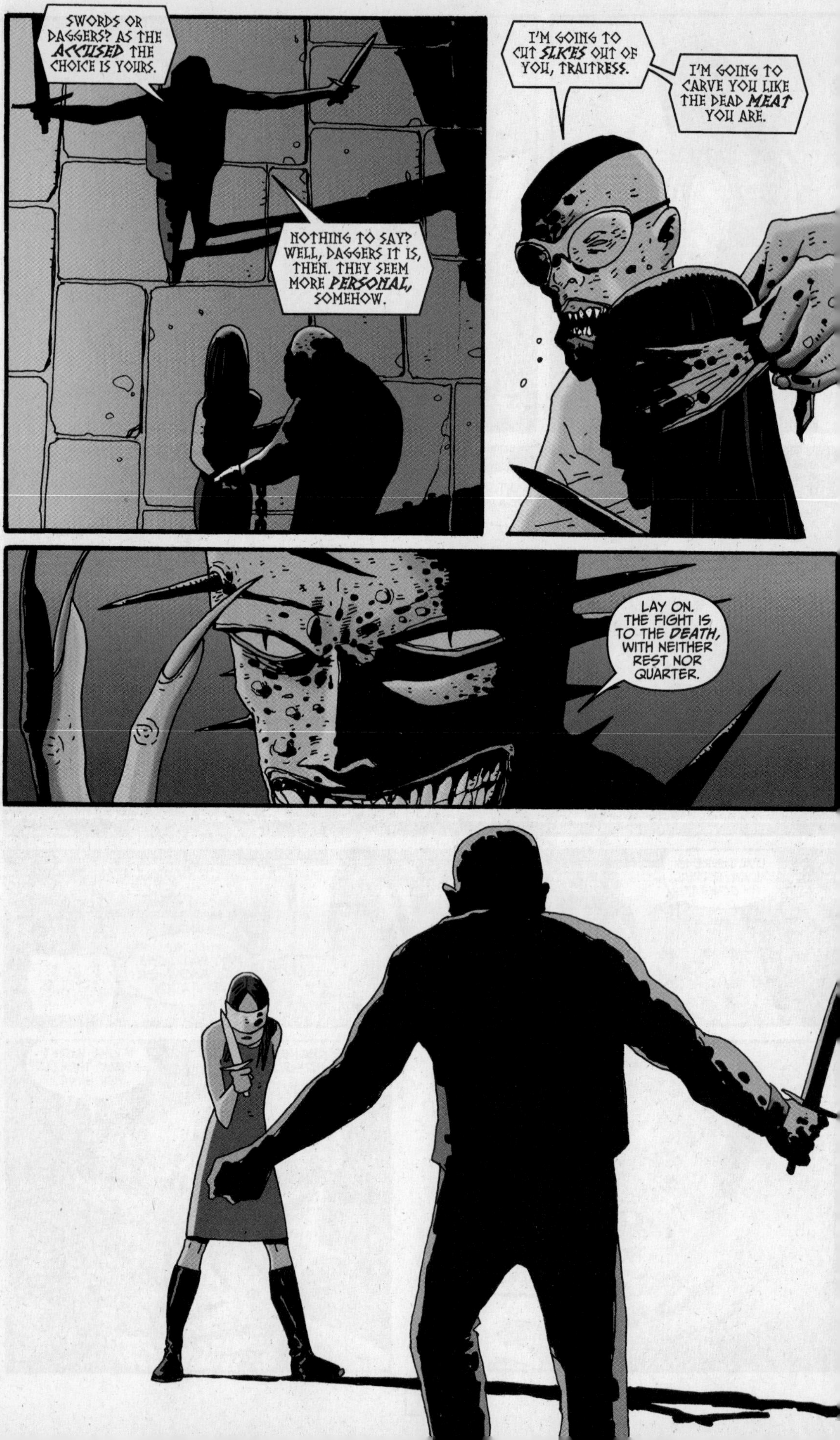
SWORDS OR DAGGERS? AS THE ACCUSED THE CHOICE IS YOURS.
NOTHING TO SAY? WELL, DAGGERS IT IS, THEN. THEY SEEM MORE PERSONAL, SOMEHOW.
I'M GOING TO CUT SLICES OUT OF YOU, TRAITRESS.
I'M GOING TO CARVE YOU LIKE THE DEAD MEAT YOU ARE.
LAY ON. THE FIGHT IS TO THE DEATH, WITH NEITHER REST NOR QUARTER.

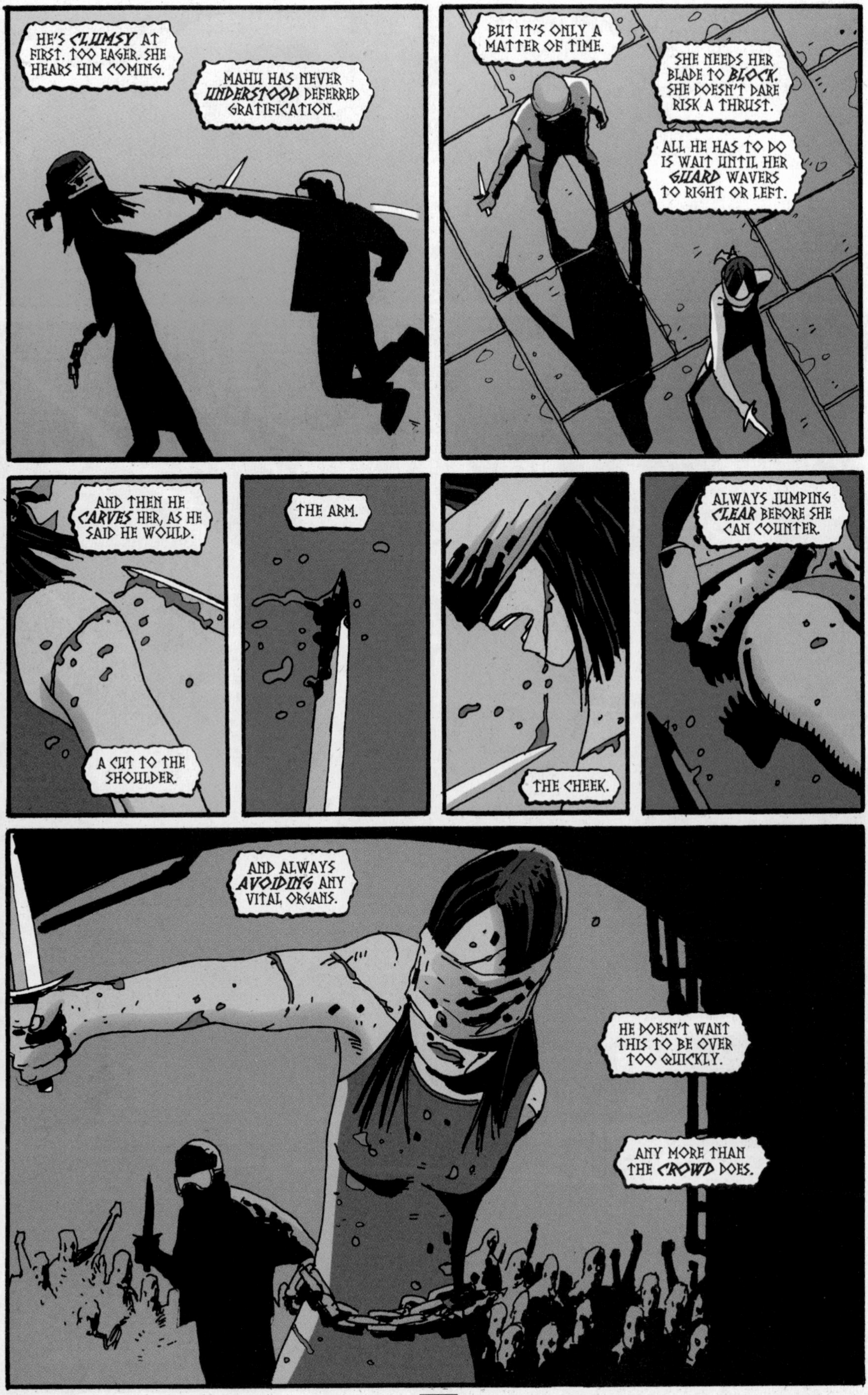
HE'S CLUMSY AT FIRST. TOO EAGER. SHE HEARS HIM COMING.
MAHU HAS NEVER UNDERSTOOD DEFERRED GRATIFICATION.
BUT IT'S ONLY A MATTER OF TIME.
SHE NEEDS HER BLADE TO BLOCK. SHE DOESN'T DARE RISK A THRUST.
ALL HE HAS TO DO IS WAIT UNTIL HER GUARD WAVERS TO RIGHT OR LEFT.
AND THEN HE CARVES HER, AS HE SAID HE WOULD.
A CUT TO THE SHOULDER.
THE ARM.
THE CHEEK.
ALWAYS JUMPING CLEAR BEFORE SHE CAN COUNTER.
AND ALWAYS AVOIDING ANY VITAL ORGANS.
HE DOESN'T WANT THIS TO BE OVER TOO QUICKLY.
ANY MORE THAN THE CROWD DOES.

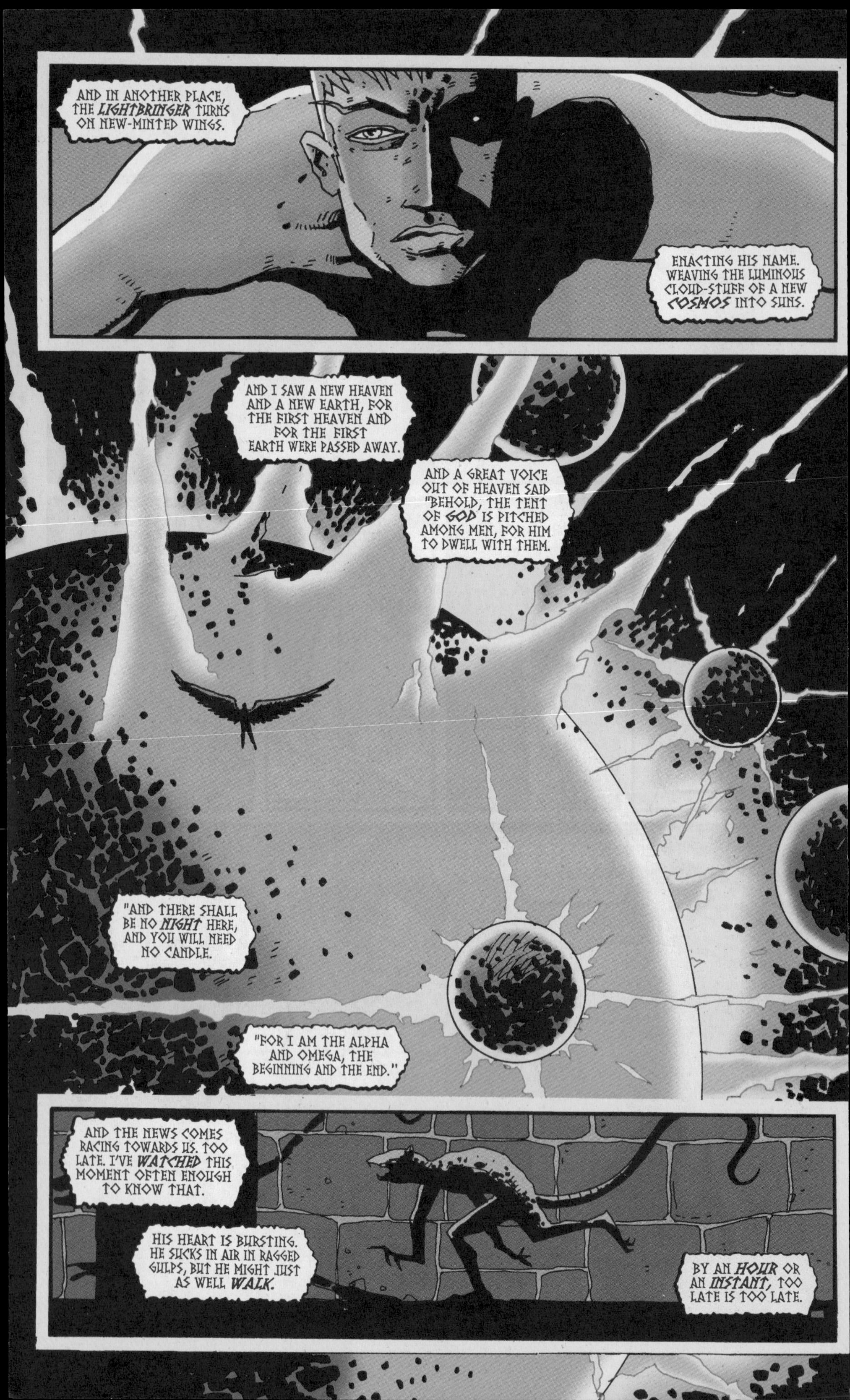
AND IN ANOTHER PLACE, THE LIGHTBRINGER TURNS ON NEW-MINTED WINGS.
ENACTING HIS NAME. WEAVING THE LUMINOUS CLOUD-STUFF OF A NEW COSMOS INTO SUNS.
AND I SAW A NEW HEAVEN AND A NEW EARTH, FOR THE FIRST HEAVEN AND FOR THE FIRST EARTH WERE PASSED AWAY.
AND A GREAT VOICE OUT OF HEAVEN SAID "BEHOLD, THE TENT OF GOD IS PITCHED AMONG MEN, FOR HIM TO DWELL WITH THEM.
"AND THERE SHALL BE NO NIGHT HERE, AND YOU WILL NEED NO CANDLE.
"FOR I AM THE ALPHA AND OMEGA, THE BEGINNING AND THE END."
AND THE NEWS COMES RACING TOWARDS US. TOO LATE. I'VE WATCHED THIS MOMENT OFTEN ENOUGH TO KNOW THAT.
HIS HEART IS BURSTING. HE SUCKS IN AIR IN RAGGED GULPS, BUT HE MIGHT JUST AS WELL WALK.
BY AN HOUR OR AN INSTANT, TOO LATE IS TOO LATE.

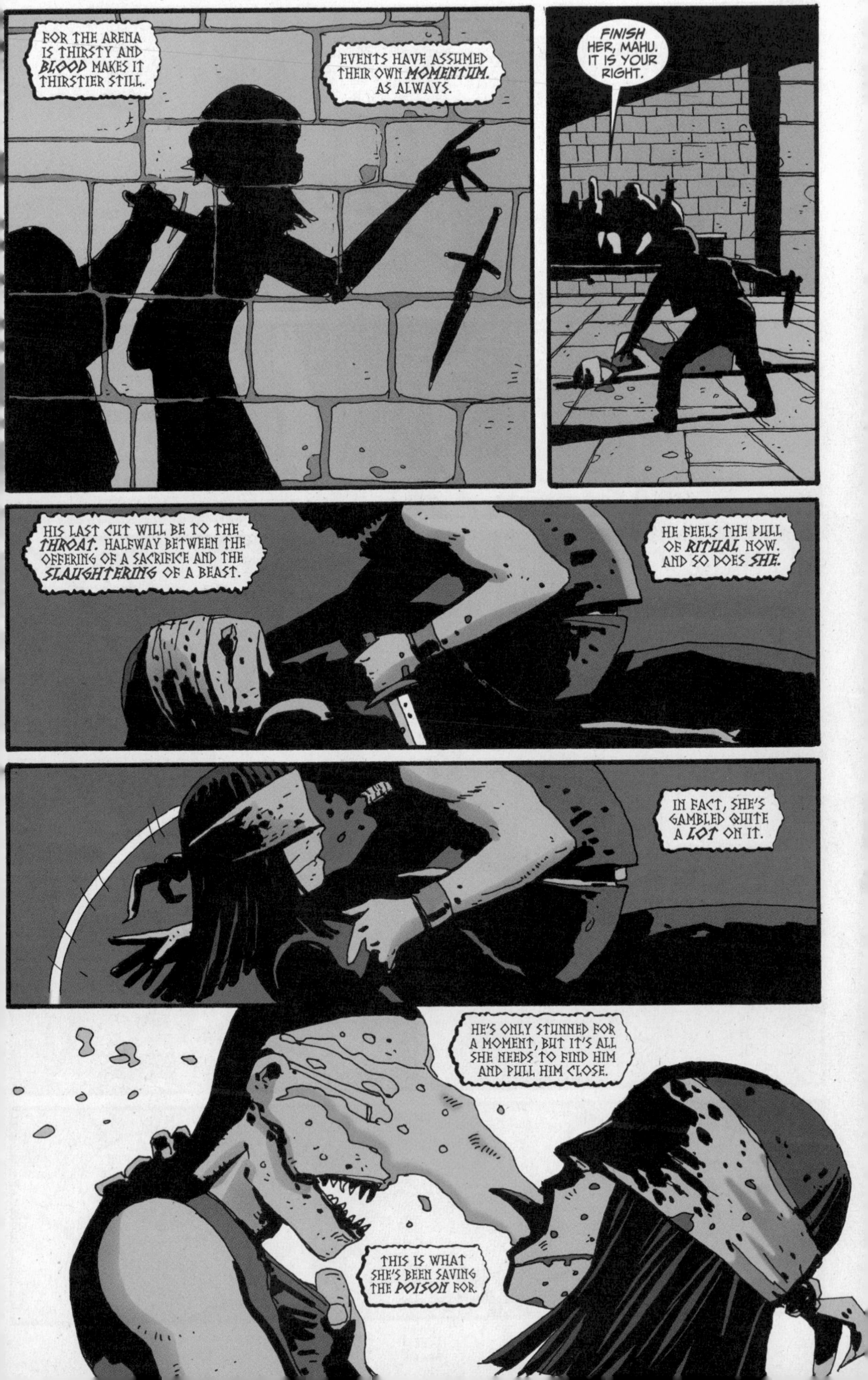
FOR THE ARENA IS THIRSTY AND BLOOD MAKES IT THIRSTIER STILL.
EVENTS HAVE ASSUMED THEIR OWN MOMENTUM. AS ALWAYS.
FINISH HER, MAHU. IT IS YOUR RIGHT.
HIS LAST CUT WILL BE TO THE THROAT. HALFWAY BETWEEN THE OFFERING OF A SACRIFICE AND THE SLAUGHTERING OF A BEAST.
HE FEELS THE PULL OF RITUAL NOW. AND SO DOES SHE.
IN FACT, SHE'S GAMBLED QUITE A LOT ON IT.
HE'S ONLY STUNNED FOR A MOMENT, BUT IT'S ALL SHE NEEDS TO FIND HIM AND PULL HIM CLOSE.
THIS IS WHAT SHE'S BEEN SAVING THE POISON FOR.

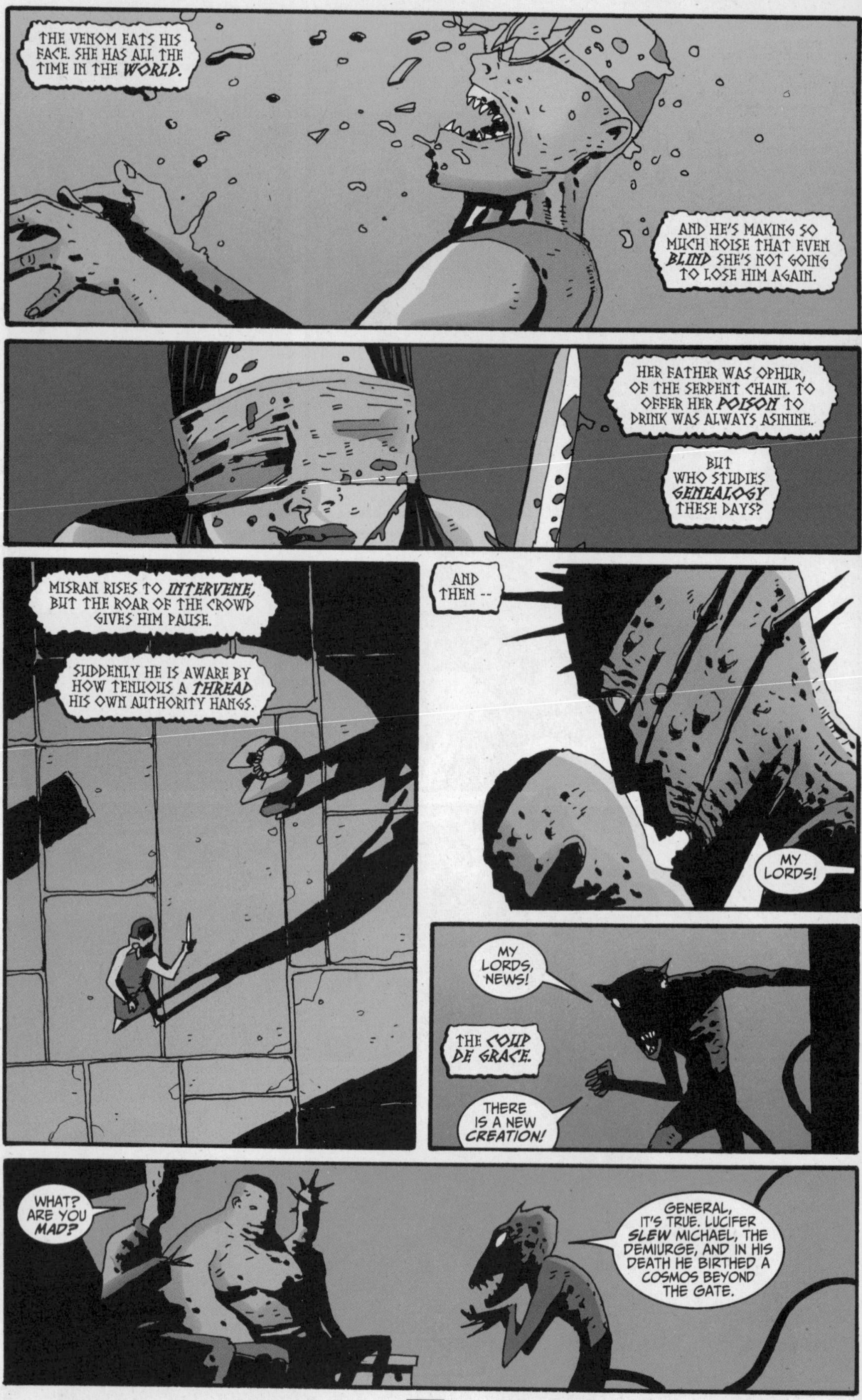

THE VENOM EATS HIS FACE. SHE HAS ALL THE TIME IN THE WORLD.
AND HE'S MAKING SO MUCH NOISE THAT EVEN BLIND SHE'S NOT GOING TO LOSE HIM AGAIN.
HER FATHER WAS OPHUR, OF THE SERPENT CHAIN. TO OFFER HER POISON TO DRINK WAS ALWAYS ASININE.
BUT WHO STUDIES GENEALOGY THESE DAYS?
MISRAN RISES TO INTERVENE, BUT THE ROAR OF THE CROWD GIVES HIM PAUSE.
SUDDENLY HE IS AWARE BY HOW TENUOUS A THREAD HIS OWN AUTHORITY HANGS.
AND THEN --
MY LORDS!
MY LORDS, NEWS!
THE COUP DE GRACE.
THERE IS A NEW CREATION!
WHAT? ARE YOU MAD?
GENERAL, IT'S TRUE. LUCIFER SLEW MICHAEL, THE DEMIURGE, AND IN HIS DEATH HE BIRTHED A COSMOS BEYOND THE GATE.

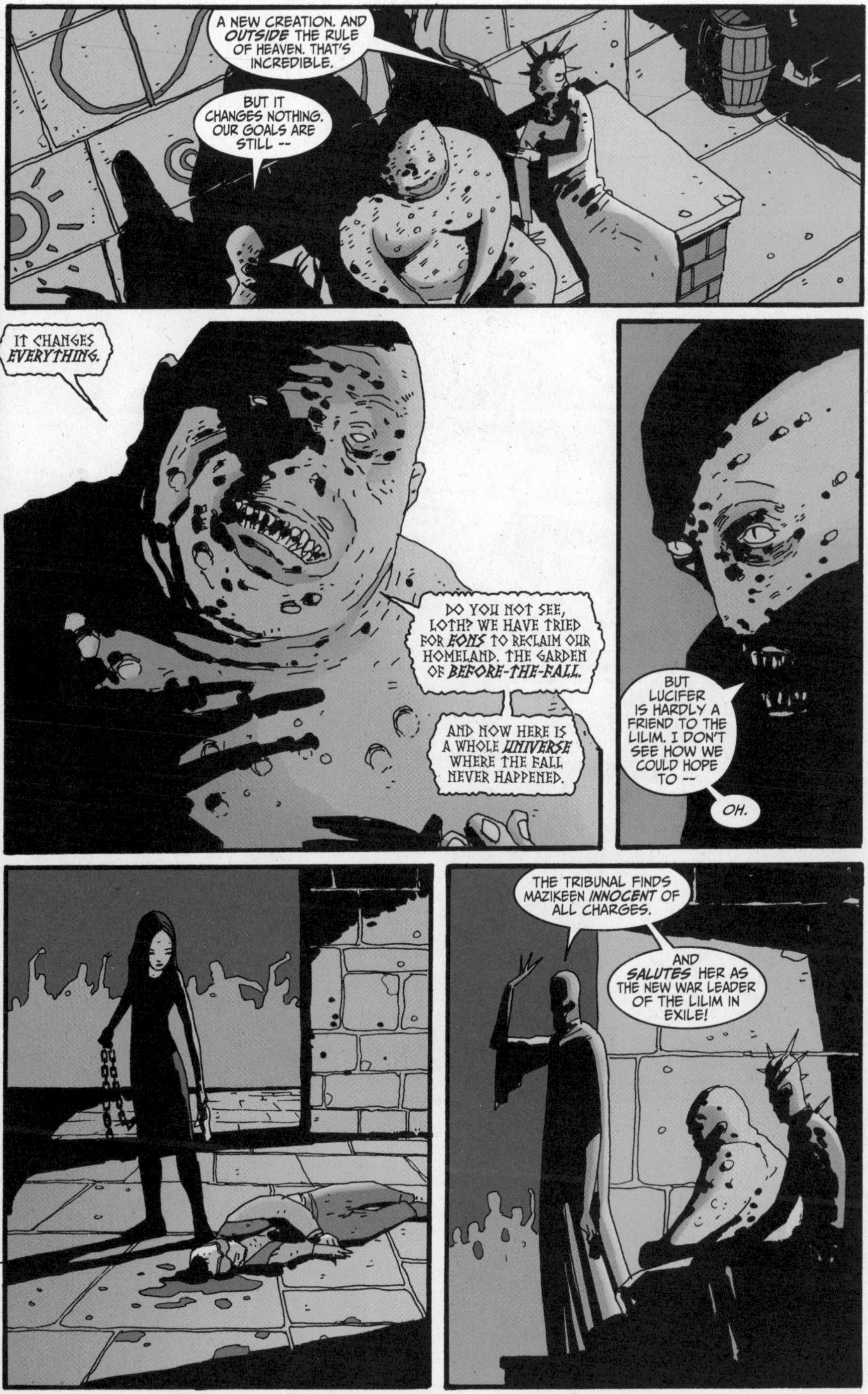
A NEW CREATION. AND *OUTSIDE* THE RULE OF HEAVEN. THAT'S INCREDIBLE.
BUT IT CHANGES NOTHING. OUR GOALS ARE STILL --
IT CHANGES *EVERYTHING.*
DO YOU NOT SEE, LOTH? WE HAVE TRIED FOR *EONS* TO RECLAIM OUR HOMELAND. THE GARDEN OF *BEFORE-THE-FALL.*
AND NOW HERE IS A WHOLE *UNIVERSE* WHERE THE FALL NEVER HAPPENED.
BUT LUCIFER IS HARDLY A FRIEND TO THE LILIM. I DON'T SEE HOW WE COULD HOPE TO --
OH.
THE TRIBUNAL FINDS MAZIKEEN *INNOCENT* OF ALL CHARGES.
AND *SALUTES* HER AS THE NEW WAR LEADER OF THE LILIM IN EXILE!

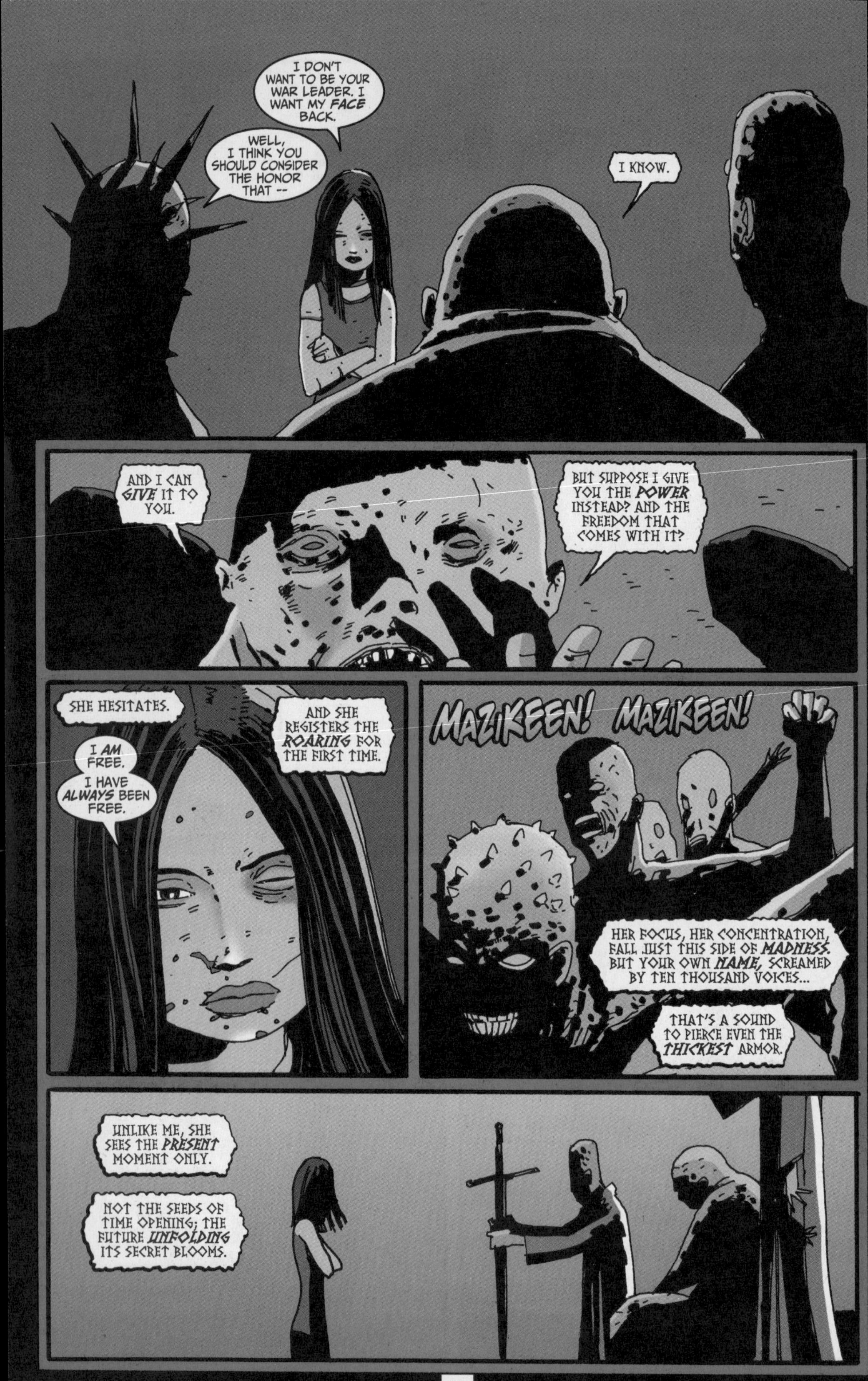
I DON'T WANT TO BE YOUR WAR LEADER. I WANT MY FACE BACK.
WELL, I THINK YOU SHOULD CONSIDER THE HONOR THAT --
I KNOW.
AND I CAN GIVE IT TO YOU.
BUT SUPPOSE I GIVE YOU THE POWER INSTEAD? AND THE FREEDOM THAT COMES WITH IT?
SHE HESITATES.
I AM FREE. I HAVE ALWAYS BEEN FREE.
AND SHE REGISTERS THE ROARING FOR THE FIRST TIME.
MAZIKEEN! MAZIKEEN!
HER FOCUS, HER CONCENTRATION, FALL JUST THIS SIDE OF MADNESS. BUT YOUR OWN NAME, SCREAMED BY TEN THOUSAND VOICES...
THAT'S A SOUND TO PIERCE EVEN THE THICKEST ARMOR.
UNLIKE ME, SHE SEES THE PRESENT MOMENT ONLY.
NOT THE SEEDS OF TIME OPENING; THE FUTURE UNFOLDING ITS SECRET BLOOMS.

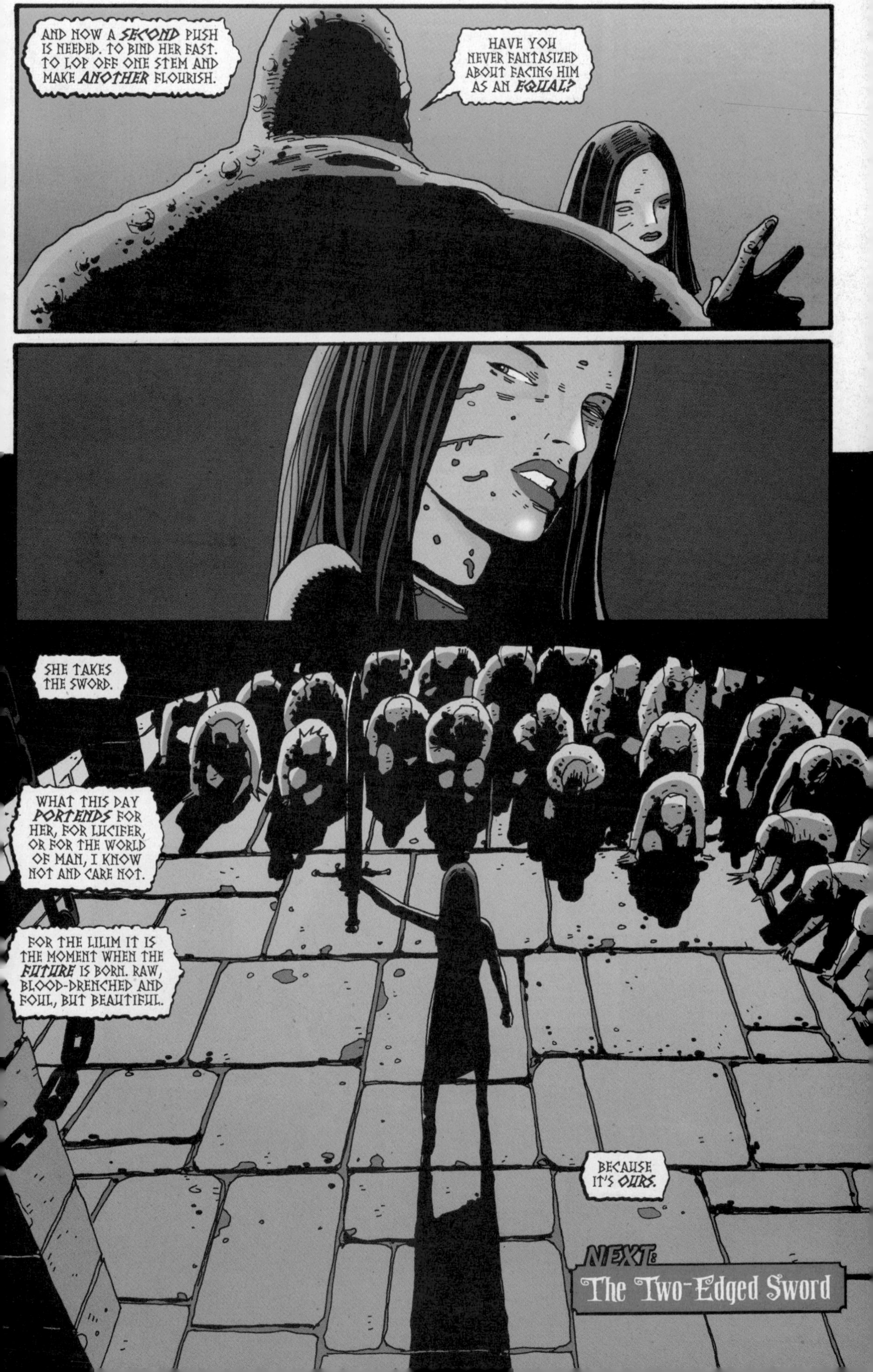

AND NOW A SECOND PUSH IS NEEDED. TO BIND HER FAST. TO LOP OFF ONE STEM AND MAKE ANOTHER FLOURISH.
HAVE YOU NEVER FANTASIZED ABOUT FACING HIM AS AN EQUAL?
SHE TAKES THE SWORD.
WHAT THIS DAY PORTENDS FOR HER, FOR LUCIFER, OR FOR THE WORLD OF MAN, I KNOW NOT AND CARE NOT.
FOR THE LILIM IT IS THE MOMENT WHEN THE FUTURE IS BORN. RAW, BLOOD-DRENCHED AND FOUL, BUT BEAUTIFUL.
BECAUSE IT'S OURS.
NEXT:
The Two-Edged Sword

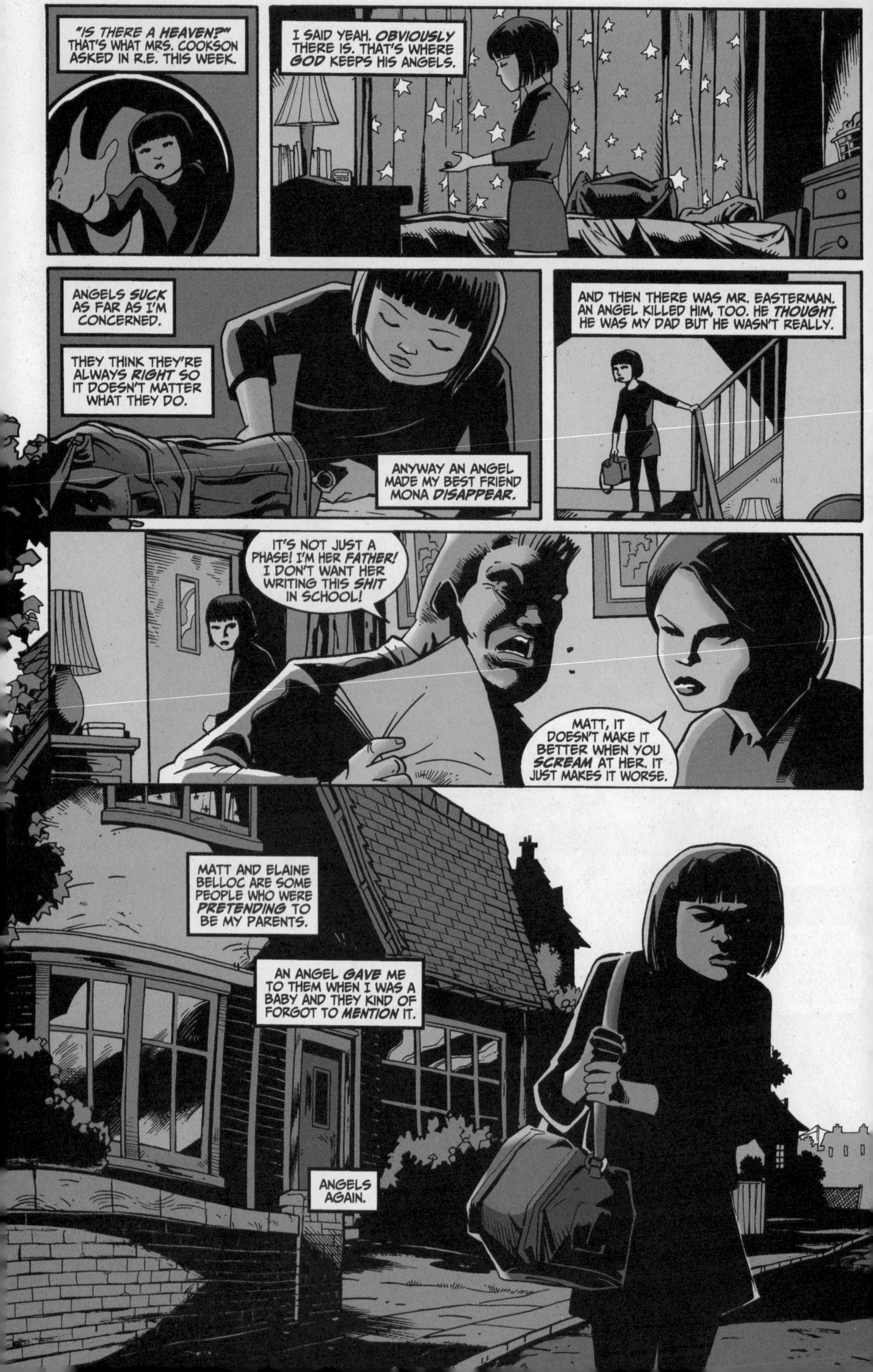
"IS THERE A HEAVEN?" THAT'S WHAT MRS. COOKSON ASKED IN R.E. THIS WEEK.
I SAID YEAH. OBVIOUSLY THERE IS. THAT'S WHERE GOD KEEPS HIS ANGELS.
ANGELS SUCK AS FAR AS I'M CONCERNED.
THEY THINK THEY'RE ALWAYS RIGHT SO IT DOESN'T MATTER WHAT THEY DO.
ANYWAY AN ANGEL MADE MY BEST FRIEND MONA DISAPPEAR.
AND THEN THERE WAS MR. EASTERMAN. AN ANGEL KILLED HIM, TOO. HE THOUGHT HE WAS MY DAD BUT HE WASN'T REALLY.
IT'S NOT JUST A PHASE! I'M HER FATHER! I DON'T WANT HER WRITING THIS SHIT IN SCHOOL!
MATT, IT DOESN'T MAKE IT BETTER WHEN YOU SCREAM AT HER. IT JUST MAKES IT WORSE.
MATT AND ELAINE BELLOC ARE SOME PEOPLE WHO WERE PRETENDING TO BE MY PARENTS.
AN ANGEL GAVE ME TO THEM WHEN I WAS A BABY AND THEY KIND OF FORGOT TO MENTION IT.
ANGELS AGAIN.

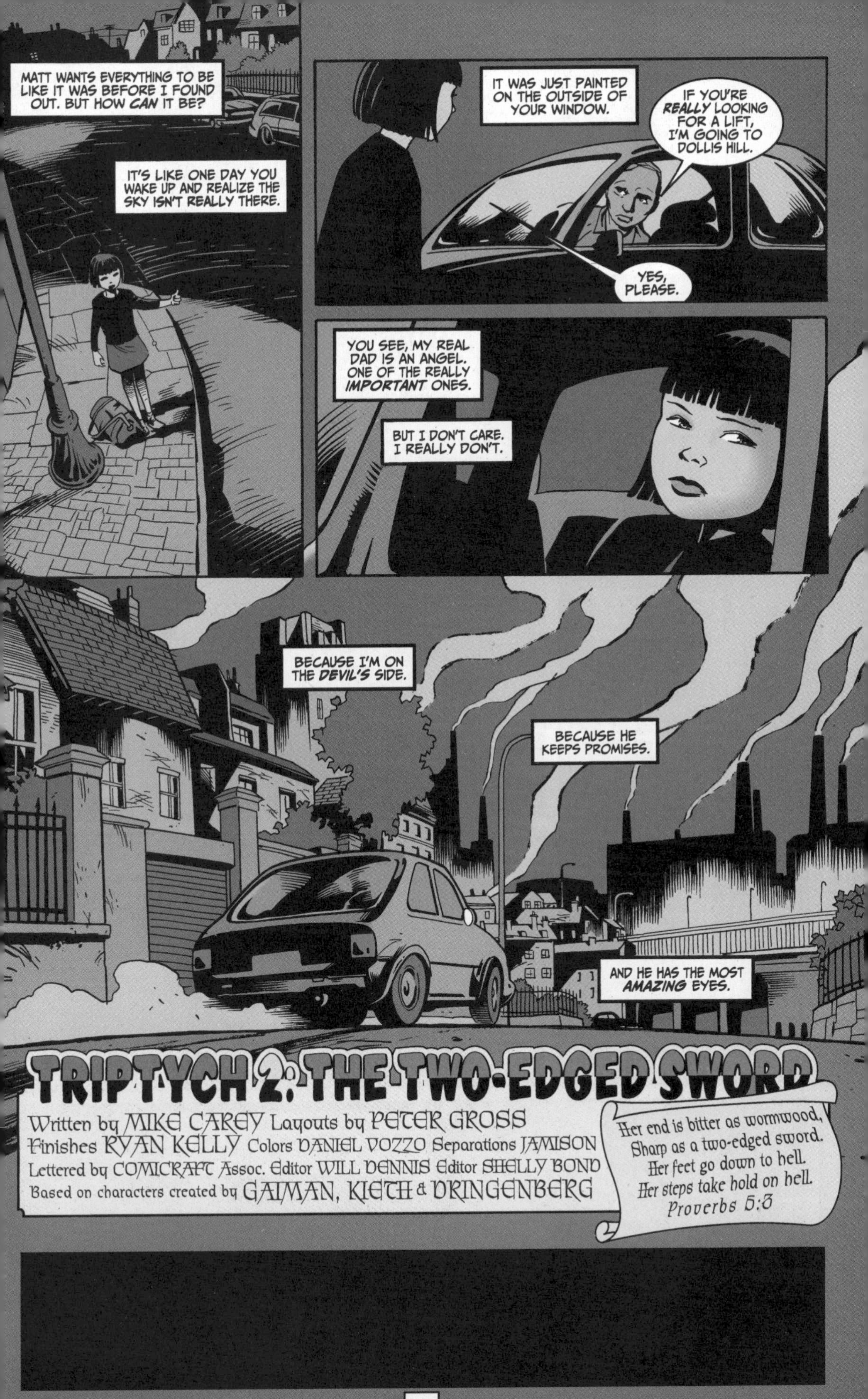

MATT WANTS EVERYTHING TO BE LIKE IT WAS BEFORE I FOUND OUT. BUT HOW *CAN* IT BE?
IT'S LIKE ONE DAY YOU WAKE UP AND REALIZE THE SKY ISN'T REALLY THERE.
IT WAS JUST PAINTED ON THE OUTSIDE OF YOUR WINDOW.
IF YOU'RE *REALLY* LOOKING FOR A LIFT, I'M GOING TO DOLLIS HILL.
YES, PLEASE.
YOU SEE, MY REAL DAD IS AN ANGEL. ONE OF THE REALLY *IMPORTANT* ONES.
BUT I DON'T CARE. I REALLY DON'T.
BECAUSE I'M ON THE *DEVIL'S* SIDE.
BECAUSE HE KEEPS PROMISES.
AND HE HAS THE MOST *AMAZING* EYES.
TRIPTYCH 2: THE TWO-EDGED SWORD
Written by MIKE CAREY Layouts by PETER GROSS
Finishes RYAN KELLY Colors DANIEL VOZZO Separations JAMISON
Lettered by COMICRAFT Assoc. Editor WILL DENNIS Editor SHELLY BOND
Based on characters created by GAIMAN, KIETH & DRINGENBERG
Her end is bitter as wormwood, Sharp as a two-edged sword. Her feet go down to hell. Her steps take hold on hell.
Proverbs 5:3

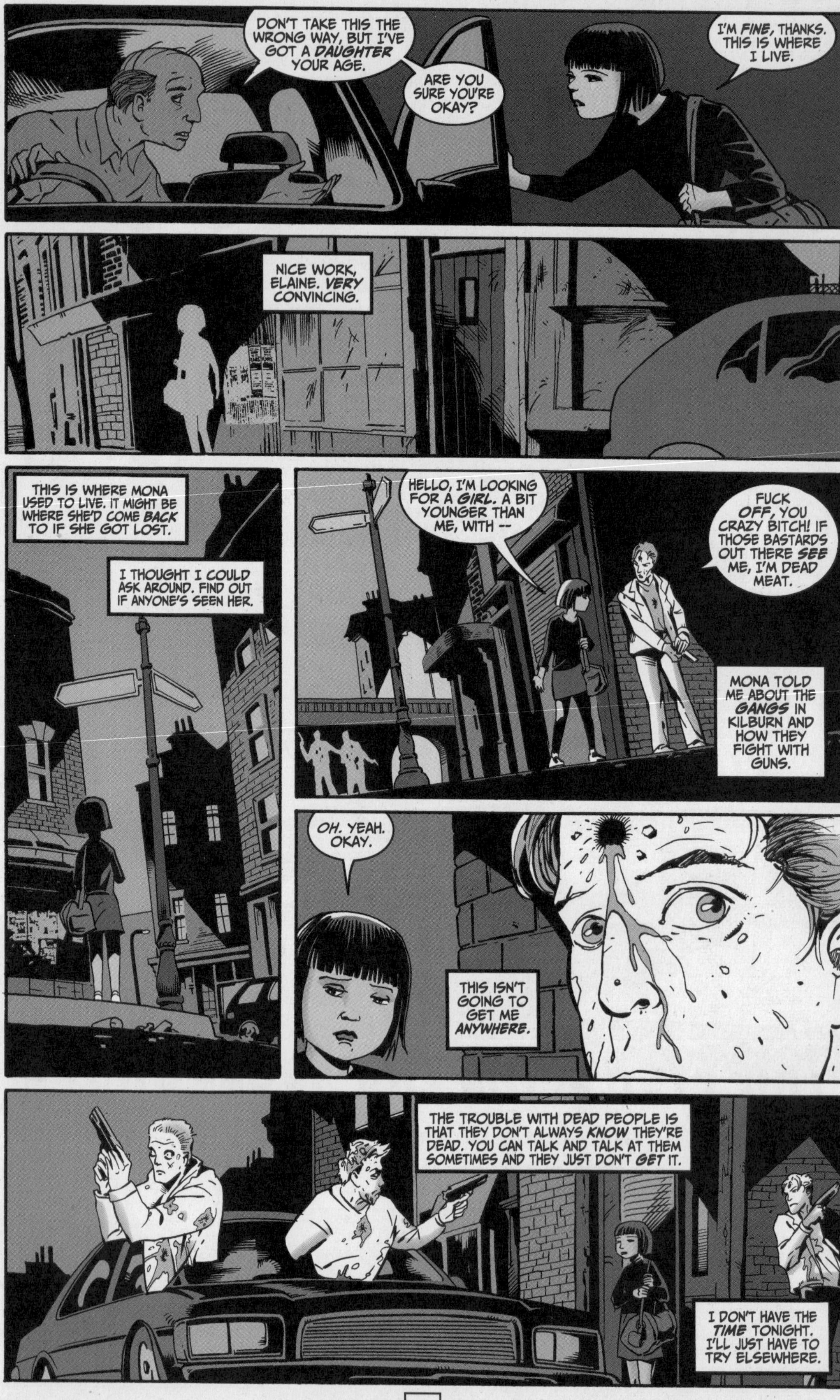

DON'T TAKE THIS THE WRONG WAY, BUT I'VE GOT A DAUGHTER YOUR AGE.
ARE YOU SURE YOU'RE OKAY?
I'M FINE, THANKS. THIS IS WHERE I LIVE.
NICE WORK, ELAINE. VERY CONVINCING.
THIS IS WHERE MONA USED TO LIVE. IT MIGHT BE WHERE SHE'D COME BACK TO IF SHE GOT LOST.
I THOUGHT I COULD ASK AROUND. FIND OUT IF ANYONE'S SEEN HER.
HELLO, I'M LOOKING FOR A GIRL. A BIT YOUNGER THAN ME, WITH --
FUCK OFF, YOU CRAZY BITCH! IF THOSE BASTARDS OUT THERE SEE ME, I'M DEAD MEAT.
MONA TOLD ME ABOUT THE GANGS IN KILBURN AND HOW THEY FIGHT WITH GUNS.
OH. YEAH. OKAY.
THIS ISN'T GOING TO GET ME ANYWHERE.
THE TROUBLE WITH DEAD PEOPLE IS THAT THEY DON'T ALWAYS KNOW THEY'RE DEAD. YOU CAN TALK AND TALK AT THEM SOMETIMES AND THEY JUST DON'T GET IT.
I DON'T HAVE THE TIME TONIGHT. I'LL JUST HAVE TO TRY ELSEWHERE.

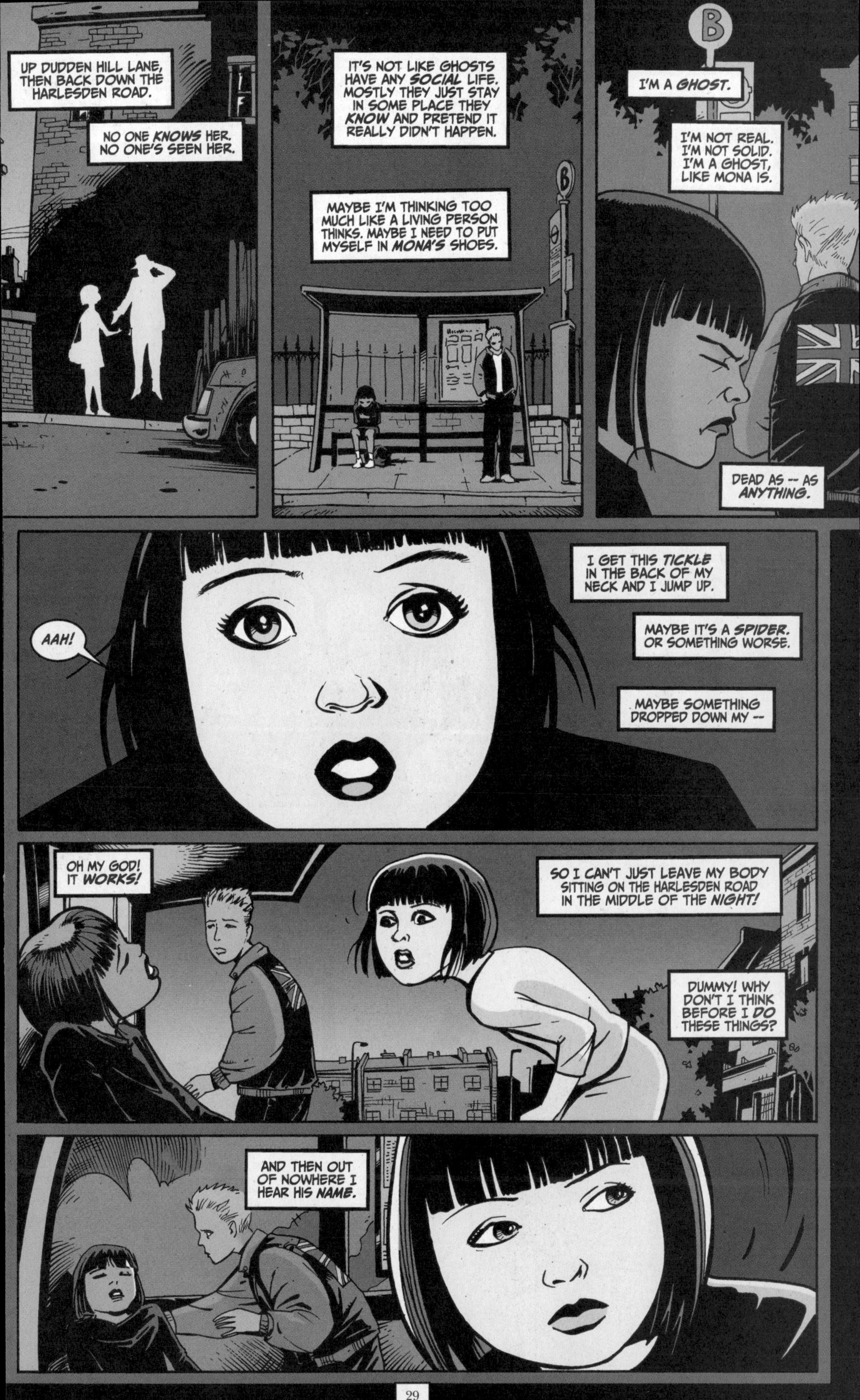
UP DUDDEN HILL LANE, THEN BACK DOWN THE HARLESDEN ROAD.
NO ONE *KNOWS* HER. NO ONE'S SEEN HER.
IT'S NOT LIKE GHOSTS HAVE ANY *SOCIAL* LIFE. MOSTLY THEY JUST STAY IN SOME PLACE THEY *KNOW* AND PRETEND IT REALLY DIDN'T HAPPEN.
MAYBE I'M THINKING TOO MUCH LIKE A LIVING PERSON THINKS. MAYBE I NEED TO PUT MYSELF IN *MONA'S* SHOES.
B
I'M A *GHOST.*
I'M NOT REAL. I'M NOT SOLID. I'M A GHOST, LIKE MONA IS.
DEAD AS -- AS *ANYTHING.*
I GET THIS *TICKLE* IN THE BACK OF MY NECK AND I JUMP UP.
AAH!
MAYBE IT'S A *SPIDER.* OR SOMETHING WORSE.
MAYBE SOMETHING DROPPED DOWN MY --
OH MY GOD! IT *WORKS!*
SO I CAN'T JUST LEAVE MY BODY SITTING ON THE HARLESDEN ROAD IN THE MIDDLE OF THE *NIGHT!*
DUMMY! WHY DON'T I THINK BEFORE I *DO* THESE THINGS?
AND THEN OUT OF NOWHERE I HEAR HIS *NAME.*

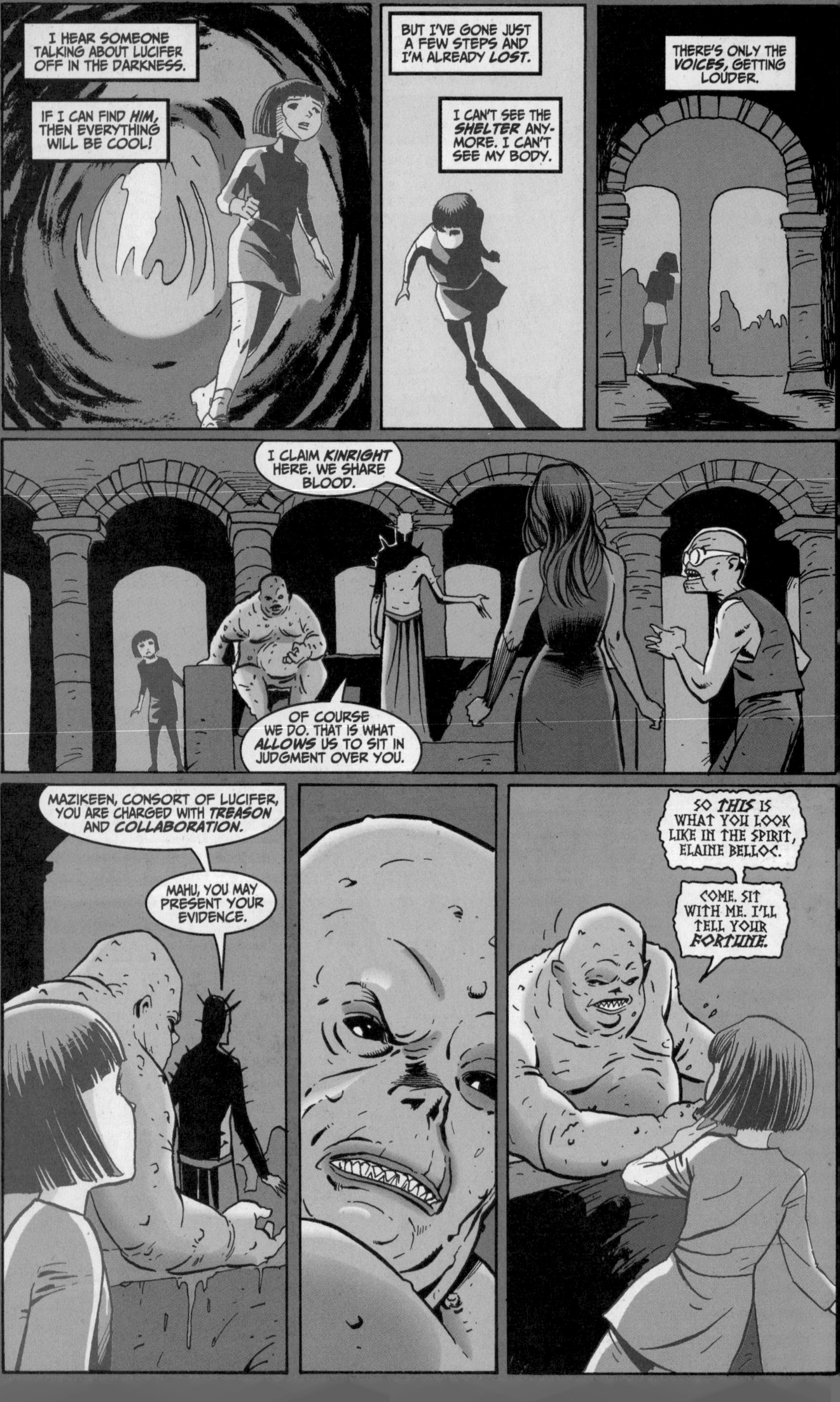
I HEAR SOMEONE TALKING ABOUT LUCIFER OFF IN THE DARKNESS.
IF I CAN FIND HIM, THEN EVERYTHING WILL BE COOL!
BUT I'VE GONE JUST A FEW STEPS AND I'M ALREADY LOST.
I CAN'T SEE THE SHELTER ANYMORE. I CAN'T SEE MY BODY.
THERE'S ONLY THE VOICES, GETTING LOUDER.
I CLAIM KINRIGHT HERE. WE SHARE BLOOD.
OF COURSE WE DO. THAT IS WHAT ALLOWS US TO SIT IN JUDGMENT OVER YOU.
MAZIKEEN, CONSORT OF LUCIFER, YOU ARE CHARGED WITH TREASON AND COLLABORATION.
MAHU, YOU MAY PRESENT YOUR EVIDENCE.
SO THIS IS WHAT YOU LOOK LIKE IN THE SPIRIT, ELAINE BELLOC.
COME. SIT WITH ME. I'LL TELL YOUR FORTUNE.

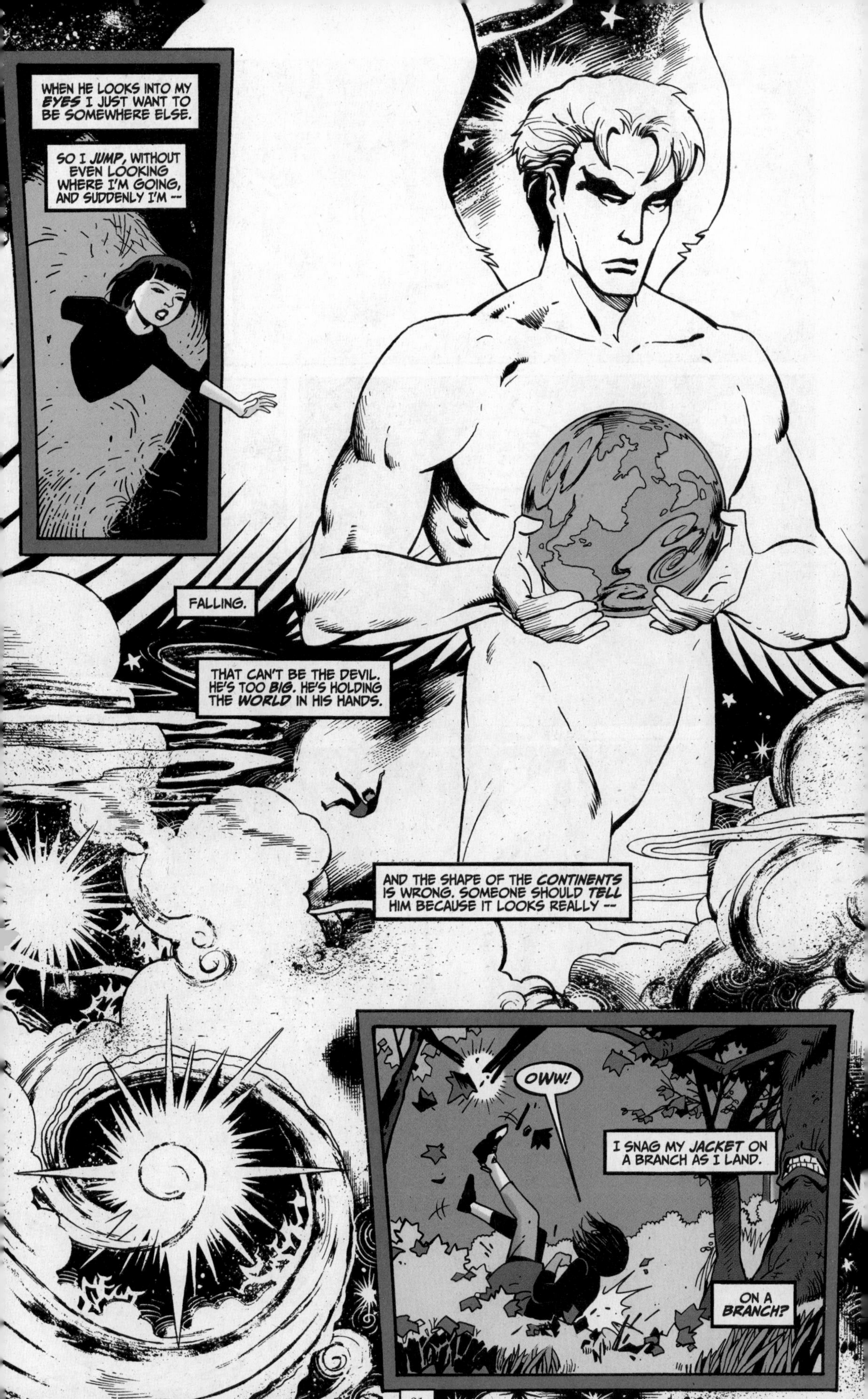

WHEN HE LOOKS INTO MY EYES I JUST WANT TO BE SOMEWHERE ELSE.
SO I JUMP, WITHOUT EVEN LOOKING WHERE I'M GOING, AND SUDDENLY I'M --
FALLING.
THAT CAN'T BE THE DEVIL. HE'S TOO BIG. HE'S HOLDING THE WORLD IN HIS HANDS.
AND THE SHAPE OF THE CONTINENTS IS WRONG. SOMEONE SHOULD TELL HIM BECAUSE IT LOOKS REALLY --
OWW!
I SNAG MY JACKET ON A BRANCH AS I LAND.
ON A BRANCH?

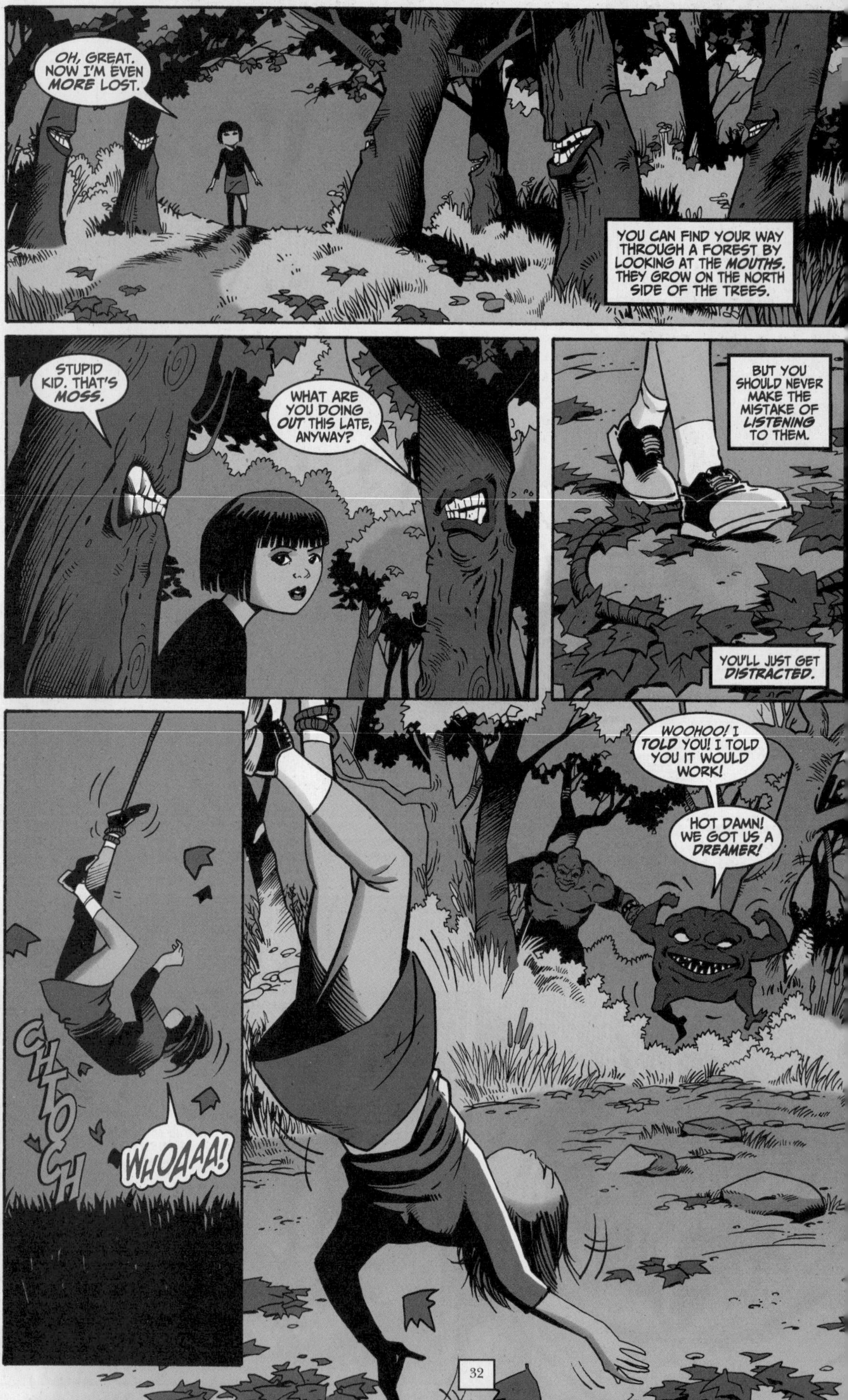
OH, GREAT. NOW I'M EVEN MORE LOST.
YOU CAN FIND YOUR WAY THROUGH A FOREST BY LOOKING AT THE MOUTHS. THEY GROW ON THE NORTH SIDE OF THE TREES.
STUPID KID. THAT'S MOSS.
WHAT ARE YOU DOING OUT THIS LATE, ANYWAY?
BUT YOU SHOULD NEVER MAKE THE MISTAKE OF LISTENING TO THEM.
YOU'LL JUST GET DISTRACTED.
CHTOCH
WHOAAA!
WOOHOO! I TOLD YOU! I TOLD YOU IT WOULD WORK!
HOT DAMN! WE GOT US A DREAMER!

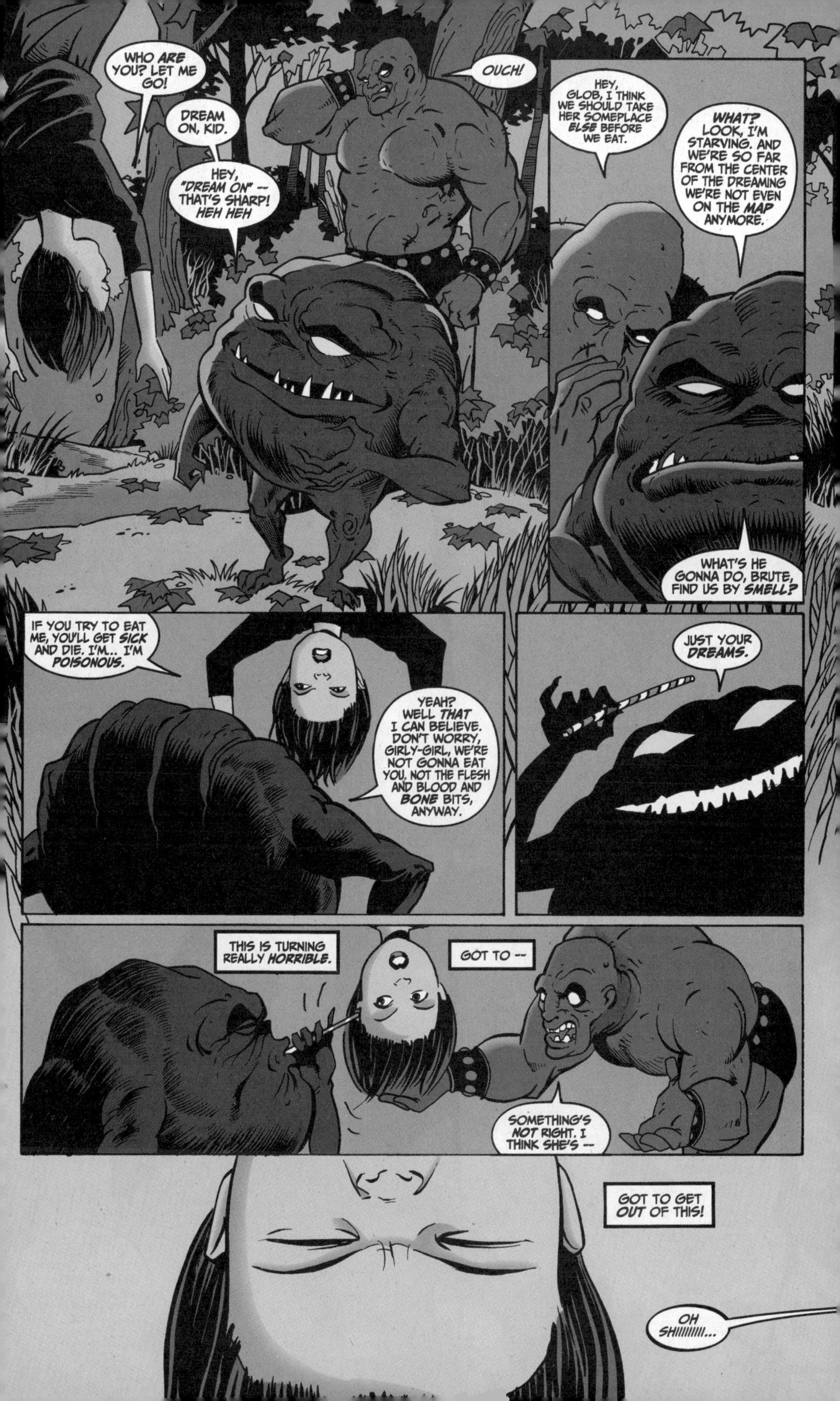
WHO ARE YOU? LET ME GO!
OUCH!
DREAM ON, KID.
HEY, "DREAM ON" -- THAT'S SHARP! HEH HEH
HEY, GLOB, I THINK WE SHOULD TAKE HER SOMEPLACE ELSE BEFORE WE EAT.
WHAT? LOOK, I'M STARVING. AND WE'RE SO FAR FROM THE CENTER OF THE DREAMING WE'RE NOT EVEN ON THE MAP ANYMORE.
WHAT'S HE GONNA DO, BRUTE, FIND US BY SMELL?
IF YOU TRY TO EAT ME, YOU'LL GET SICK AND DIE. I'M... I'M POISONOUS.
YEAH? WELL THAT I CAN BELIEVE. DON'T WORRY, GIRLY-GIRL, WE'RE NOT GONNA EAT YOU. NOT THE FLESH AND BLOOD AND BONE BITS, ANYWAY.
JUST YOUR DREAMS.
THIS IS TURNING REALLY HORRIBLE.
GOT TO --
SOMETHING'S NOT RIGHT. I THINK SHE'S --
GOT TO GET OUT OF THIS!
OH SHIIIIIIII...

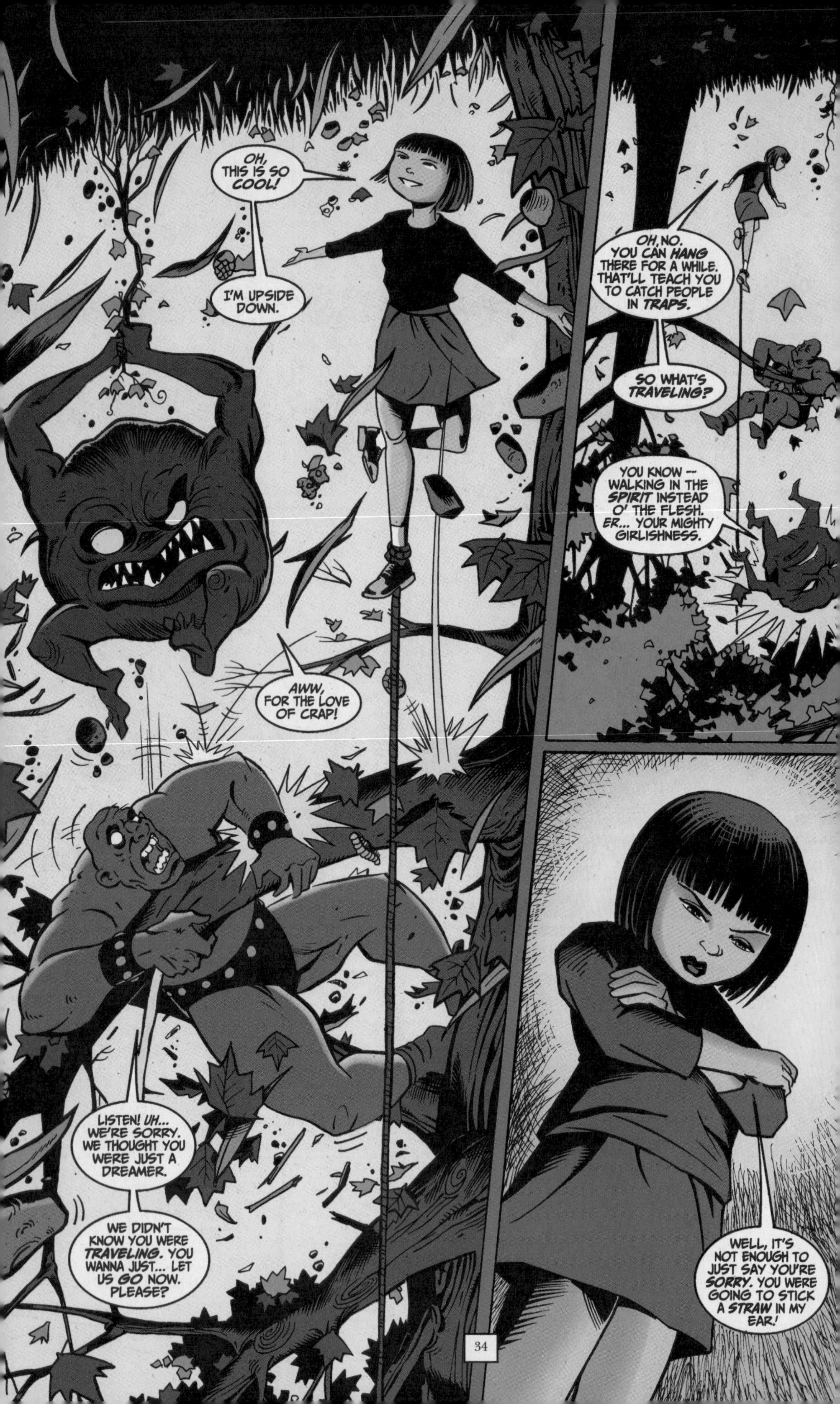

OH, THIS IS SO COOL!
I'M UPSIDE DOWN.
AWW, FOR THE LOVE OF CRAP!
LISTEN! UH... WE'RE SORRY. WE THOUGHT YOU WERE JUST A DREAMER.
WE DIDN'T KNOW YOU WERE TRAVELING. YOU WANNA JUST... LET US GO NOW. PLEASE?
OH, NO. YOU CAN HANG THERE FOR A WHILE. THAT'LL TEACH YOU TO CATCH PEOPLE IN TRAPS.
SO WHAT'S TRAVELING?
YOU KNOW -- WALKING IN THE SPIRIT INSTEAD O' THE FLESH. ER... YOUR MIGHTY GIRLISHNESS.
WELL, IT'S NOT ENOUGH TO JUST SAY YOU'RE SORRY. YOU WERE GOING TO STICK A STRAW IN MY EAR!

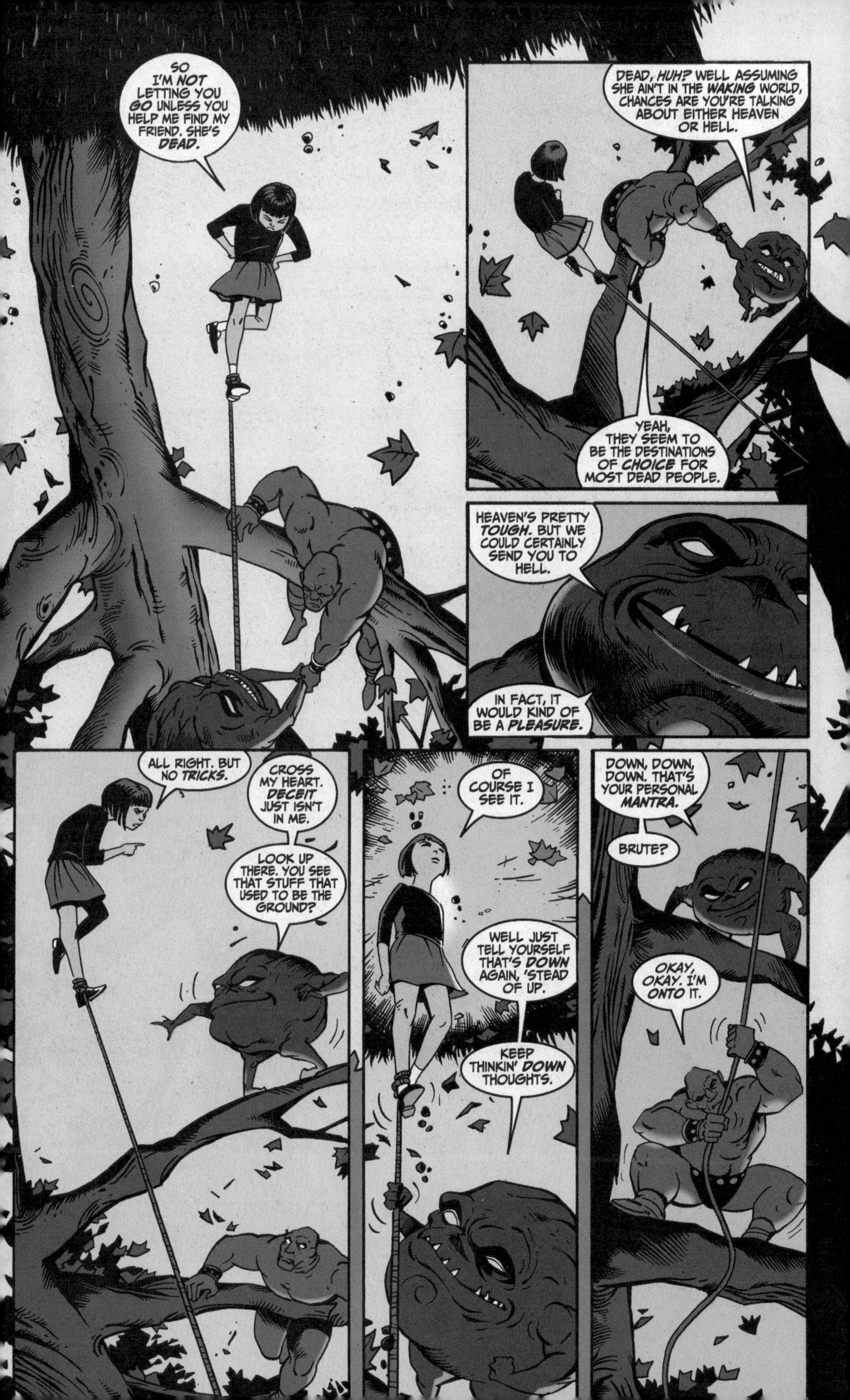

SO I'M NOT LETTING YOU GO UNLESS YOU HELP ME FIND MY FRIEND. SHE'S DEAD.
DEAD, HUH? WELL ASSUMING SHE AIN'T IN THE WAKING WORLD, CHANCES ARE YOU'RE TALKING ABOUT EITHER HEAVEN OR HELL.
YEAH, THEY SEEM TO BE THE DESTINATIONS OF CHOICE FOR MOST DEAD PEOPLE.
HEAVEN'S PRETTY TOUGH. BUT WE COULD CERTAINLY SEND YOU TO HELL.
IN FACT, IT WOULD KIND OF BE A PLEASURE.
ALL RIGHT. BUT NO TRICKS.
CROSS MY HEART. DECEIT JUST ISN'T IN ME.
LOOK UP THERE. YOU SEE THAT STUFF THAT USED TO BE THE GROUND?
OF COURSE I SEE IT.
WELL JUST TELL YOURSELF THAT'S DOWN AGAIN, 'STEAD OF UP.
KEEP THINKIN' DOWN THOUGHTS.
DOWN, DOWN, DOWN. THAT'S YOUR PERSONAL MANTRA.
BRUTE?
OKAY, OKAY. I'M ONTO IT.

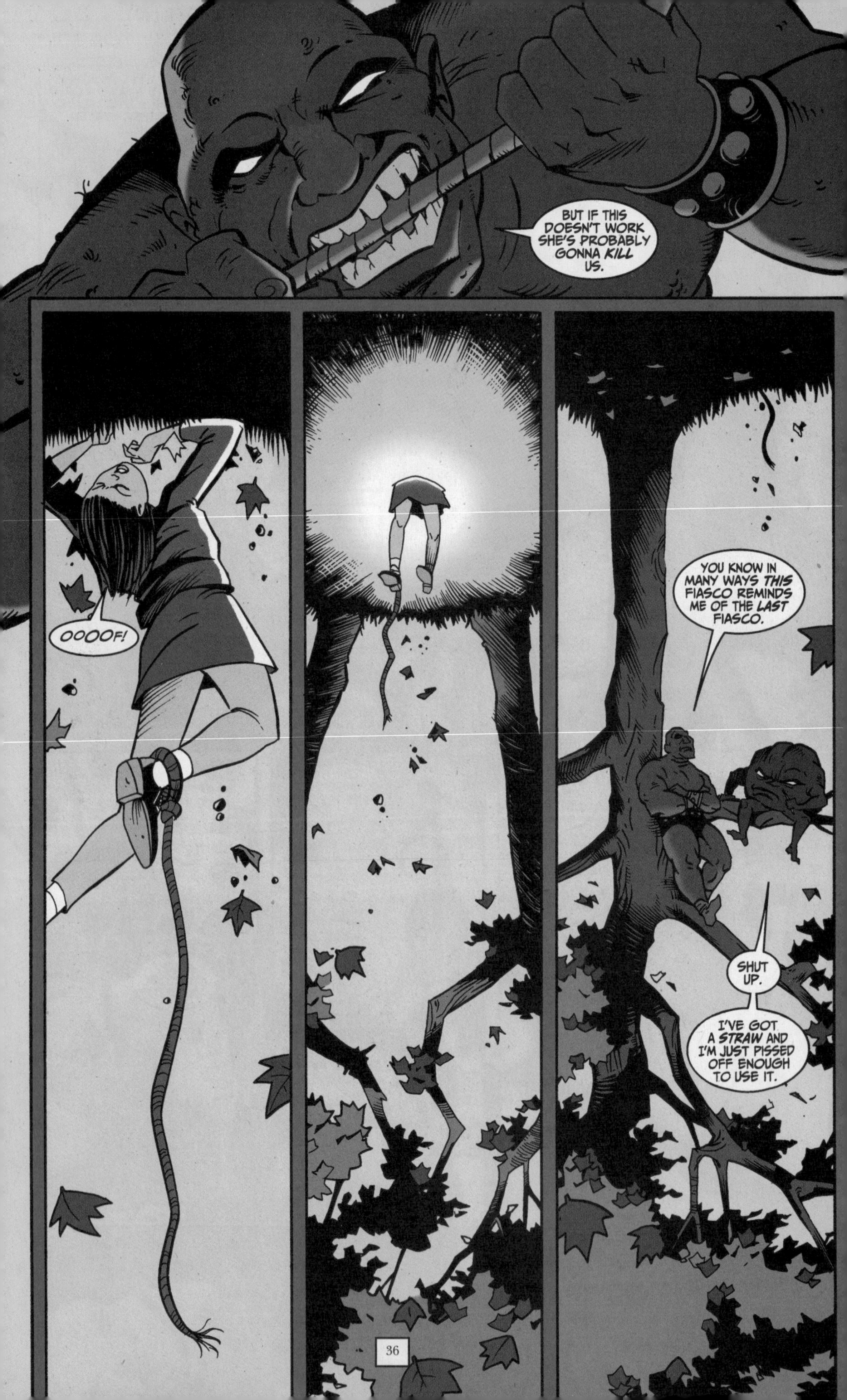
BUT IF THIS DOESN'T WORK SHE'S PROBABLY GONNA KILL US.
OOOOF!
YOU KNOW IN MANY WAYS THIS FIASCO REMINDS ME OF THE LAST FIASCO.
SHUT UP.
I'VE GOT A STRAW AND I'M JUST PISSED OFF ENOUGH TO USE IT.

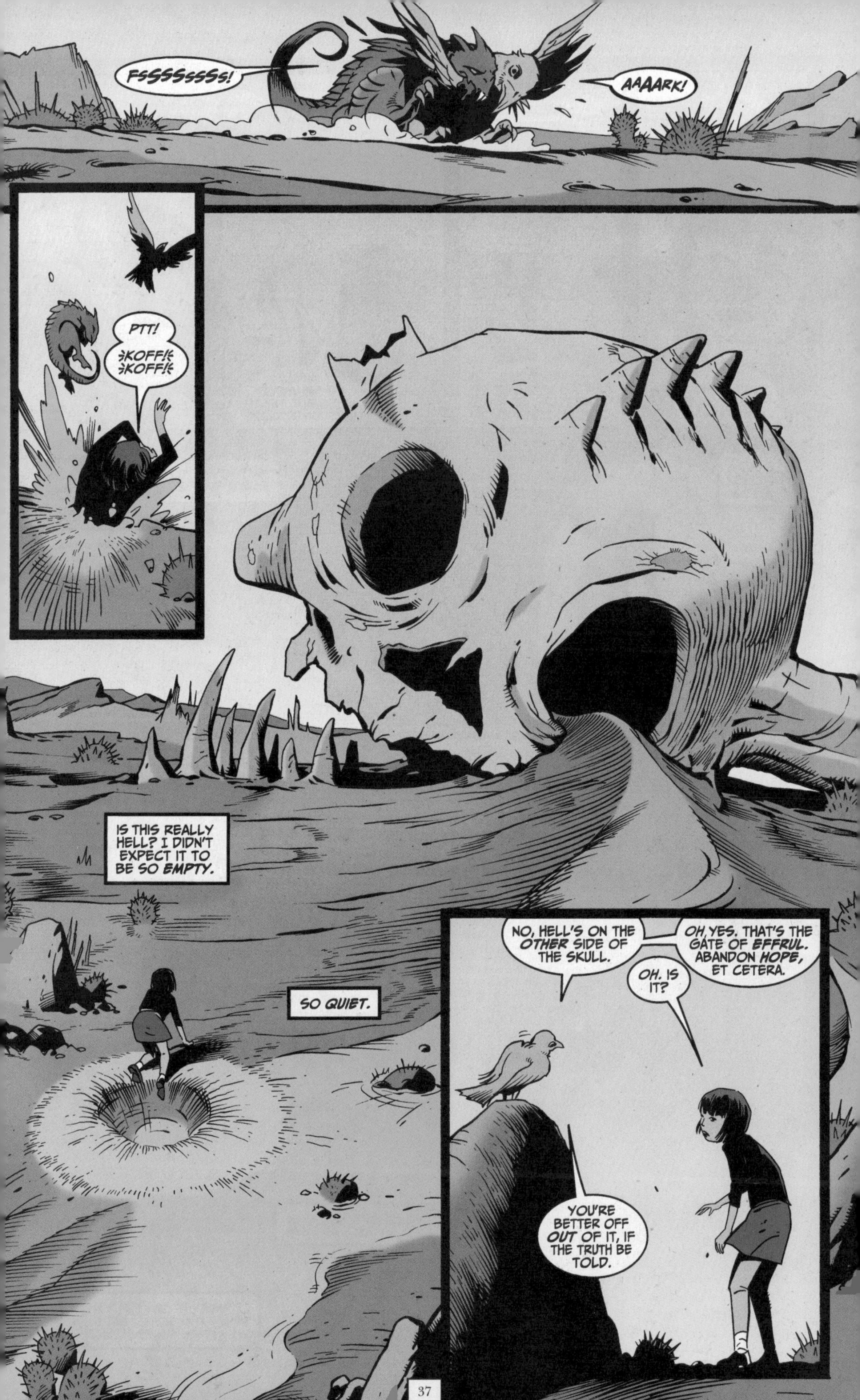
FSSSSSSSS!
AAAARK!
PTT!
KOFF!
KOFF!
IS THIS REALLY HELL? I DIDN'T EXPECT IT TO BE SO EMPTY.
SO QUIET.
NO, HELL'S ON THE OTHER SIDE OF THE SKULL.
OH. IS IT?
OH, YES. THAT'S THE GATE OF EFFRUL. ABANDON HOPE, ET CETERA.
YOU'RE BETTER OFF OUT OF IT, IF THE TRUTH BE TOLD.

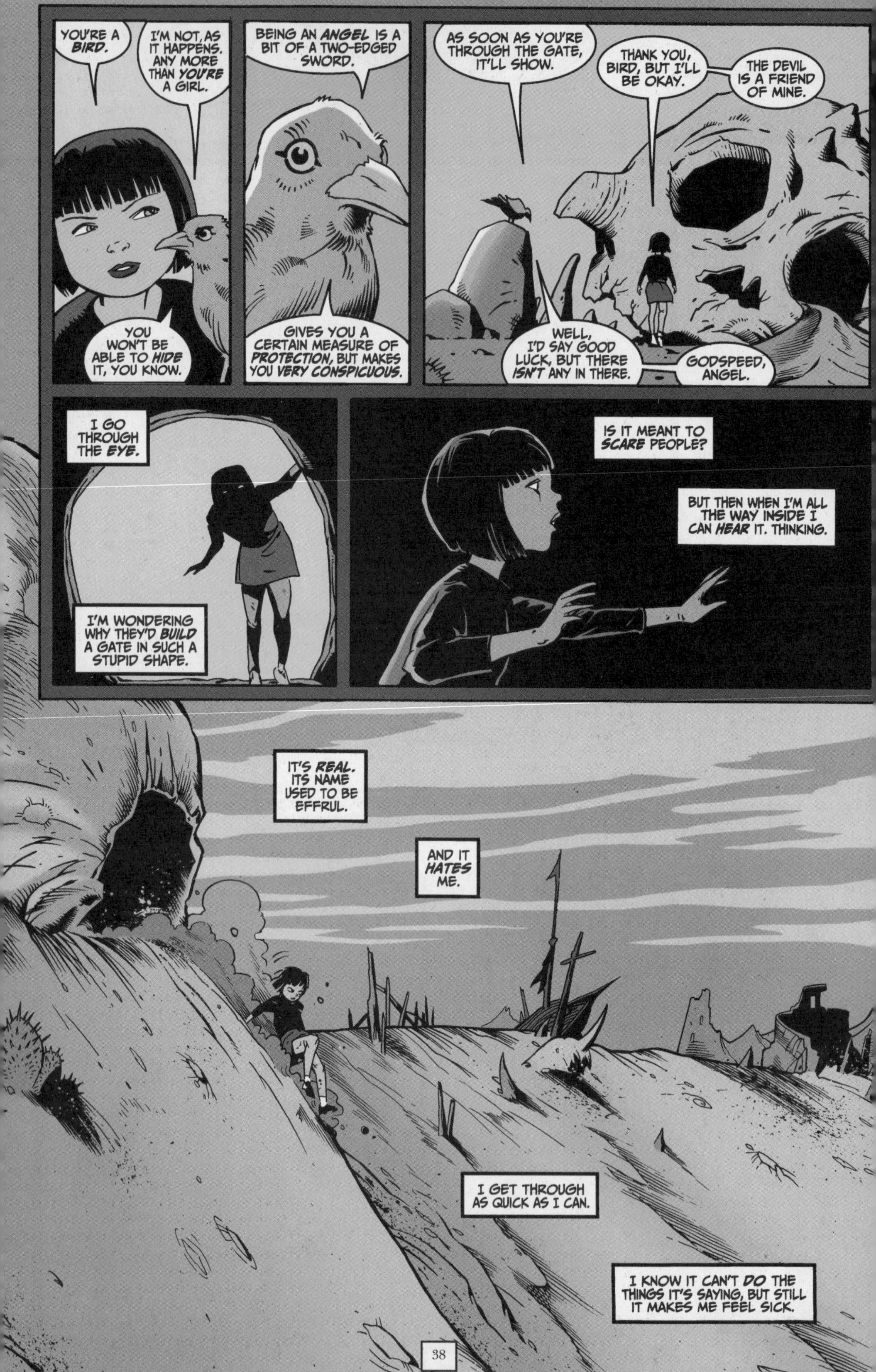
YOU'RE A BIRD.
I'M NOT, AS IT HAPPENS. ANY MORE THAN YOU'RE A GIRL.
YOU WON'T BE ABLE TO HIDE IT, YOU KNOW.
BEING AN ANGEL IS A BIT OF A TWO-EDGED SWORD.
GIVES YOU A CERTAIN MEASURE OF PROTECTION, BUT MAKES YOU VERY CONSPICUOUS.
AS SOON AS YOU'RE THROUGH THE GATE, IT'LL SHOW.
THANK YOU, BIRD, BUT I'LL BE OKAY.
THE DEVIL IS A FRIEND OF MINE.
WELL, I'D SAY GOOD LUCK, BUT THERE ISN'T ANY IN THERE.
GODSPEED, ANGEL.
I GO THROUGH THE EYE.
I'M WONDERING WHY THEY'D BUILD A GATE IN SUCH A STUPID SHAPE.
IS IT MEANT TO SCARE PEOPLE?
BUT THEN WHEN I'M ALL THE WAY INSIDE I CAN HEAR IT. THINKING.
IT'S REAL. ITS NAME USED TO BE EFFRUL.
AND IT HATES ME.
I GET THROUGH AS QUICK AS I CAN.
I KNOW IT CAN'T DO THE THINGS IT'S SAYING, BUT STILL IT MAKES ME FEEL SICK.

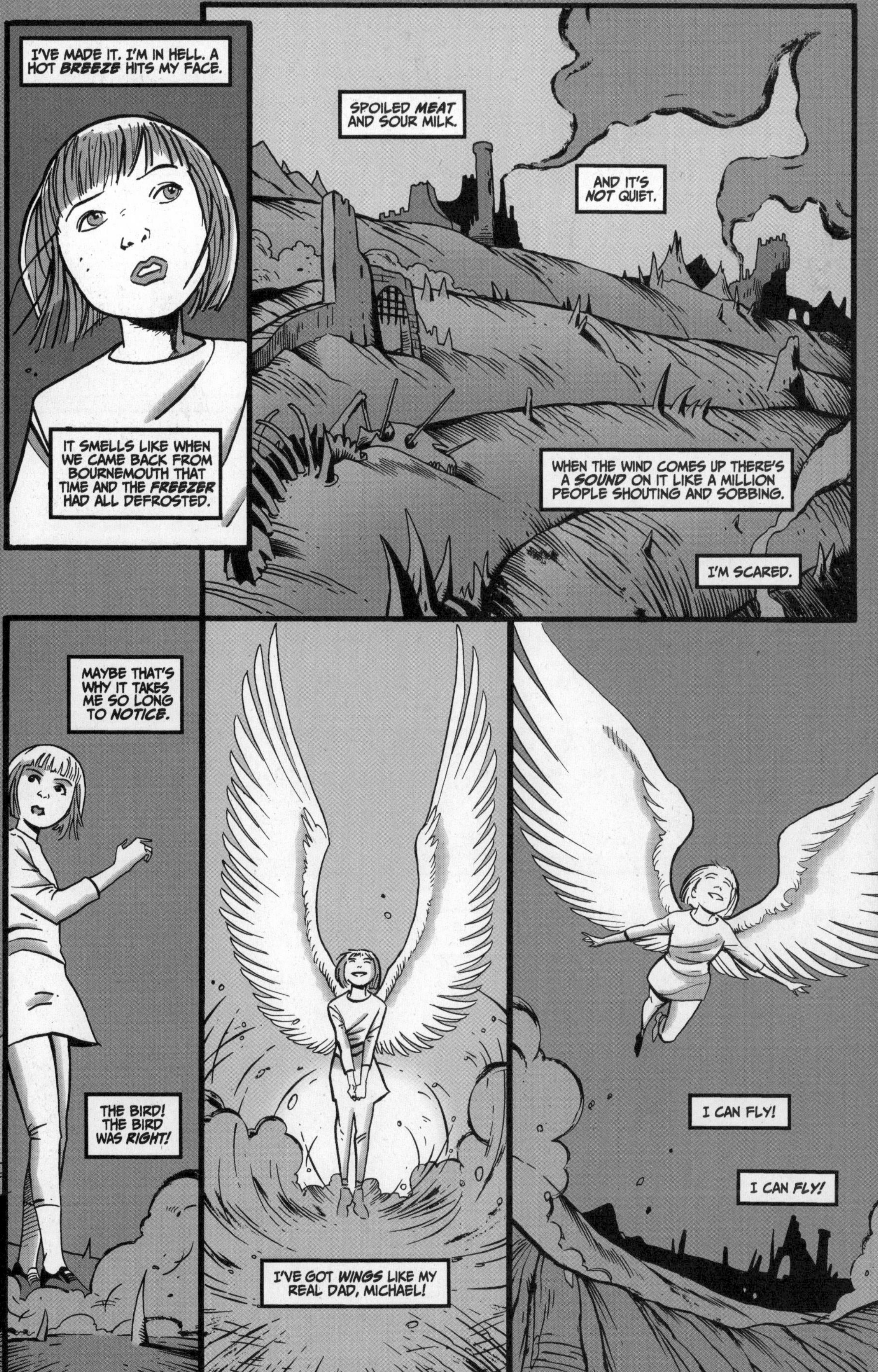
I'VE MADE IT. I'M IN HELL. A HOT BREEZE HITS MY FACE.
IT SMELLS LIKE WHEN WE CAME BACK FROM BOURNEMOUTH THAT TIME AND THE FREEZER HAD ALL DEFROSTED.
SPOILED MEAT AND SOUR MILK.
AND IT'S NOT QUIET.
WHEN THE WIND COMES UP THERE'S A SOUND ON IT LIKE A MILLION PEOPLE SHOUTING AND SOBBING.
I'M SCARED.
MAYBE THAT'S WHY IT TAKES ME SO LONG TO NOTICE.
THE BIRD! THE BIRD WAS RIGHT!
I'VE GOT WINGS LIKE MY REAL DAD, MICHAEL!
I CAN FLY!
I CAN FLY!

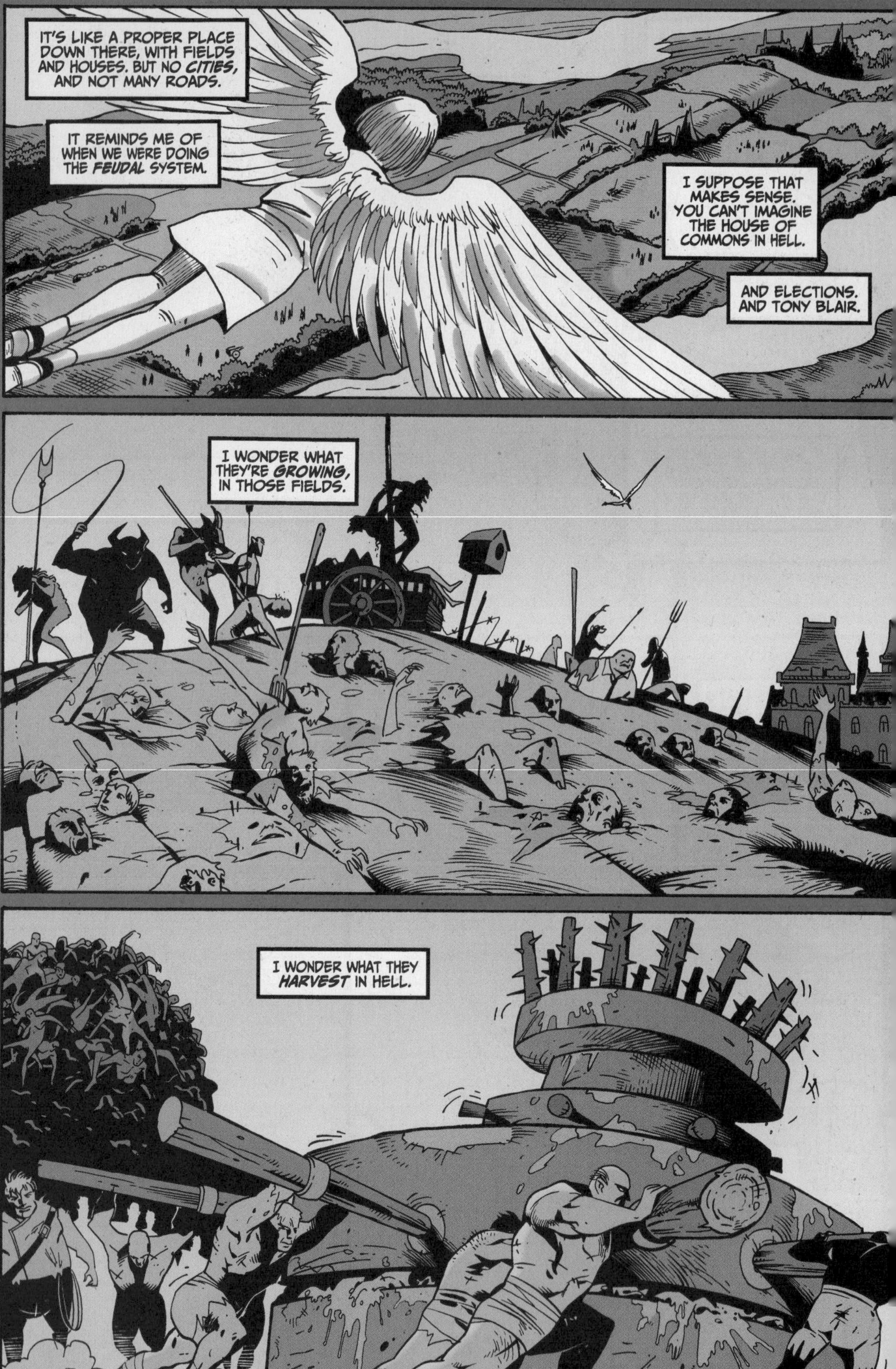
IT'S LIKE A PROPER PLACE DOWN THERE, WITH FIELDS AND HOUSES. BUT NO *CITIES*, AND NOT MANY ROADS.
IT REMINDS ME OF WHEN WE WERE DOING THE *FEUDAL* SYSTEM.
I SUPPOSE THAT MAKES SENSE. YOU CAN'T IMAGINE THE HOUSE OF COMMONS IN HELL.
AND ELECTIONS. AND TONY BLAIR.
I WONDER WHAT THEY'RE *GROWING*, IN THOSE FIELDS.
I WONDER WHAT THEY *HARVEST* IN HELL.

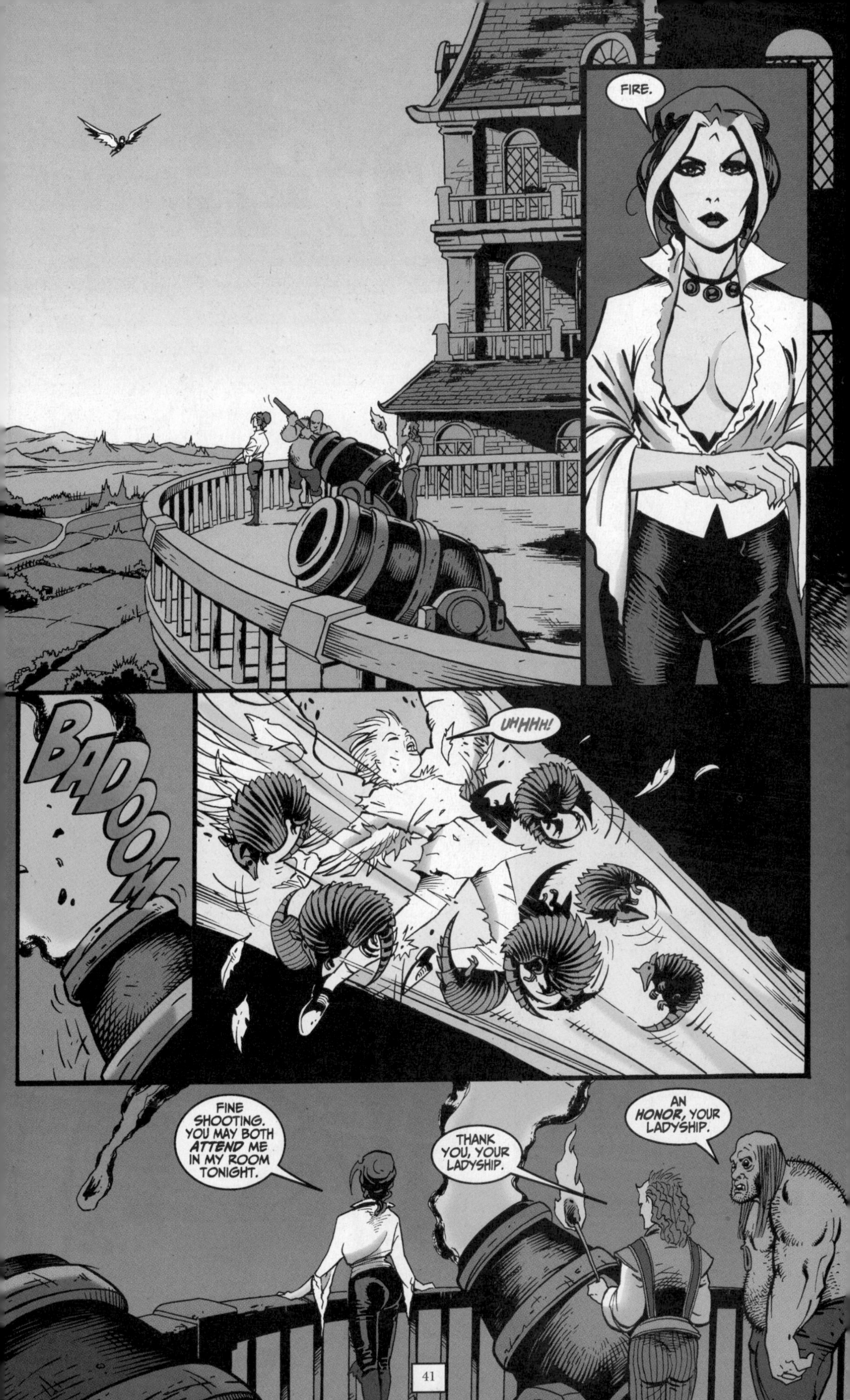
FIRE.
BADOOOM
UHHHH!
FINE SHOOTING. YOU MAY BOTH ATTEND ME IN MY ROOM TONIGHT.
THANK YOU, YOUR LADYSHIP.
AN HONOR, YOUR LADYSHIP.

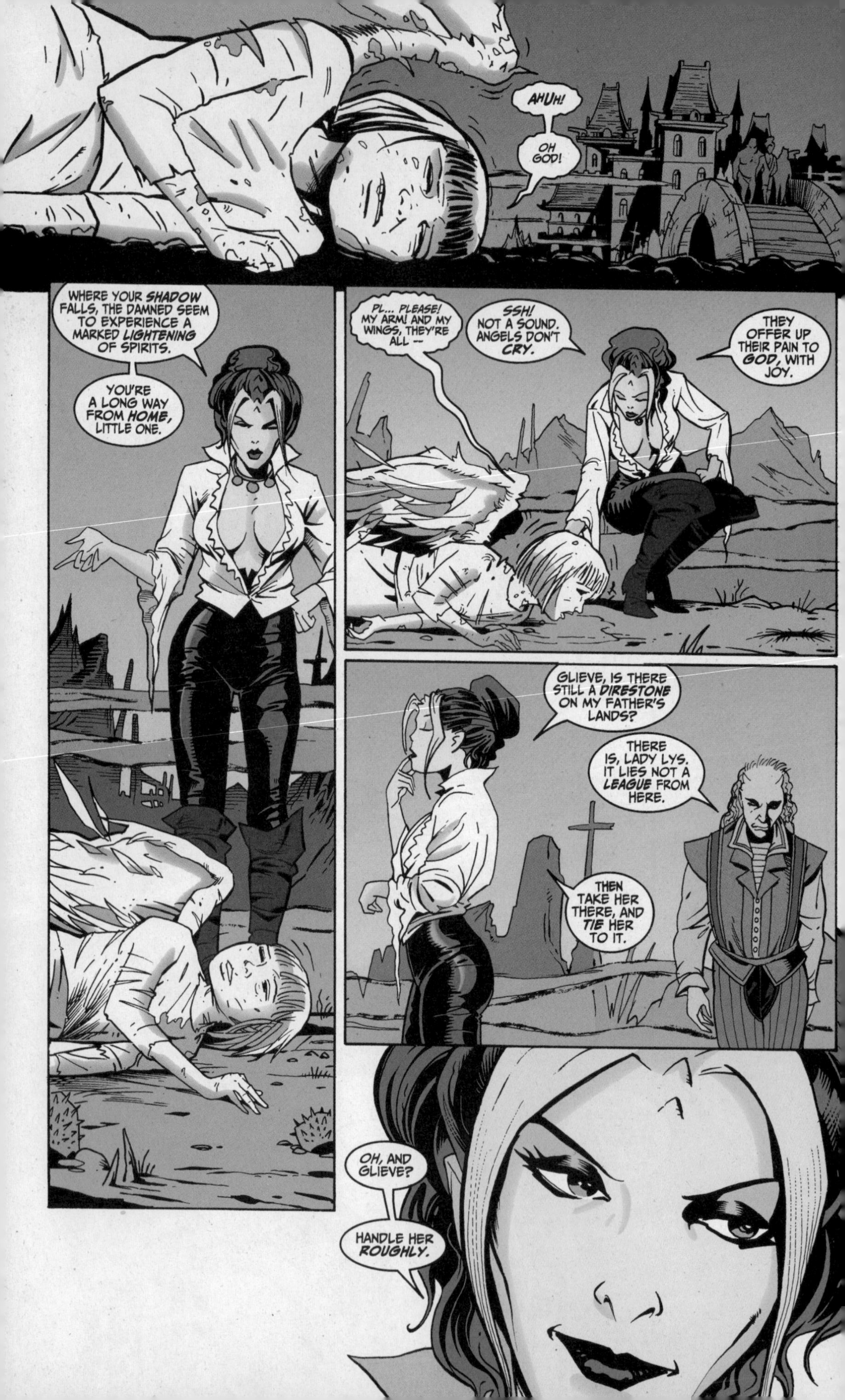
AHUH!
OH GOD!
WHERE YOUR SHADOW FALLS, THE DAMNED SEEM TO EXPERIENCE A MARKED LIGHTENING OF SPIRITS.
YOU'RE A LONG WAY FROM HOME, LITTLE ONE.
PL... PLEASE! MY ARM! AND MY WINGS, THEY'RE ALL --
SSH! NOT A SOUND. ANGELS DON'T CRY.
THEY OFFER UP THEIR PAIN TO GOD, WITH JOY.
GLIEVE, IS THERE STILL A DIRESTONE ON MY FATHER'S LANDS?
THERE IS, LADY LYS. IT LIES NOT A LEAGUE FROM HERE.
THEN TAKE HER THERE, AND TIE HER TO IT.
OH, AND GLIEVE?
HANDLE HER ROUGHLY.

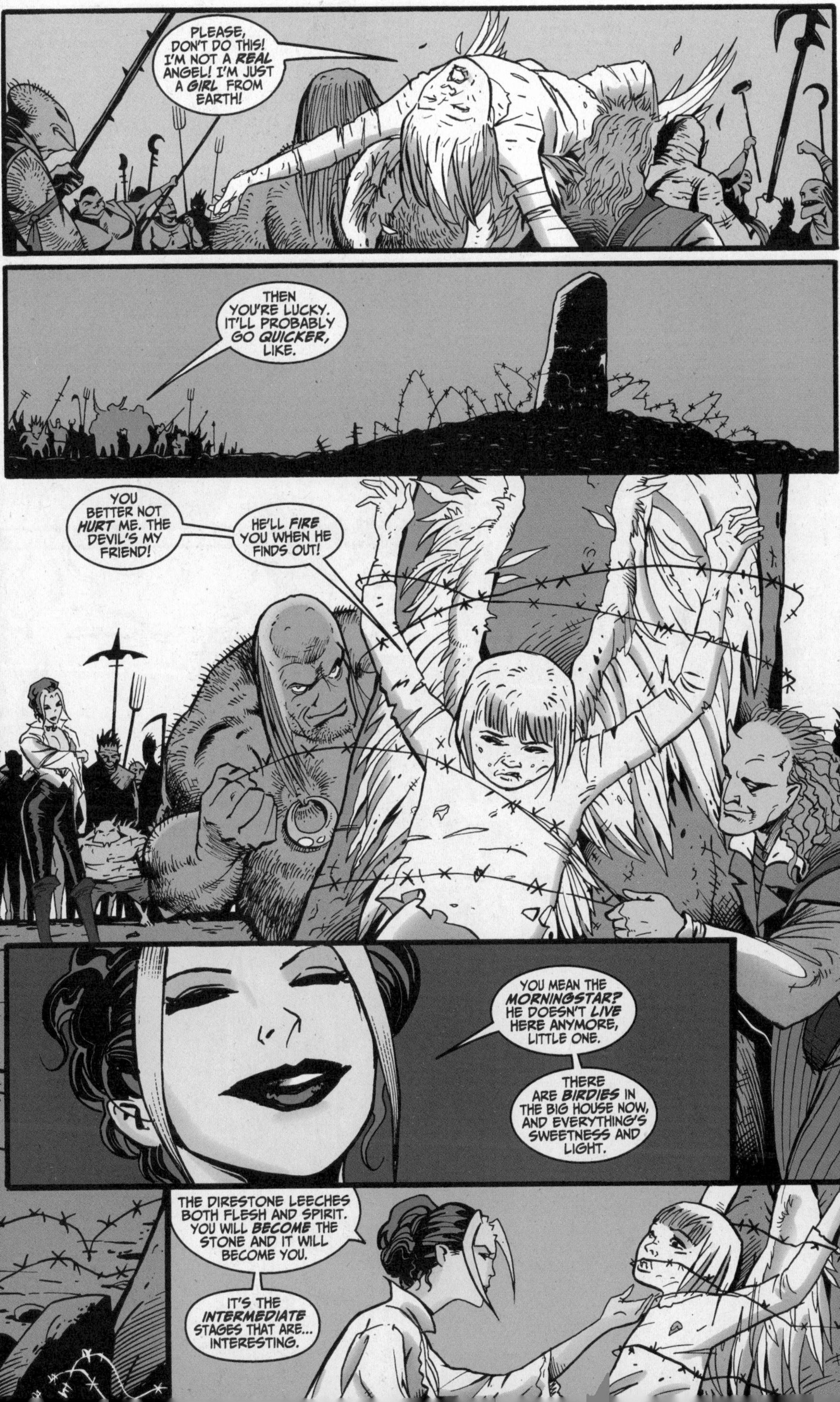
PLEASE, DON'T DO THIS! I'M NOT A REAL ANGEL! I'M JUST A GIRL FROM EARTH!
THEN YOU'RE LUCKY. IT'LL PROBABLY GO QUICKER, LIKE.
YOU BETTER NOT HURT ME. THE DEVIL'S MY FRIEND!
HE'LL FIRE YOU WHEN HE FINDS OUT!
YOU MEAN THE MORNINGSTAR? HE DOESN'T LIVE HERE ANYMORE, LITTLE ONE.
THERE ARE BIRDIES IN THE BIG HOUSE NOW, AND EVERYTHING'S SWEETNESS AND LIGHT.
THE DIRESTONE LEECHES BOTH FLESH AND SPIRIT. YOU WILL BECOME THE STONE AND IT WILL BECOME YOU.
IT'S THE INTERMEDIATE STAGES THAT ARE... INTERESTING.

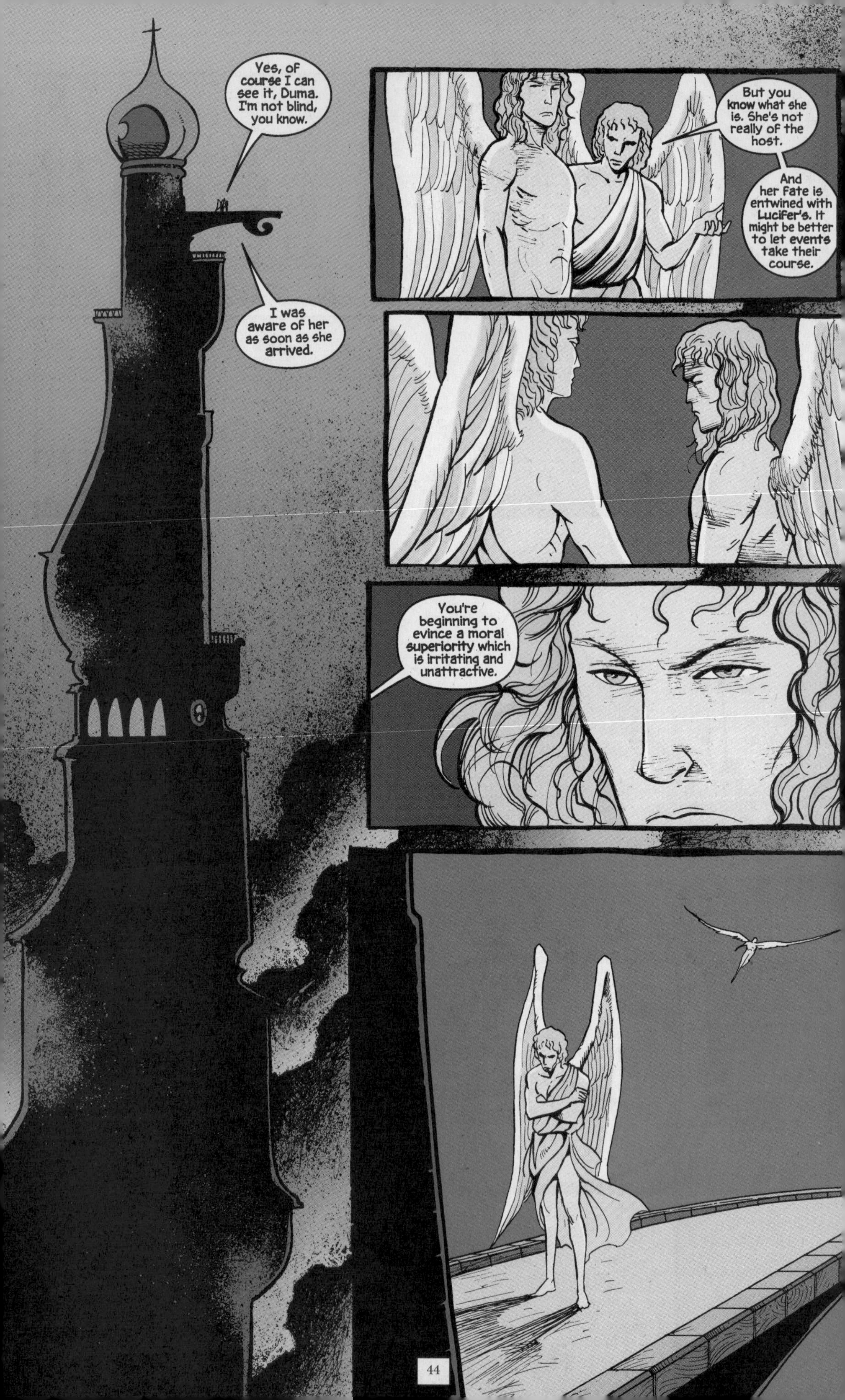

Yes, of course I can see it, Duma. I'm not blind, you know.
I was aware of her as soon as she arrived.
But you know what she is. She's not really of the host.
And her fate is entwined with Lucifer's. It might be better to let events take their course.
You're beginning to evince a moral superiority which is irritating and unattractive.

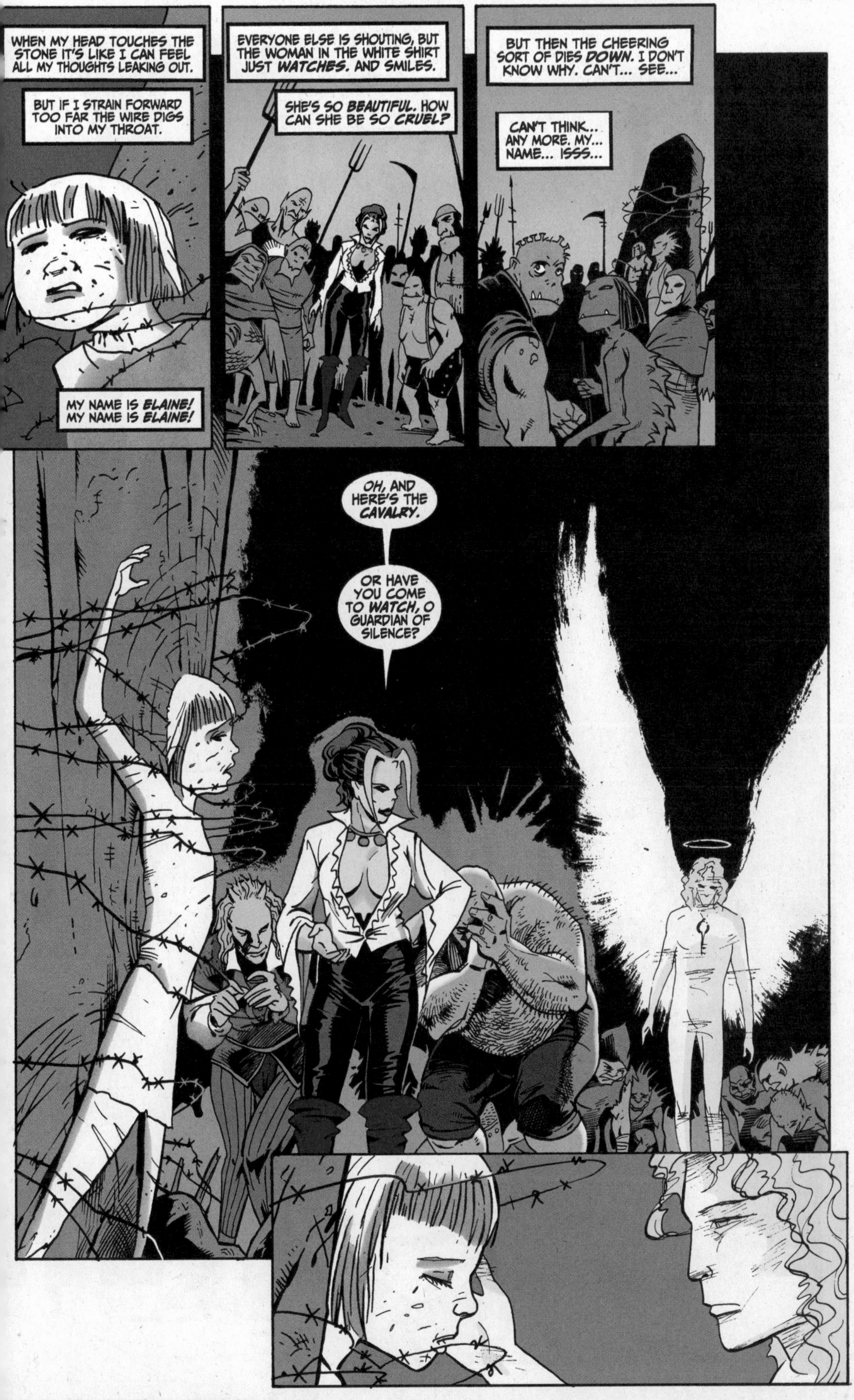

WHEN MY HEAD TOUCHES THE STONE IT'S LIKE I CAN FEEL ALL MY THOUGHTS LEAKING OUT.
BUT IF I STRAIN FORWARD TOO FAR THE WIRE DIGS INTO MY THROAT.
MY NAME IS *ELAINE!* MY NAME IS *ELAINE!*
EVERYONE ELSE IS SHOUTING, BUT THE WOMAN IN THE WHITE SHIRT JUST *WATCHES.* AND SMILES.
SHE'S SO *BEAUTIFUL.* HOW CAN SHE BE SO *CRUEL?*
BUT THEN THE CHEERING SORT OF DIES *DOWN.* I DON'T KNOW WHY. CAN'T... SEE...
CAN'T THINK... ANY MORE. MY... NAME... ISSS...
OH, AND HERE'S THE *CAVALRY.*
OR HAVE YOU COME TO *WATCH,* O GUARDIAN OF SILENCE?

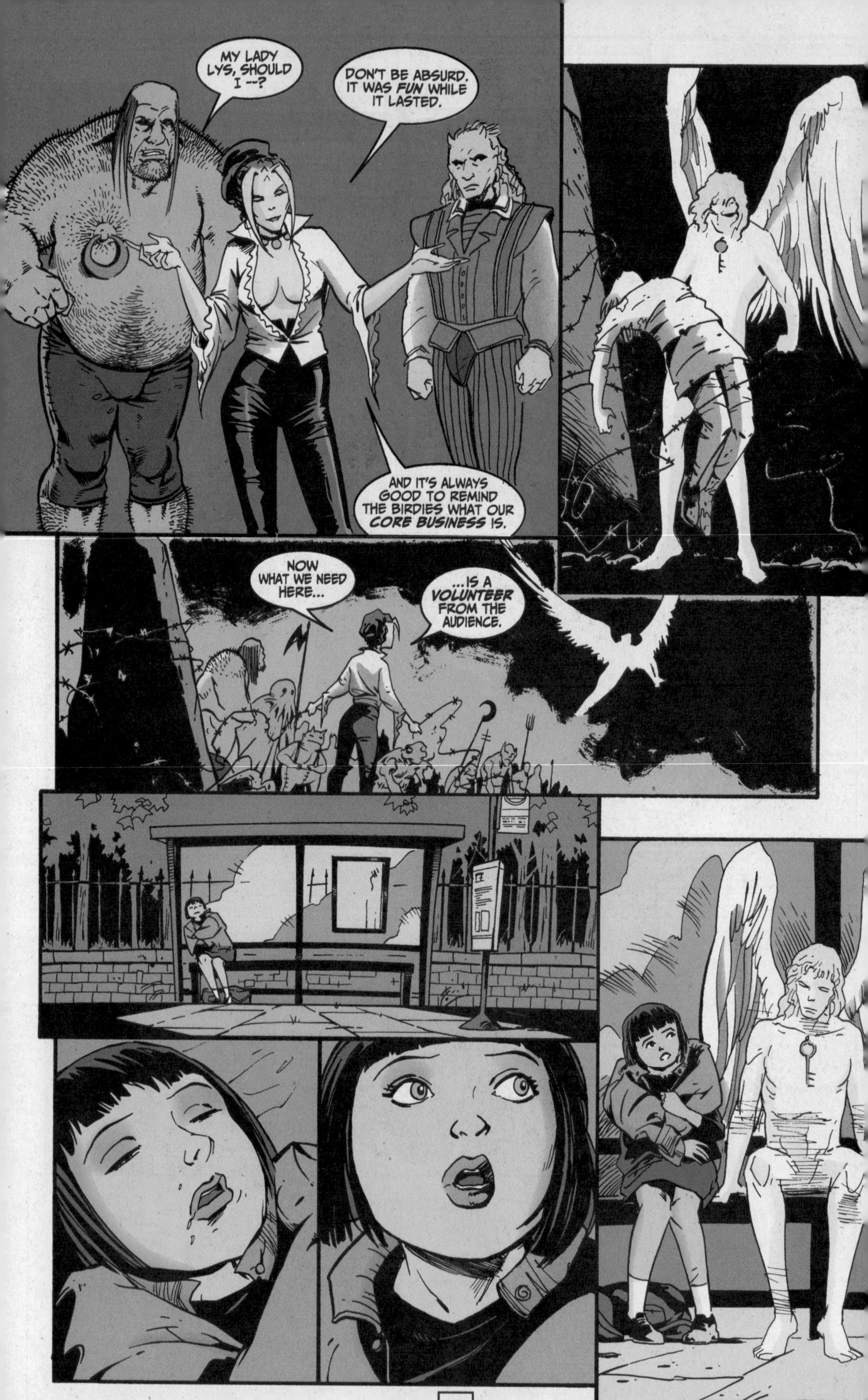
MY LADY LYS, SHOULD I --?
DON'T BE ABSURD. IT WAS FUN WHILE IT LASTED.
AND IT'S ALWAYS GOOD TO REMIND THE BIRDIES WHAT OUR CORE BUSINESS IS.
NOW WHAT WE NEED HERE...
...IS A VOLUNTEER FROM THE AUDIENCE.

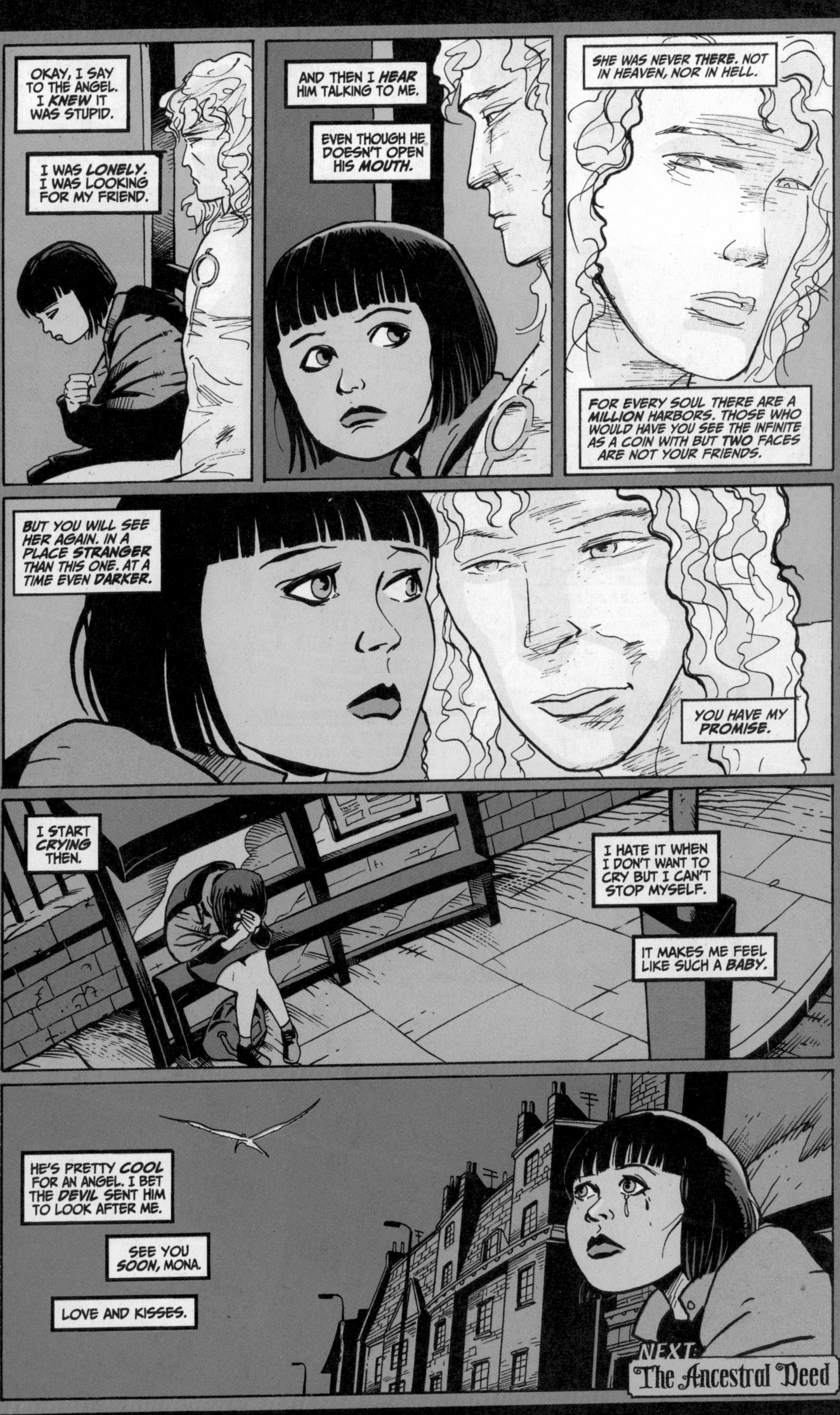
OKAY, I SAY TO THE ANGEL. I KNEW IT WAS STUPID.
I WAS LONELY. I WAS LOOKING FOR MY FRIEND.
AND THEN I HEAR HIM TALKING TO ME.
EVEN THOUGH HE DOESN'T OPEN HIS MOUTH.
SHE WAS NEVER THERE. NOT IN HEAVEN, NOR IN HELL.
FOR EVERY SOUL THERE ARE A MILLION HARBORS. THOSE WHO WOULD HAVE YOU SEE THE INFINITE AS A COIN WITH BUT TWO FACES ARE NOT YOUR FRIENDS.
BUT YOU WILL SEE HER AGAIN. IN A PLACE STRANGER THAN THIS ONE. AT A TIME EVEN DARKER.
YOU HAVE MY PROMISE.
I START CRYING THEN.
I HATE IT WHEN I DON'T WANT TO CRY BUT I CAN'T STOP MYSELF.
IT MAKES ME FEEL LIKE SUCH A BABY.
HE'S PRETTY COOL FOR AN ANGEL. I BET THE DEVIL SENT HIM TO LOOK AFTER ME.
SEE YOU SOON, MONA.
LOVE AND KISSES.
NEXT: The Ancestral Deed

LOS ANGELES HAS CHANGED SINCE SHE LEFT. IT APPEARS TO BE *HAUNTED* NOW.

HAUNTED BY AN ABSENCE, PERHAPS. A FUGUE. A BREAK IN CONTINUITY.

SHE TURNS ONTO GREGORY AT LA CIENEGA PARK. THE STREET IS BLOCKED OFF WHERE A FOURTEEN-WHEELER SMASHED THROUGH A CONCRETE BARRIER AND FELL DOWN ONTO THE SIDEWALK.

PEOPLE LOOK AWAY AS THEY GO BY, WITH TROUBLED, HAUNTED EYES

THE FIRST CHURCH OF THE SILENT GOD PREACHES THAT *CHRIST* RETURNED LAST TUESDAY, BUT THAT THE DEVIL KILLED HIM WHILE THE CITY SLEPT.

THERE ARE DOZENS OF NEW CULTS SPRINGING UP, BUT THAT ONE STRIKES HER AS PARTICULARLY AMUSING.

STRIKE TWO
PRAY THAT HE WILL COME AGAIN.
Scully Hill, Sunday. 3:00pm
First Church of the Silent God

EVERYONE REMEMBERS SOMETHING. EVERYONE HAS THEIR OWN WAY OF EVADING THE TRUTH.

MINDQUAKE

ST LOST MY MIND FOR A MOMENT THE

norm conscious will b resume

THAT THERE WAS A WAR HERE. AND NONE OF THEM WERE INVITED.

A BLOCK AWAY FROM LUX SHE SEES THE SMALL ENCAMPMENT THAT THE SENSITIVES HAVE MADE. THE ONES DRAWN HERE BY THE GATE. AND HELD HERE, IN SPITE OF FIRE AND SWORD.

SHE'S ON FAMILIAR GROUND NOW.

OR AT LEAST SHE THINKS SHE IS.

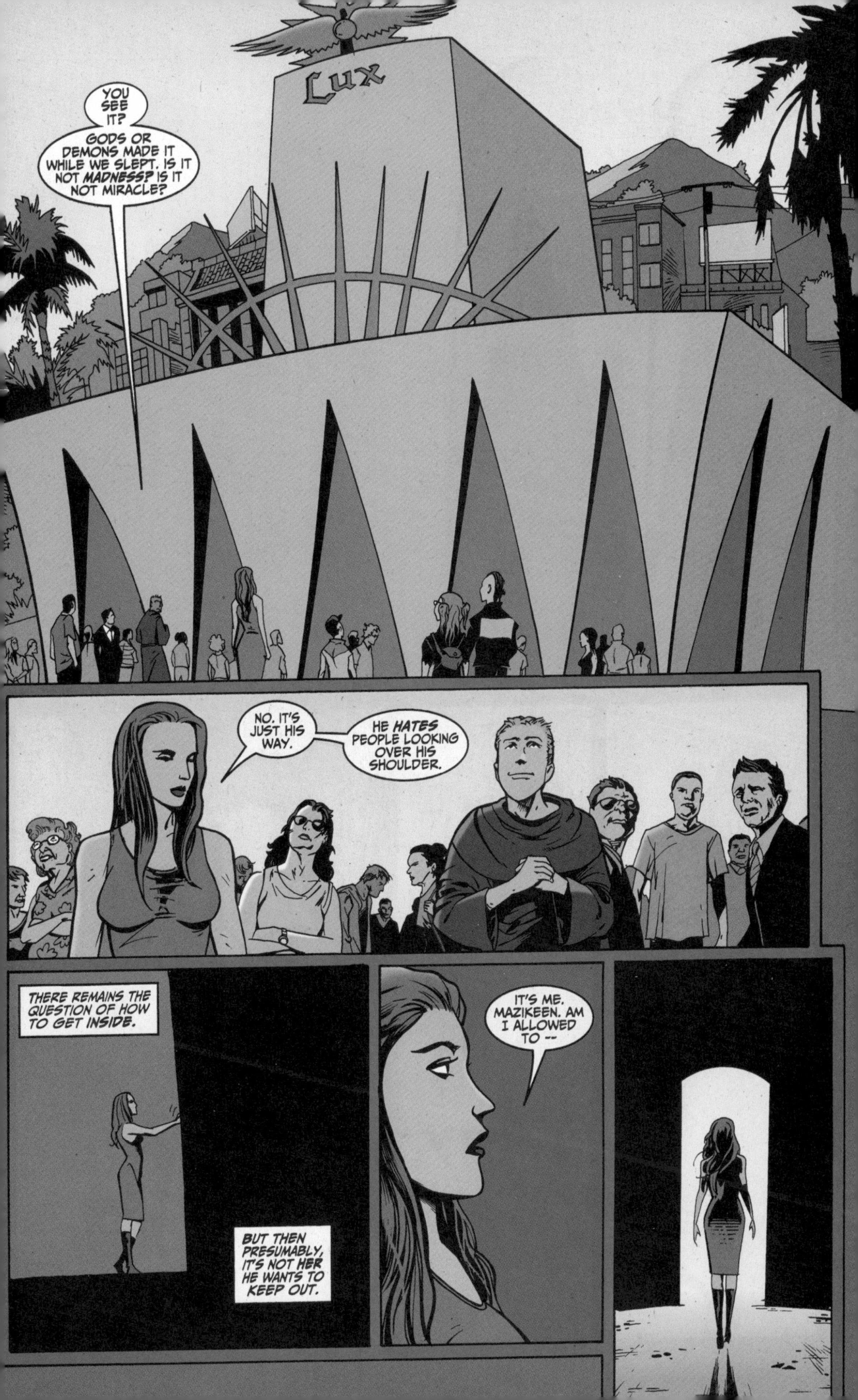
Lux
YOU SEE IT? GODS OR DEMONS MADE IT WHILE WE SLEPT. IS IT NOT MADNESS? IS IT NOT MIRACLE?
NO. IT'S JUST HIS WAY.
HE HATES PEOPLE LOOKING OVER HIS SHOULDER.
THERE REMAINS THE QUESTION OF HOW TO GET INSIDE.
BUT THEN PRESUMABLY, IT'S NOT HER HE WANTS TO KEEP OUT.
IT'S ME. MAZIKEEN. AM I ALLOWED TO --

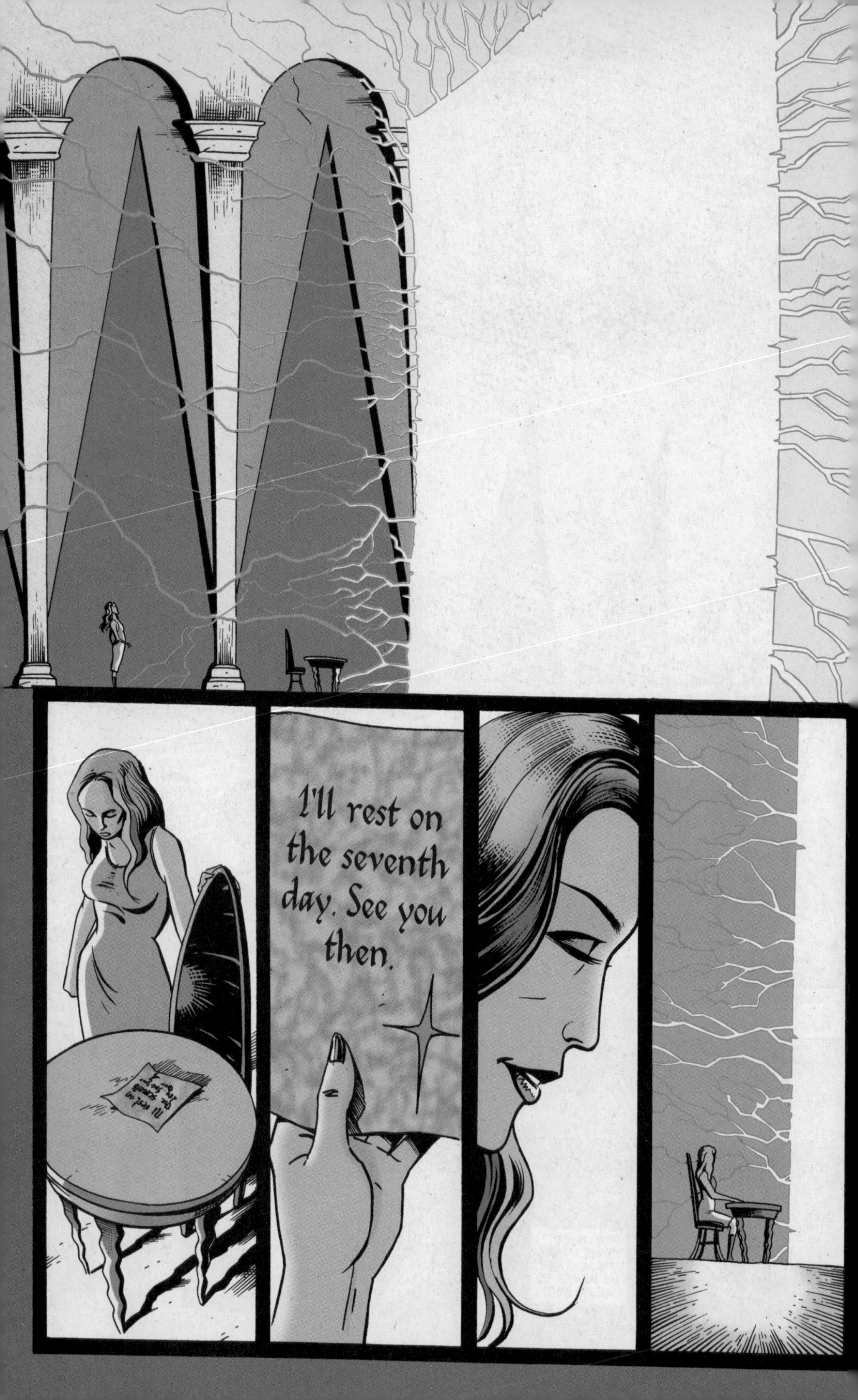
I'll rest on the seventh day. See you then.

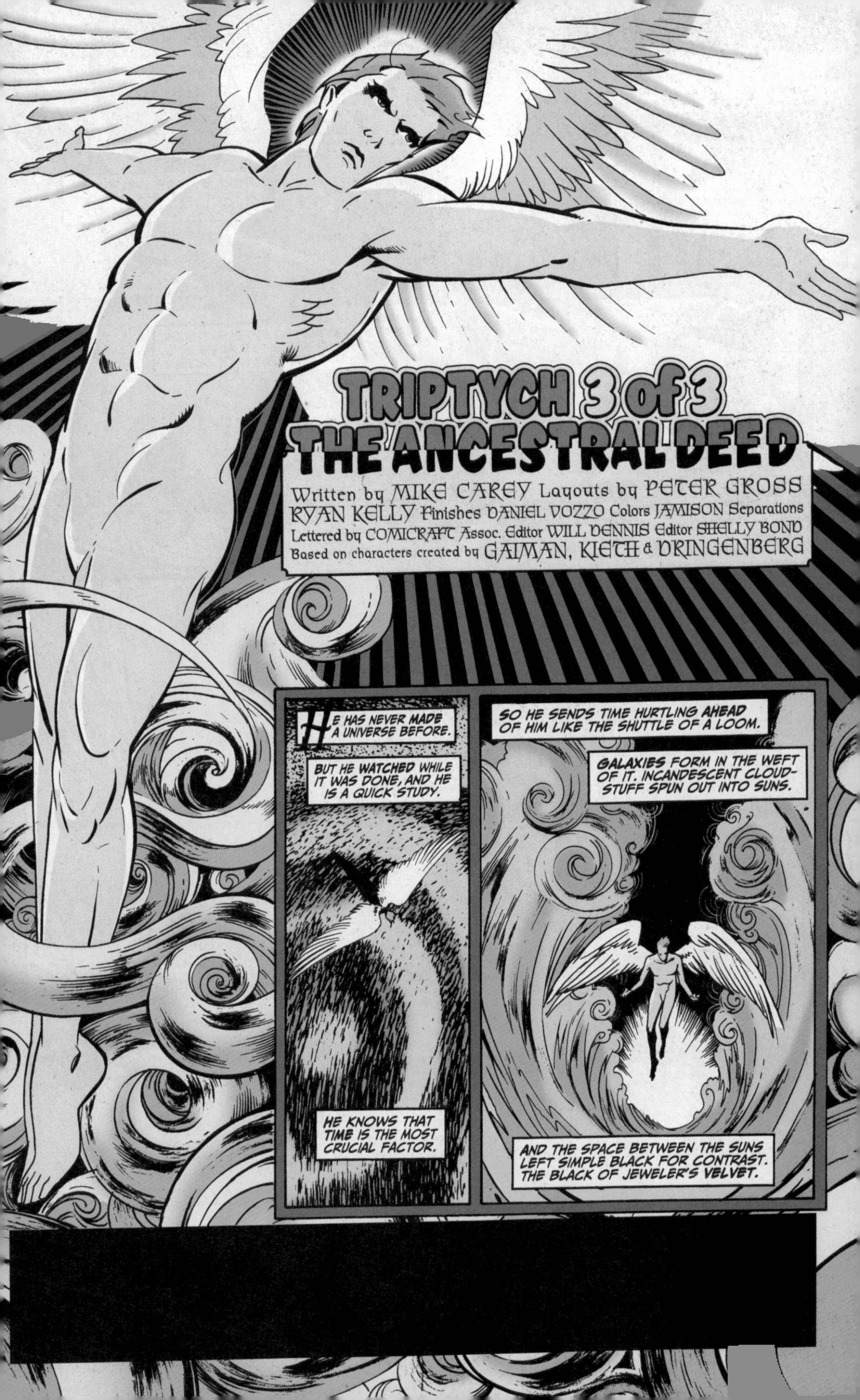
TRIPTYCH 3 of 3
THE ANCESTRAL DEED
Written by MIKE CAREY Layouts by PETER GROSS
RYAN KELLY Finishes DANIEL VOZZO Colors JAMISON Separations
Lettered by COMICRAFT Assoc. Editor WILL DENNIS Editor SHELLY BOND
Based on characters created by GAIMAN, KIETH & DRINGENBERG
HE HAS NEVER MADE A UNIVERSE BEFORE.
BUT HE WATCHED WHILE IT WAS DONE, AND HE IS A QUICK STUDY.
HE KNOWS THAT TIME IS THE MOST CRUCIAL FACTOR.
SO HE SENDS TIME HURTLING AHEAD OF HIM LIKE THE SHUTTLE OF A LOOM.
GALAXIES FORM IN THE WEFT OF IT. INCANDESCENT CLOUD-STUFF SPUN OUT INTO SUNS.
AND THE SPACE BETWEEN THE SUNS LEFT SIMPLE BLACK FOR CONTRAST. THE BLACK OF JEWELER'S VELVET.

[redacted]

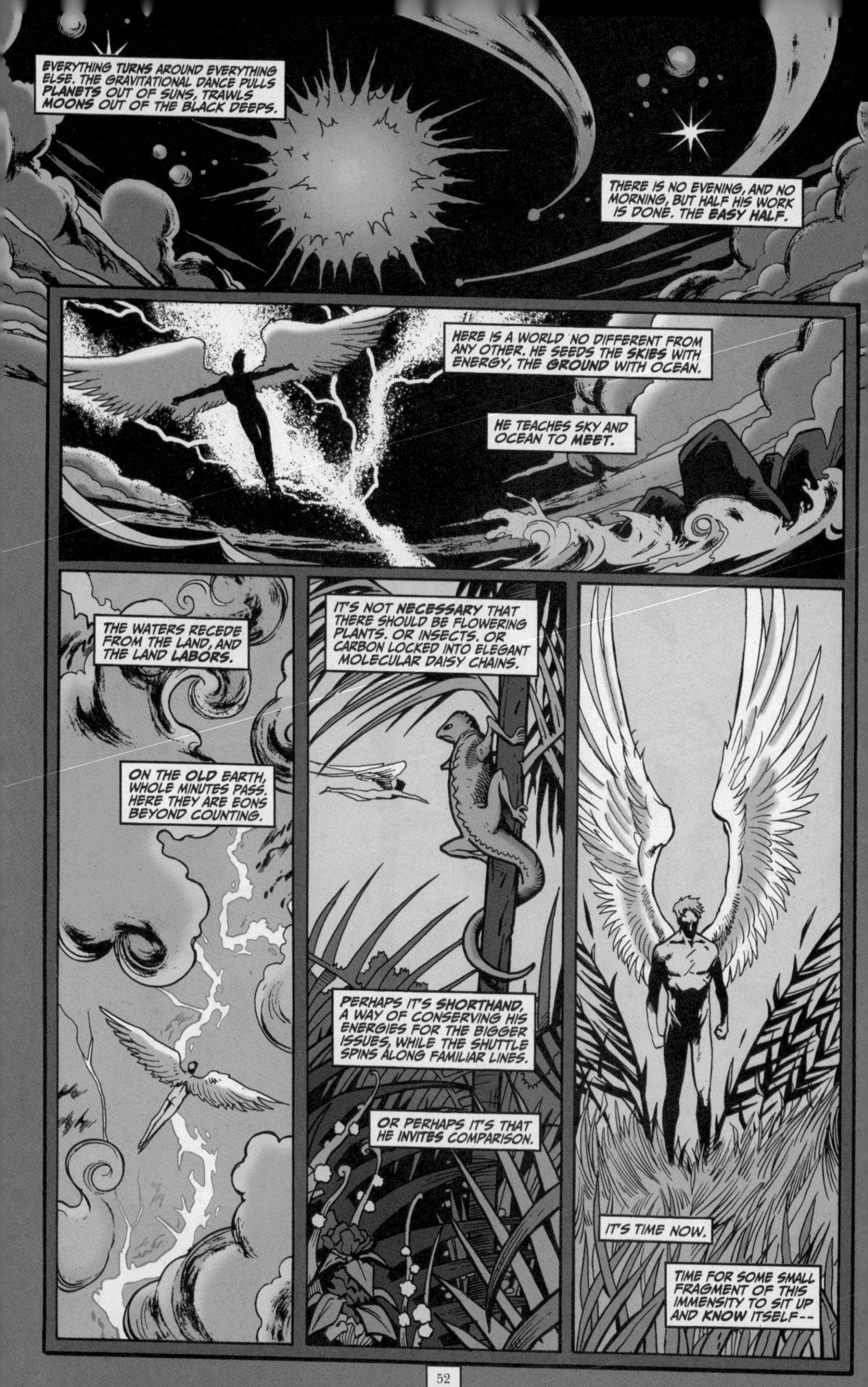
EVERYTHING TURNS AROUND EVERYTHING ELSE. THE GRAVITATIONAL DANCE PULLS PLANETS OUT OF SUNS, TRAWLS MOONS OUT OF THE BLACK DEEPS.
THERE IS NO EVENING, AND NO MORNING, BUT HALF HIS WORK IS DONE. THE EASY HALF.
HERE IS A WORLD NO DIFFERENT FROM ANY OTHER. HE SEEDS THE SKIES WITH ENERGY, THE GROUND WITH OCEAN.
HE TEACHES SKY AND OCEAN TO MEET.
THE WATERS RECEDE FROM THE LAND, AND THE LAND LABORS.
ON THE OLD EARTH, WHOLE MINUTES PASS. HERE THEY ARE EONS BEYOND COUNTING.
IT'S NOT NECESSARY THAT THERE SHOULD BE FLOWERING PLANTS. OR INSECTS. OR CARBON LOCKED INTO ELEGANT MOLECULAR DAISY CHAINS.
PERHAPS IT'S SHORTHAND, A WAY OF CONSERVING HIS ENERGIES FOR THE BIGGER ISSUES, WHILE THE SHUTTLE SPINS ALONG FAMILIAR LINES.
OR PERHAPS IT'S THAT HE INVITES COMPARISON.
IT'S TIME NOW.
TIME FOR SOME SMALL FRAGMENT OF THIS IMMENSITY TO SIT UP AND KNOW ITSELF--

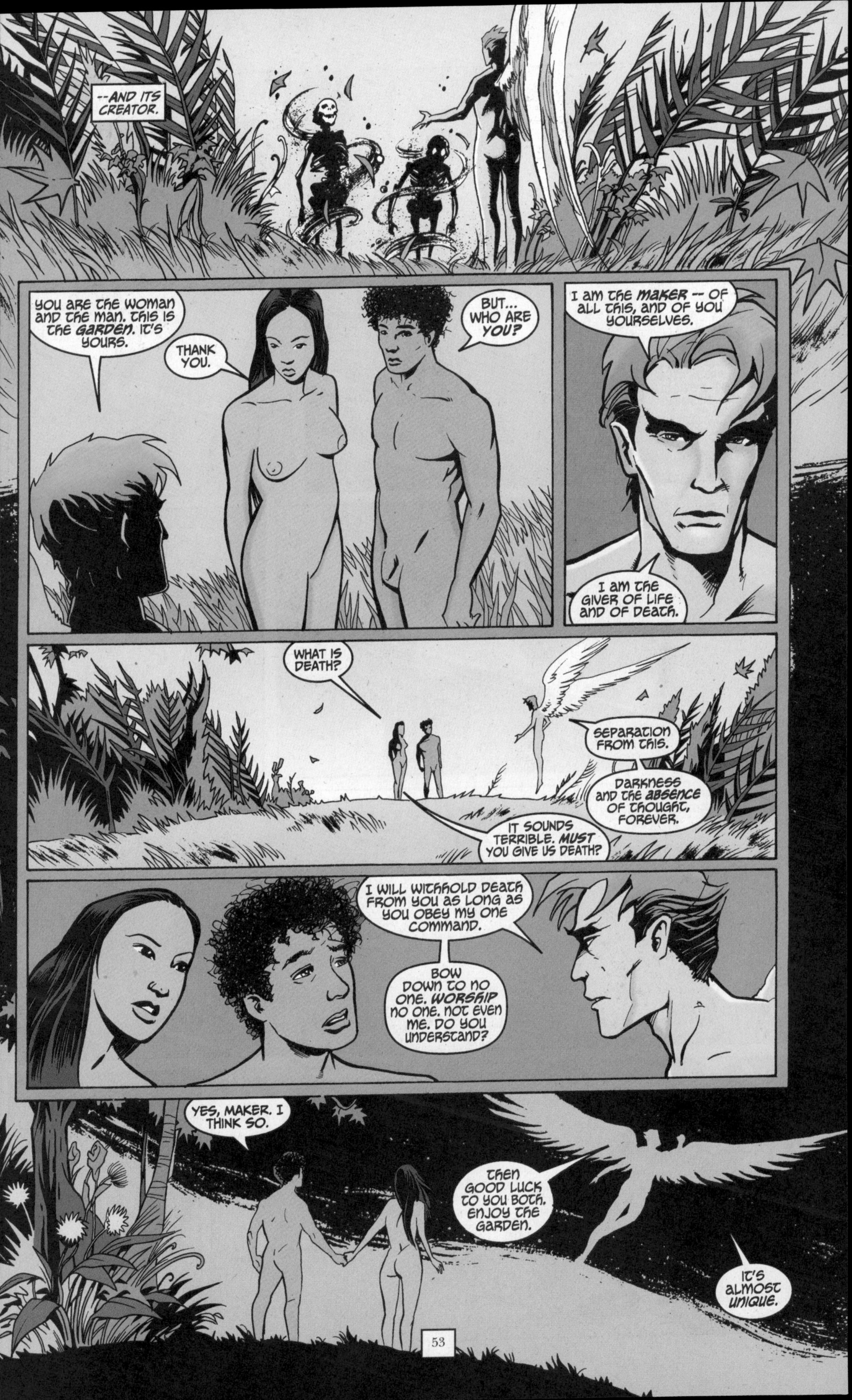
--AND ITS CREATOR.
YOU ARE THE WOMAN AND THE MAN. THIS IS THE GARDEN. IT'S YOURS.
THANK YOU.
BUT... WHO ARE YOU?
I AM THE MAKER -- OF ALL THIS, AND OF YOU YOURSELVES.
I AM THE GIVER OF LIFE AND OF DEATH.
WHAT IS DEATH?
SEPARATION FROM THIS.
DARKNESS AND THE ABSENCE OF THOUGHT, FOREVER.
IT SOUNDS TERRIBLE. MUST YOU GIVE US DEATH?
I WILL WITHHOLD DEATH FROM YOU AS LONG AS YOU OBEY MY ONE COMMAND.
BOW DOWN TO NO ONE. WORSHIP NO ONE. NOT EVEN ME. DO YOU UNDERSTAND?
YES, MAKER. I THINK SO.
THEN GOOD LUCK TO YOU BOTH. ENJOY THE GARDEN.
IT'S ALMOST UNIQUE.

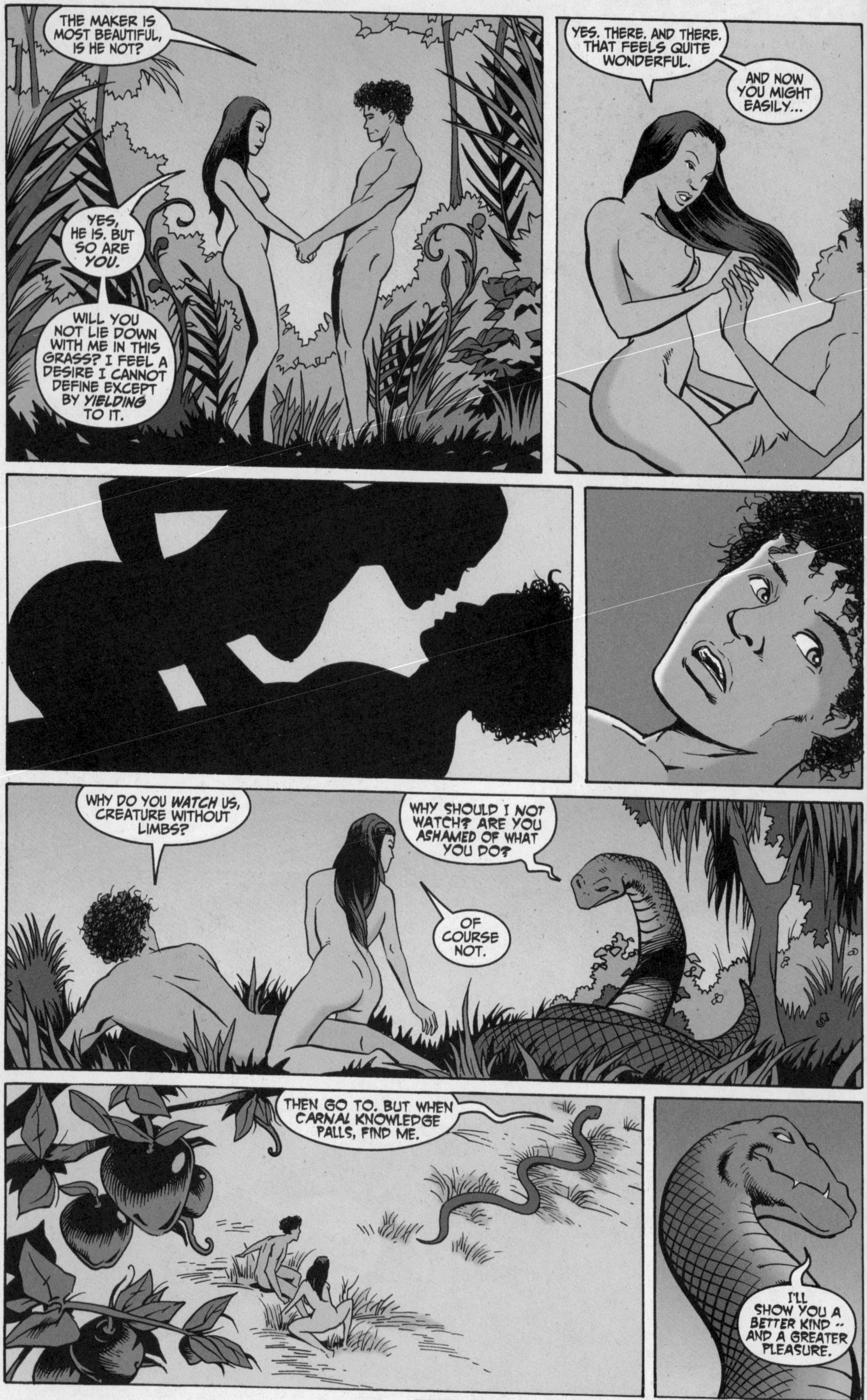
THE MAKER IS MOST BEAUTIFUL, IS HE NOT?
YES, HE IS. BUT SO ARE *YOU*.
WILL YOU NOT LIE DOWN WITH ME IN THIS GRASS? I FEEL A DESIRE I CANNOT DEFINE EXCEPT BY *YIELDING* TO IT.
YES. THERE. AND THERE. THAT FEELS QUITE WONDERFUL.
AND NOW YOU MIGHT EASILY...
WHY DO YOU *WATCH* US, CREATURE WITHOUT LIMBS?
WHY SHOULD I *NOT* WATCH? ARE YOU *ASHAMED* OF WHAT YOU DO?
OF COURSE NOT.
THEN GO TO. BUT WHEN *CARNAL* KNOWLEDGE PALLS, FIND ME.
I'LL SHOW YOU A BETTER KIND -- AND A GREATER PLEASURE.

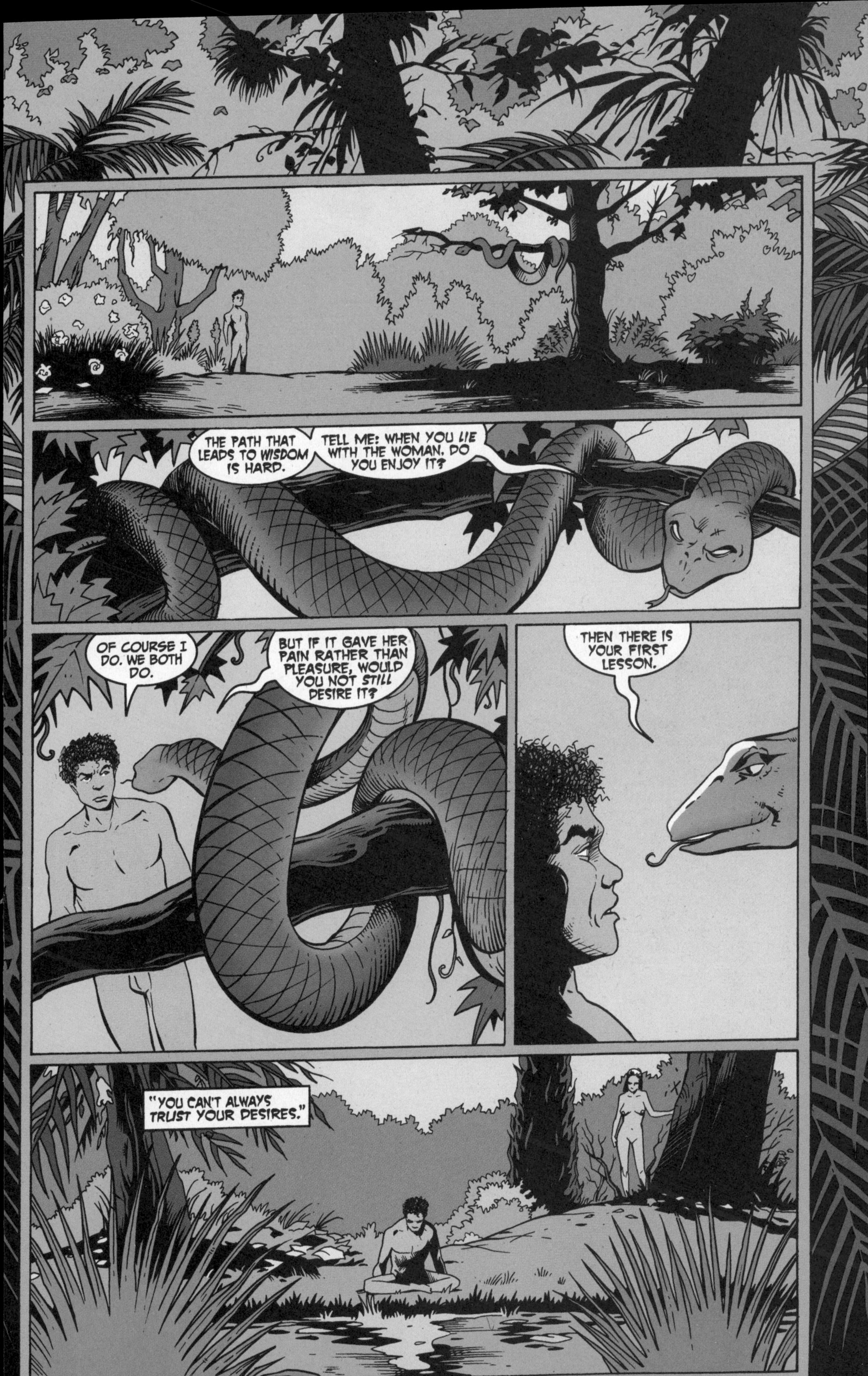
THE PATH THAT LEADS TO WISDOM IS HARD.
TELL ME: WHEN YOU LIE WITH THE WOMAN, DO YOU ENJOY IT?
OF COURSE I DO. WE BOTH DO.
BUT IF IT GAVE HER PAIN RATHER THAN PLEASURE, WOULD YOU NOT STILL DESIRE IT?
THEN THERE IS YOUR FIRST LESSON.
"YOU CAN'T ALWAYS TRUST YOUR DESIRES."

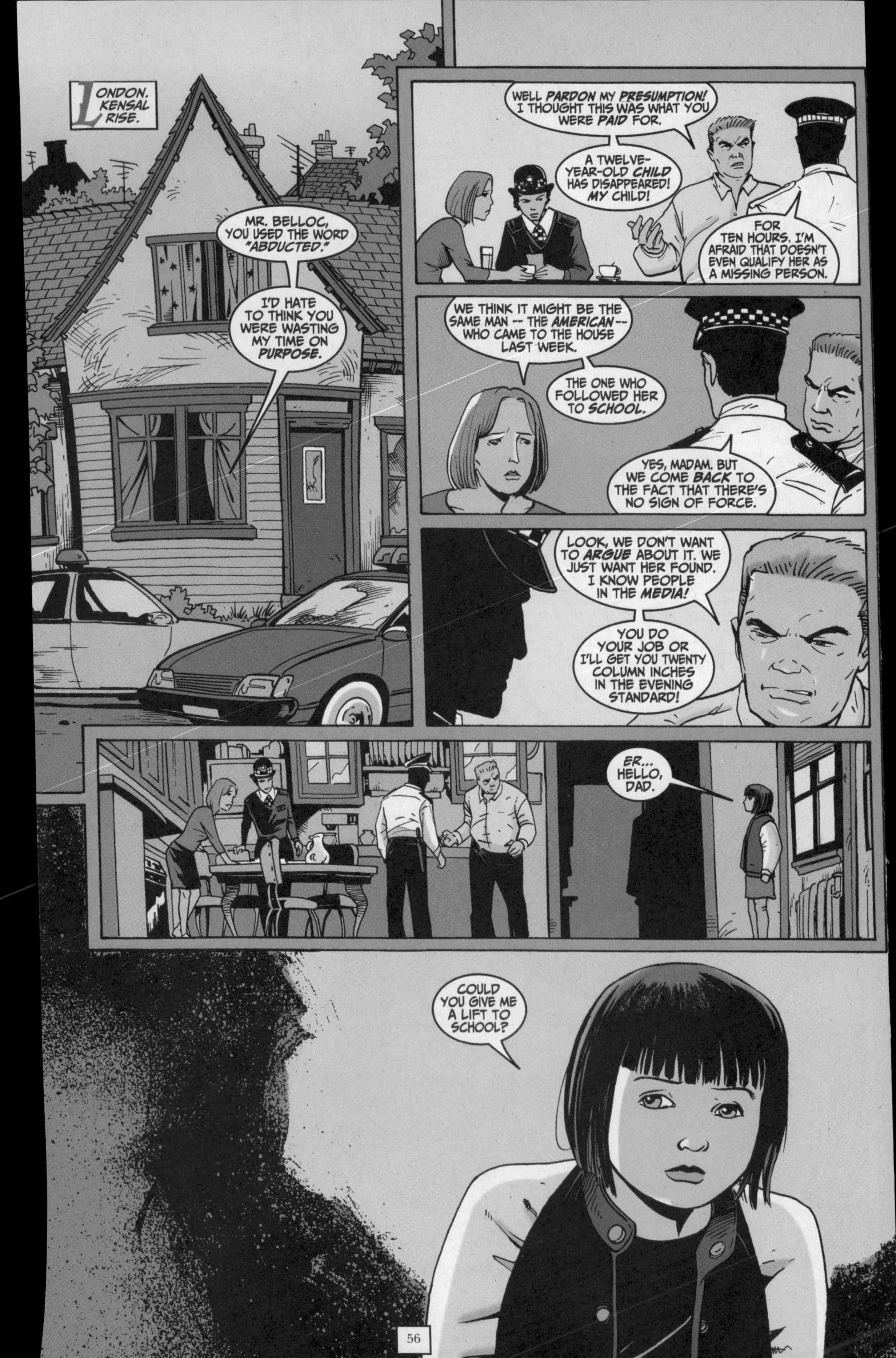
LONDON. KENSAL RISE.
MR. BELLOC, YOU USED THE WORD "ABDUCTED."
I'D HATE TO THINK YOU WERE WASTING MY TIME ON PURPOSE.
WELL PARDON MY PRESUMPTION! I THOUGHT THIS WAS WHAT YOU WERE PAID FOR.
A TWELVE-YEAR-OLD CHILD HAS DISAPPEARED! MY CHILD!
FOR TEN HOURS. I'M AFRAID THAT DOESN'T EVEN QUALIFY HER AS A MISSING PERSON.
WE THINK IT MIGHT BE THE SAME MAN -- THE AMERICAN -- WHO CAME TO THE HOUSE LAST WEEK.
THE ONE WHO FOLLOWED HER TO SCHOOL.
YES, MADAM. BUT WE COME BACK TO THE FACT THAT THERE'S NO SIGN OF FORCE.
LOOK, WE DON'T WANT TO ARGUE ABOUT IT. WE JUST WANT HER FOUND. I KNOW PEOPLE IN THE MEDIA!
YOU DO YOUR JOB OR I'LL GET YOU TWENTY COLUMN INCHES IN THE EVENING STANDARD!
ER... HELLO, DAD.
COULD YOU GIVE ME A LIFT TO SCHOOL?

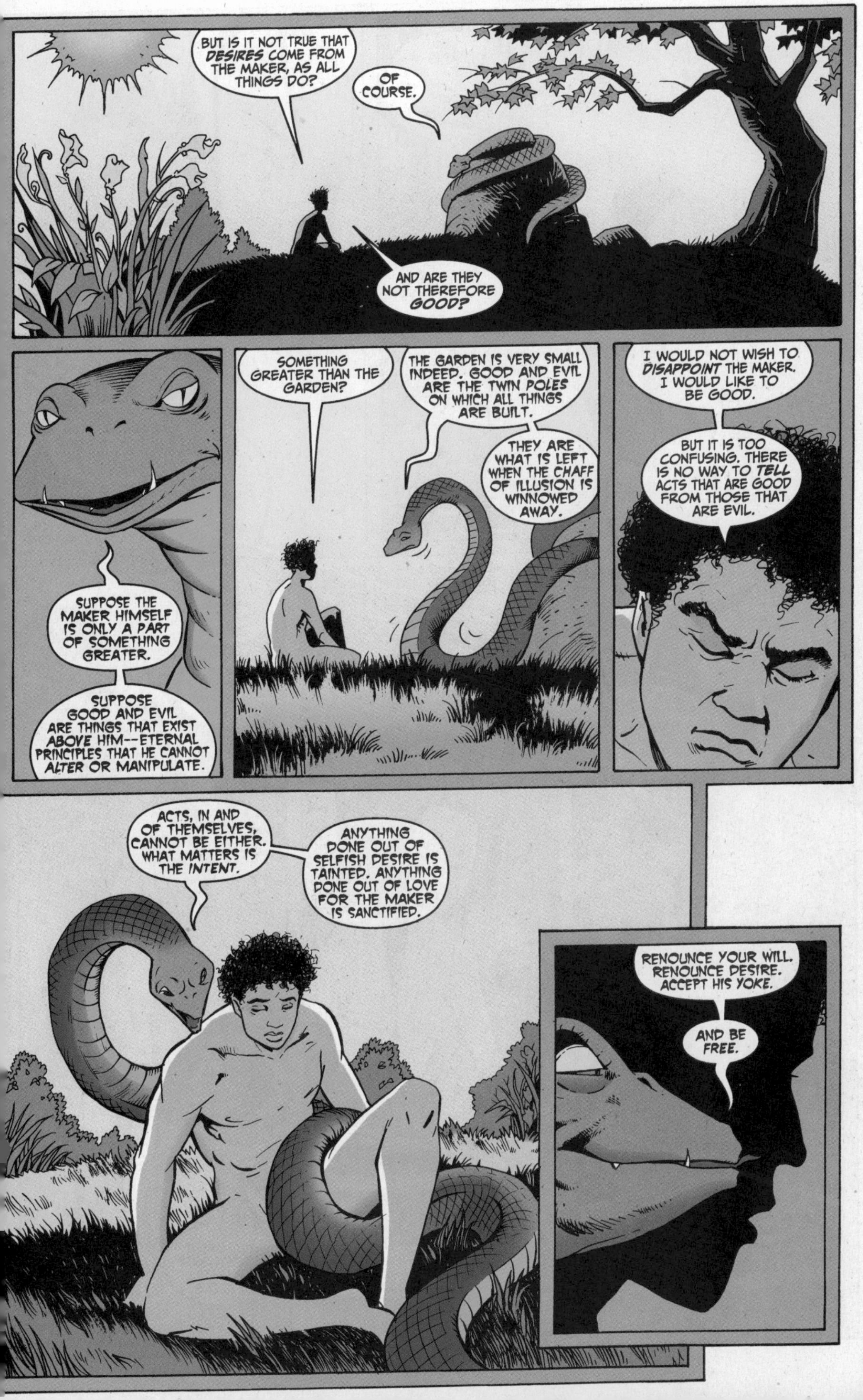
BUT IS IT NOT TRUE THAT DESIRES COME FROM THE MAKER, AS ALL THINGS DO?
OF COURSE.
AND ARE THEY NOT THEREFORE GOOD?
SUPPOSE THE MAKER HIMSELF IS ONLY A PART OF SOMETHING GREATER.
SUPPOSE GOOD AND EVIL ARE THINGS THAT EXIST ABOVE HIM--ETERNAL PRINCIPLES THAT HE CANNOT ALTER OR MANIPULATE.
SOMETHING GREATER THAN THE GARDEN?
THE GARDEN IS VERY SMALL INDEED. GOOD AND EVIL ARE THE TWIN POLES ON WHICH ALL THINGS ARE BUILT.
THEY ARE WHAT IS LEFT WHEN THE CHAFF OF ILLUSION IS WINNOWED AWAY.
I WOULD NOT WISH TO DISAPPOINT THE MAKER. I WOULD LIKE TO BE GOOD.
BUT IT IS TOO CONFUSING. THERE IS NO WAY TO TELL ACTS THAT ARE GOOD FROM THOSE THAT ARE EVIL.
ACTS, IN AND OF THEMSELVES, CANNOT BE EITHER. WHAT MATTERS IS THE INTENT.
ANYTHING DONE OUT OF SELFISH DESIRE IS TAINTED. ANYTHING DONE OUT OF LOVE FOR THE MAKER IS SANCTIFIED.
RENOUNCE YOUR WILL. RENOUNCE DESIRE. ACCEPT HIS YOKE.
AND BE FREE.

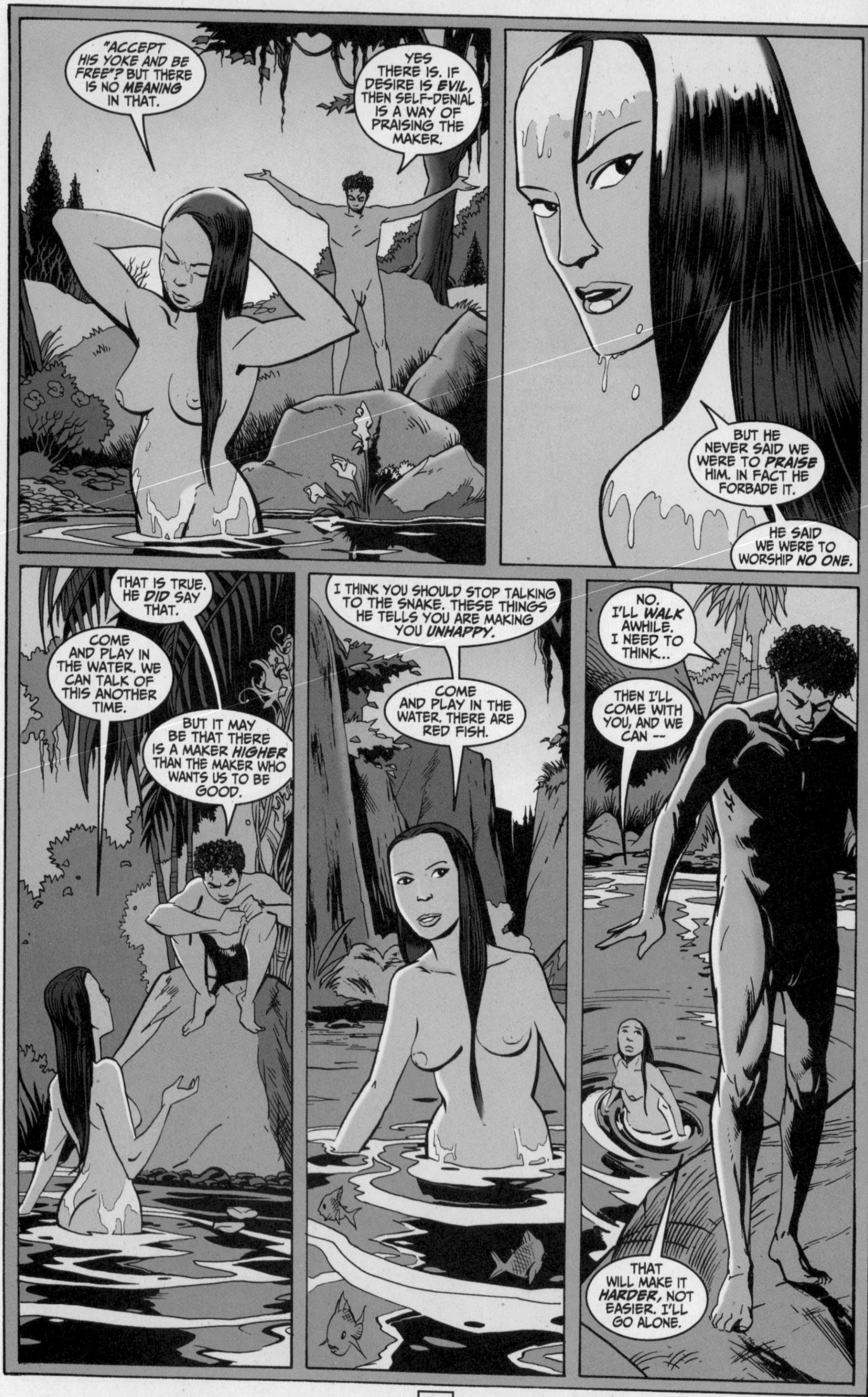
"ACCEPT HIS YOKE AND BE FREE"? BUT THERE IS NO MEANING IN THAT.
YES THERE IS. IF DESIRE IS EVIL, THEN SELF-DENIAL IS A WAY OF PRAISING THE MAKER.
BUT HE NEVER SAID WE WERE TO PRAISE HIM. IN FACT HE FORBADE IT.
HE SAID WE WERE TO WORSHIP NO ONE.
THAT IS TRUE. HE DID SAY THAT.
COME AND PLAY IN THE WATER. WE CAN TALK OF THIS ANOTHER TIME.
BUT IT MAY BE THAT THERE IS A MAKER HIGHER THAN THE MAKER WHO WANTS US TO BE GOOD.
I THINK YOU SHOULD STOP TALKING TO THE SNAKE. THESE THINGS HE TELLS YOU ARE MAKING YOU UNHAPPY.
COME AND PLAY IN THE WATER. THERE ARE RED FISH.
NO. I'LL WALK AWHILE. I NEED TO THINK...
THEN I'LL COME WITH YOU, AND WE CAN --
THAT WILL MAKE IT HARDER, NOT EASIER. I'LL GO ALONE.

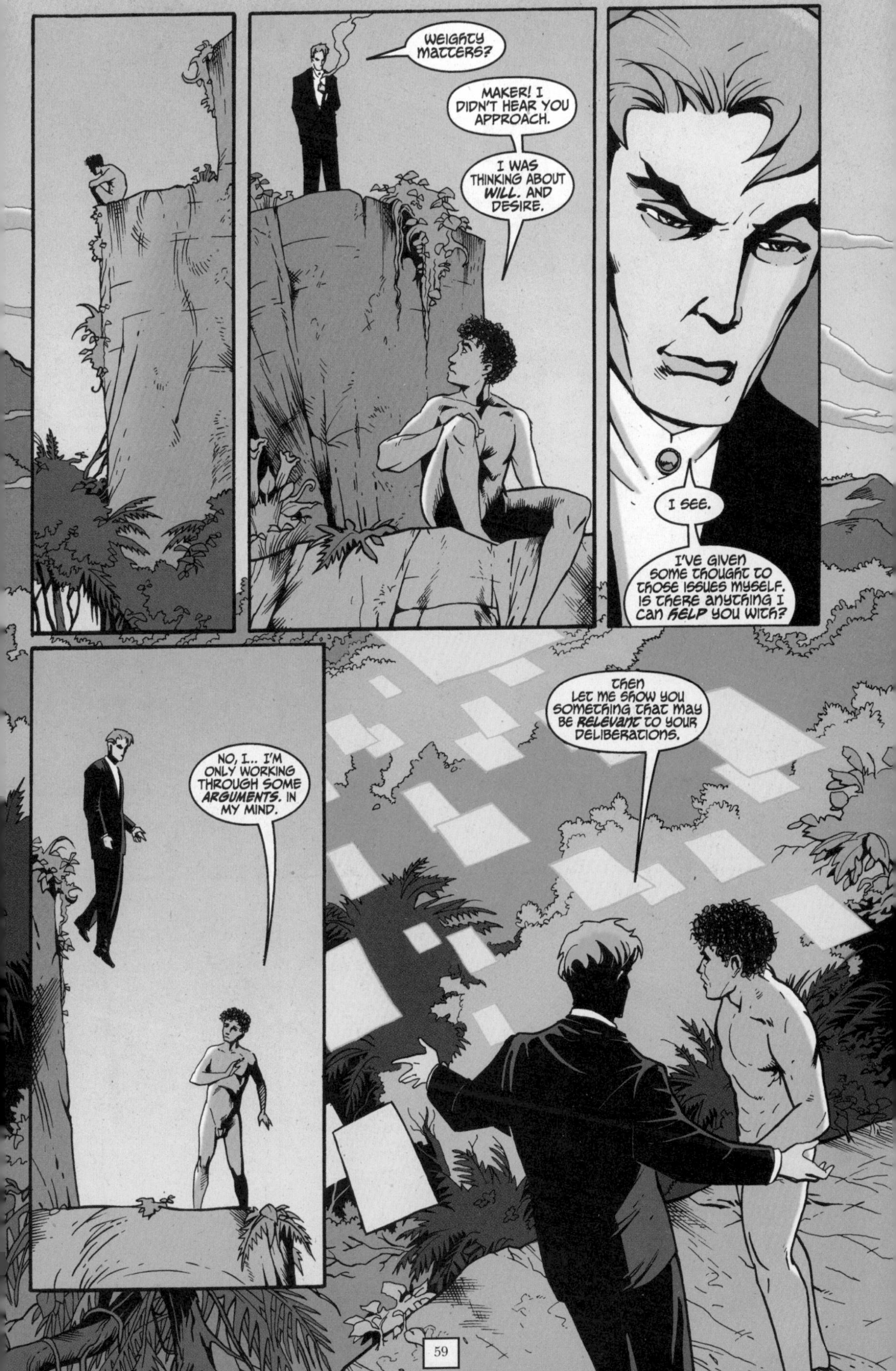
WEIGHTY MATTERS?
MAKER! I DIDN'T HEAR YOU APPROACH.
I WAS THINKING ABOUT *WILL*. AND DESIRE.
I SEE.
I'VE GIVEN SOME THOUGHT TO THOSE ISSUES MYSELF. IS THERE ANYTHING I CAN *HELP* YOU WITH?
NO, I.. I'M ONLY WORKING THROUGH SOME *ARGUMENTS*. IN MY MIND.
THEN LET ME SHOW YOU SOMETHING THAT MAY BE *RELEVANT* TO YOUR DELIBERATIONS.

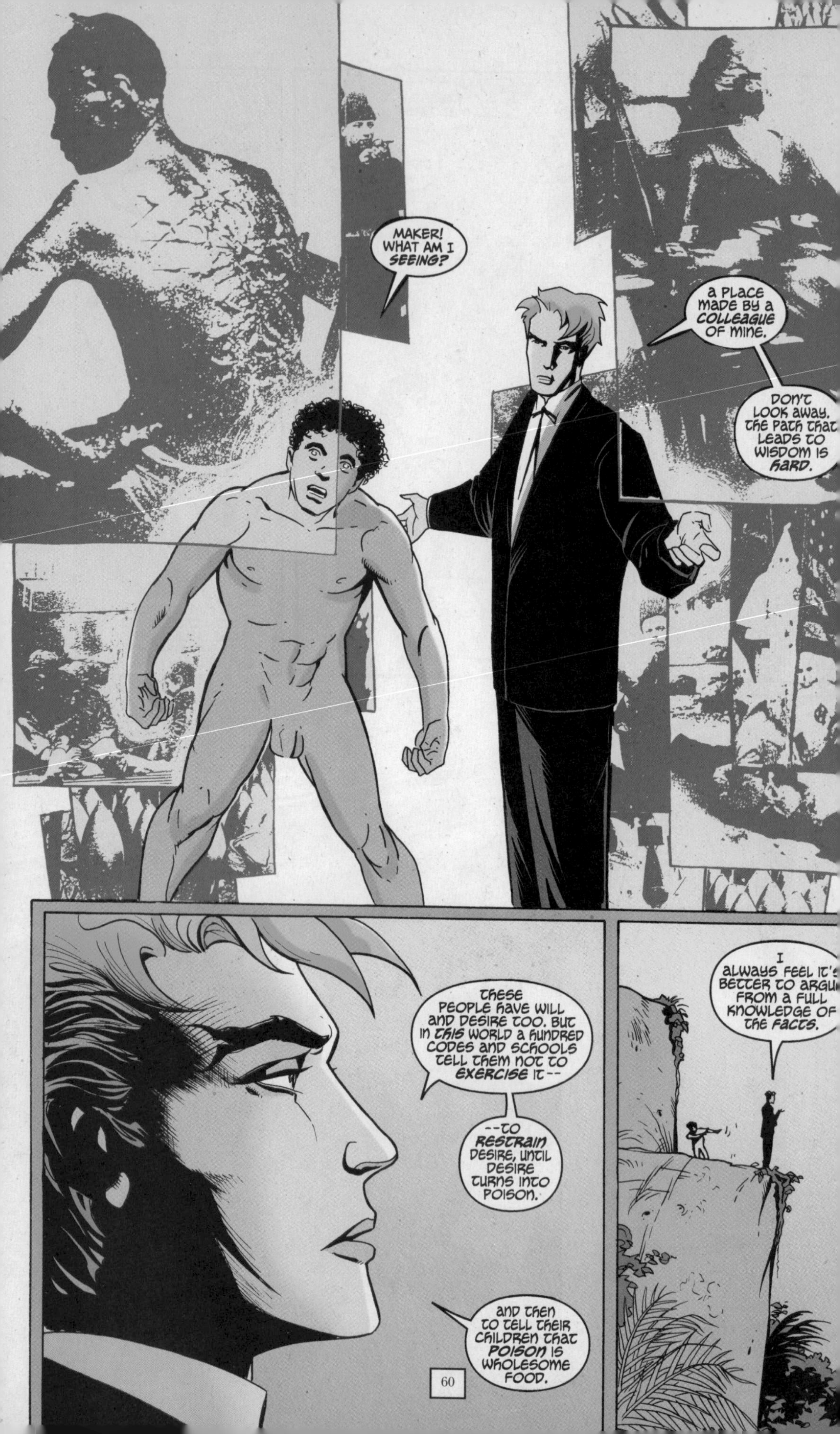
MAKER! WHAT AM I SEEING?
A PLACE MADE BY A COLLEAGUE OF MINE.
DON'T LOOK AWAY. THE PATH THAT LEADS TO WISDOM IS HARD.
THESE PEOPLE HAVE WILL AND DESIRE TOO. BUT IN THIS WORLD A HUNDRED CODES AND SCHOOLS TELL THEM NOT TO EXERCISE IT--
--TO RESTRAIN DESIRE, UNTIL DESIRE TURNS INTO POISON.
AND THEN TO TELL THEIR CHILDREN THAT POISON IS WHOLESOME FOOD.
I ALWAYS FEEL IT'S BETTER TO ARGU FROM A FULL KNOWLEDGE OF THE FACTS.

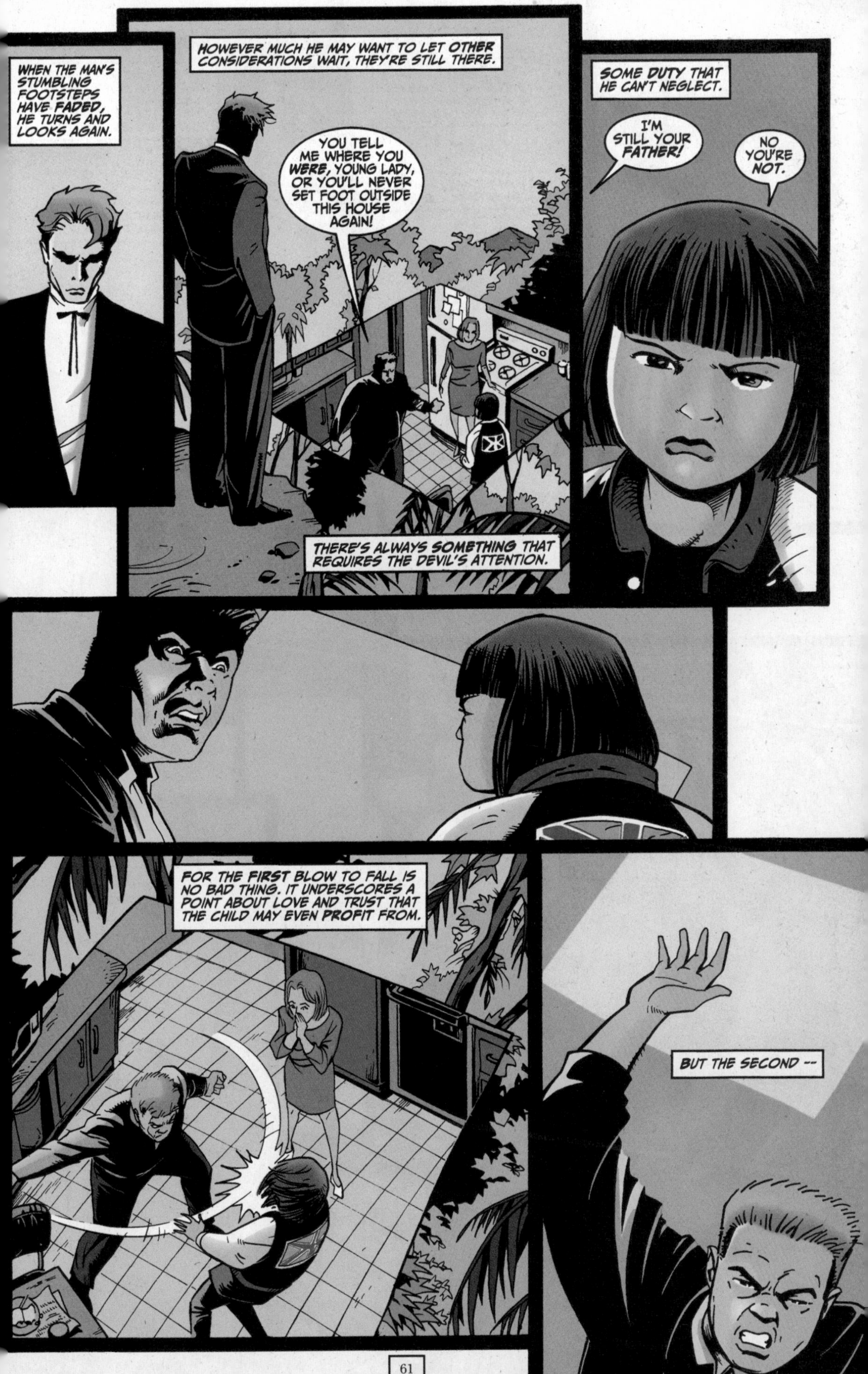
WHEN THE MAN'S STUMBLING FOOTSTEPS HAVE FADED, HE TURNS AND LOOKS AGAIN.
HOWEVER MUCH HE MAY WANT TO LET OTHER CONSIDERATIONS WAIT, THEY'RE STILL THERE.
YOU TELL ME WHERE YOU WERE, YOUNG LADY, OR YOU'LL NEVER SET FOOT OUTSIDE THIS HOUSE AGAIN!
THERE'S ALWAYS SOMETHING THAT REQUIRES THE DEVIL'S ATTENTION.
SOME DUTY THAT HE CAN'T NEGLECT.
I'M STILL YOUR FATHER!
NO YOU'RE NOT.
FOR THE FIRST BLOW TO FALL IS NO BAD THING. IT UNDERSCORES A POINT ABOUT LOVE AND TRUST THAT THE CHILD MAY EVEN PROFIT FROM.
BUT THE SECOND --

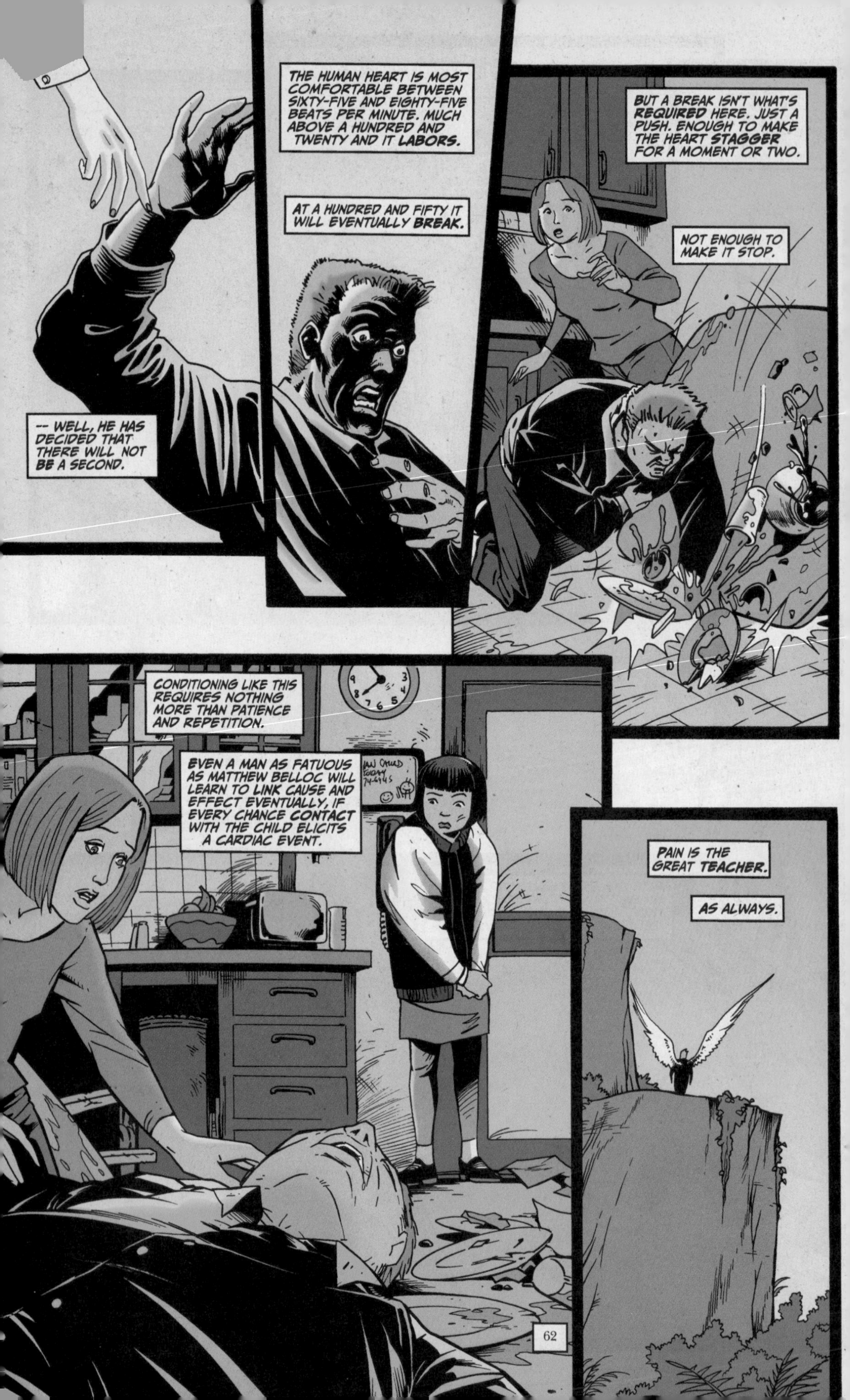
-- WELL, HE HAS DECIDED THAT THERE WILL NOT BE A SECOND.
THE HUMAN HEART IS MOST COMFORTABLE BETWEEN SIXTY-FIVE AND EIGHTY-FIVE BEATS PER MINUTE. MUCH ABOVE A HUNDRED AND TWENTY AND IT LABORS.
AT A HUNDRED AND FIFTY IT WILL EVENTUALLY BREAK.
BUT A BREAK ISN'T WHAT'S REQUIRED HERE. JUST A PUSH. ENOUGH TO MAKE THE HEART STAGGER FOR A MOMENT OR TWO.
NOT ENOUGH TO MAKE IT STOP.
CONDITIONING LIKE THIS REQUIRES NOTHING MORE THAN PATIENCE AND REPETITION.
EVEN A MAN AS FATUOUS AS MATTHEW BELLOC WILL LEARN TO LINK CAUSE AND EFFECT EVENTUALLY, IF EVERY CHANCE CONTACT WITH THE CHILD ELICITS A CARDIAC EVENT.
PAIN IS THE GREAT TEACHER.
AS ALWAYS.

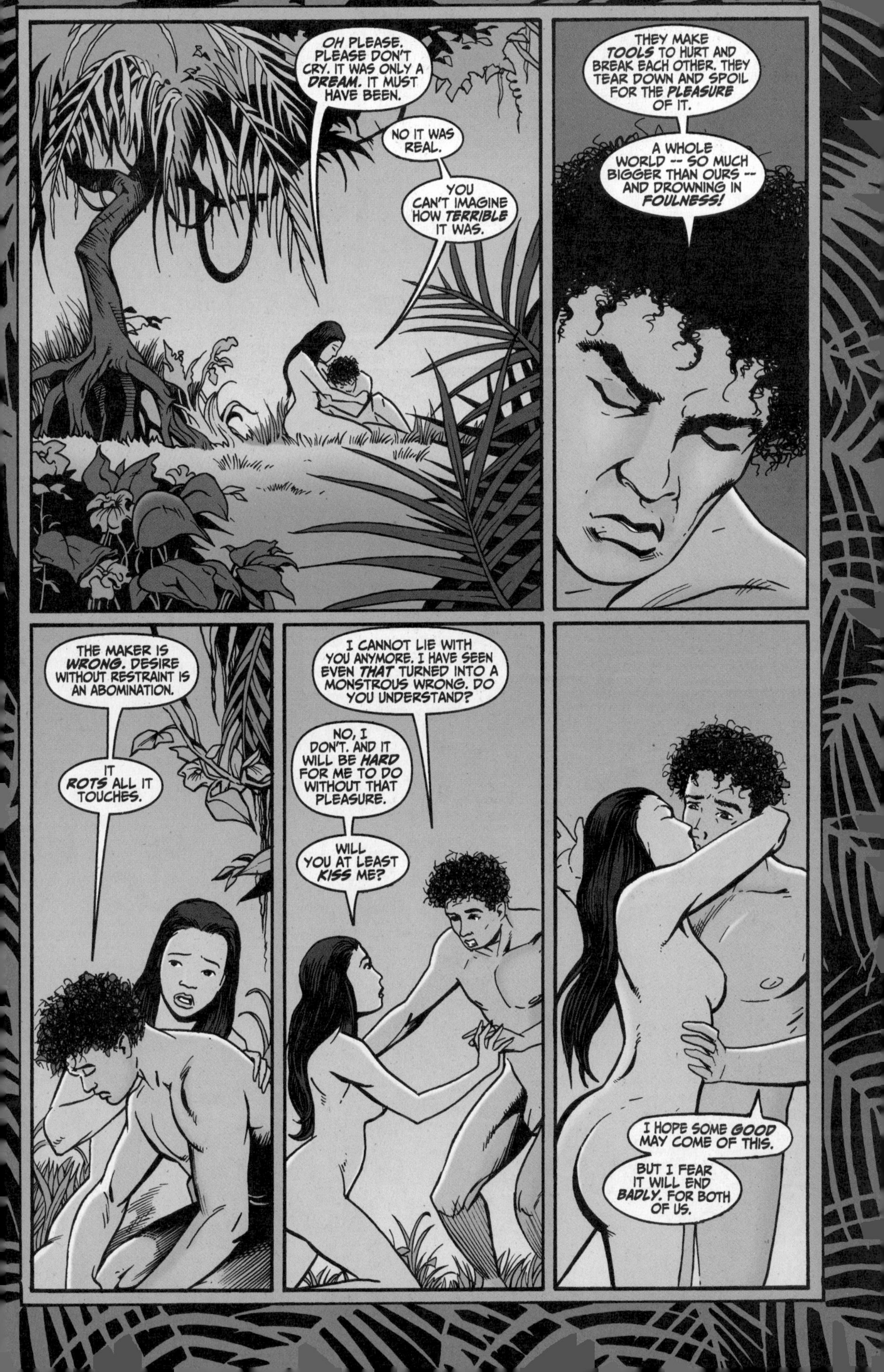
OH PLEASE. PLEASE DON'T CRY. IT WAS ONLY A DREAM. IT MUST HAVE BEEN.
NO IT WAS REAL.
YOU CAN'T IMAGINE HOW TERRIBLE IT WAS.
THEY MAKE TOOLS TO HURT AND BREAK EACH OTHER. THEY TEAR DOWN AND SPOIL FOR THE PLEASURE OF IT.
A WHOLE WORLD -- SO MUCH BIGGER THAN OURS -- AND DROWNING IN FOULNESS!
THE MAKER IS WRONG. DESIRE WITHOUT RESTRAINT IS AN ABOMINATION.
IT ROTS ALL IT TOUCHES.
I CANNOT LIE WITH YOU ANYMORE. I HAVE SEEN EVEN THAT TURNED INTO A MONSTROUS WRONG. DO YOU UNDERSTAND?
NO, I DON'T. AND IT WILL BE HARD FOR ME TO DO WITHOUT THAT PLEASURE.
WILL YOU AT LEAST KISS ME?
I HOPE SOME GOOD MAY COME OF THIS.
BUT I FEAR IT WILL END BADLY. FOR BOTH OF US.

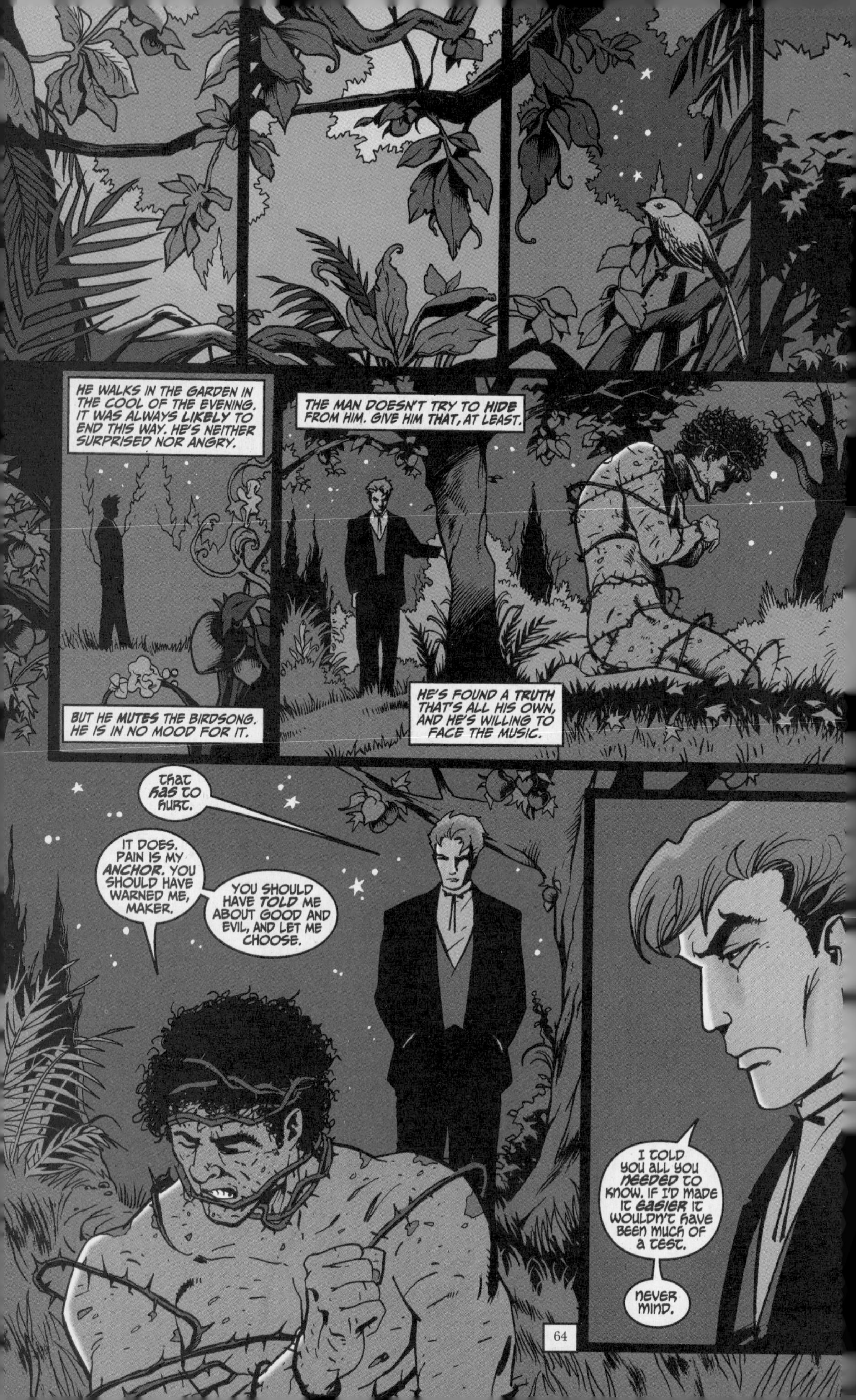
HE WALKS IN THE GARDEN IN THE COOL OF THE EVENING. IT WAS ALWAYS LIKELY TO END THIS WAY. HE'S NEITHER SURPRISED NOR ANGRY.
BUT HE MUTES THE BIRDSONG. HE IS IN NO MOOD FOR IT.
THE MAN DOESN'T TRY TO HIDE FROM HIM. GIVE HIM THAT, AT LEAST.
HE'S FOUND A TRUTH THAT'S ALL HIS OWN, AND HE'S WILLING TO FACE THE MUSIC.
THAT HAS TO HURT.
IT DOES. PAIN IS MY ANCHOR. YOU SHOULD HAVE WARNED ME, MAKER.
YOU SHOULD HAVE TOLD ME ABOUT GOOD AND EVIL, AND LET ME CHOOSE.
I TOLD YOU ALL YOU NEEDED TO KNOW. IF I'D MADE IT EASIER IT WOULDN'T HAVE BEEN MUCH OF A TEST.
NEVER MIND.

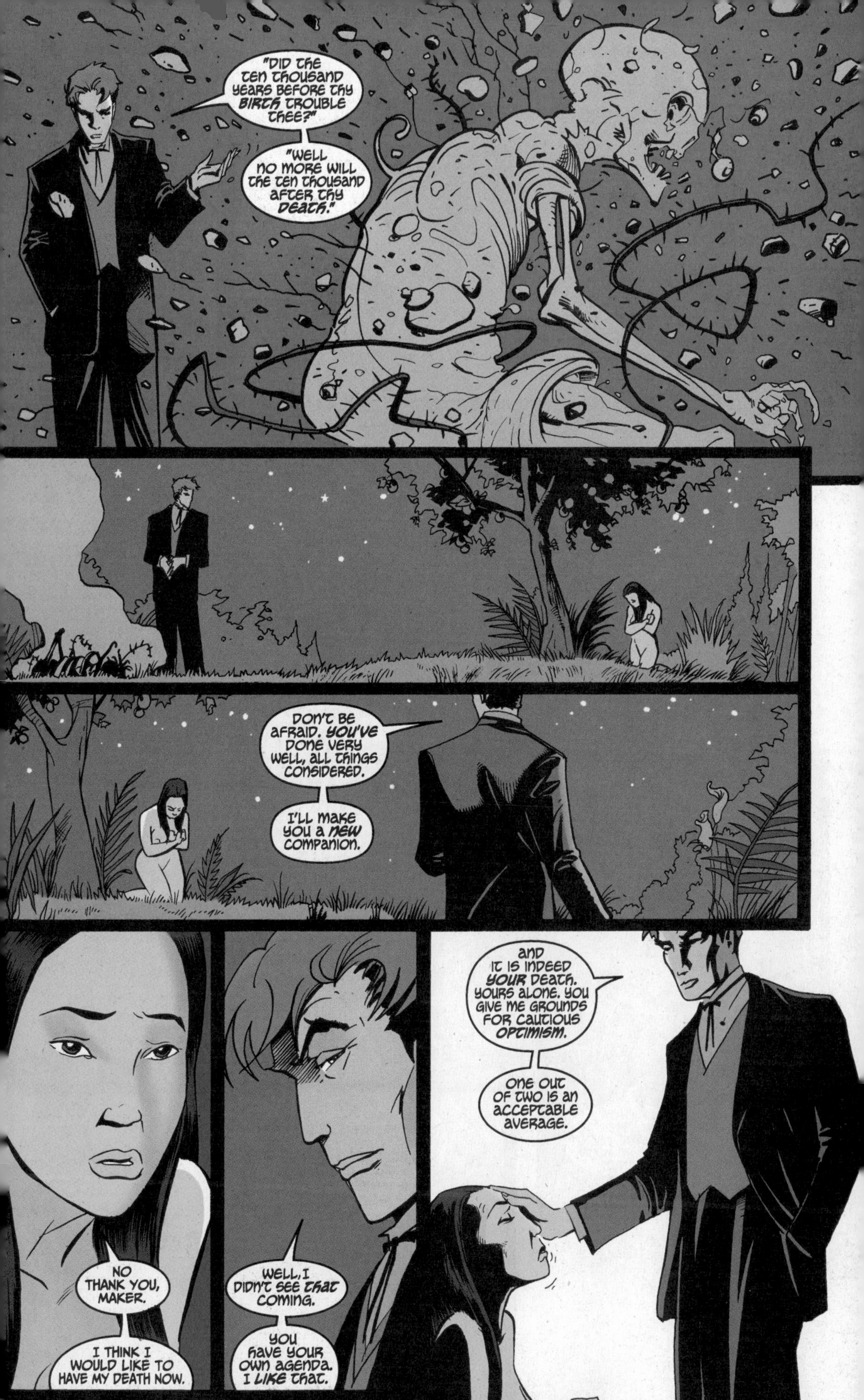

"DID THE TEN THOUSAND YEARS BEFORE THY BIRTH TROUBLE THEE?"
"WELL NO MORE WILL THE TEN THOUSAND AFTER THY DEATH."
DON'T BE AFRAID. YOU'VE DONE VERY WELL, ALL THINGS CONSIDERED.
I'LL MAKE YOU A NEW COMPANION.
NO THANK YOU, MAKER.
I THINK I WOULD LIKE TO HAVE MY DEATH NOW.
WELL, I DIDN'T SEE THAT COMING.
YOU HAVE YOUR OWN AGENDA. I LIKE THAT.
AND IT IS INDEED YOUR DEATH. YOURS ALONE. YOU GIVE ME GROUNDS FOR CAUTIOUS OPTIMISM.
ONE OUT OF TWO IS AN ACCEPTABLE AVERAGE.

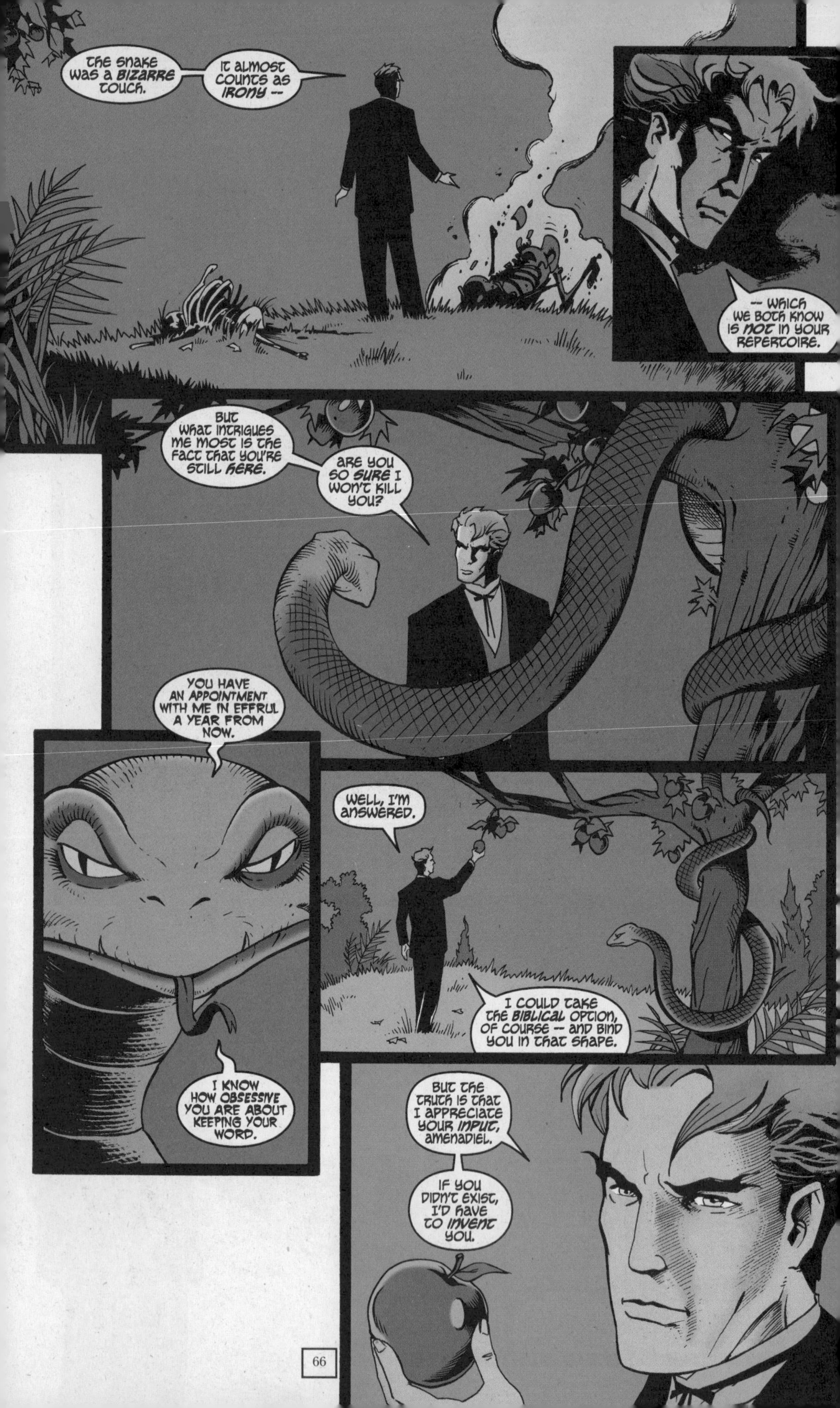

THE SNAKE WAS A BIZARRE TOUCH.
IT ALMOST COUNTS AS IRONY --
-- WHICH WE BOTH KNOW IS NOT IN YOUR REPERTOIRE.
BUT WHAT INTRIGUES ME MOST IS THE FACT THAT YOU'RE STILL HERE.
ARE YOU SO SURE I WON'T KILL YOU?
YOU HAVE AN APPOINTMENT WITH ME IN EFFRUL A YEAR FROM NOW.
I KNOW HOW OBSESSIVE YOU ARE ABOUT KEEPING YOUR WORD.
WELL, I'M ANSWERED.
I COULD TAKE THE BIBLICAL OPTION, OF COURSE -- AND BIND YOU IN THAT SHAPE.
BUT THE TRUTH IS THAT I APPRECIATE YOUR INPUT, AMENADIEL.
IF YOU DIDN'T EXIST, I'D HAVE TO INVENT YOU.

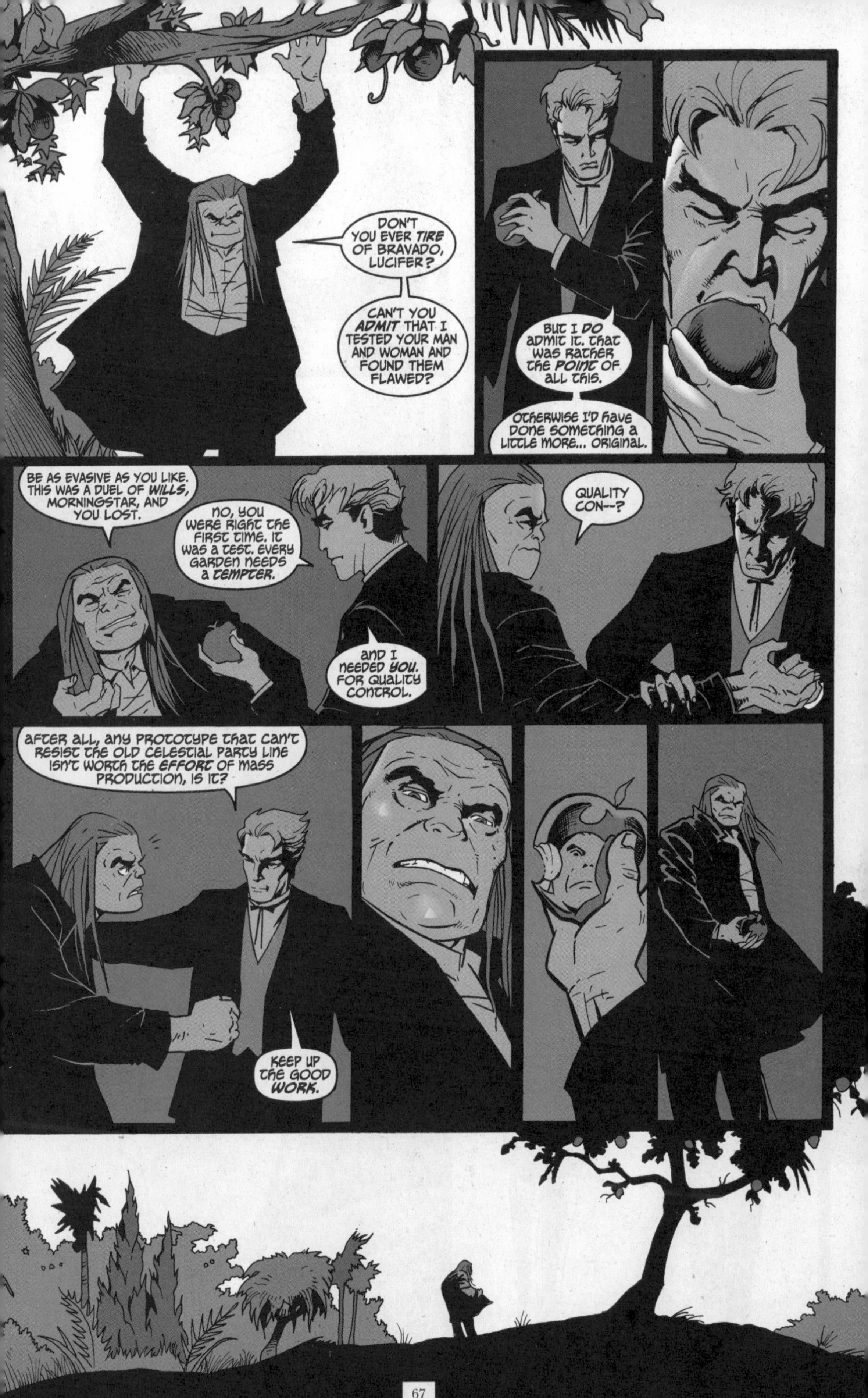
DON'T YOU EVER TIRE OF BRAVADO, LUCIFER?
CAN'T YOU ADMIT THAT I TESTED YOUR MAN AND WOMAN AND FOUND THEM FLAWED?
BUT I DO ADMIT IT. THAT WAS RATHER THE POINT OF ALL THIS.
OTHERWISE I'D HAVE DONE SOMETHING A LITTLE MORE... ORIGINAL.
BE AS EVASIVE AS YOU LIKE. THIS WAS A DUEL OF WILLS, MORNINGSTAR, AND YOU LOST.
NO, YOU WERE RIGHT THE FIRST TIME. IT WAS A TEST. EVERY GARDEN NEEDS A TEMPTER.
AND I NEEDED YOU. FOR QUALITY CONTROL.
QUALITY CON--?
AFTER ALL, ANY PROTOTYPE THAT CAN'T RESIST THE OLD CELESTIAL PARTY LINE ISN'T WORTH THE EFFORT OF MASS PRODUCTION, IS IT?
KEEP UP THE GOOD WORK.

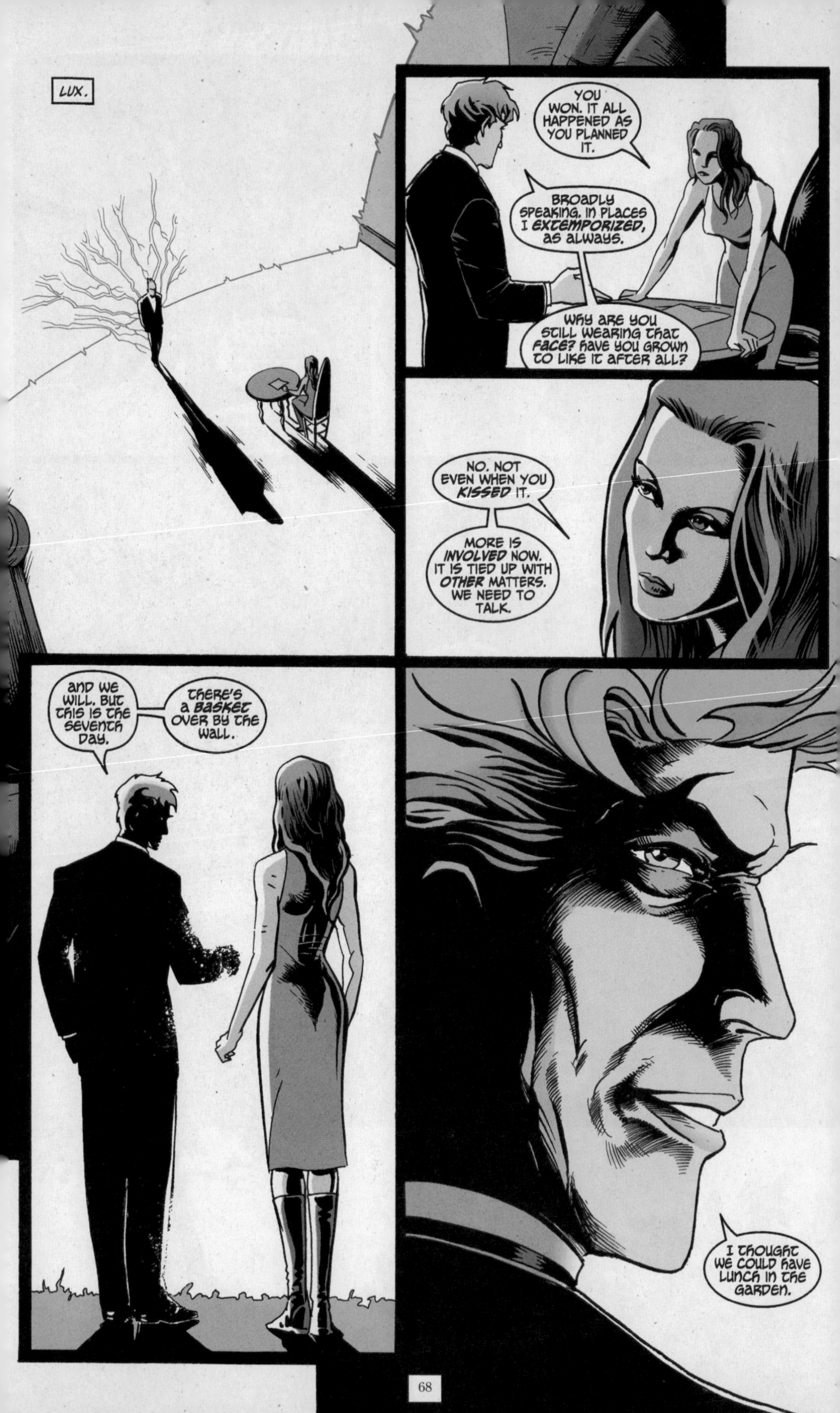
LUX.
YOU WON. IT ALL HAPPENED AS YOU PLANNED IT.
BROADLY SPEAKING. IN PLACES I EXTEMPORIZED, AS ALWAYS.
WHY ARE YOU STILL WEARING THAT FACE? HAVE YOU GROWN TO LIKE IT AFTER ALL?
NO. NOT EVEN WHEN YOU KISSED IT.
MORE IS INVOLVED NOW. IT IS TIED UP WITH OTHER MATTERS. WE NEED TO TALK.
AND WE WILL. BUT THIS IS THE SEVENTH DAY.
THERE'S A BASKET OVER BY THE WALL.
I THOUGHT WE COULD HAVE LUNCH IN THE GARDEN.

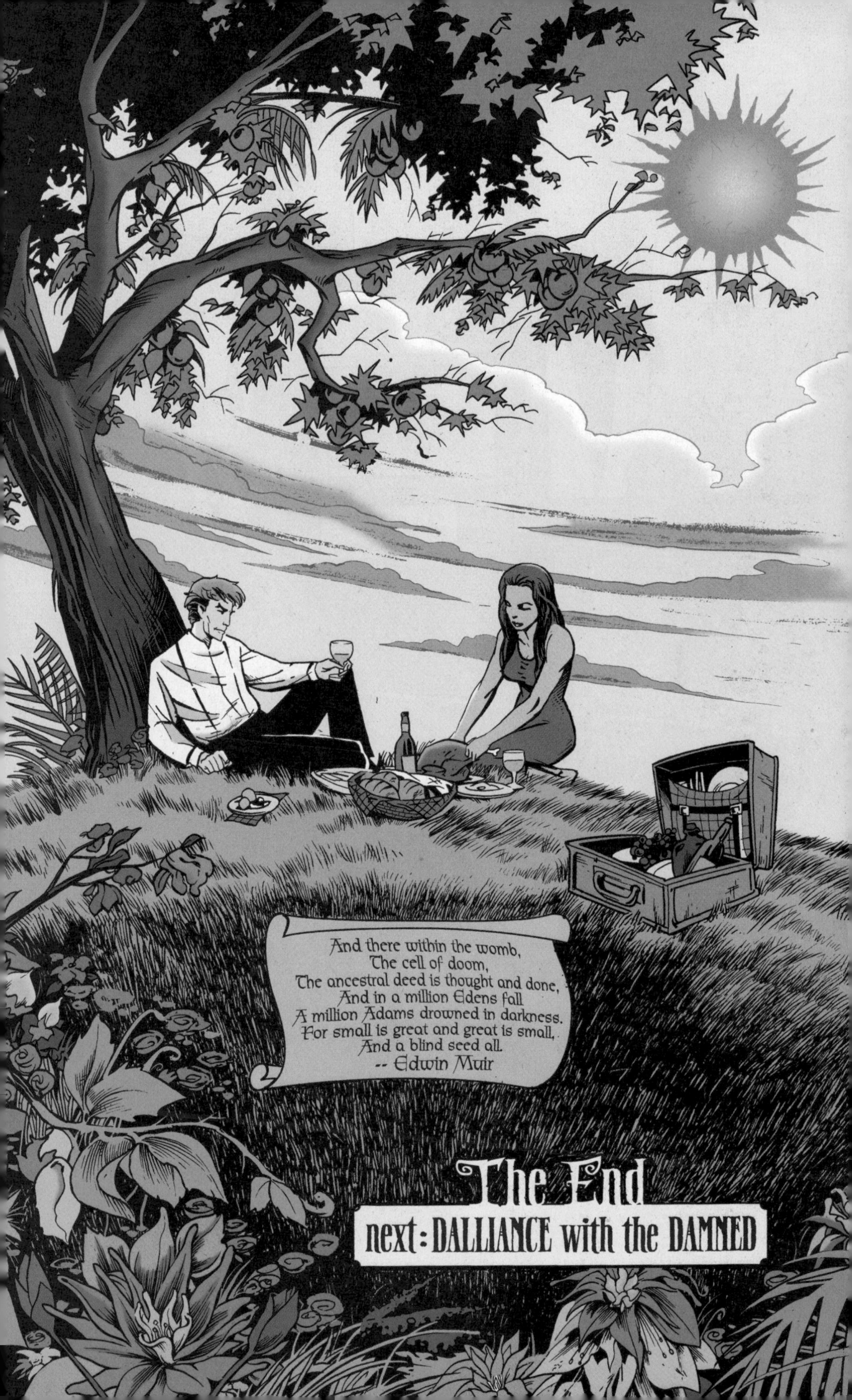
And there within the womb,
The cell of doom,
The ancestral deed is thought and done,
And in a million Edens fall
A million Adams drowned in darkness.
For small is great and great is small,
And a blind seed all.
-- Edwin Muir
The End
next: DALLIANCE with the DAMNED

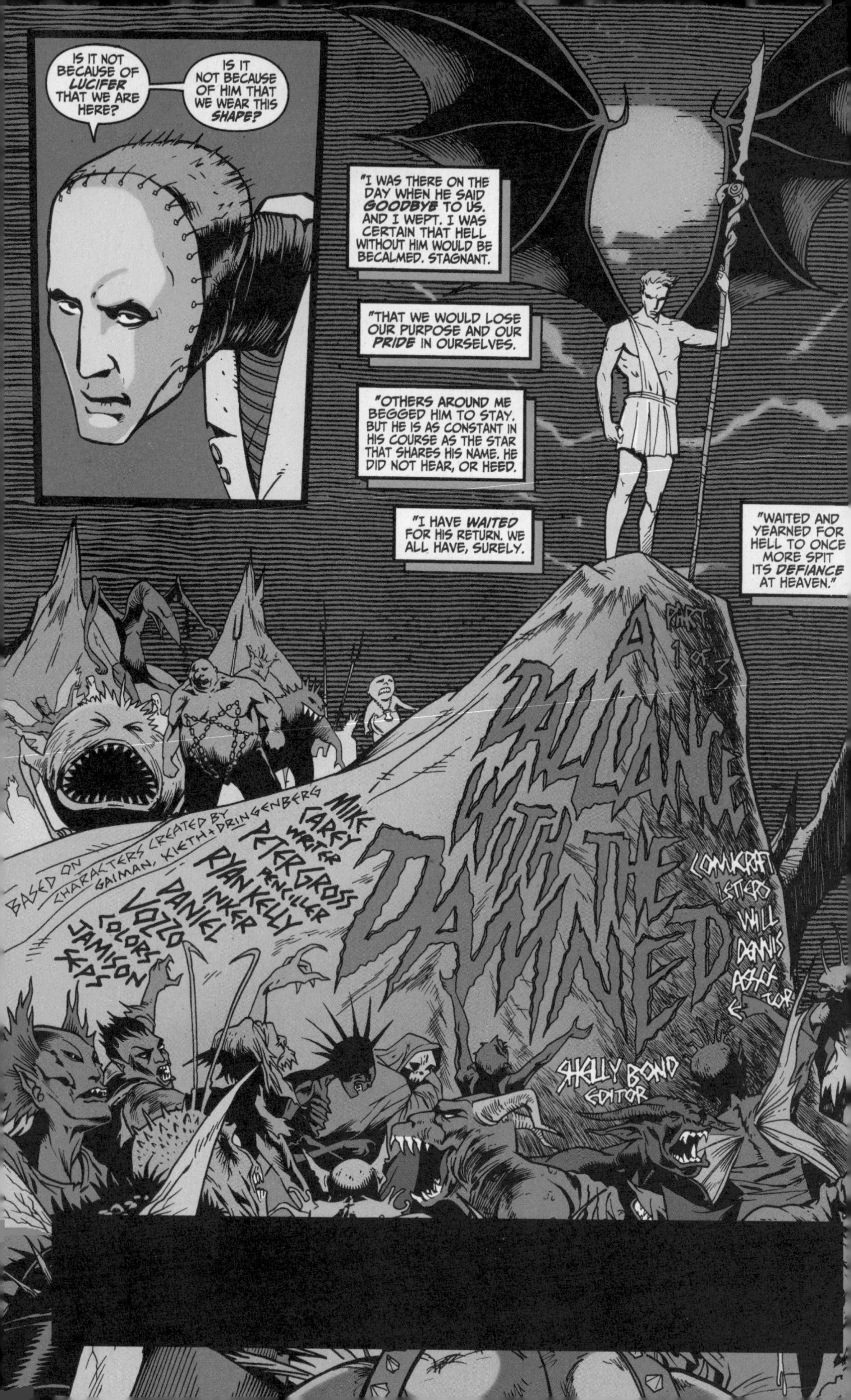
IS IT NOT BECAUSE OF LUCIFER THAT WE ARE HERE?
IS IT NOT BECAUSE OF HIM THAT WE WEAR THIS SHAPE?
"I WAS THERE ON THE DAY WHEN HE SAID GOODBYE TO US. AND I WEPT. I WAS CERTAIN THAT HELL WITHOUT HIM WOULD BE BECALMED. STAGNANT.
"THAT WE WOULD LOSE OUR PURPOSE AND OUR PRIDE IN OURSELVES.
"OTHERS AROUND ME BEGGED HIM TO STAY. BUT HE IS AS CONSTANT IN HIS COURSE AS THE STAR THAT SHARES HIS NAME. HE DID NOT HEAR, OR HEED.
"I HAVE WAITED FOR HIS RETURN. WE ALL HAVE, SURELY.
"WAITED AND YEARNED FOR HELL TO ONCE MORE SPIT ITS DEFIANCE AT HEAVEN."
A DALLIANCE WITH THE DAMNED
PART 1 OF 3
BASED ON CHARACTERS CREATED BY GAIMAN, KIETH + DRINGENBERG
MIKE CAREY WRITER
PETER GROSS PENCILLER
RYAN KELLY INKER
DANIEL VOZZO COLORS
JAMISON SEPS
COMICRAFT LETTERS
WILL DENNIS ASS'T EDITOR
SHELLY BOND EDITOR
[redacted]

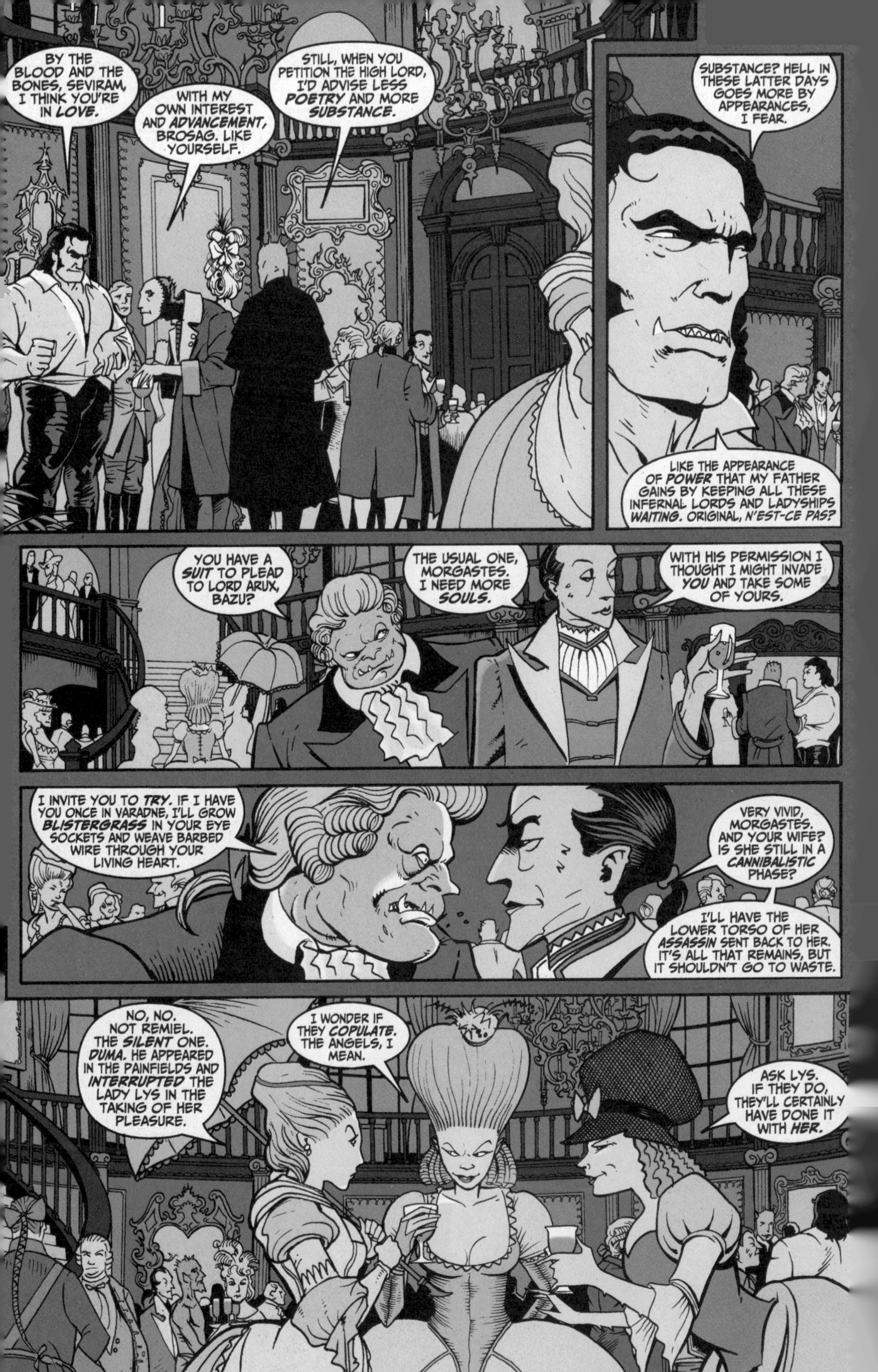
BY THE BLOOD AND THE BONES, SEVIRAM, I THINK YOU'RE IN LOVE.
WITH MY OWN INTEREST AND ADVANCEMENT, BROSAG. LIKE YOURSELF.
STILL, WHEN YOU PETITION THE HIGH LORD, I'D ADVISE LESS POETRY AND MORE SUBSTANCE.
SUBSTANCE? HELL IN THESE LATTER DAYS GOES MORE BY APPEARANCES, I FEAR.
LIKE THE APPEARANCE OF POWER THAT MY FATHER GAINS BY KEEPING ALL THESE INFERNAL LORDS AND LADYSHIPS WAITING. ORIGINAL, N'EST-CE PAS?
YOU HAVE A SUIT TO PLEAD TO LORD ARUX, BAZU?
THE USUAL ONE, MORGASTES. I NEED MORE SOULS.
WITH HIS PERMISSION I THOUGHT I MIGHT INVADE YOU AND TAKE SOME OF YOURS.
I INVITE YOU TO TRY. IF I HAVE YOU ONCE IN VARADNE, I'LL GROW BLISTERGRASS IN YOUR EYE SOCKETS AND WEAVE BARBED WIRE THROUGH YOUR LIVING HEART.
VERY VIVID, MORGASTES. AND YOUR WIFE? IS SHE STILL IN A CANNIBALISTIC PHASE?
I'LL HAVE THE LOWER TORSO OF HER ASSASSIN SENT BACK TO HER. IT'S ALL THAT REMAINS, BUT IT SHOULDN'T GO TO WASTE.
NO, NO. NOT REMIEL. THE SILENT ONE. DUMA. HE APPEARED IN THE PAINFIELDS AND INTERRUPTED THE LADY LYS IN THE TAKING OF HER PLEASURE.
I WONDER IF THEY COPULATE. THE ANGELS, I MEAN.
ASK LYS. IF THEY DO, THEY'LL CERTAINLY HAVE DONE IT WITH HER.

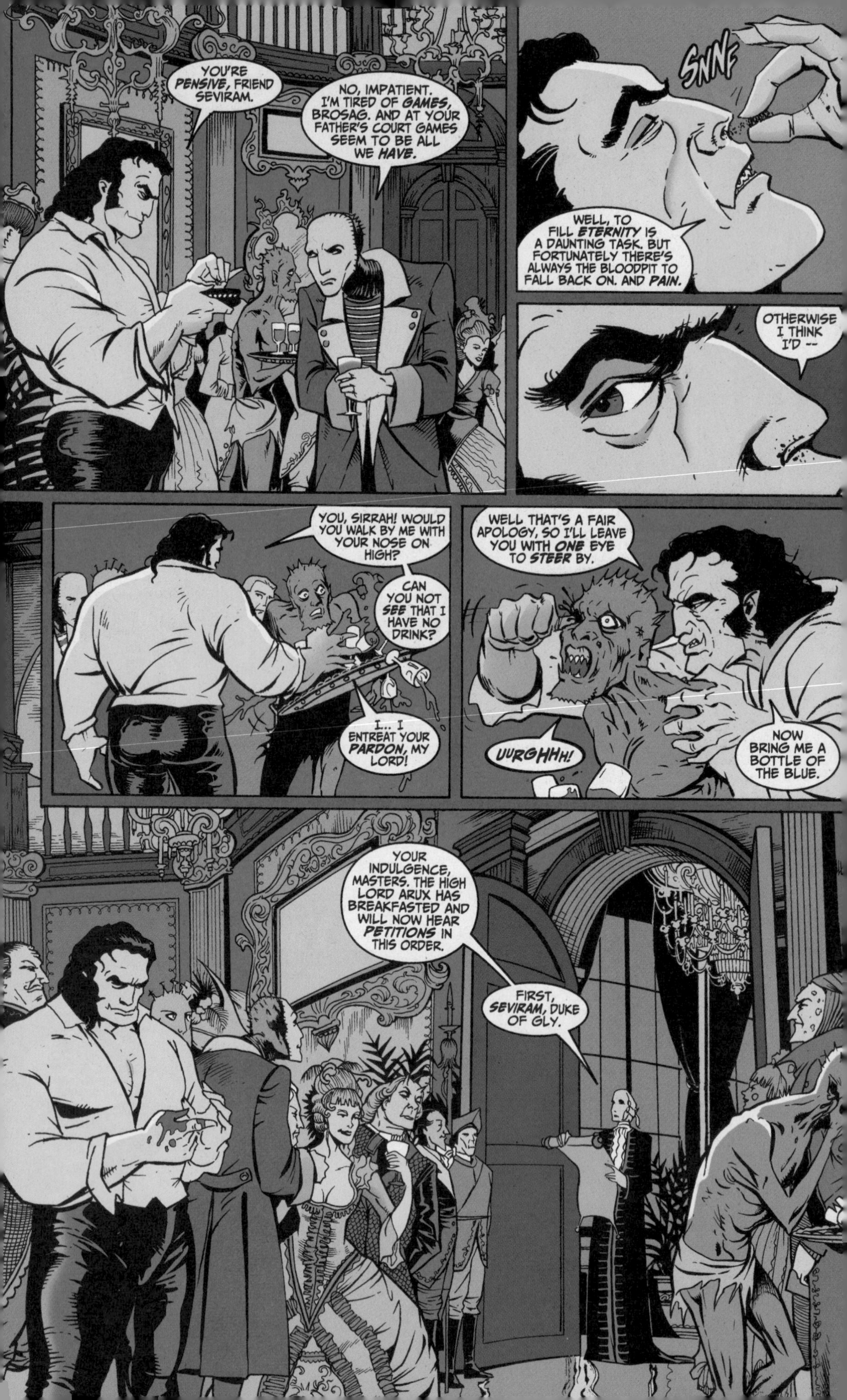
YOU'RE PENSIVE, FRIEND SEVIRAM.
NO, IMPATIENT. I'M TIRED OF GAMES, BROSAG. AND AT YOUR FATHER'S COURT GAMES SEEM TO BE ALL WE HAVE.
SNNF
WELL, TO FILL ETERNITY IS A DAUNTING TASK. BUT FORTUNATELY THERE'S ALWAYS THE BLOODPIT TO FALL BACK ON. AND PAIN.
OTHERWISE I THINK I'D --
YOU, SIRRAH! WOULD YOU WALK BY ME WITH YOUR NOSE ON HIGH?
CAN YOU NOT SEE THAT I HAVE NO DRINK?
I... I ENTREAT YOUR PARDON, MY LORD!
WELL THAT'S A FAIR APOLOGY, SO I'LL LEAVE YOU WITH ONE EYE TO STEER BY.
UURGHHH!
NOW BRING ME A BOTTLE OF THE BLUE.
YOUR INDULGENCE, MASTERS. THE HIGH LORD ARUX HAS BREAKFASTED AND WILL NOW HEAR PETITIONS IN THIS ORDER.
FIRST, SEVIRAM, DUKE OF GLY.

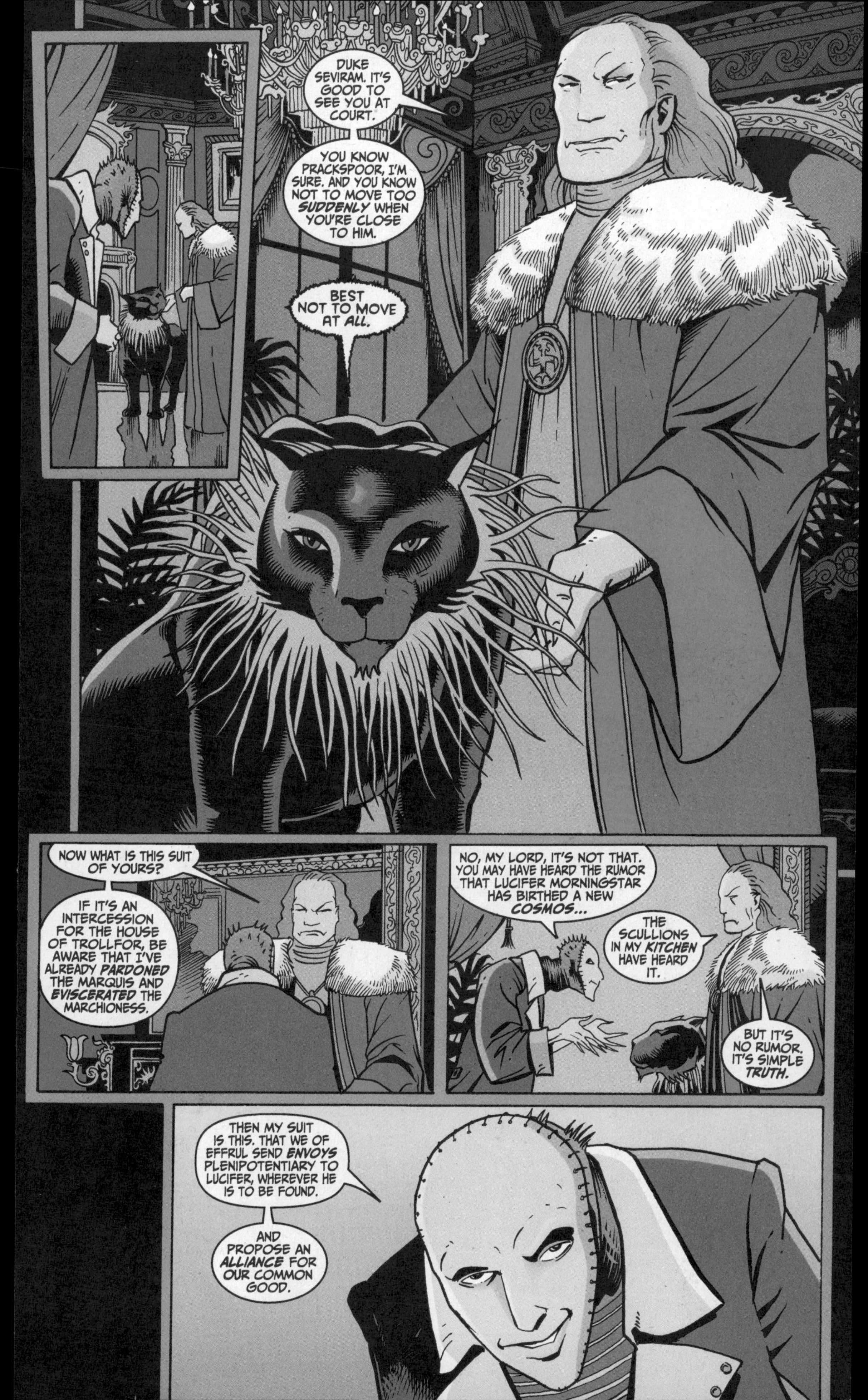

DUKE SEVIRAM. IT'S GOOD TO SEE YOU AT COURT.
YOU KNOW PRACKSPOOR, I'M SURE. AND YOU KNOW NOT TO MOVE TOO SUDDENLY WHEN YOU'RE CLOSE TO HIM.
BEST NOT TO MOVE AT ALL.
NOW WHAT IS THIS SUIT OF YOURS?
IF IT'S AN INTERCESSION FOR THE HOUSE OF TROLLFOR, BE AWARE THAT I'VE ALREADY PARDONED THE MARQUIS AND EVISCERATED THE MARCHIONESS.
NO, MY LORD, IT'S NOT THAT. YOU MAY HAVE HEARD THE RUMOR THAT LUCIFER MORNINGSTAR HAS BIRTHED A NEW COSMOS...
THE SCULLIONS IN MY KITCHEN HAVE HEARD IT.
BUT IT'S NO RUMOR. IT'S SIMPLE TRUTH.
THEN MY SUIT IS THIS. THAT WE OF EFFRUL SEND ENVOYS PLENIPOTENTIARY TO LUCIFER, WHEREVER HE IS TO BE FOUND.
AND PROPOSE AN ALLIANCE FOR OUR COMMON GOOD.

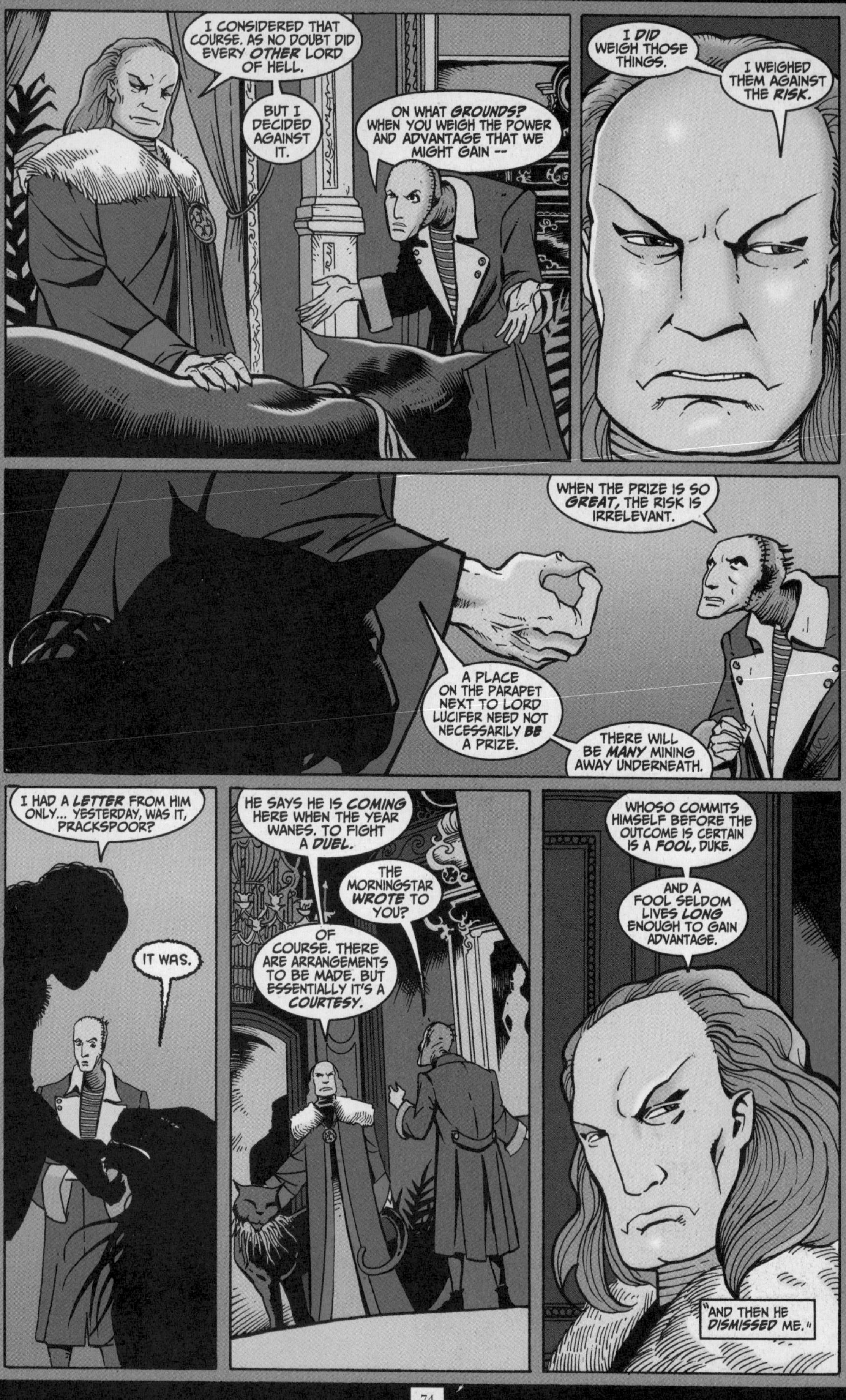
I CONSIDERED THAT COURSE. AS NO DOUBT DID EVERY OTHER LORD OF HELL.
BUT I DECIDED AGAINST IT.
ON WHAT GROUNDS? WHEN YOU WEIGH THE POWER AND ADVANTAGE THAT WE MIGHT GAIN --
I DID WEIGH THOSE THINGS.
I WEIGHED THEM AGAINST THE RISK.
WHEN THE PRIZE IS SO GREAT, THE RISK IS IRRELEVANT.
A PLACE ON THE PARAPET NEXT TO LORD LUCIFER NEED NOT NECESSARILY BE A PRIZE.
THERE WILL BE MANY MINING AWAY UNDERNEATH.
I HAD A LETTER FROM HIM ONLY... YESTERDAY, WAS IT, PRACKSPOOR?
IT WAS.
HE SAYS HE IS COMING HERE WHEN THE YEAR WANES. TO FIGHT A DUEL.
THE MORNINGSTAR WROTE TO YOU?
OF COURSE. THERE ARE ARRANGEMENTS TO BE MADE. BUT ESSENTIALLY IT'S A COURTESY.
WHOSO COMMITS HIMSELF BEFORE THE OUTCOME IS CERTAIN IS A FOOL, DUKE.
AND A FOOL SELDOM LIVES LONG ENOUGH TO GAIN ADVANTAGE.
"AND THEN HE DISMISSED ME."

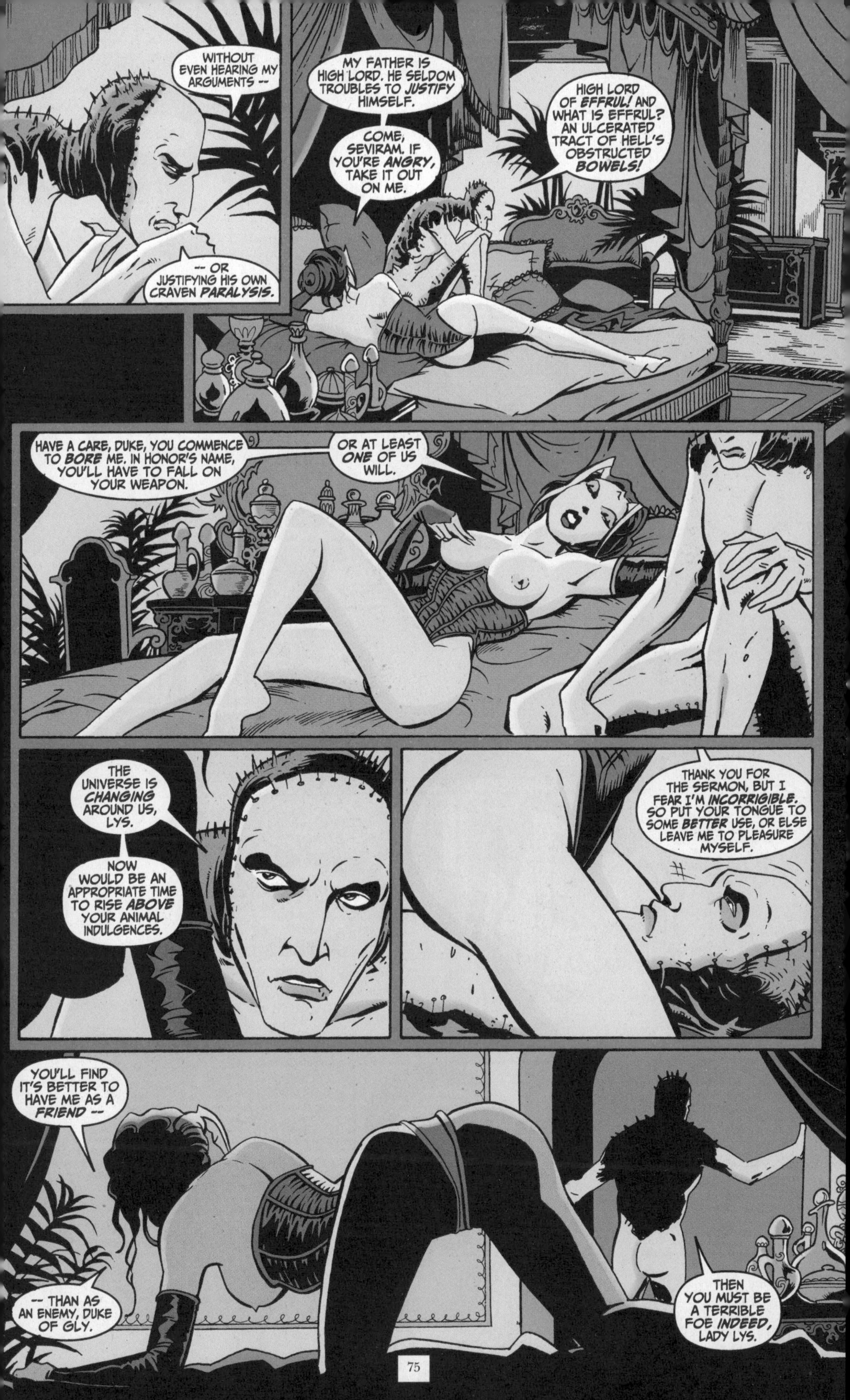

WITHOUT EVEN HEARING MY ARGUMENTS --
-- OR JUSTIFYING HIS OWN CRAVEN PARALYSIS.
MY FATHER IS HIGH LORD. HE SELDOM TROUBLES TO JUSTIFY HIMSELF.
COME, SEVIRAM. IF YOU'RE ANGRY, TAKE IT OUT ON ME.
HIGH LORD OF EFFRUL! AND WHAT IS EFFRUL? AN ULCERATED TRACT OF HELL'S OBSTRUCTED BOWELS!
HAVE A CARE, DUKE, YOU COMMENCE TO BORE ME. IN HONOR'S NAME, YOU'LL HAVE TO FALL ON YOUR WEAPON.
OR AT LEAST ONE OF US WILL.
THE UNIVERSE IS CHANGING AROUND US, LYS.
NOW WOULD BE AN APPROPRIATE TIME TO RISE ABOVE YOUR ANIMAL INDULGENCES.
THANK YOU FOR THE SERMON, BUT I FEAR I'M INCORRIGIBLE. SO PUT YOUR TONGUE TO SOME BETTER USE, OR ELSE LEAVE ME TO PLEASURE MYSELF.
YOU'LL FIND IT'S BETTER TO HAVE ME AS A FRIEND --
-- THAN AS AN ENEMY, DUKE OF GLY.
THEN YOU MUST BE A TERRIBLE FOE INDEED, LADY LYS.

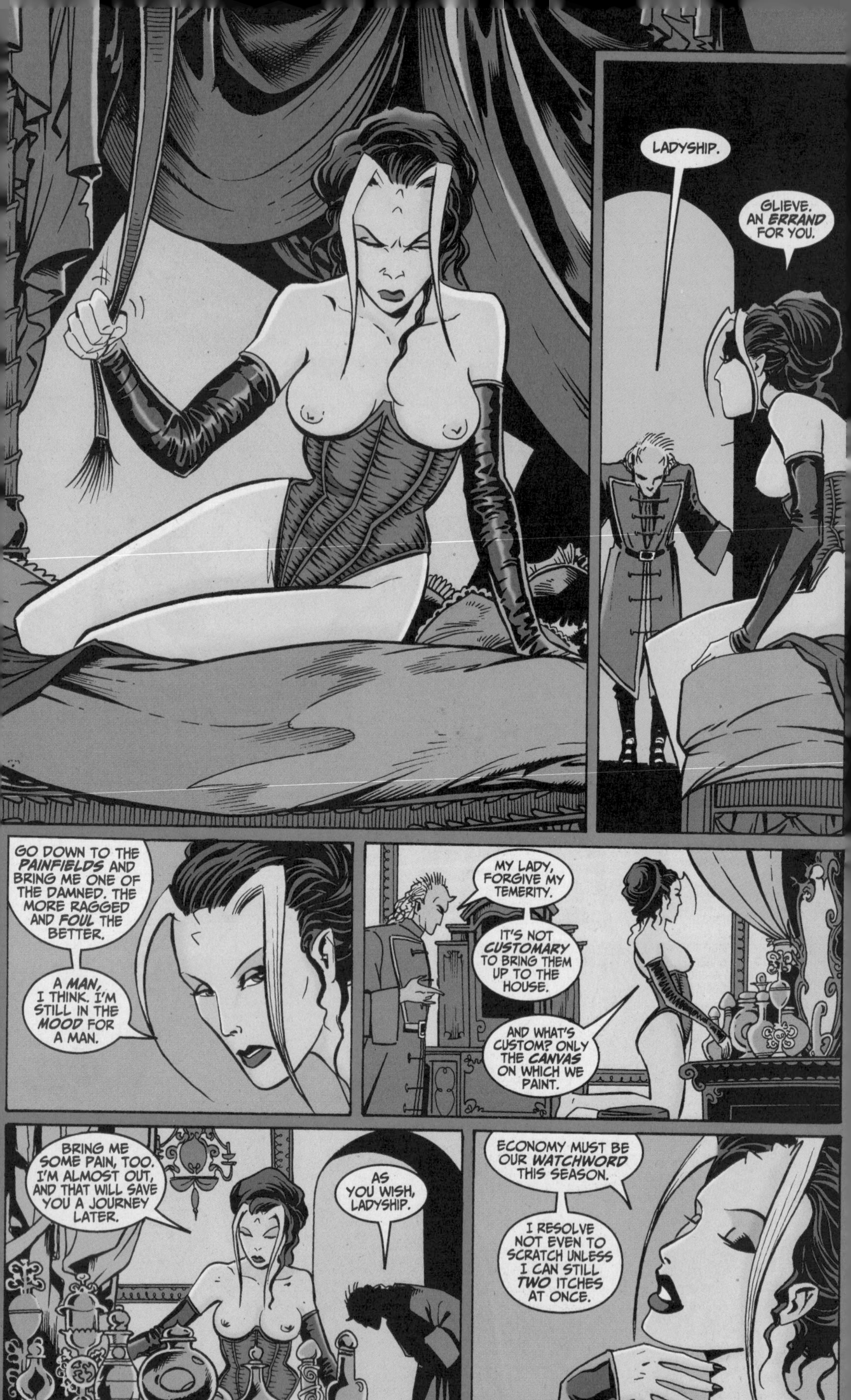
LADYSHIP.
GLIEVE. AN ERRAND FOR YOU.
GO DOWN TO THE PAINFIELDS AND BRING ME ONE OF THE DAMNED. THE MORE RAGGED AND FOUL THE BETTER.
A MAN, I THINK. I'M STILL IN THE MOOD FOR A MAN.
MY LADY, FORGIVE MY TEMERITY.
IT'S NOT CUSTOMARY TO BRING THEM UP TO THE HOUSE.
AND WHAT'S CUSTOM? ONLY THE CANVAS ON WHICH WE PAINT.
BRING ME SOME PAIN, TOO. I'M ALMOST OUT, AND THAT WILL SAVE YOU A JOURNEY LATER.
AS YOU WISH, LADYSHIP.
ECONOMY MUST BE OUR WATCHWORD THIS SEASON.
I RESOLVE NOT EVEN TO SCRATCH UNLESS I CAN STILL TWO ITCHES AT ONCE.

I ANSWER TO THE HIGH LORD, NOT TO HIS *DAUGHTER.*

THE DAMNED OF EFFRUL ARE IN MY CHARGE. I MAY NOT RELEASE A SINGLE SOUL, SAVE UNDER ARUX'S SEAL.

I UNDERSTAND. AND *SYMPATHIZE.*

BUT THE FACT REMAINS THAT MY LADY WILL FLAY YOUR BACK TO *JELLY* IF I GO BACK TO HER EMPTY-HANDED.

AND THE HIGH LORD WILL COMMEND YOUR STAUNCH PRINCIPLES *POSTHUMOUSLY.*

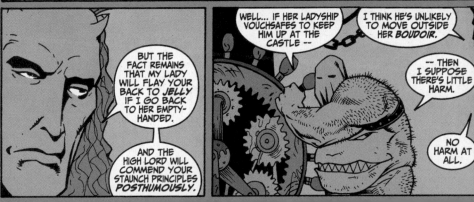

WELL... IF HER LADYSHIP VOUCHSAFES TO KEEP HIM UP AT THE CASTLE --

I THINK HE'S UNLIKELY TO MOVE OUTSIDE HER *BOUDOIR.*

-- THEN I SUPPOSE THERE'S LITTLE HARM.

NO HARM AT ALL.

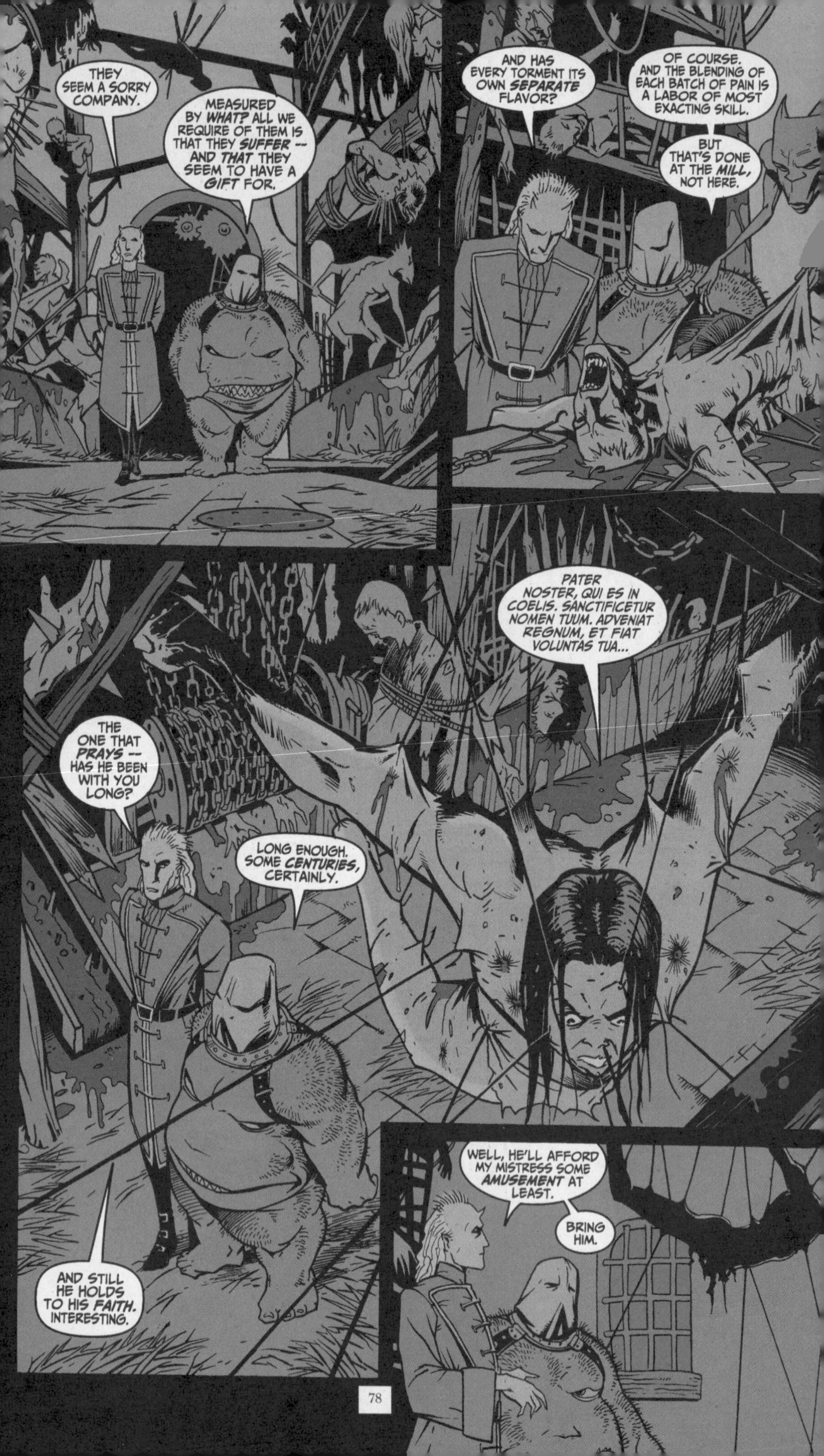

THEY SEEM A SORRY COMPANY.
MEASURED BY WHAT? ALL WE REQUIRE OF THEM IS THAT THEY SUFFER -- AND THAT THEY SEEM TO HAVE A GIFT FOR.
AND HAS EVERY TORMENT ITS OWN SEPARATE FLAVOR?
OF COURSE. AND THE BLENDING OF EACH BATCH OF PAIN IS A LABOR OF MOST EXACTING SKILL.
BUT THAT'S DONE AT THE MILL, NOT HERE.
PATER NOSTER, QUI ES IN COELIS. SANCTIFICETUR NOMEN TUUM. ADVENIAT REGNUM, ET FIAT VOLUNTAS TUA...
THE ONE THAT PRAYS -- HAS HE BEEN WITH YOU LONG?
LONG ENOUGH. SOME CENTURIES, CERTAINLY.
AND STILL HE HOLDS TO HIS FAITH. INTERESTING.
WELL, HE'LL AFFORD MY MISTRESS SOME AMUSEMENT AT LEAST.
BRING HIM.

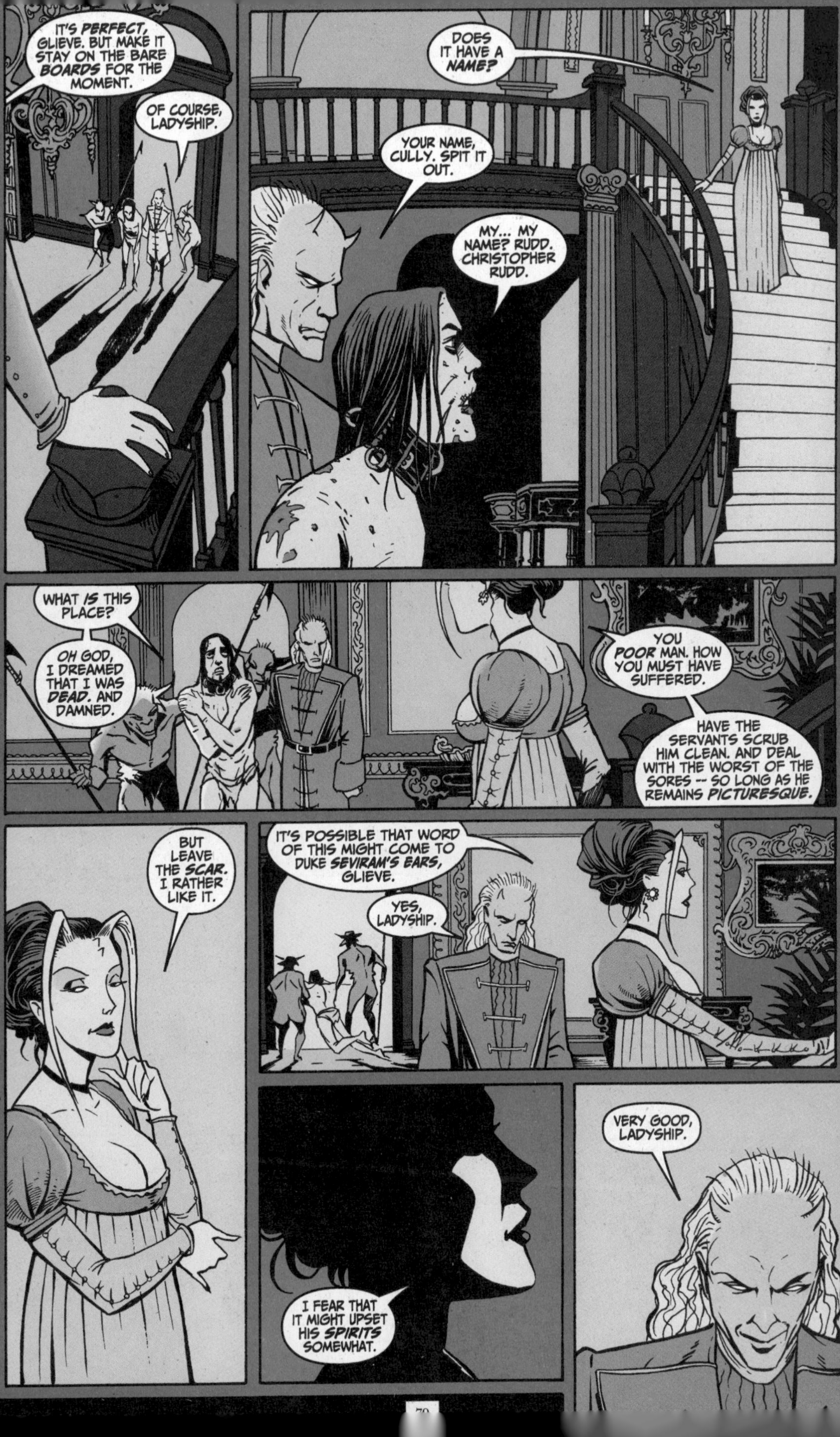
IT'S PERFECT, GLIEVE. BUT MAKE IT STAY ON THE BARE BOARDS FOR THE MOMENT.
OF COURSE, LADYSHIP.
DOES IT HAVE A NAME?
YOUR NAME, CULLY. SPIT IT OUT.
MY... MY NAME? RUDD. CHRISTOPHER RUDD.
WHAT IS THIS PLACE?
OH GOD, I DREAMED THAT I WAS DEAD. AND DAMNED.
YOU POOR MAN. HOW YOU MUST HAVE SUFFERED.
HAVE THE SERVANTS SCRUB HIM CLEAN. AND DEAL WITH THE WORST OF THE SORES -- SO LONG AS HE REMAINS PICTURESQUE.
BUT LEAVE THE SCAR. I RATHER LIKE IT.
IT'S POSSIBLE THAT WORD OF THIS MIGHT COME TO DUKE SEVIRAM'S EARS, GLIEVE.
YES, LADYSHIP.
I FEAR THAT IT MIGHT UPSET HIS SPIRITS SOMEWHAT.
VERY GOOD, LADYSHIP.

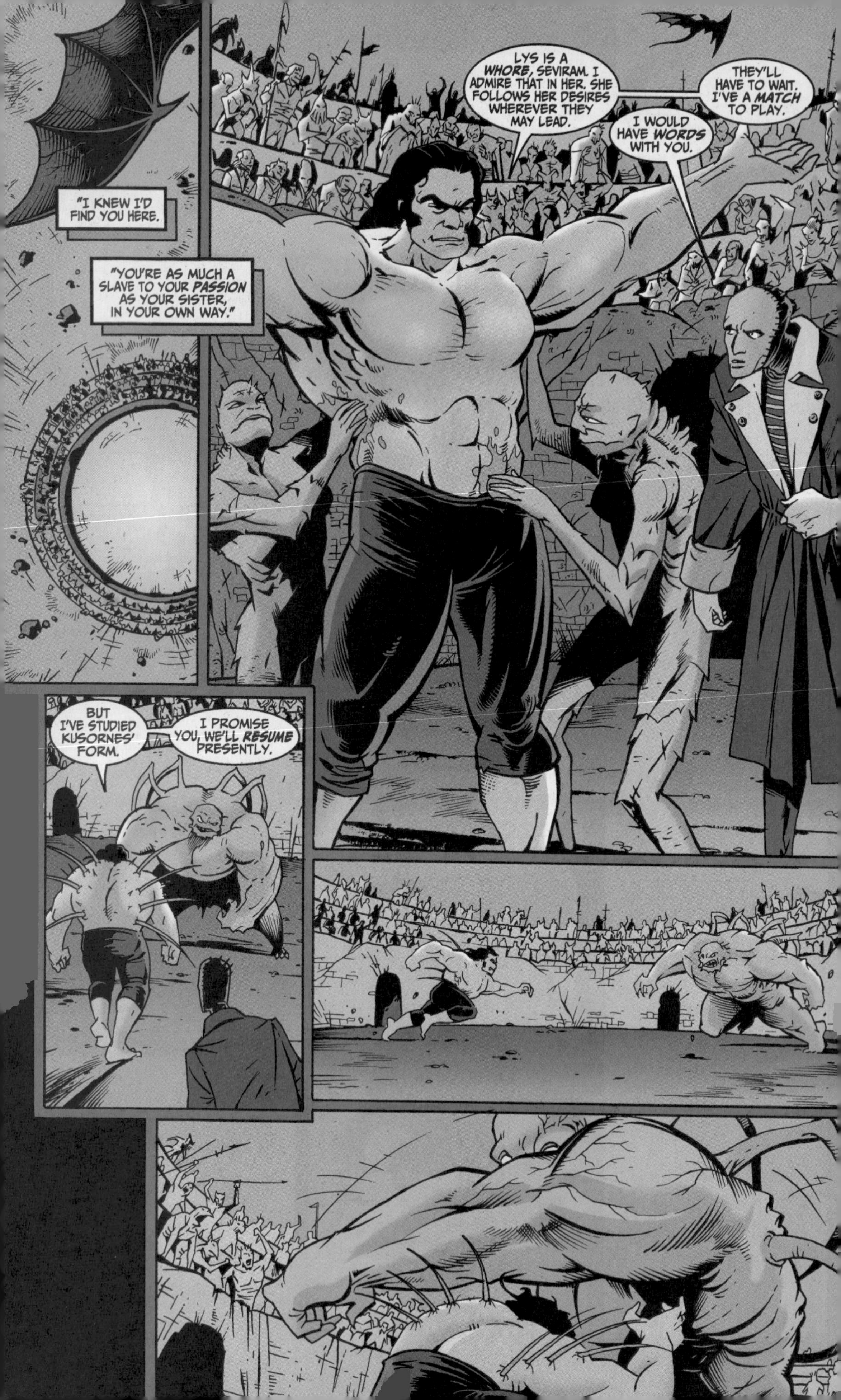
"I KNEW I'D FIND YOU HERE.
"YOU'RE AS MUCH A SLAVE TO YOUR PASSION AS YOUR SISTER, IN YOUR OWN WAY."
LYS IS A WHORE, SEVIRAM. I ADMIRE THAT IN HER. SHE FOLLOWS HER DESIRES WHEREVER THEY MAY LEAD.
I WOULD HAVE WORDS WITH YOU.
THEY'LL HAVE TO WAIT. I'VE A MATCH TO PLAY.
BUT I'VE STUDIED KUSORNES' FORM.
I PROMISE YOU, WE'LL RESUME PRESENTLY.

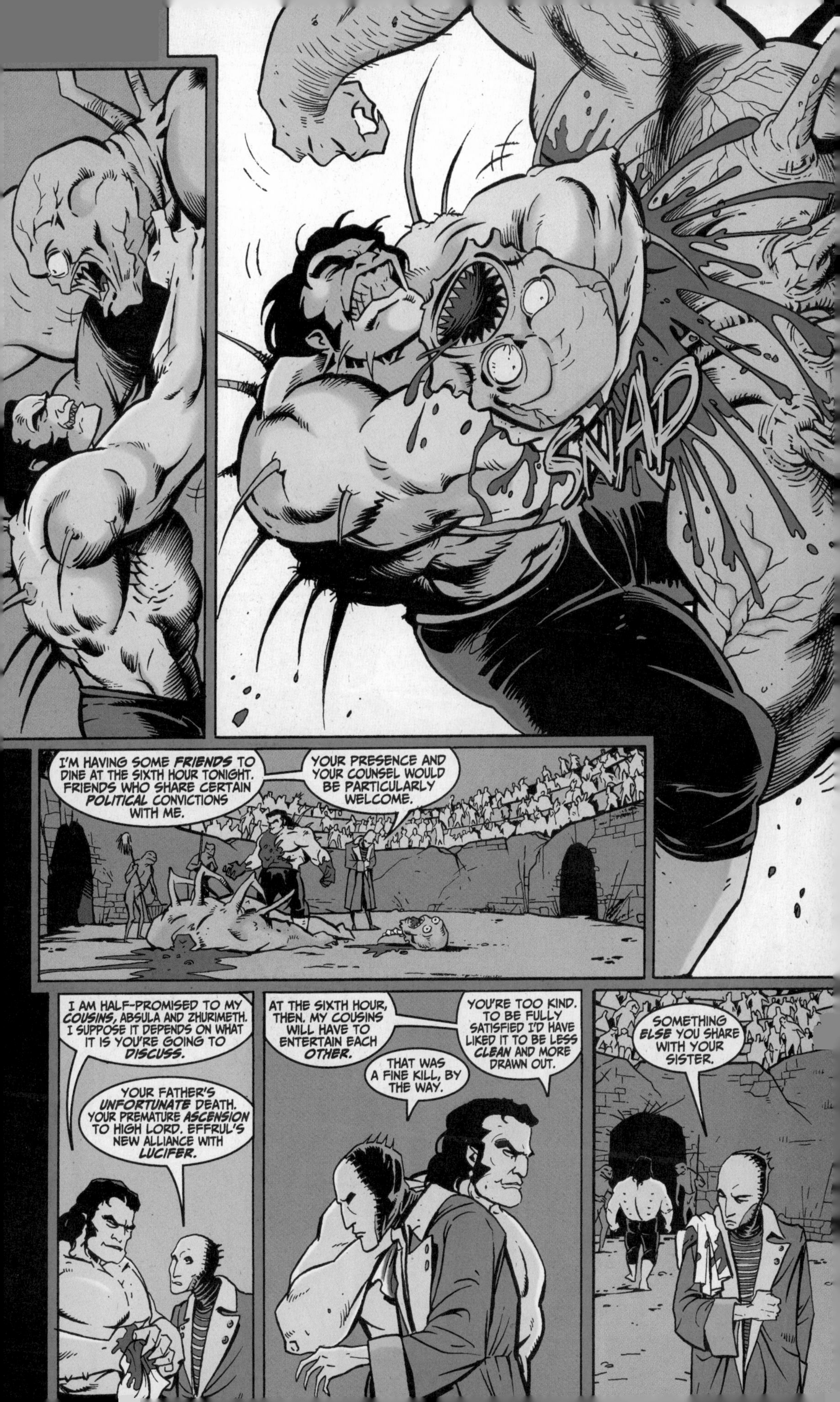

SNAP
I'M HAVING SOME FRIENDS TO DINE AT THE SIXTH HOUR TONIGHT. FRIENDS WHO SHARE CERTAIN POLITICAL CONVICTIONS WITH ME.
YOUR PRESENCE AND YOUR COUNSEL WOULD BE PARTICULARLY WELCOME.
I AM HALF-PROMISED TO MY COUSINS, ABSULA AND ZHURIMETH. I SUPPOSE IT DEPENDS ON WHAT IT IS YOU'RE GOING TO DISCUSS.
YOUR FATHER'S UNFORTUNATE DEATH. YOUR PREMATURE ASCENSION TO HIGH LORD. EFFRUL'S NEW ALLIANCE WITH LUCIFER.
AT THE SIXTH HOUR, THEN. MY COUSINS WILL HAVE TO ENTERTAIN EACH OTHER.
THAT WAS A FINE KILL, BY THE WAY.
YOU'RE TOO KIND. TO BE FULLY SATISFIED I'D HAVE LIKED IT TO BE LESS CLEAN AND MORE DRAWN OUT.
SOMETHING ELSE YOU SHARE WITH YOUR SISTER.

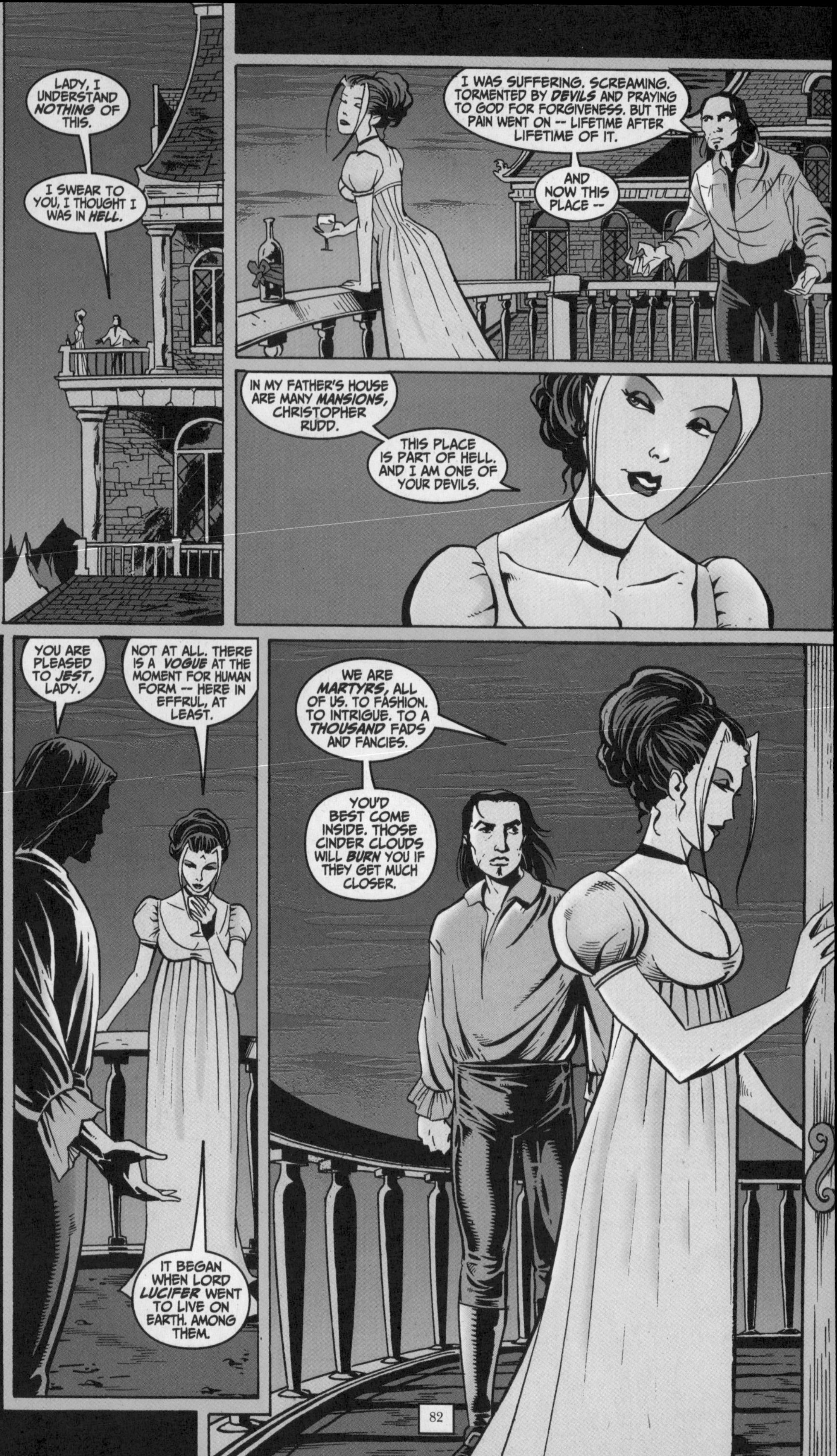
LADY, I UNDERSTAND NOTHING OF THIS.
I SWEAR TO YOU, I THOUGHT I WAS IN HELL.
I WAS SUFFERING. SCREAMING. TORMENTED BY DEVILS AND PRAYING TO GOD FOR FORGIVENESS. BUT THE PAIN WENT ON -- LIFETIME AFTER LIFETIME OF IT.
AND NOW THIS PLACE --
IN MY FATHER'S HOUSE ARE MANY MANSIONS, CHRISTOPHER RUDD.
THIS PLACE IS PART OF HELL. AND I AM ONE OF YOUR DEVILS.
YOU ARE PLEASED TO JEST, LADY.
NOT AT ALL. THERE IS A VOGUE AT THE MOMENT FOR HUMAN FORM -- HERE IN EFFRUL, AT LEAST.
IT BEGAN WHEN LORD LUCIFER WENT TO LIVE ON EARTH. AMONG THEM.
WE ARE MARTYRS, ALL OF US. TO FASHION. TO INTRIGUE. TO A THOUSAND FADS AND FANCIES.
YOU'D BEST COME INSIDE. THOSE CINDER CLOUDS WILL BURN YOU IF THEY GET MUCH CLOSER.

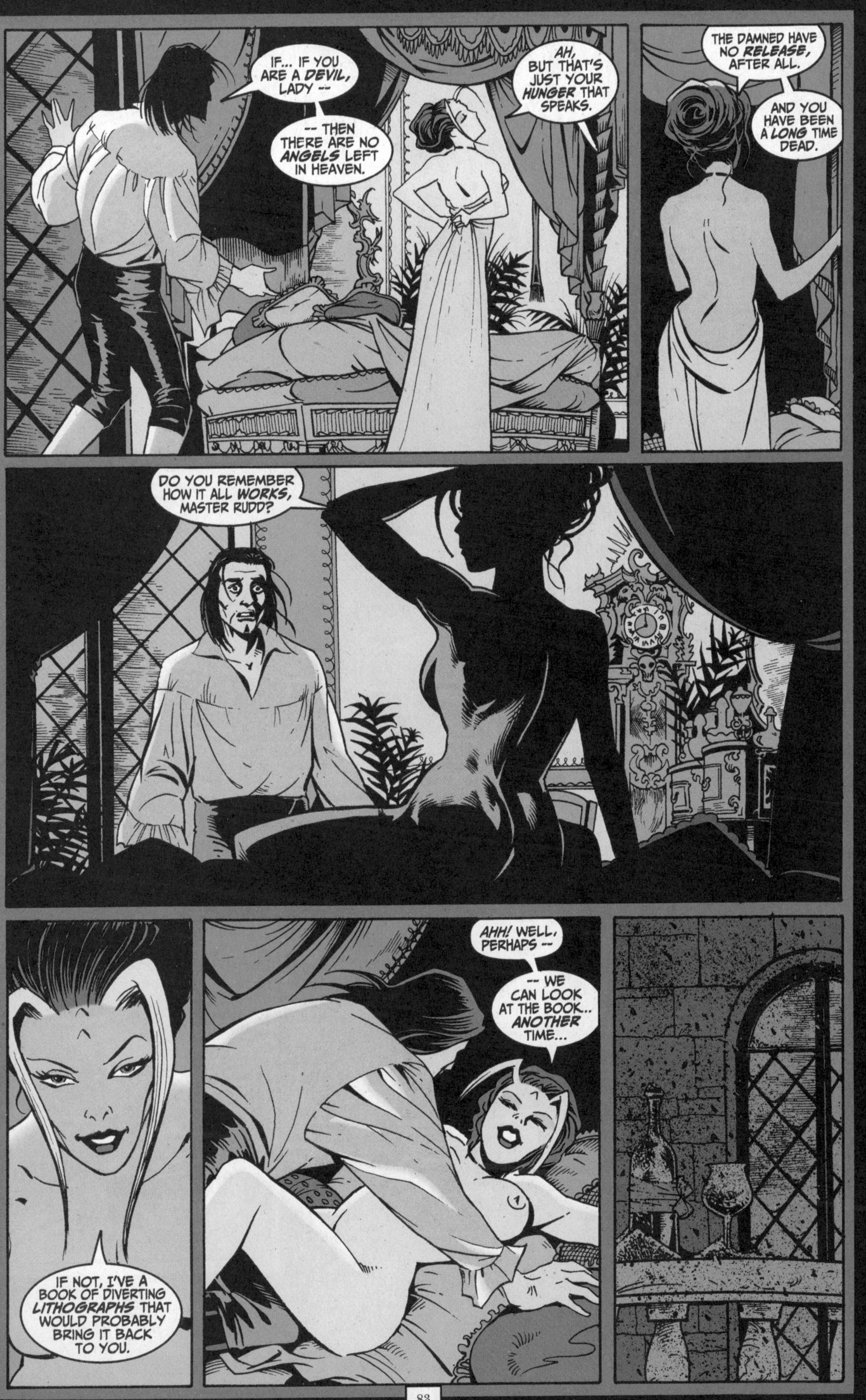
IF... IF YOU ARE A DEVIL, LADY --
-- THEN THERE ARE NO ANGELS LEFT IN HEAVEN.
AH, BUT THAT'S JUST YOUR HUNGER THAT SPEAKS.
THE DAMNED HAVE NO RELEASE, AFTER ALL.
AND YOU HAVE BEEN A LONG TIME DEAD.
DO YOU REMEMBER HOW IT ALL WORKS, MASTER RUDD?
IF NOT, I'VE A BOOK OF DIVERTING LITHOGRAPHS THAT WOULD PROBABLY BRING IT BACK TO YOU.
AHH! WELL, PERHAPS --
-- WE CAN LOOK AT THE BOOK... ANOTHER TIME...

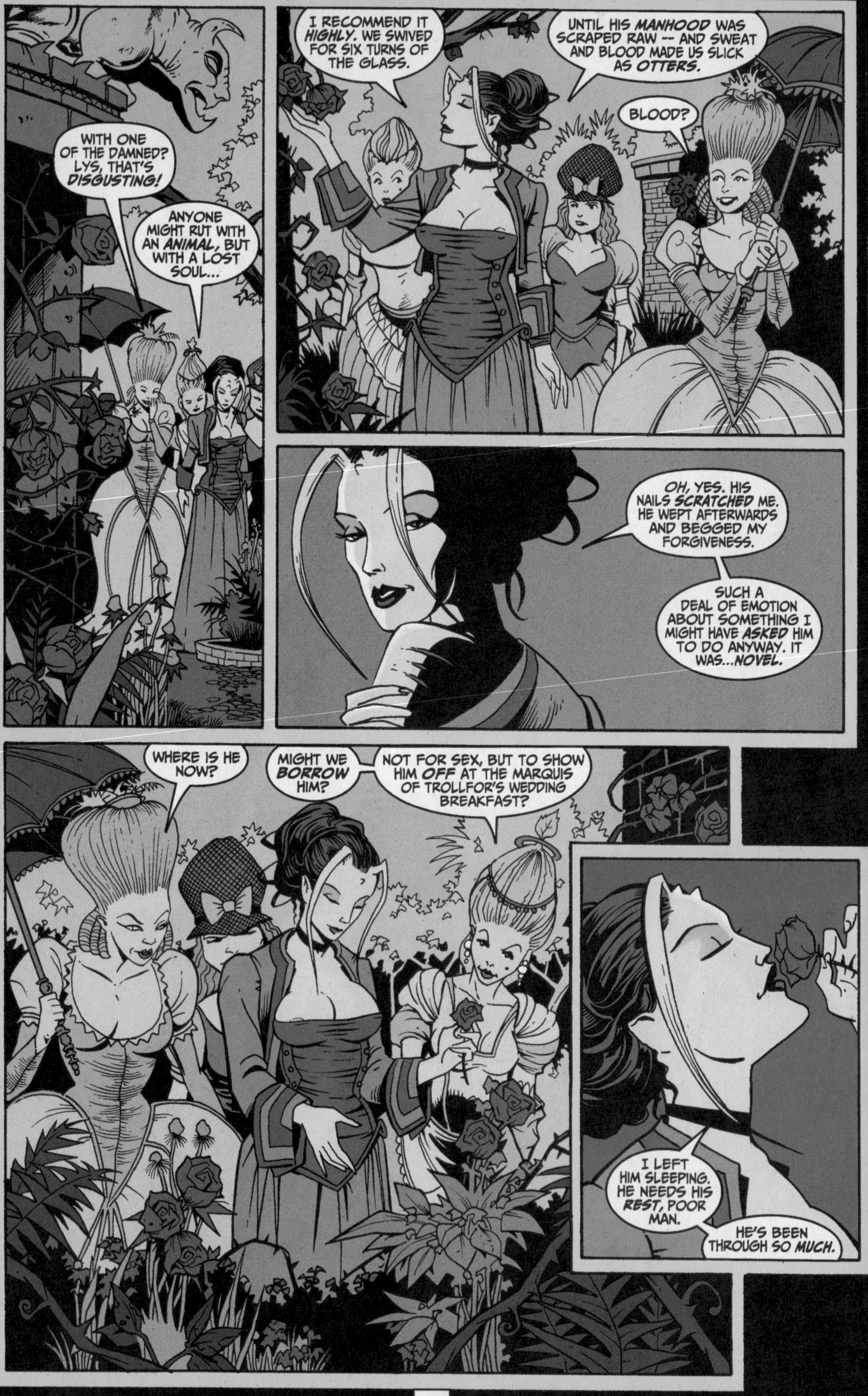
WITH ONE OF THE DAMNED? LYS, THAT'S DISGUSTING!
ANYONE MIGHT RUT WITH AN ANIMAL, BUT WITH A LOST SOUL...
I RECOMMEND IT HIGHLY. WE SWIVED FOR SIX TURNS OF THE GLASS.
UNTIL HIS MANHOOD WAS SCRAPED RAW -- AND SWEAT AND BLOOD MADE US SLICK AS OTTERS.
BLOOD?
OH, YES. HIS NAILS SCRATCHED ME. HE WEPT AFTERWARDS AND BEGGED MY FORGIVENESS.
SUCH A DEAL OF EMOTION ABOUT SOMETHING I MIGHT HAVE ASKED HIM TO DO ANYWAY. IT WAS...NOVEL.
WHERE IS HE NOW?
MIGHT WE BORROW HIM?
NOT FOR SEX, BUT TO SHOW HIM OFF AT THE MARQUIS OF TROLLFOR'S WEDDING BREAKFAST?
I LEFT HIM SLEEPING. HE NEEDS HIS REST, POOR MAN.
HE'S BEEN THROUGH SO MUCH.

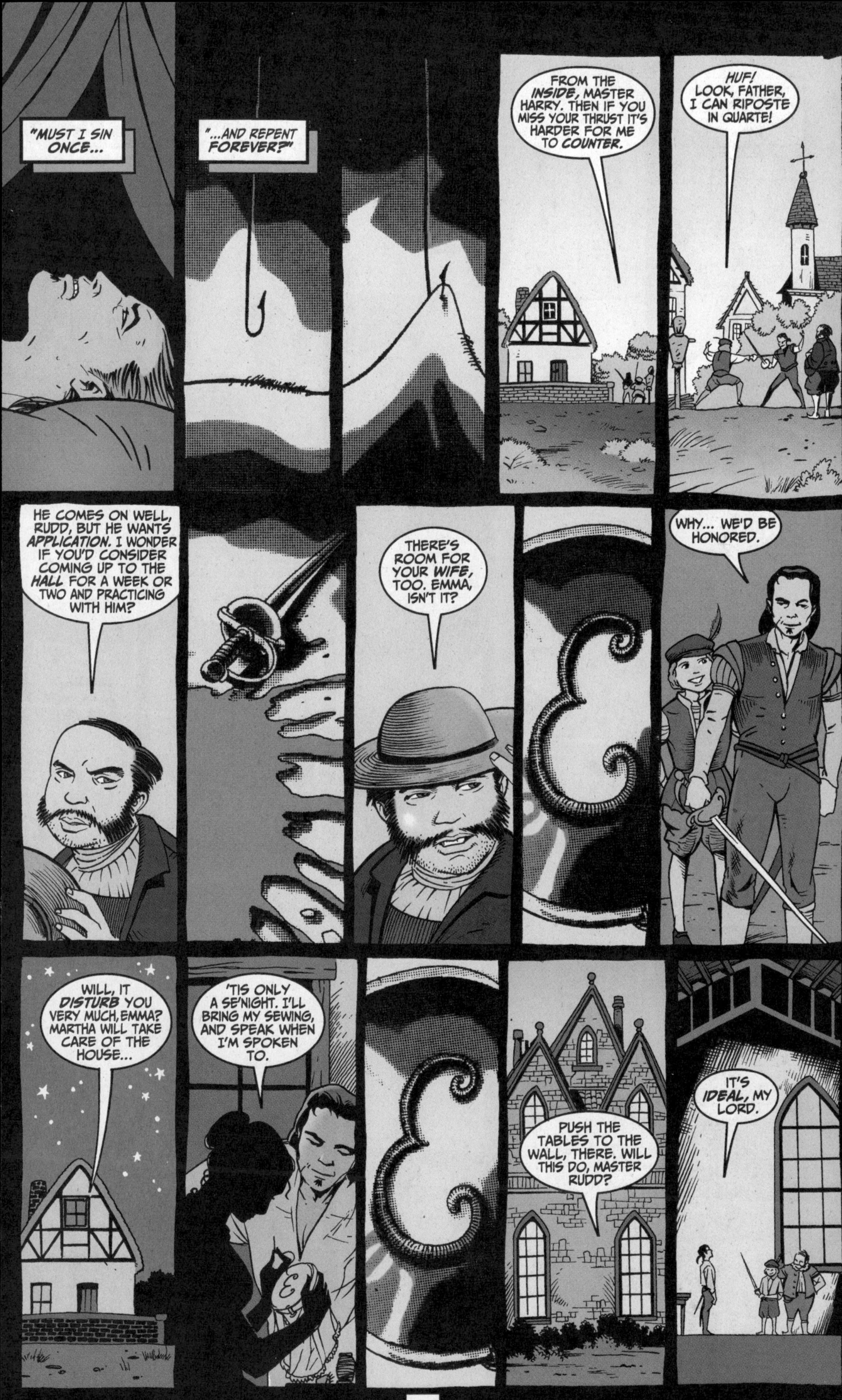
"MUST I SIN ONCE...
"...AND REPENT FOREVER?"
FROM THE INSIDE, MASTER HARRY. THEN IF YOU MISS YOUR THRUST IT'S HARDER FOR ME TO COUNTER.
HUF! LOOK, FATHER, I CAN RIPOSTE IN QUARTE!
HE COMES ON WELL, RUDD, BUT HE WANTS APPLICATION. I WONDER IF YOU'D CONSIDER COMING UP TO THE HALL FOR A WEEK OR TWO AND PRACTICING WITH HIM?
THERE'S ROOM FOR YOUR WIFE, TOO. EMMA, ISN'T IT?
WHY... WE'D BE HONORED.
WILL, IT DISTURB YOU VERY MUCH, EMMA? MARTHA WILL TAKE CARE OF THE HOUSE...
'TIS ONLY A SE'NIGHT. I'LL BRING MY SEWING, AND SPEAK WHEN I'M SPOKEN TO.
PUSH THE TABLES TO THE WALL, THERE. WILL THIS DO, MASTER RUDD?
IT'S IDEAL, MY LORD.

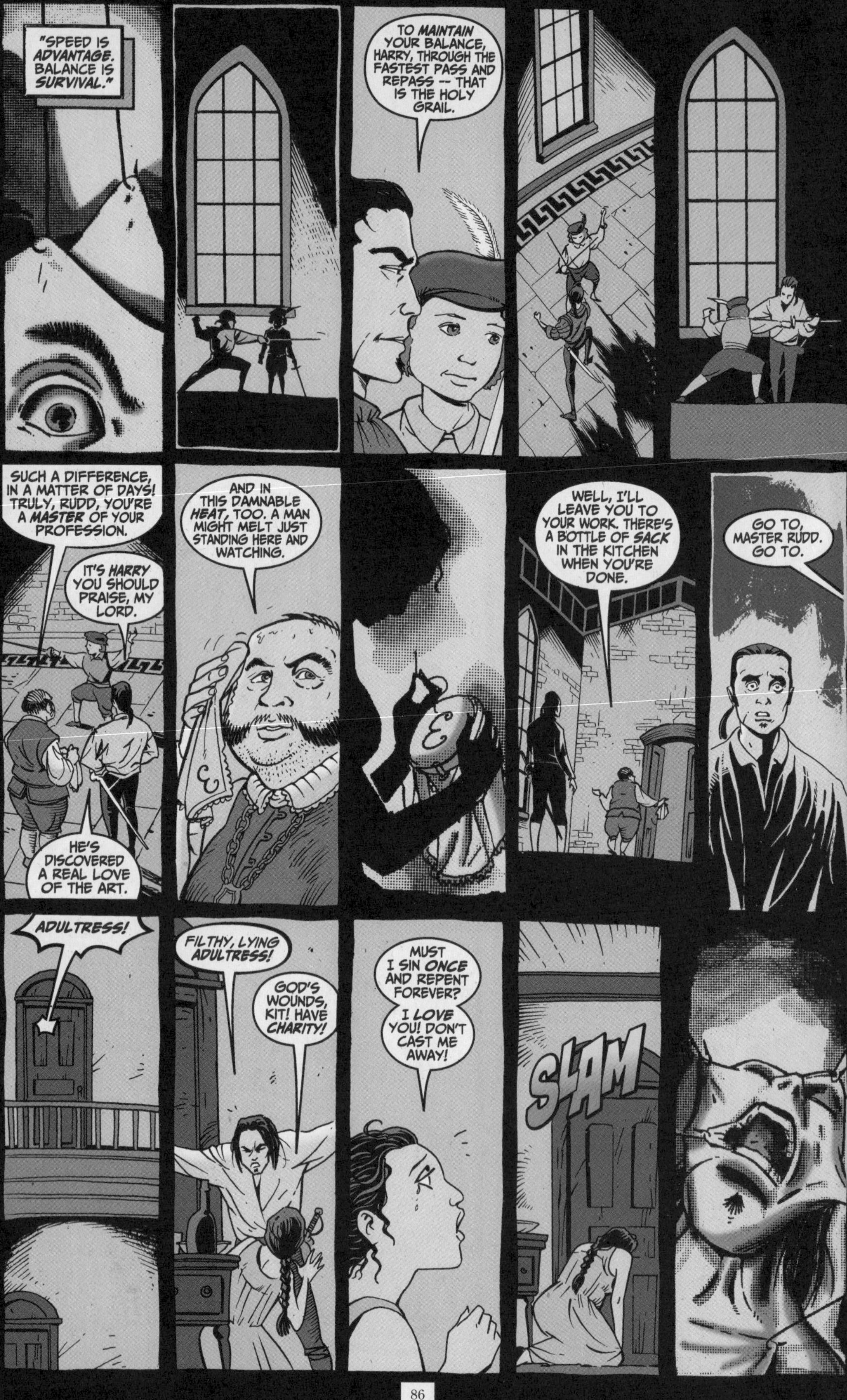
"SPEED IS ADVANTAGE. BALANCE IS SURVIVAL."
TO MAINTAIN YOUR BALANCE, HARRY, THROUGH THE FASTEST PASS AND REPASS -- THAT IS THE HOLY GRAIL.
SUCH A DIFFERENCE, IN A MATTER OF DAYS! TRULY, RUDD, YOU'RE A MASTER OF YOUR PROFESSION.
IT'S HARRY YOU SHOULD PRAISE, MY LORD.
HE'S DISCOVERED A REAL LOVE OF THE ART.
AND IN THIS DAMNABLE HEAT, TOO. A MAN MIGHT MELT JUST STANDING HERE AND WATCHING.
WELL, I'LL LEAVE YOU TO YOUR WORK. THERE'S A BOTTLE OF SACK IN THE KITCHEN WHEN YOU'RE DONE.
GO TO, MASTER RUDD. GO TO.
ADULTRESS!
FILTHY, LYING ADULTRESS!
GOD'S WOUNDS, KIT! HAVE CHARITY!
MUST I SIN ONCE AND REPENT FOREVER?
I LOVE YOU! DON'T CAST ME AWAY!
SLAM

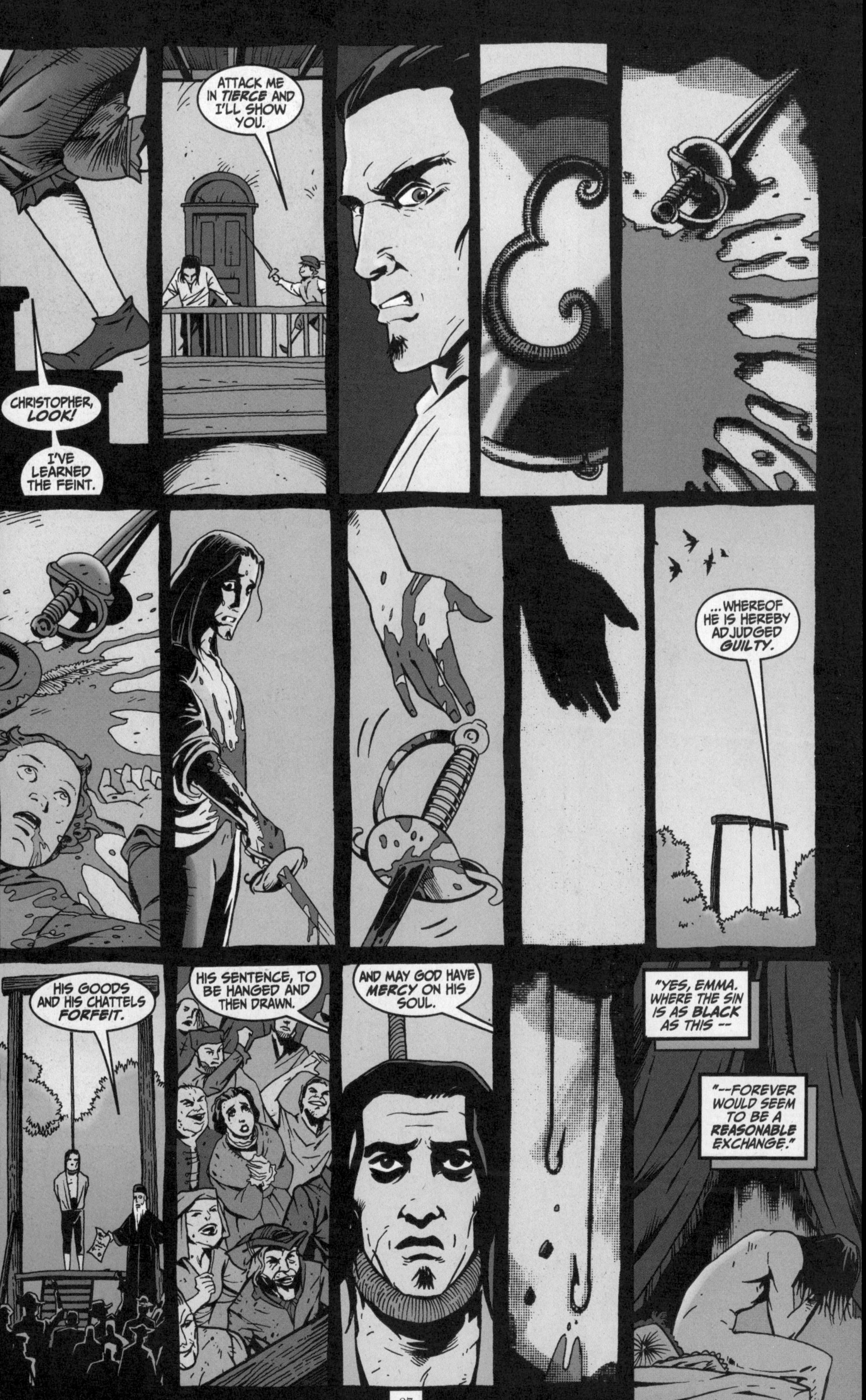
CHRISTOPHER, LOOK!
I'VE LEARNED THE FEINT.
ATTACK ME IN TIERCE AND I'LL SHOW YOU.
...WHEREOF HE IS HEREBY ADJUDGED GUILTY.
HIS GOODS AND HIS CHATTELS FORFEIT.
HIS SENTENCE, TO BE HANGED AND THEN DRAWN.
AND MAY GOD HAVE MERCY ON HIS SOUL.
"YES, EMMA. WHERE THE SIN IS AS BLACK AS THIS --
"--FOREVER WOULD SEEM TO BE A REASONABLE EXCHANGE."

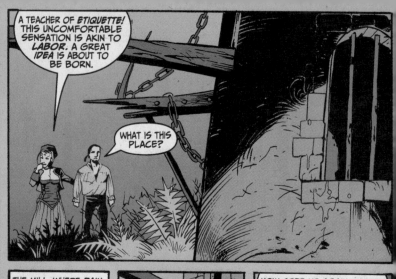

YOU WERE A TEACHER?

A TEACHER OF *ETIQUETTE!* THIS UNCOMFORTABLE SENSATION IS AKIN TO *LABOR.* A GREAT *IDEA* IS ABOUT TO BE BORN.

WHAT IS THIS PLACE?

OF SWORDPLAY AND ETIQUETTE. BUT THAT WAS IN ANOTHER *COUNTRY.*

AND MANY LIFETIMES AGO.

THE MILL. WHERE *PAIN* IS REFINED AND GROUND INTO GRANULAR FORM FOR OUR DELIGHT AND DIVERSION.

HERE. TAKE SOME.

IT'S LIKE *SNUFF.* I WAS NEVER ABLE TO ABIDE ITS SMELL.

AS YOU LIKE.

NOW COPE ME *AGAIN,* MASTER RUDD. BUT THIS TIME YOU MUST *BITE* AS WELL AS SCRATCH.

AND AFTERWARDS --

-- I'LL INTRODUCE YOU TO MY *FATHER.*

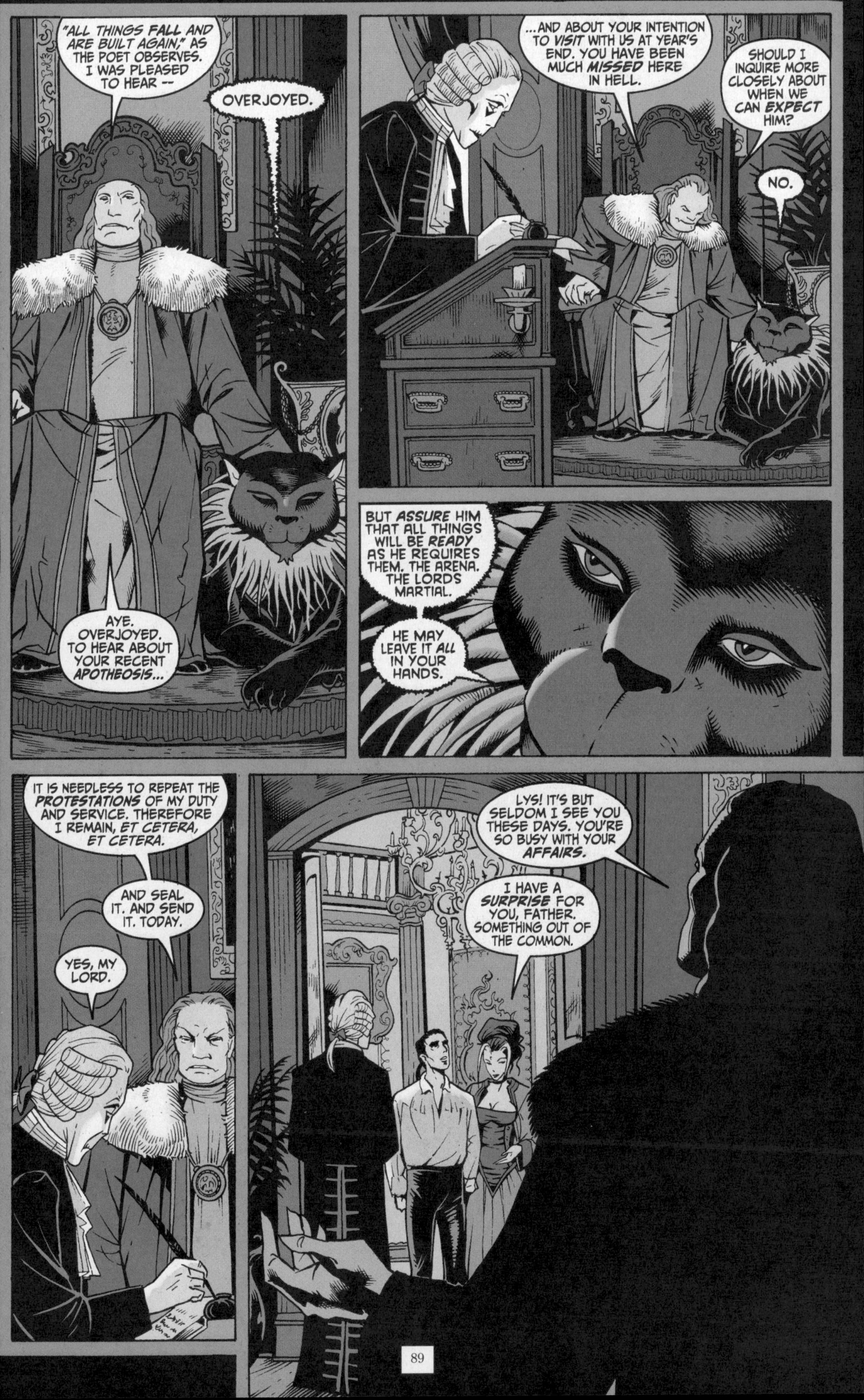
"ALL THINGS FALL AND ARE BUILT AGAIN," AS THE POET OBSERVES. I WAS PLEASED TO HEAR --
OVERJOYED.
AYE. OVERJOYED. TO HEAR ABOUT YOUR RECENT APOTHEOSIS...
...AND ABOUT YOUR INTENTION TO VISIT WITH US AT YEAR'S END. YOU HAVE BEEN MUCH MISSED HERE IN HELL.
SHOULD I INQUIRE MORE CLOSELY ABOUT WHEN WE CAN EXPECT HIM?
NO.
BUT ASSURE HIM THAT ALL THINGS WILL BE READY AS HE REQUIRES THEM. THE ARENA. THE LORDS MARTIAL.
HE MAY LEAVE IT ALL IN YOUR HANDS.
IT IS NEEDLESS TO REPEAT THE PROTESTATIONS OF MY DUTY AND SERVICE. THEREFORE I REMAIN, ET CETERA, ET CETERA.
AND SEAL IT. AND SEND IT. TODAY.
YES, MY LORD.
LYS! IT'S BUT SELDOM I SEE YOU THESE DAYS. YOU'RE SO BUSY WITH YOUR AFFAIRS.
I HAVE A SURPRISE FOR YOU, FATHER. SOMETHING OUT OF THE COMMON.

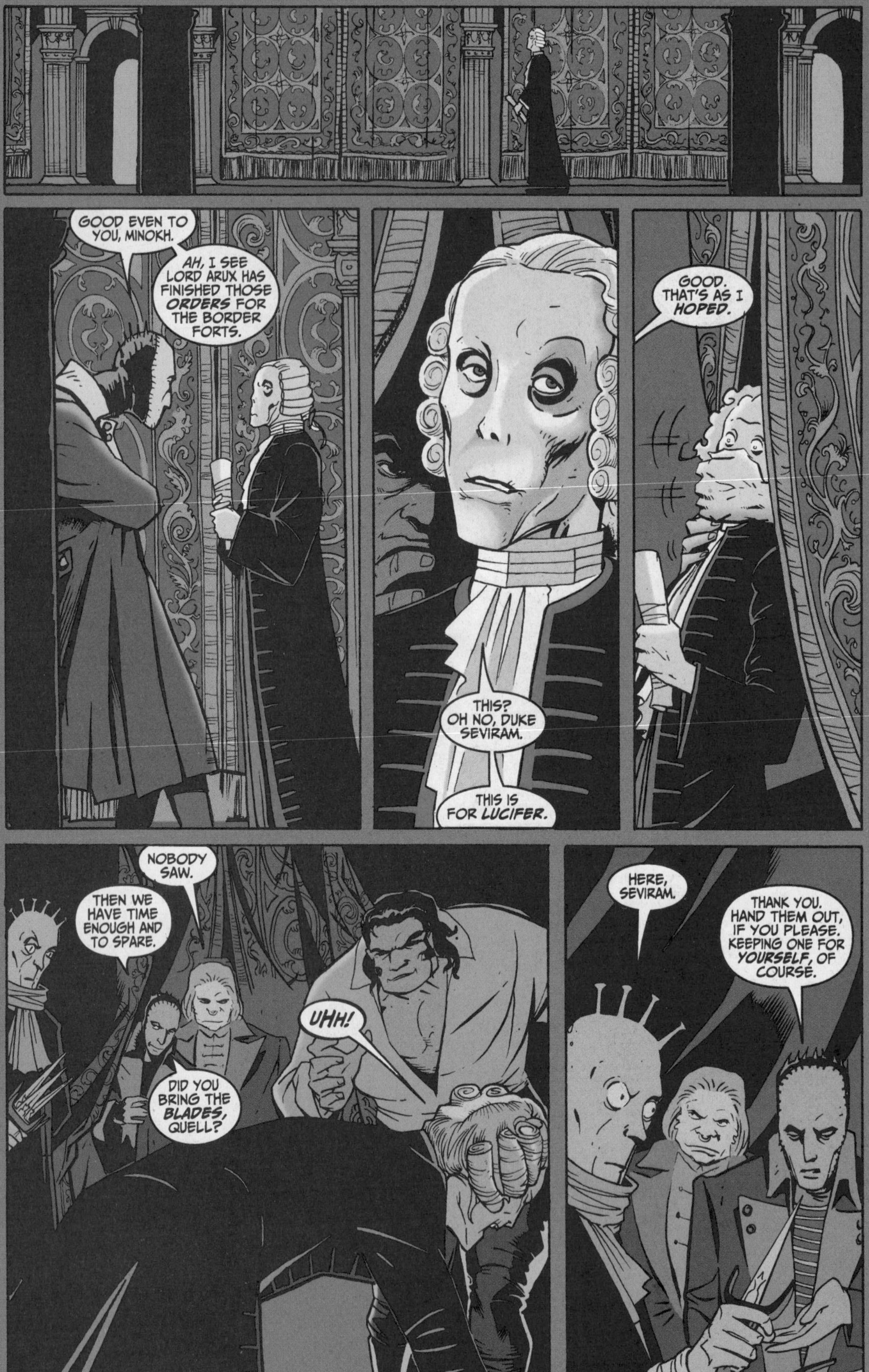
GOOD EVEN TO YOU, MINOKH.
AH, I SEE LORD ARUX HAS FINISHED THOSE ORDERS FOR THE BORDER FORTS.
THIS? OH NO, DUKE SEVIRAM.
THIS IS FOR LUCIFER.
GOOD. THAT'S AS I HOPED.
NOBODY SAW.
THEN WE HAVE TIME ENOUGH AND TO SPARE.
DID YOU BRING THE BLADES, QUELL?
UHH!
HERE, SEVIRAM.
THANK YOU. HAND THEM OUT, IF YOU PLEASE. KEEPING ONE FOR YOURSELF, OF COURSE.

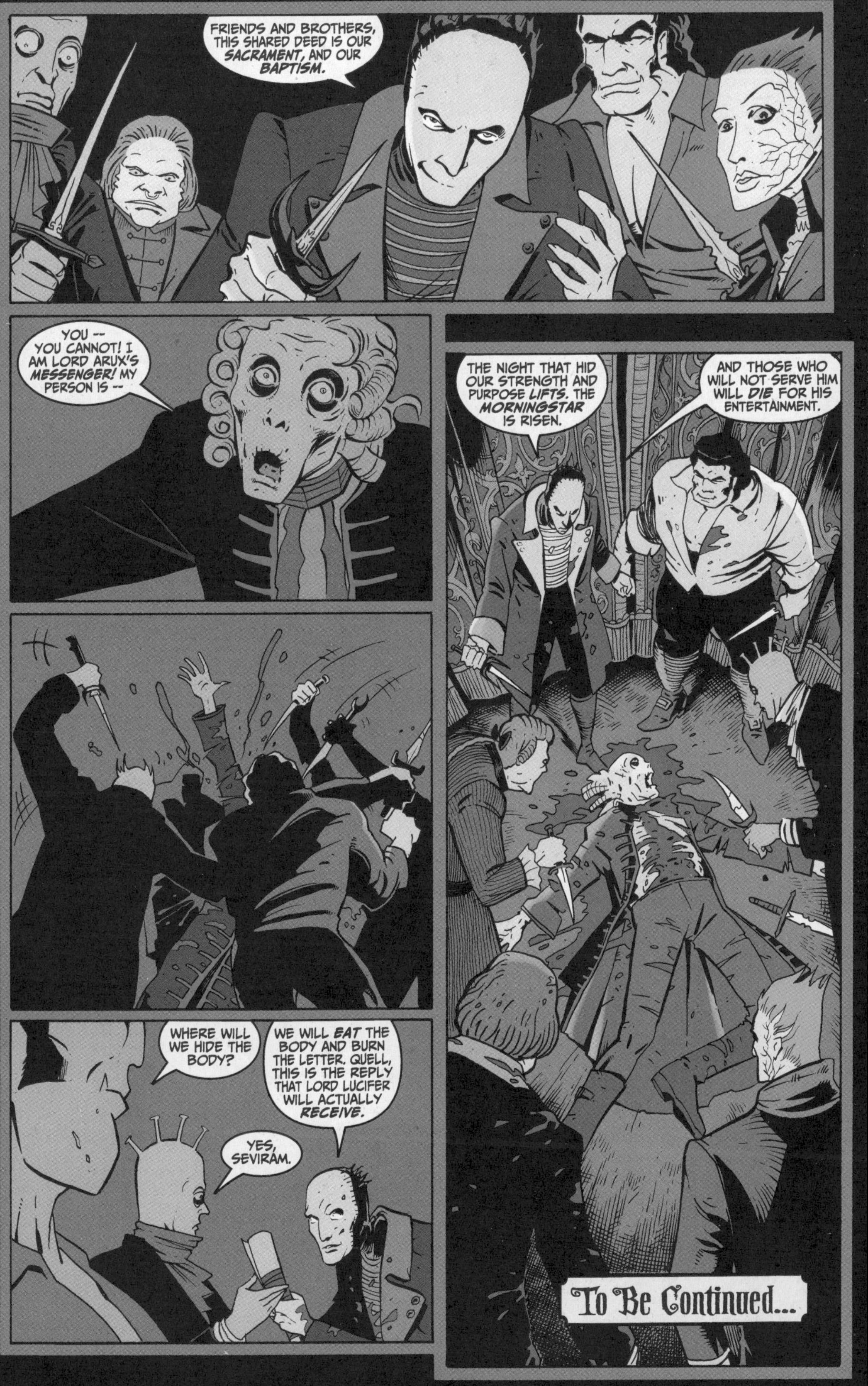
FRIENDS AND BROTHERS, THIS SHARED DEED IS OUR *SACRAMENT*, AND OUR *BAPTISM*.
YOU -- YOU CANNOT! I AM LORD ARUX'S *MESSENGER!* MY PERSON IS --
WHERE WILL WE HIDE THE BODY?
WE WILL *EAT* THE BODY AND BURN THE LETTER. QUELL, THIS IS THE REPLY THAT LORD LUCIFER WILL ACTUALLY *RECEIVE*.
YES, SEVIRAM.
THE NIGHT THAT HID OUR STRENGTH AND PURPOSE *LIFTS*. THE *MORNINGSTAR* IS RISEN.
AND THOSE WHO WILL NOT SERVE HIM WILL *DIE* FOR HIS ENTERTAINMENT.
To Be Continued...

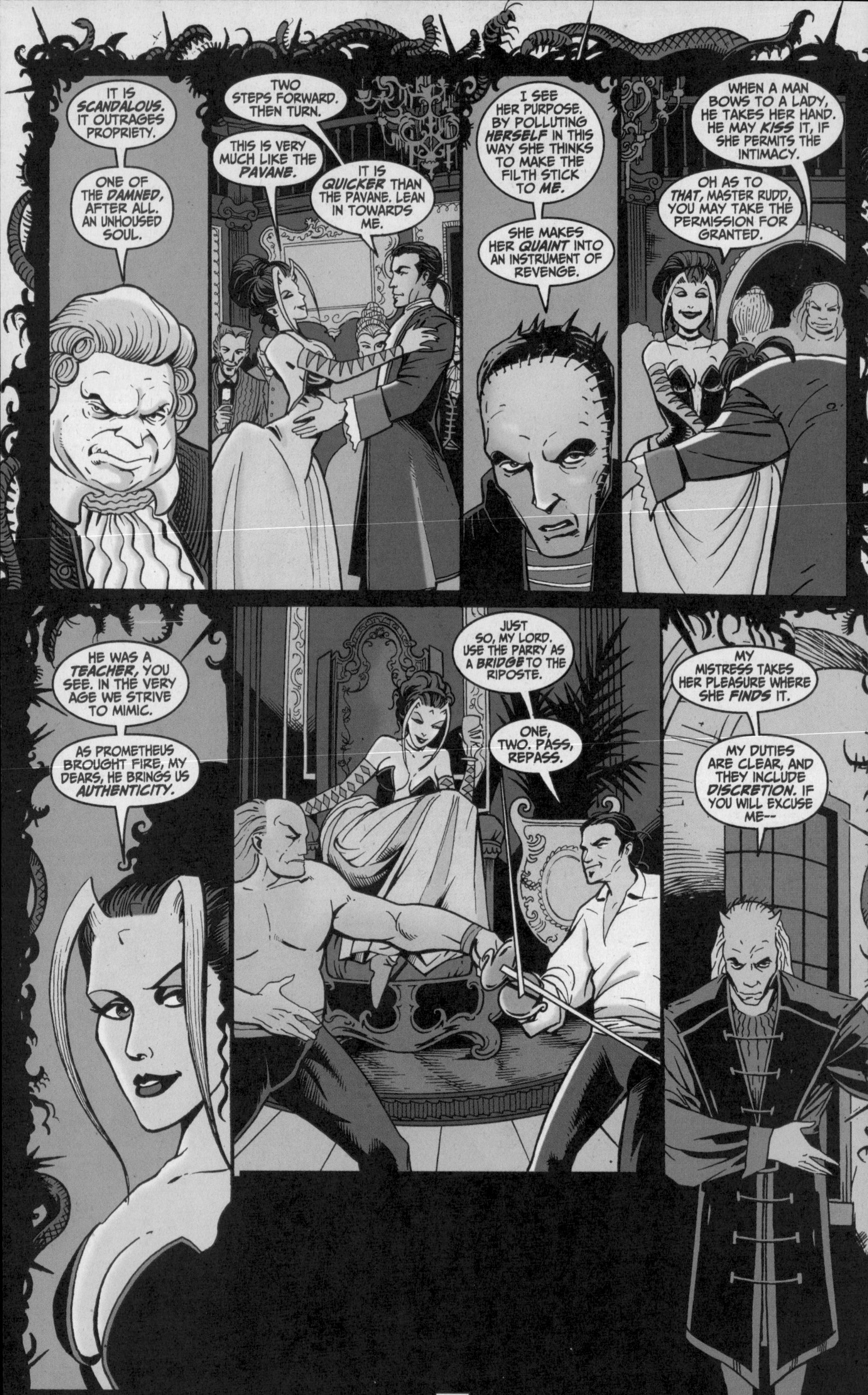
IT IS SCANDALOUS. IT OUTRAGES PROPRIETY.
ONE OF THE DAMNED, AFTER ALL. AN UNHOUSED SOUL.
TWO STEPS FORWARD. THEN TURN.
THIS IS VERY MUCH LIKE THE PAVANE.
IT IS QUICKER THAN THE PAVANE. LEAN IN TOWARDS ME.
I SEE HER PURPOSE. BY POLLUTING HERSELF IN THIS WAY SHE THINKS TO MAKE THE FILTH STICK TO ME.
SHE MAKES HER QUAINT INTO AN INSTRUMENT OF REVENGE.
WHEN A MAN BOWS TO A LADY, HE TAKES HER HAND. HE MAY KISS IT, IF SHE PERMITS THE INTIMACY.
OH AS TO THAT, MASTER RUDD, YOU MAY TAKE THE PERMISSION FOR GRANTED.
HE WAS A TEACHER, YOU SEE. IN THE VERY AGE WE STRIVE TO MIMIC.
AS PROMETHEUS BROUGHT FIRE, MY DEARS, HE BRINGS US AUTHENTICITY.
JUST SO, MY LORD. USE THE PARRY AS A BRIDGE TO THE RIPOSTE.
ONE, TWO. PASS, REPASS.
MY MISTRESS TAKES HER PLEASURE WHERE SHE FINDS IT.
MY DUTIES ARE CLEAR, AND THEY INCLUDE DISCRETION. IF YOU WILL EXCUSE ME--

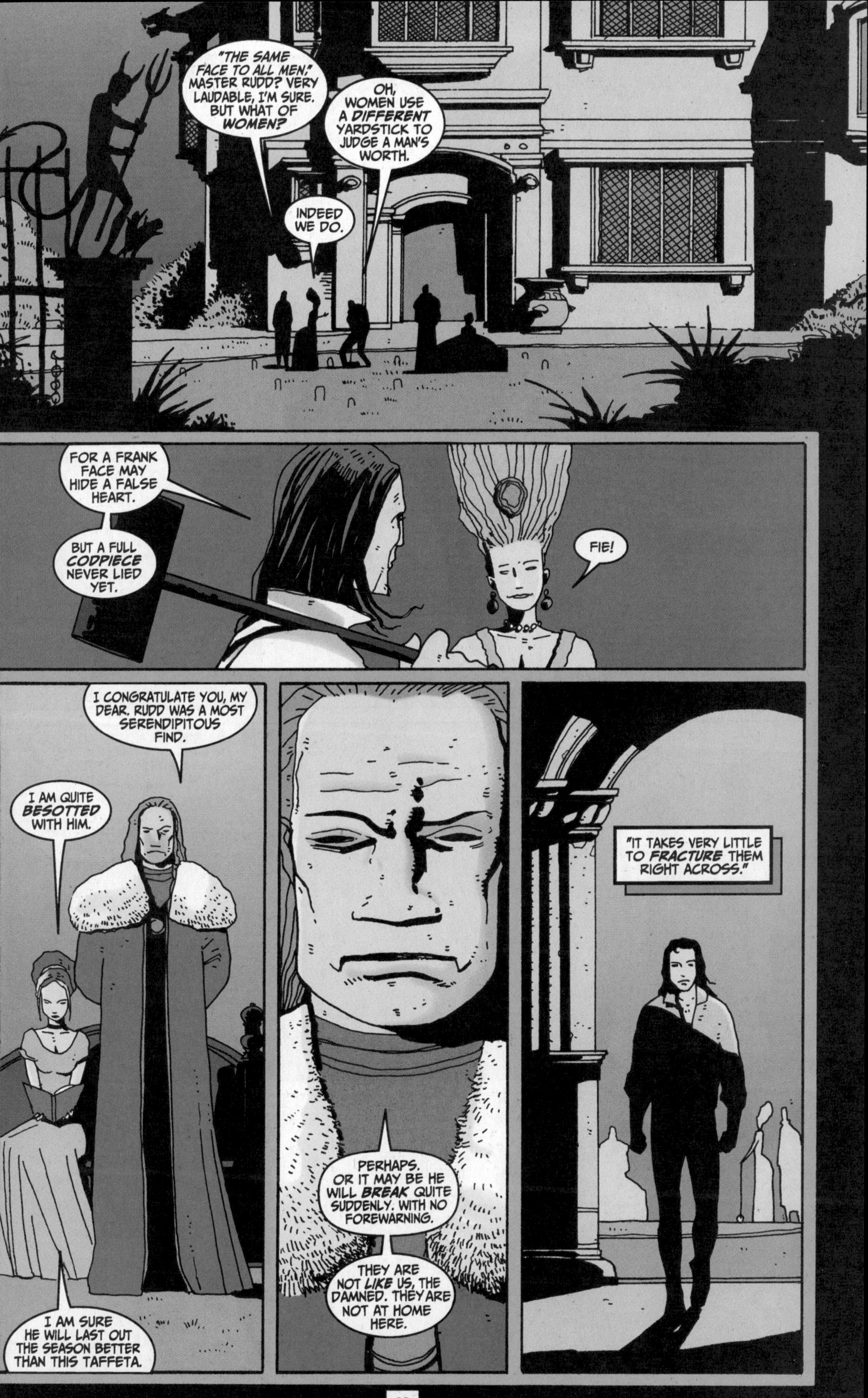
"THE SAME FACE TO ALL MEN," MASTER RUDD? VERY LAUDABLE, I'M SURE. BUT WHAT OF WOMEN?
OH, WOMEN USE A DIFFERENT YARDSTICK TO JUDGE A MAN'S WORTH.
INDEED WE DO.
FOR A FRANK FACE MAY HIDE A FALSE HEART.
BUT A FULL CODPIECE NEVER LIED YET.
FIE!
I CONGRATULATE YOU, MY DEAR. RUDD WAS A MOST SERENDIPITOUS FIND.
I AM QUITE BESOTTED WITH HIM.
I AM SURE HE WILL LAST OUT THE SEASON BETTER THAN THIS TAFFETA.
PERHAPS. OR IT MAY BE HE WILL BREAK QUITE SUDDENLY. WITH NO FOREWARNING.
THEY ARE NOT LIKE US, THE DAMNED. THEY ARE NOT AT HOME HERE.
"IT TAKES VERY LITTLE TO FRACTURE THEM RIGHT ACROSS."

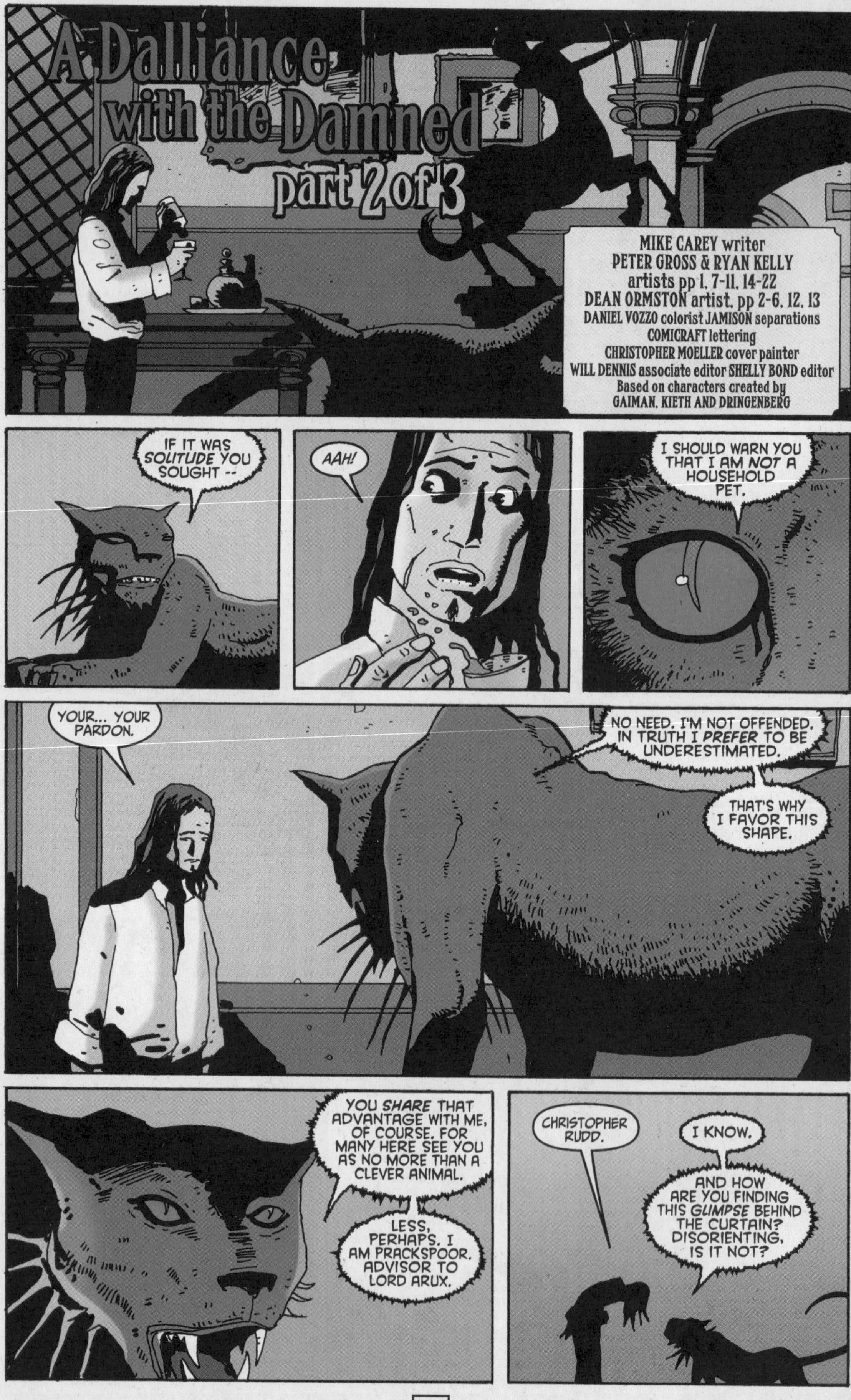
A Dalliance with the Damned
part 2 of 3
MIKE CAREY writer
PETER GROSS & RYAN KELLY artists pp 1, 7-11, 14-22
DEAN ORMSTON artist, pp 2-6, 12, 13
DANIEL VOZZO colorist JAMISON separations
COMICRAFT lettering
CHRISTOPHER MOELLER cover painter
WILL DENNIS associate editor SHELLY BOND editor
Based on characters created by
GAIMAN, KIETH AND DRINGENBERG
IF IT WAS SOLITUDE YOU SOUGHT --
AAH!
I SHOULD WARN YOU THAT I AM NOT A HOUSEHOLD PET.
YOUR... YOUR PARDON.
NO NEED. I'M NOT OFFENDED. IN TRUTH I PREFER TO BE UNDERESTIMATED.
THAT'S WHY I FAVOR THIS SHAPE.
YOU SHARE THAT ADVANTAGE WITH ME, OF COURSE. FOR MANY HERE SEE YOU AS NO MORE THAN A CLEVER ANIMAL.
LESS, PERHAPS. I AM PRACKSPOOR, ADVISOR TO LORD ARUX.
CHRISTOPHER RUDD.
I KNOW.
AND HOW ARE YOU FINDING THIS GLIMPSE BEHIND THE CURTAIN? DISORIENTING, IS IT NOT?

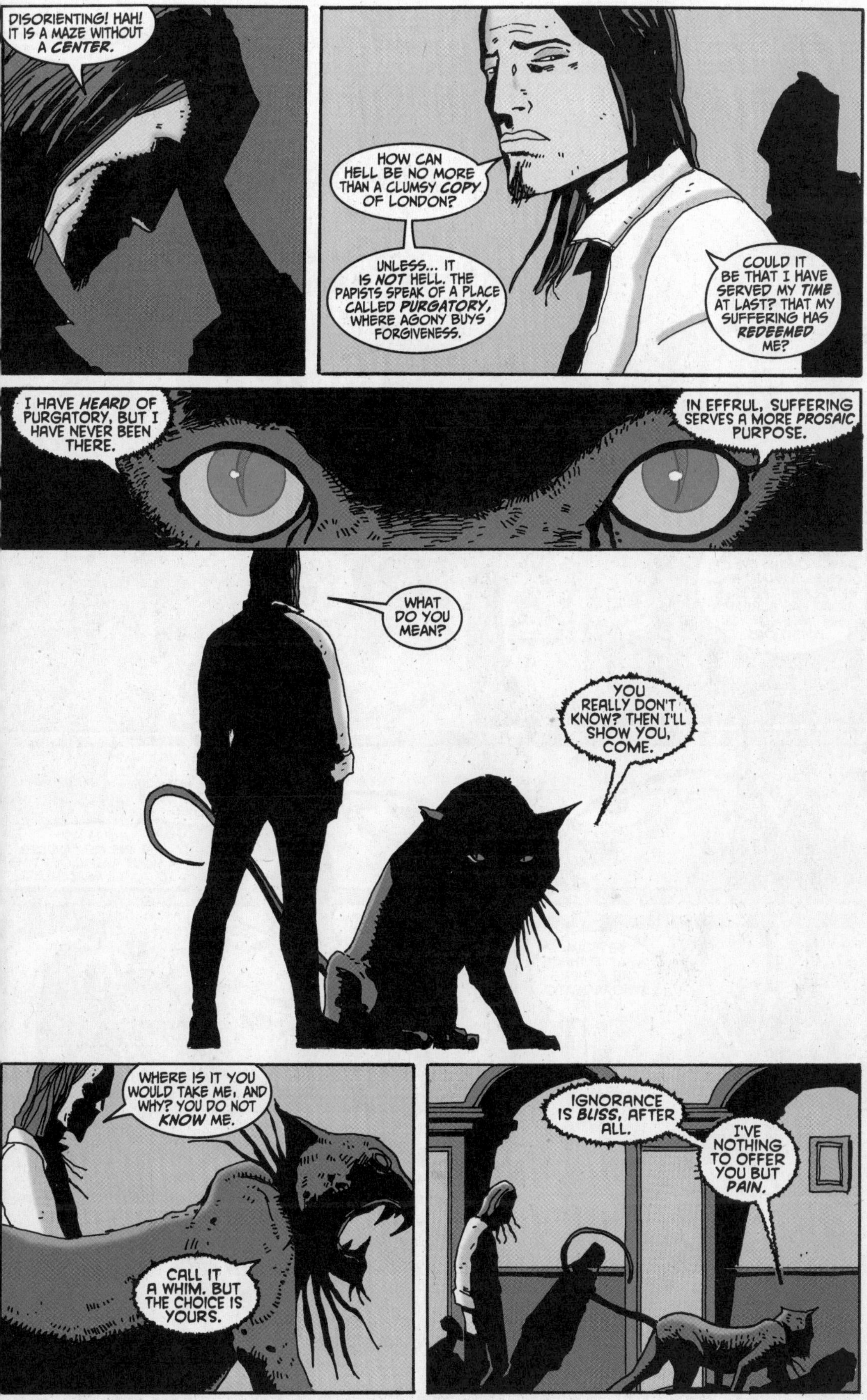

DISORIENTING! HAH! IT IS A MAZE WITHOUT A CENTER.
HOW CAN HELL BE NO MORE THAN A CLUMSY COPY OF LONDON?
UNLESS... IT IS NOT HELL. THE PAPISTS SPEAK OF A PLACE CALLED PURGATORY, WHERE AGONY BUYS FORGIVENESS.
COULD IT BE THAT I HAVE SERVED MY TIME AT LAST? THAT MY SUFFERING HAS REDEEMED ME?
I HAVE HEARD OF PURGATORY, BUT I HAVE NEVER BEEN THERE.
IN EFFRUL, SUFFERING SERVES A MORE PROSAIC PURPOSE.
WHAT DO YOU MEAN?
YOU REALLY DON'T KNOW? THEN I'LL SHOW YOU, COME.
WHERE IS IT YOU WOULD TAKE ME, AND WHY? YOU DO NOT KNOW ME.
CALL IT A WHIM. BUT THE CHOICE IS YOURS.
IGNORANCE IS BLISS, AFTER ALL.
I'VE NOTHING TO OFFER YOU BUT PAIN.

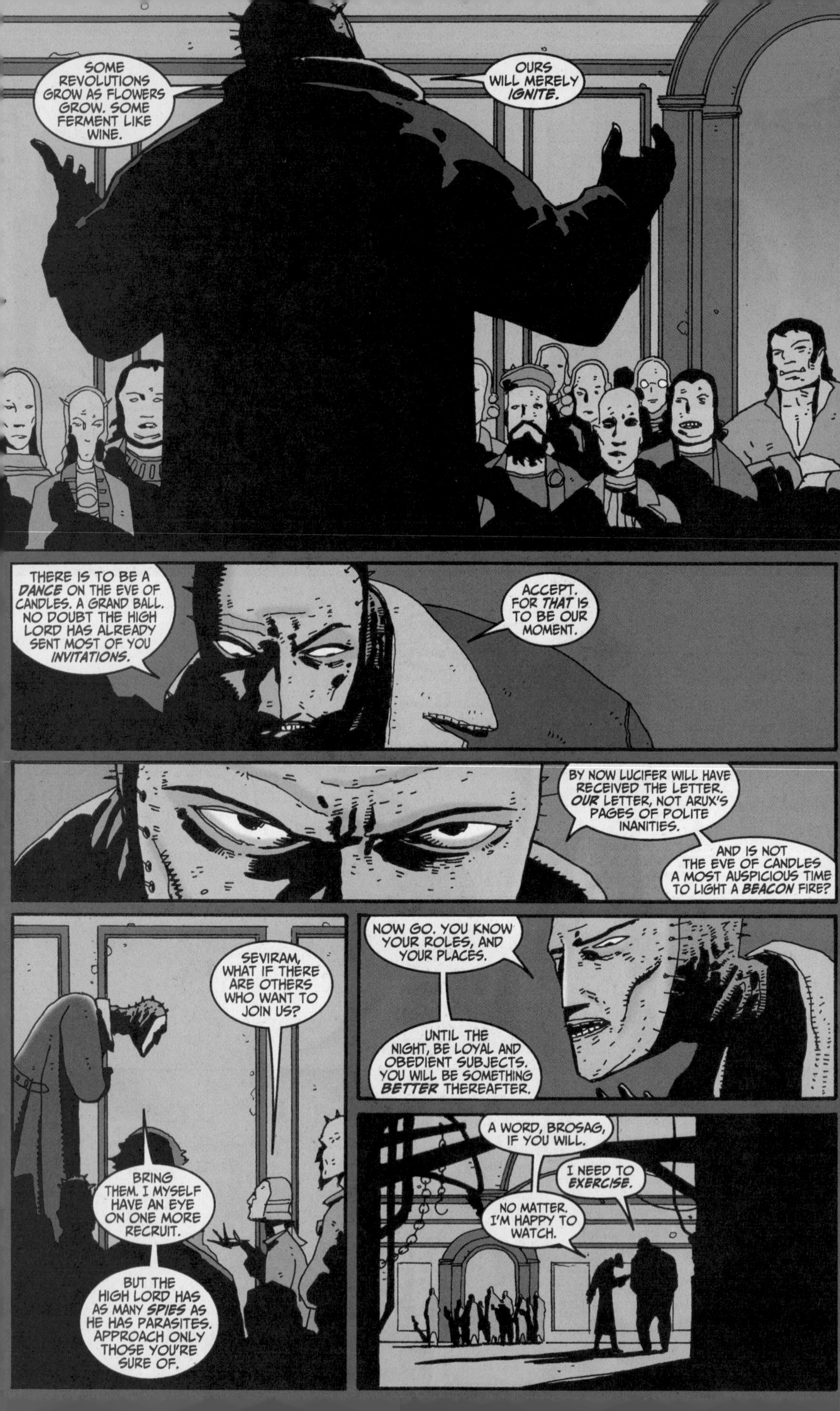
SOME REVOLUTIONS GROW AS FLOWERS GROW. SOME FERMENT LIKE WINE.
OURS WILL MERELY *IGNITE.*
THERE IS TO BE A *DANCE* ON THE EVE OF CANDLES. A GRAND BALL. NO DOUBT THE HIGH LORD HAS ALREADY SENT MOST OF YOU *INVITATIONS.*
ACCEPT. FOR *THAT* IS TO BE OUR MOMENT.
BY NOW LUCIFER WILL HAVE RECEIVED THE LETTER. *OUR* LETTER, NOT ARUX'S PAGES OF POLITE INANITIES.
AND IS NOT THE EVE OF CANDLES A MOST AUSPICIOUS TIME TO LIGHT A *BEACON* FIRE?
SEVIRAM, WHAT IF THERE ARE OTHERS WHO WANT TO JOIN US?
BRING THEM. I MYSELF HAVE AN EYE ON ONE MORE RECRUIT.
BUT THE HIGH LORD HAS AS MANY *SPIES* AS HE HAS PARASITES. APPROACH ONLY THOSE YOU'RE SURE OF.
NOW GO. YOU KNOW YOUR ROLES, AND YOUR PLACES.
UNTIL THE NIGHT, BE LOYAL AND OBEDIENT SUBJECTS. YOU WILL BE SOMETHING *BETTER* THEREAFTER.
A WORD, BROSAG, IF YOU WILL.
I NEED TO *EXERCISE.*
NO MATTER. I'M HAPPY TO WATCH.

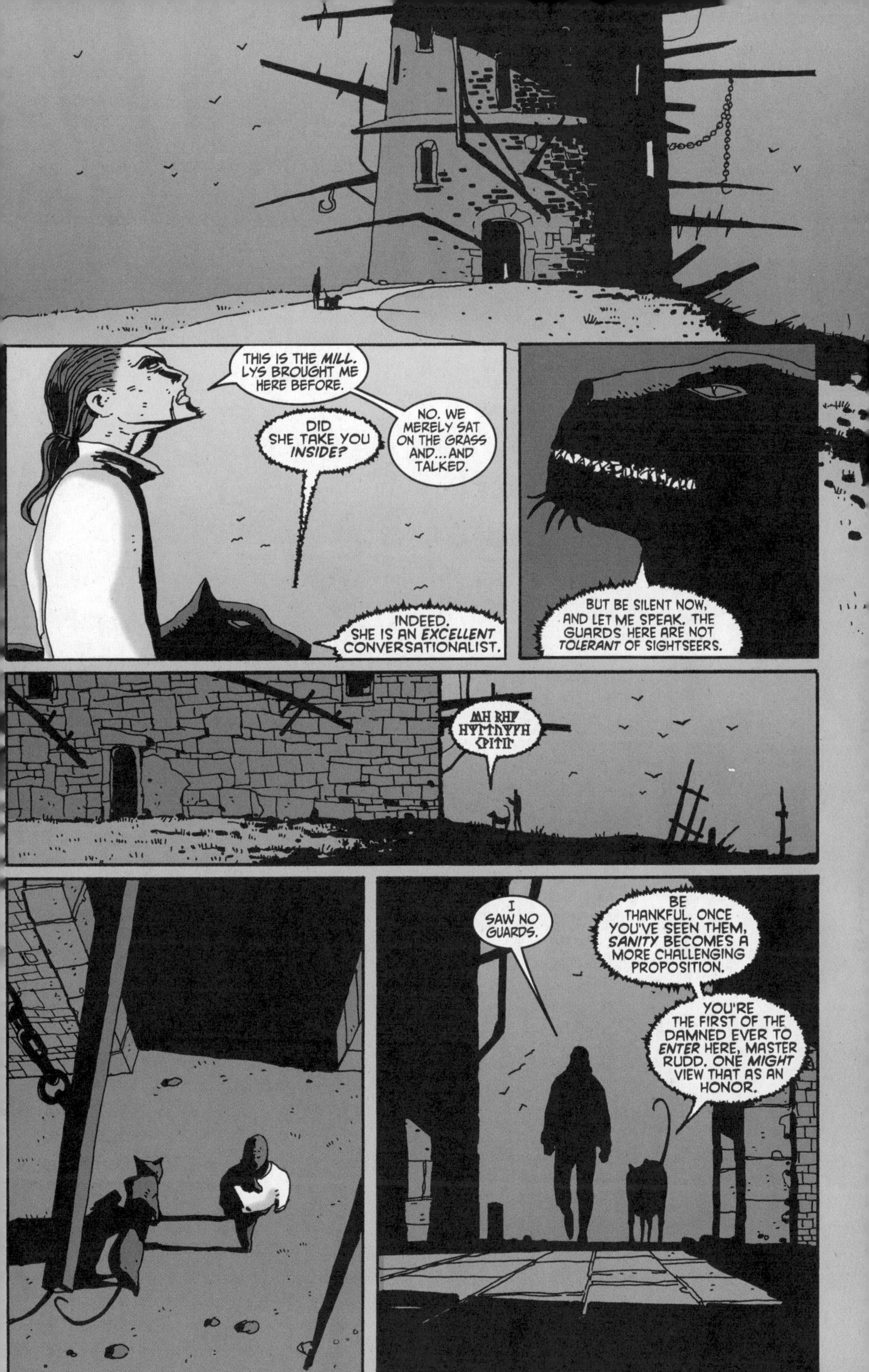
THIS IS THE MILL. LYS BROUGHT ME HERE BEFORE.
DID SHE TAKE YOU INSIDE?
NO. WE MERELY SAT ON THE GRASS AND...AND TALKED.
INDEED. SHE IS AN EXCELLENT CONVERSATIONALIST.
BUT BE SILENT NOW, AND LET ME SPEAK. THE GUARDS HERE ARE NOT TOLERANT OF SIGHTSEERS.
I SAW NO GUARDS.
BE THANKFUL. ONCE YOU'VE SEEN THEM, SANITY BECOMES A MORE CHALLENGING PROPOSITION.
YOU'RE THE FIRST OF THE DAMNED EVER TO ENTER HERE, MASTER RUDD. ONE MIGHT VIEW THAT AS AN HONOR.

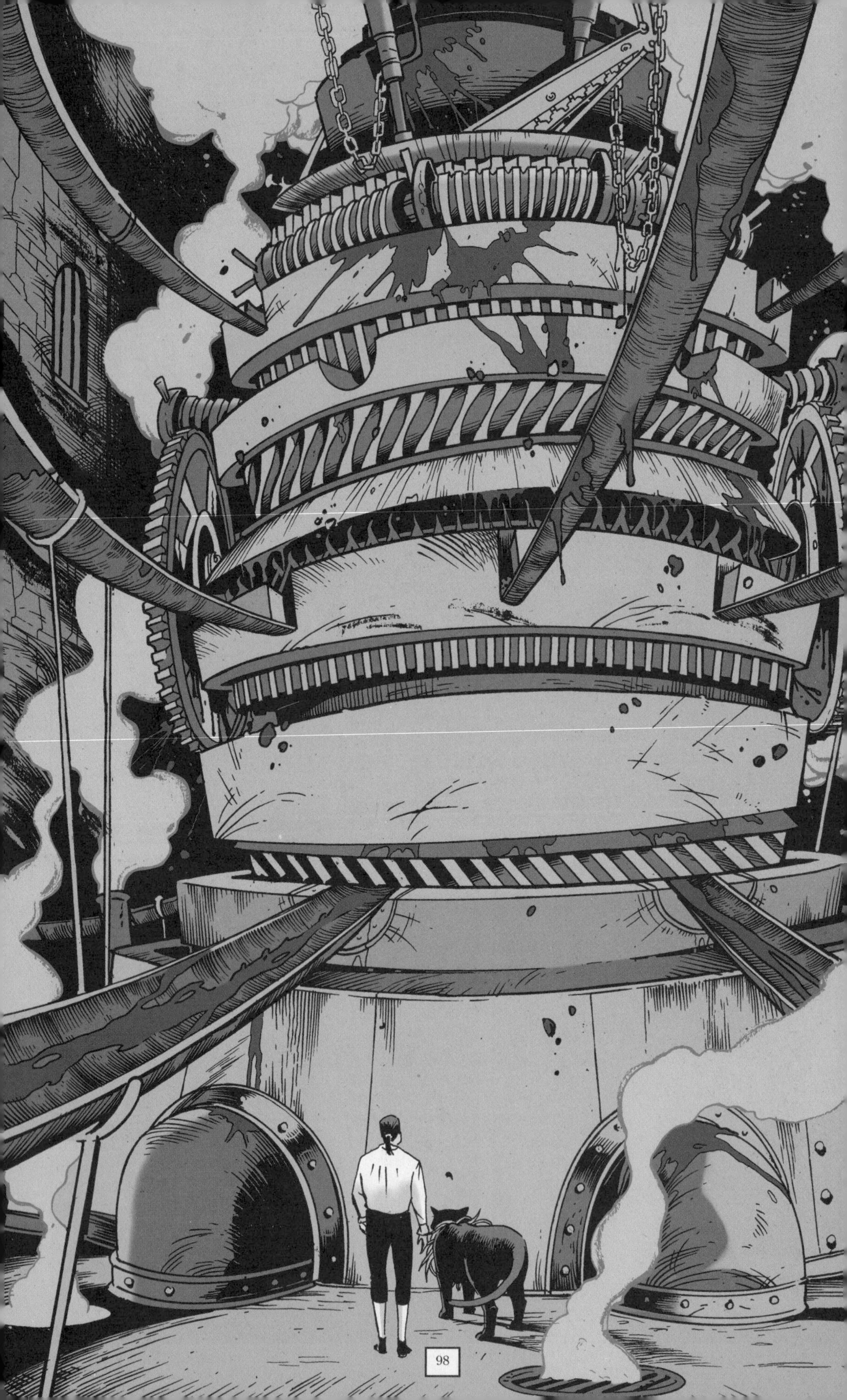

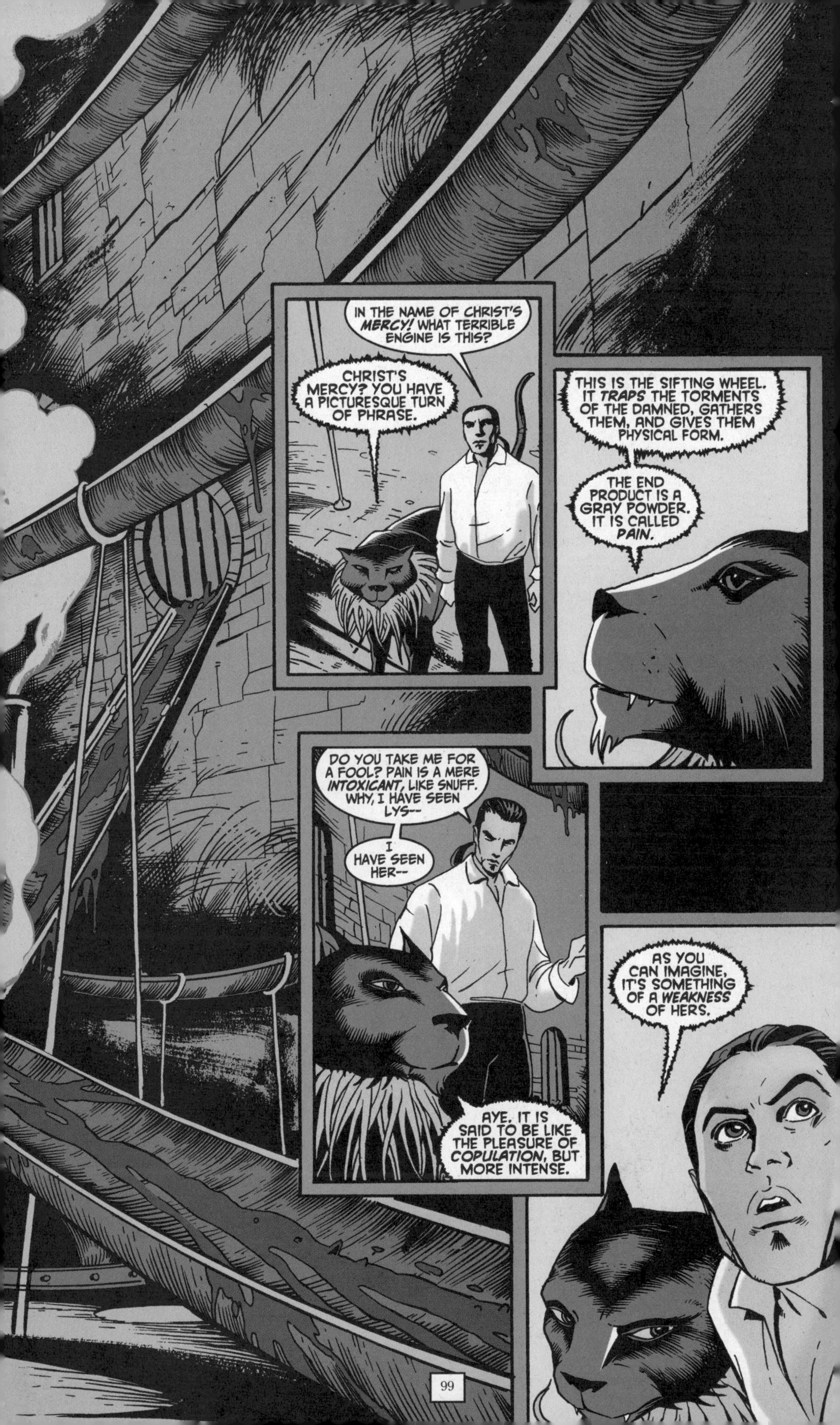
IN THE NAME OF CHRIST'S *MERCY!* WHAT TERRIBLE ENGINE IS THIS?
CHRIST'S MERCY? YOU HAVE A PICTURESQUE TURN OF PHRASE.
THIS IS THE SIFTING WHEEL. IT *TRAPS* THE TORMENTS OF THE DAMNED, GATHERS THEM, AND GIVES THEM PHYSICAL FORM.
THE END PRODUCT IS A GRAY POWDER. IT IS CALLED *PAIN.*
DO YOU TAKE ME FOR A FOOL? PAIN IS A MERE *INTOXICANT,* LIKE SNUFF. WHY, I HAVE SEEN LYS--
I HAVE SEEN HER--
AYE. IT IS SAID TO BE LIKE THE PLEASURE OF *COPULATION,* BUT MORE INTENSE.
AS YOU CAN IMAGINE, IT'S SOMETHING OF A *WEAKNESS* OF HERS.

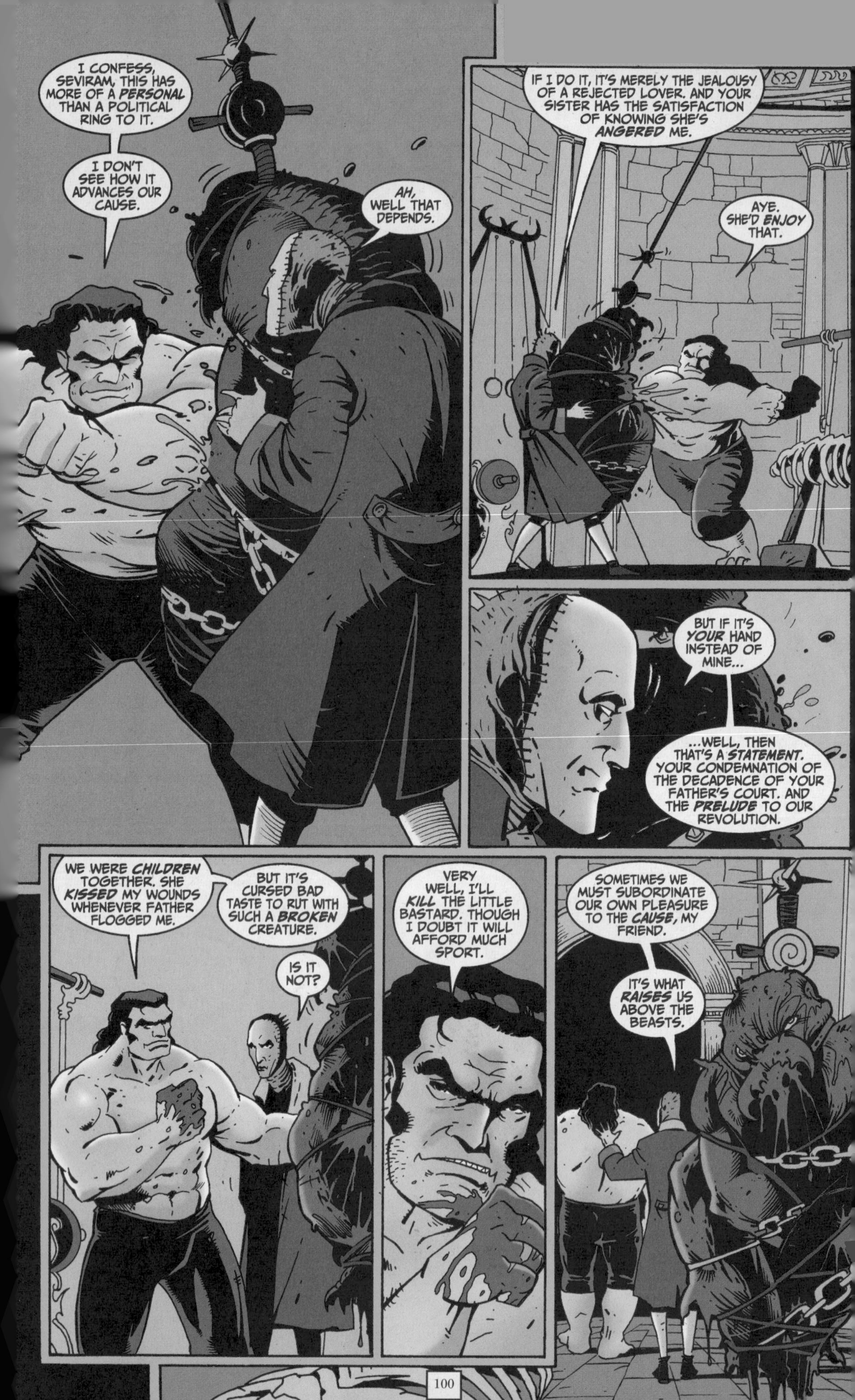
I CONFESS, SEVIRAM, THIS HAS MORE OF A PERSONAL THAN A POLITICAL RING TO IT.
I DON'T SEE HOW IT ADVANCES OUR CAUSE.
AH, WELL THAT DEPENDS.
IF I DO IT, IT'S MERELY THE JEALOUSY OF A REJECTED LOVER. AND YOUR SISTER HAS THE SATISFACTION OF KNOWING SHE'S ANGERED ME.
AYE. SHE'D ENJOY THAT.
BUT IF IT'S YOUR HAND INSTEAD OF MINE...
...WELL, THEN THAT'S A STATEMENT. YOUR CONDEMNATION OF THE DECADENCE OF YOUR FATHER'S COURT. AND THE PRELUDE TO OUR REVOLUTION.
WE WERE CHILDREN TOGETHER. SHE KISSED MY WOUNDS WHENEVER FATHER FLOGGED ME.
BUT IT'S CURSED BAD TASTE TO RUT WITH SUCH A BROKEN CREATURE.
IS IT NOT?
VERY WELL, I'LL KILL THE LITTLE BASTARD. THOUGH I DOUBT IT WILL AFFORD MUCH SPORT.
SOMETIMES WE MUST SUBORDINATE OUR OWN PLEASURE TO THE CAUSE, MY FRIEND.
IT'S WHAT RAISES US ABOVE THE BEASTS.

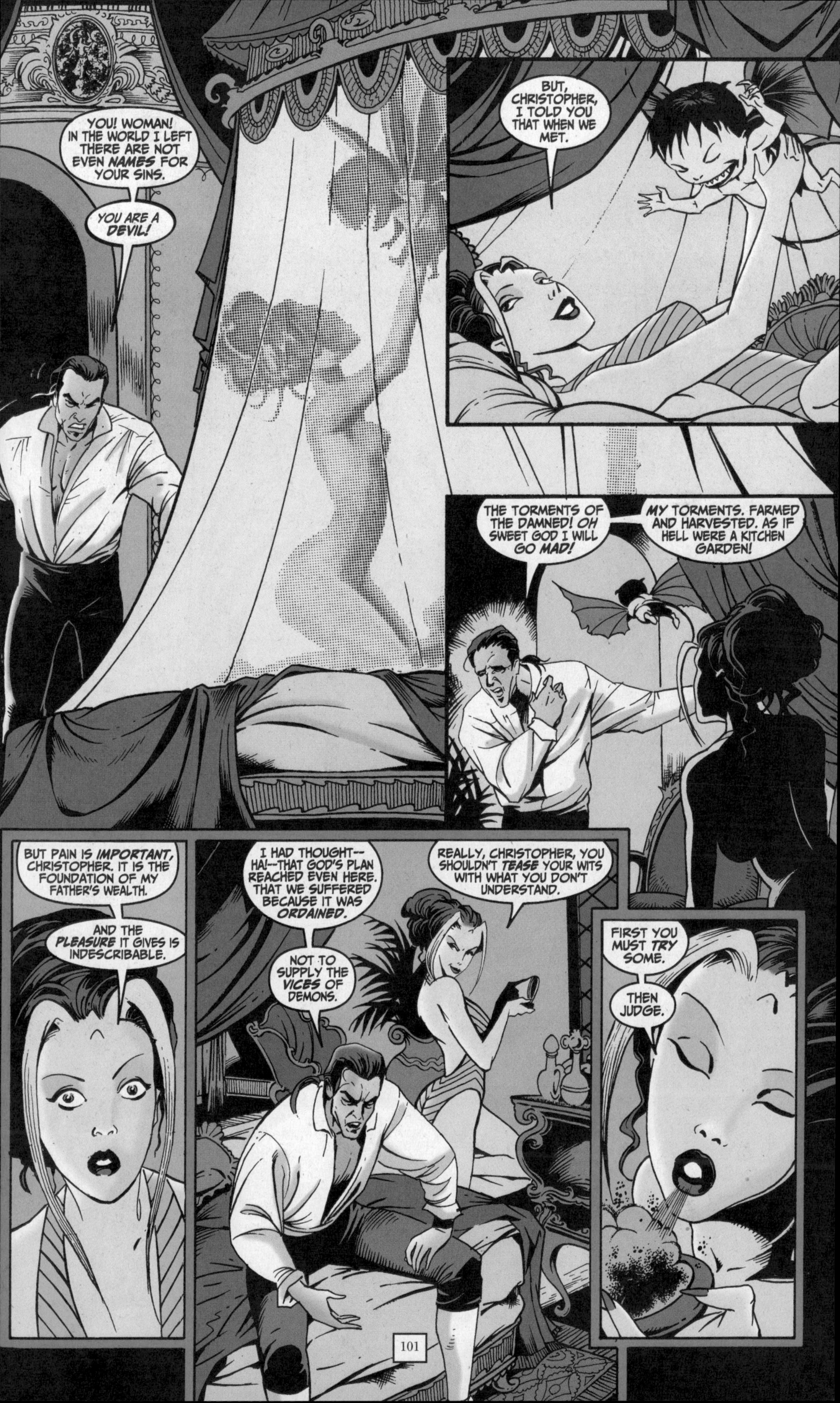

YOU! WOMAN! IN THE WORLD I LEFT THERE ARE NOT EVEN NAMES FOR YOUR SINS.
YOU ARE A DEVIL!
BUT, CHRISTOPHER, I TOLD YOU THAT WHEN WE MET.
THE TORMENTS OF THE DAMNED! OH SWEET GOD I WILL GO MAD!
MY TORMENTS. FARMED AND HARVESTED. AS IF HELL WERE A KITCHEN GARDEN!
BUT PAIN IS IMPORTANT, CHRISTOPHER. IT IS THE FOUNDATION OF MY FATHER'S WEALTH.
AND THE PLEASURE IT GIVES IS INDESCRIBABLE.
I HAD THOUGHT-- HA!--THAT GOD'S PLAN REACHED EVEN HERE. THAT WE SUFFERED BECAUSE IT WAS ORDAINED.
NOT TO SUPPLY THE VICES OF DEMONS.
REALLY, CHRISTOPHER, YOU SHOULDN'T TEASE YOUR WITS WITH WHAT YOU DON'T UNDERSTAND.
FIRST YOU MUST TRY SOME.
THEN JUDGE.

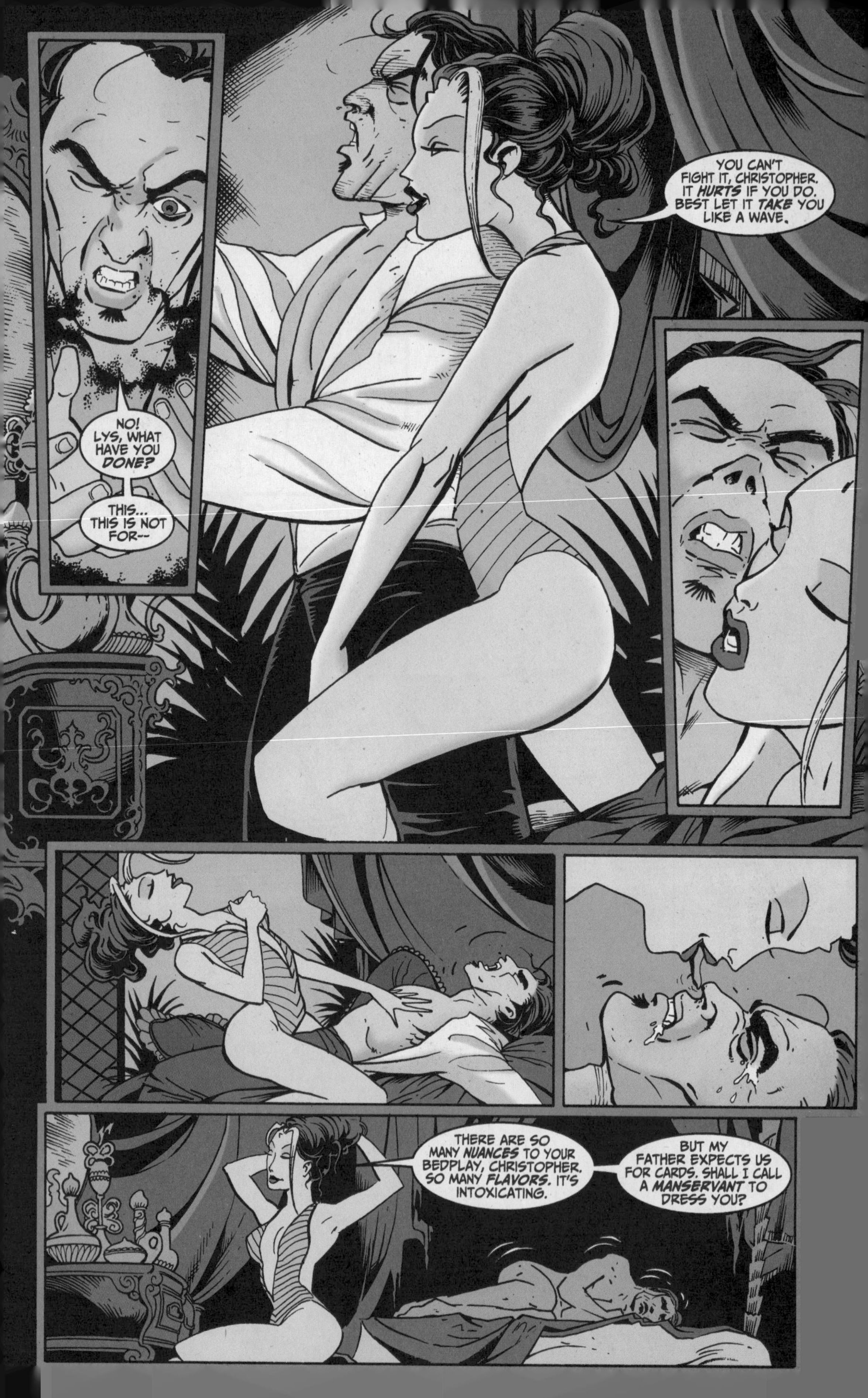
YOU CAN'T FIGHT IT, CHRISTOPHER. IT HURTS IF YOU DO. BEST LET IT TAKE YOU LIKE A WAVE.
NO! LYS, WHAT HAVE YOU DONE?
THIS... THIS IS NOT FOR--
THERE ARE SO MANY NUANCES TO YOUR BEDPLAY, CHRISTOPHER. SO MANY FLAVORS. IT'S INTOXICATING.
BUT MY FATHER EXPECTS US FOR CARDS. SHALL I CALL A MANSERVANT TO DRESS YOU?

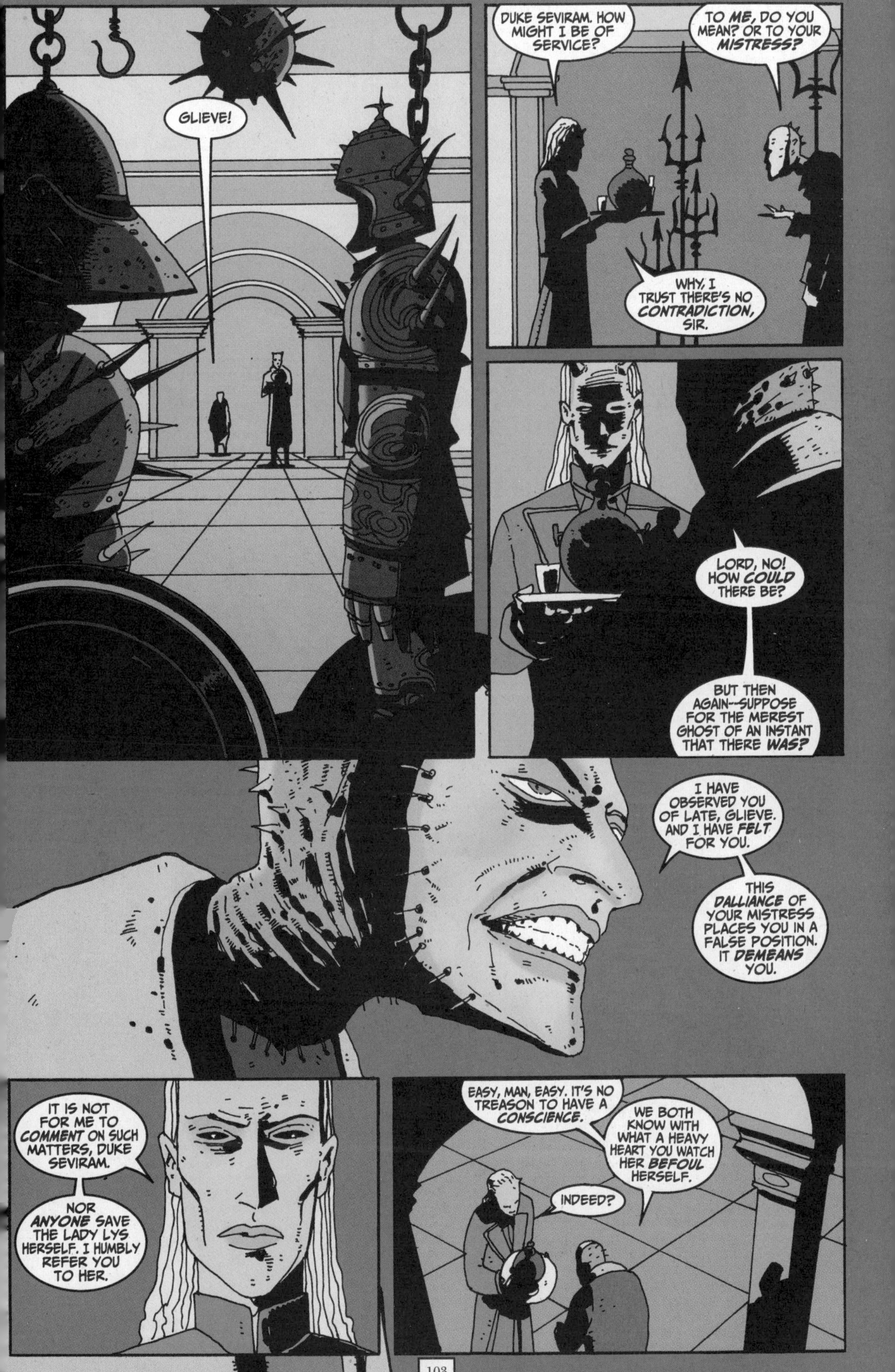
GLIEVE!
DUKE SEVIRAM. HOW MIGHT I BE OF SERVICE?
TO ME, DO YOU MEAN? OR TO YOUR MISTRESS?
WHY, I TRUST THERE'S NO CONTRADICTION, SIR.
LORD, NO! HOW COULD THERE BE?
BUT THEN AGAIN--SUPPOSE FOR THE MEREST GHOST OF AN INSTANT THAT THERE WAS?
I HAVE OBSERVED YOU OF LATE, GLIEVE. AND I HAVE FELT FOR YOU.
THIS DALLIANCE OF YOUR MISTRESS PLACES YOU IN A FALSE POSITION. IT DEMEANS YOU.
IT IS NOT FOR ME TO COMMENT ON SUCH MATTERS, DUKE SEVIRAM.
NOR ANYONE SAVE THE LADY LYS HERSELF. I HUMBLY REFER YOU TO HER.
EASY, MAN, EASY. IT'S NO TREASON TO HAVE A CONSCIENCE.
WE BOTH KNOW WITH WHAT A HEAVY HEART YOU WATCH HER BEFOUL HERSELF.
INDEED?

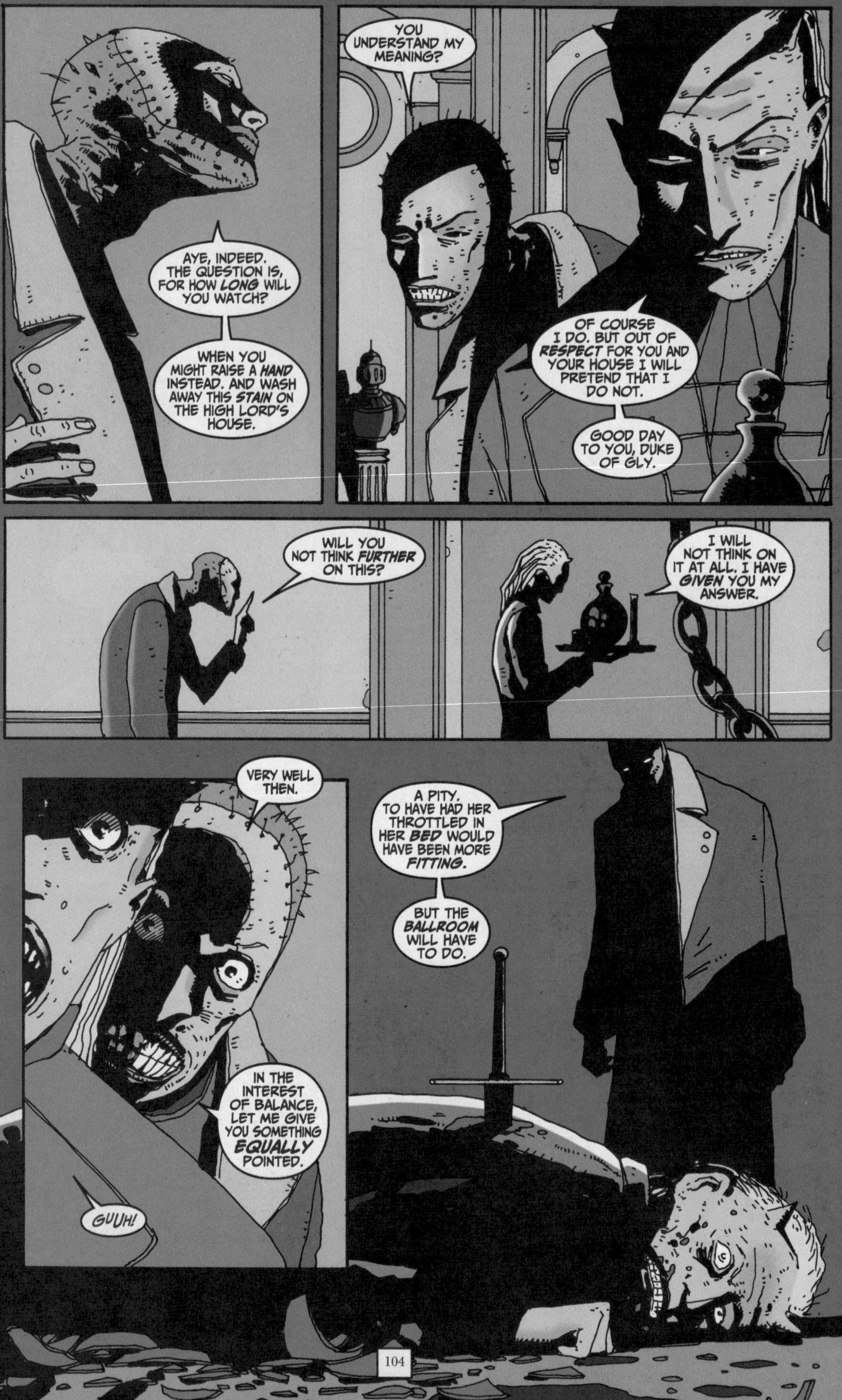

AYE, INDEED. THE QUESTION IS, FOR HOW LONG WILL YOU WATCH?
WHEN YOU MIGHT RAISE A HAND INSTEAD. AND WASH AWAY THIS STAIN ON THE HIGH LORD'S HOUSE.
YOU UNDERSTAND MY MEANING?
OF COURSE I DO. BUT OUT OF RESPECT FOR YOU AND YOUR HOUSE I WILL PRETEND THAT I DO NOT.
GOOD DAY TO YOU, DUKE OF GLY.
WILL YOU NOT THINK FURTHER ON THIS?
I WILL NOT THINK ON IT AT ALL. I HAVE GIVEN YOU MY ANSWER.
VERY WELL THEN.
IN THE INTEREST OF BALANCE, LET ME GIVE YOU SOMETHING EQUALLY POINTED.
GUUH!
A PITY. TO HAVE HAD HER THROTTLED IN HER BED WOULD HAVE BEEN MORE FITTING.
BUT THE BALLROOM WILL HAVE TO DO.

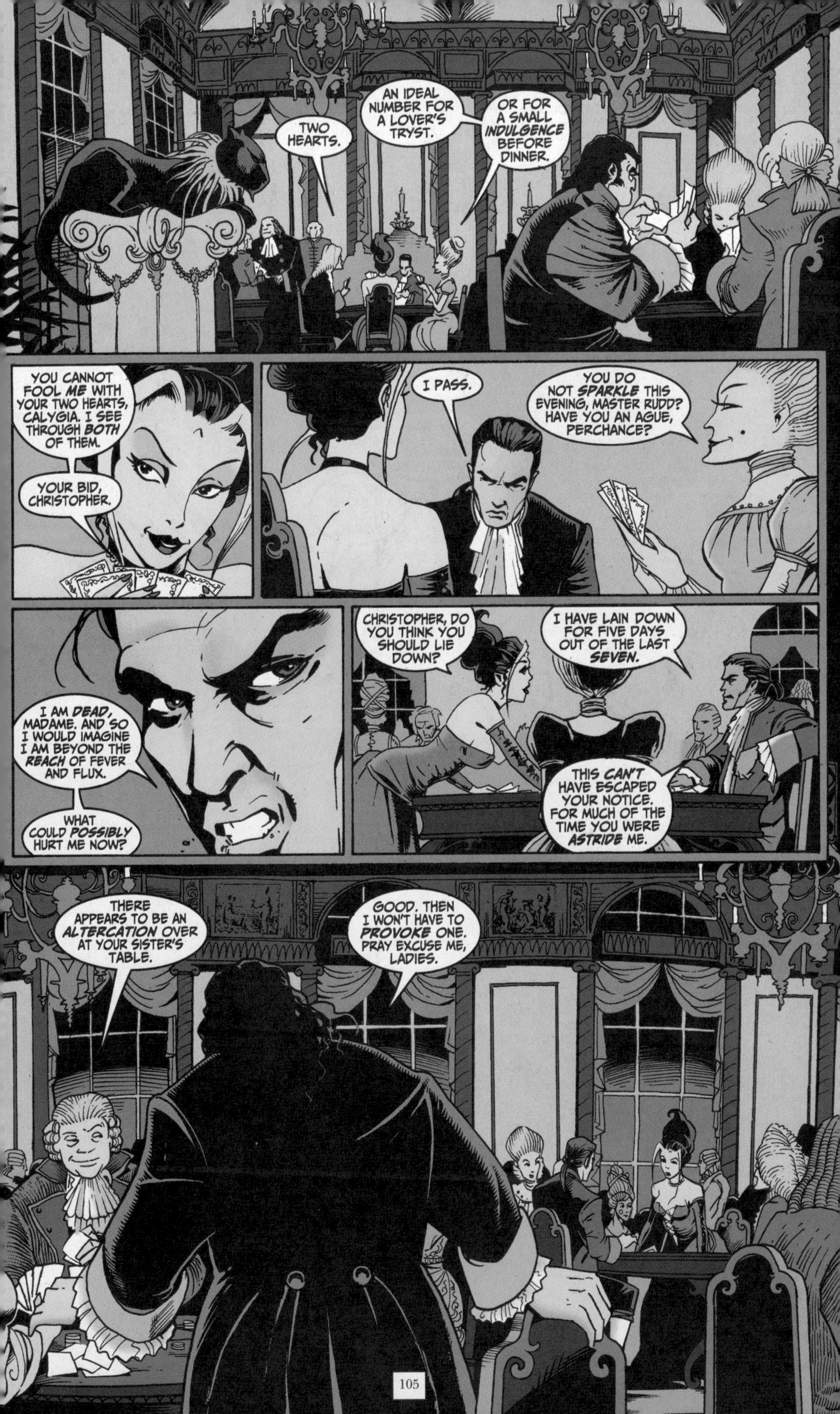
TWO HEARTS.
AN IDEAL NUMBER FOR A LOVER'S TRYST.
OR FOR A SMALL INDULGENCE BEFORE DINNER.
YOU CANNOT FOOL ME WITH YOUR TWO HEARTS, CALYGIA. I SEE THROUGH BOTH OF THEM.
YOUR BID, CHRISTOPHER.
I PASS.
YOU DO NOT SPARKLE THIS EVENING, MASTER RUDD? HAVE YOU AN AGUE, PERCHANCE?
I AM DEAD, MADAME. AND SO I WOULD IMAGINE I AM BEYOND THE REACH OF FEVER AND FLUX.
WHAT COULD POSSIBLY HURT ME NOW?
CHRISTOPHER, DO YOU THINK YOU SHOULD LIE DOWN?
I HAVE LAIN DOWN FOR FIVE DAYS OUT OF THE LAST SEVEN.
THIS CAN'T HAVE ESCAPED YOUR NOTICE. FOR MUCH OF THE TIME YOU WERE ASTRIDE ME.
THERE APPEARS TO BE AN ALTERCATION OVER AT YOUR SISTER'S TABLE.
GOOD. THEN I WON'T HAVE TO PROVOKE ONE. PRAY EXCUSE ME, LADIES.

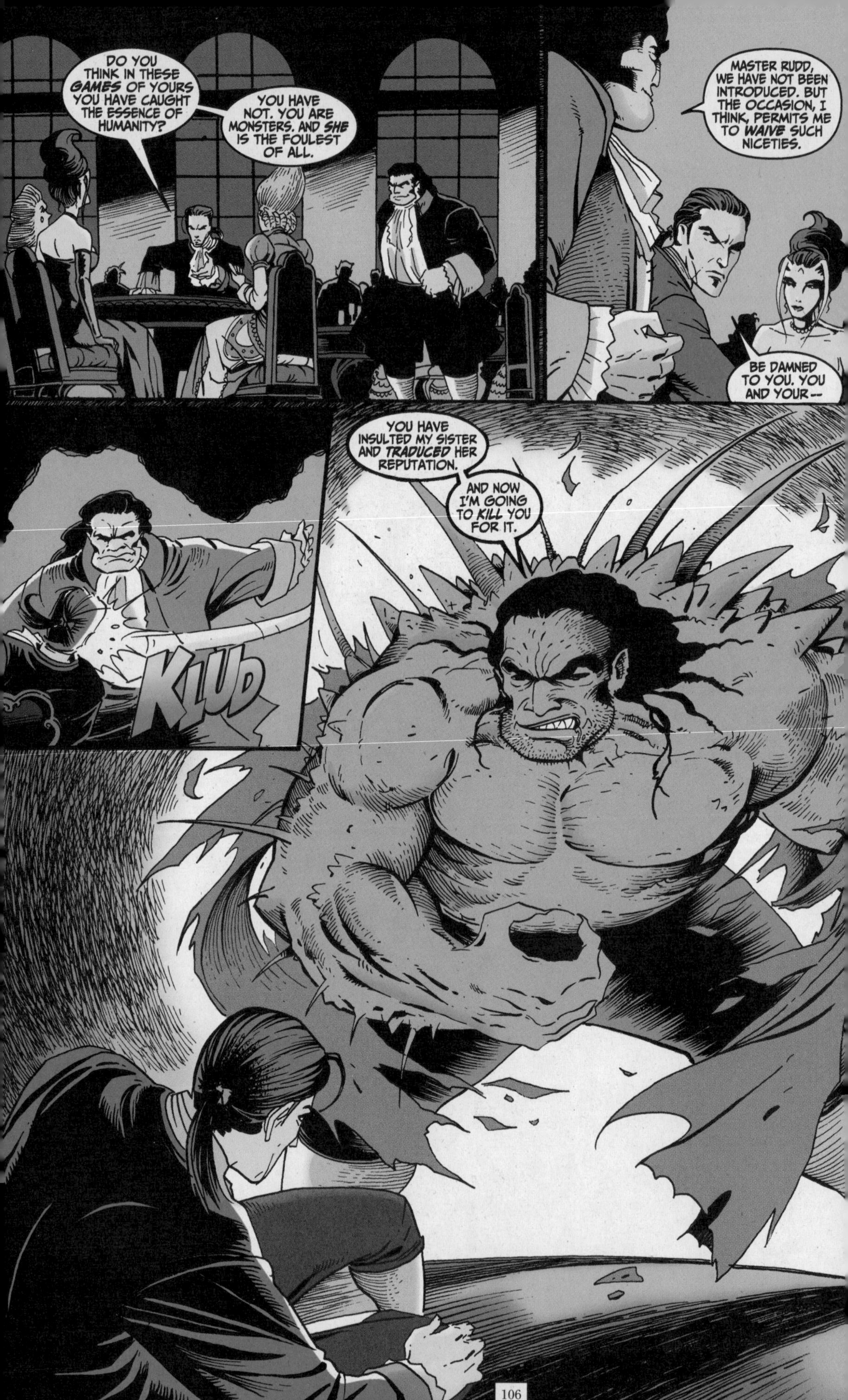
DO YOU THINK IN THESE GAMES OF YOURS YOU HAVE CAUGHT THE ESSENCE OF HUMANITY?
YOU HAVE NOT. YOU ARE MONSTERS. AND SHE IS THE FOULEST OF ALL.
MASTER RUDD, WE HAVE NOT BEEN INTRODUCED. BUT THE OCCASION, I THINK, PERMITS ME TO WAIVE SUCH NICETIES.
BE DAMNED TO YOU. YOU AND YOUR --
KLUD
YOU HAVE INSULTED MY SISTER AND TRADUCED HER REPUTATION.
AND NOW I'M GOING TO KILL YOU FOR IT.

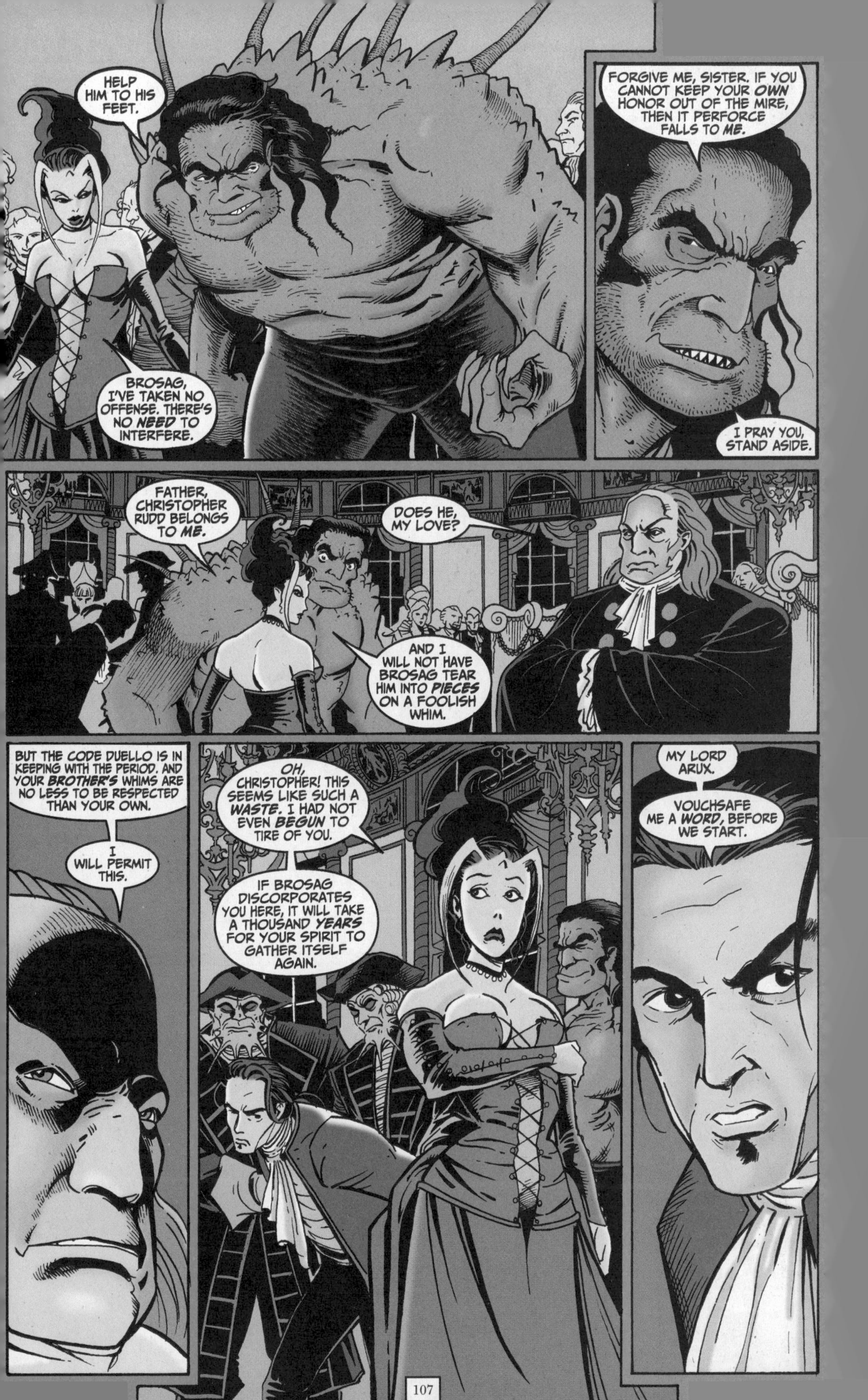
HELP HIM TO HIS FEET.
BROSAG, I'VE TAKEN NO OFFENSE. THERE'S NO NEED TO INTERFERE.
FORGIVE ME, SISTER. IF YOU CANNOT KEEP YOUR OWN HONOR OUT OF THE MIRE, THEN IT PERFORCE FALLS TO ME.
I PRAY YOU, STAND ASIDE.
FATHER, CHRISTOPHER RUDD BELONGS TO ME.
DOES HE, MY LOVE?
AND I WILL NOT HAVE BROSAG TEAR HIM INTO PIECES ON A FOOLISH WHIM.
BUT THE CODE DUELLO IS IN KEEPING WITH THE PERIOD. AND YOUR BROTHER'S WHIMS ARE NO LESS TO BE RESPECTED THAN YOUR OWN.
I WILL PERMIT THIS.
OH, CHRISTOPHER! THIS SEEMS LIKE SUCH A WASTE. I HAD NOT EVEN BEGUN TO TIRE OF YOU.
IF BROSAG DISCORPORATES YOU HERE, IT WILL TAKE A THOUSAND YEARS FOR YOUR SPIRIT TO GATHER ITSELF AGAIN.
MY LORD ARUX.
VOUCHSAFE ME A WORD, BEFORE WE START.

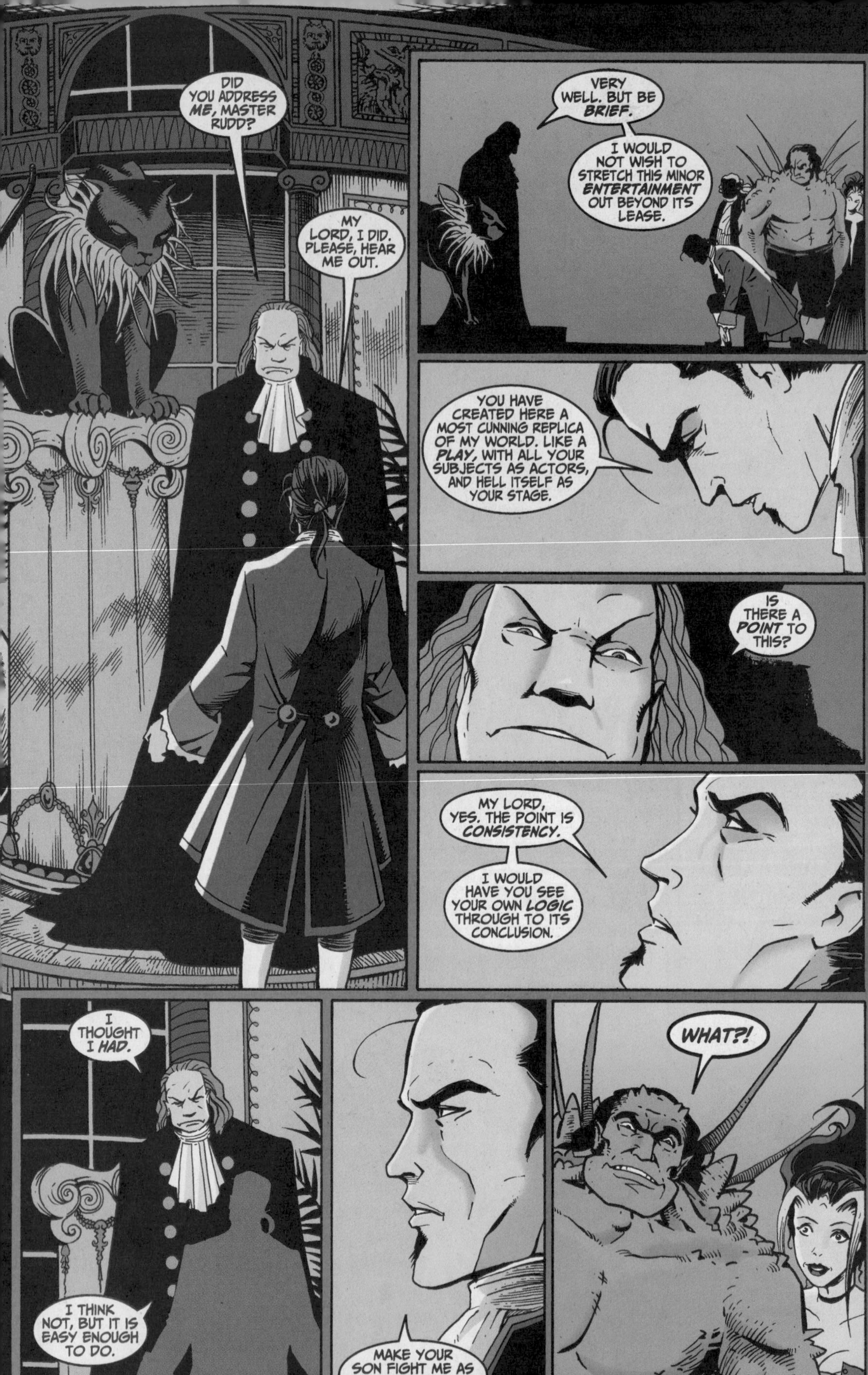
DID YOU ADDRESS *ME*, MASTER RUDD?
MY LORD, I DID. PLEASE, HEAR ME OUT.
VERY WELL. BUT BE *BRIEF*.
I WOULD NOT WISH TO STRETCH THIS MINOR *ENTERTAINMENT* OUT BEYOND ITS LEASE.
YOU HAVE CREATED HERE A MOST CUNNING REPLICA OF MY WORLD. LIKE A *PLAY*, WITH ALL YOUR SUBJECTS AS ACTORS, AND HELL ITSELF AS YOUR STAGE.
IS THERE A *POINT* TO THIS?
MY LORD, YES. THE POINT IS *CONSISTENCY*.
I WOULD HAVE YOU SEE YOUR OWN *LOGIC* THROUGH TO ITS CONCLUSION.
I THOUGHT I *HAD*.
I THINK NOT, BUT IT IS EASY ENOUGH TO DO.
MAKE YOUR SON FIGHT ME AS A *MAN*, RATHER THAN A *DEMON*.
WHAT?!

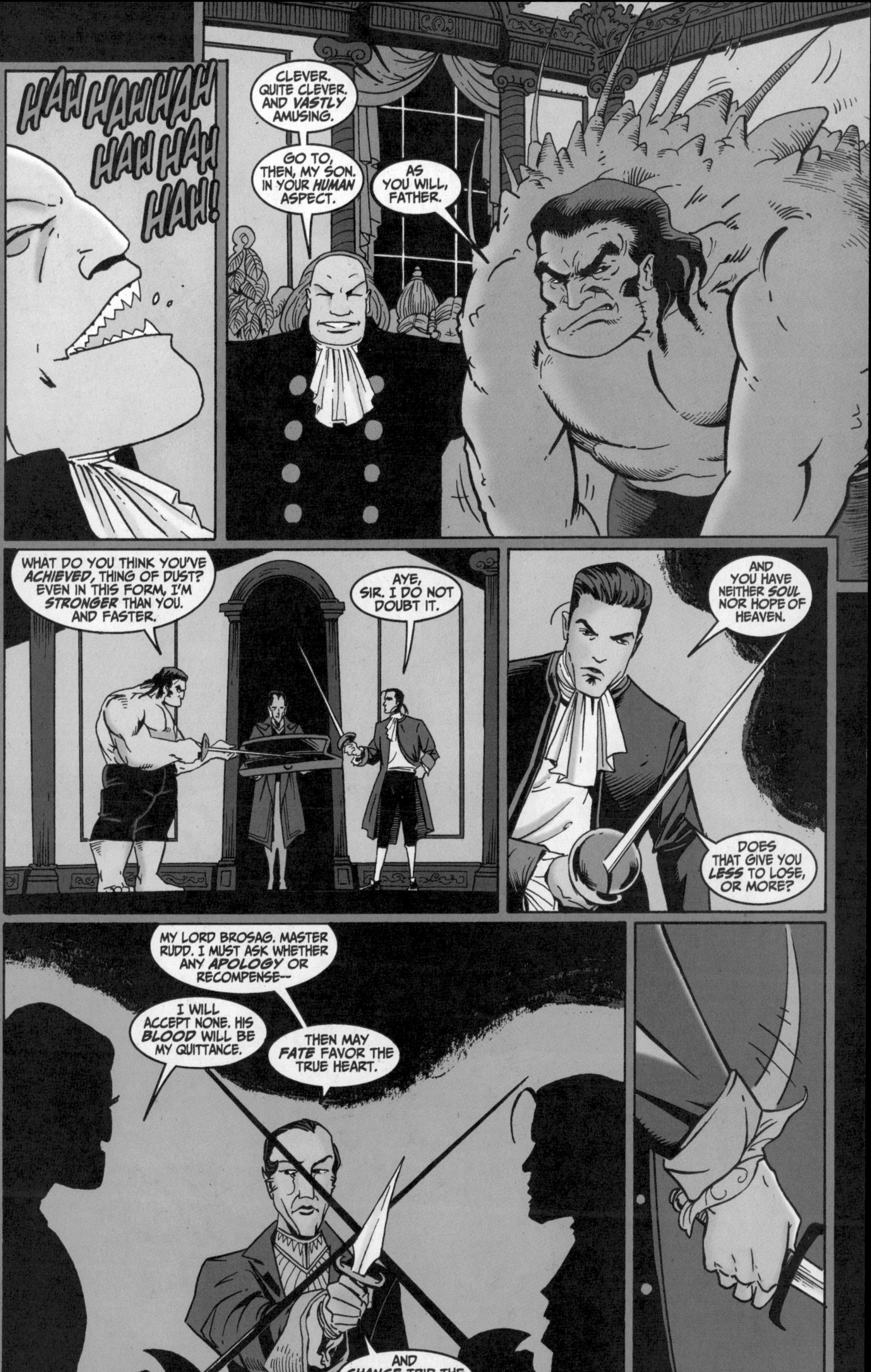

HAH HAH HAH HAH HAH HAH!
CLEVER. QUITE CLEVER. AND VASTLY AMUSING.
GO TO, THEN, MY SON. IN YOUR HUMAN ASPECT.
AS YOU WILL, FATHER.
WHAT DO YOU THINK YOU'VE ACHIEVED, THING OF DUST? EVEN IN THIS FORM, I'M STRONGER THAN YOU. AND FASTER.
AYE, SIR. I DO NOT DOUBT IT.
AND YOU HAVE NEITHER SOUL NOR HOPE OF HEAVEN.
DOES THAT GIVE YOU LESS TO LOSE, OR MORE?
MY LORD BROSAG. MASTER RUDD. I MUST ASK WHETHER ANY APOLOGY OR RECOMPENSE--
I WILL ACCEPT NONE. HIS BLOOD WILL BE MY QUITTANCE.
THEN MAY FATE FAVOR THE TRUE HEART.
AND CHANCE TRIP THE BLACKGUARD.

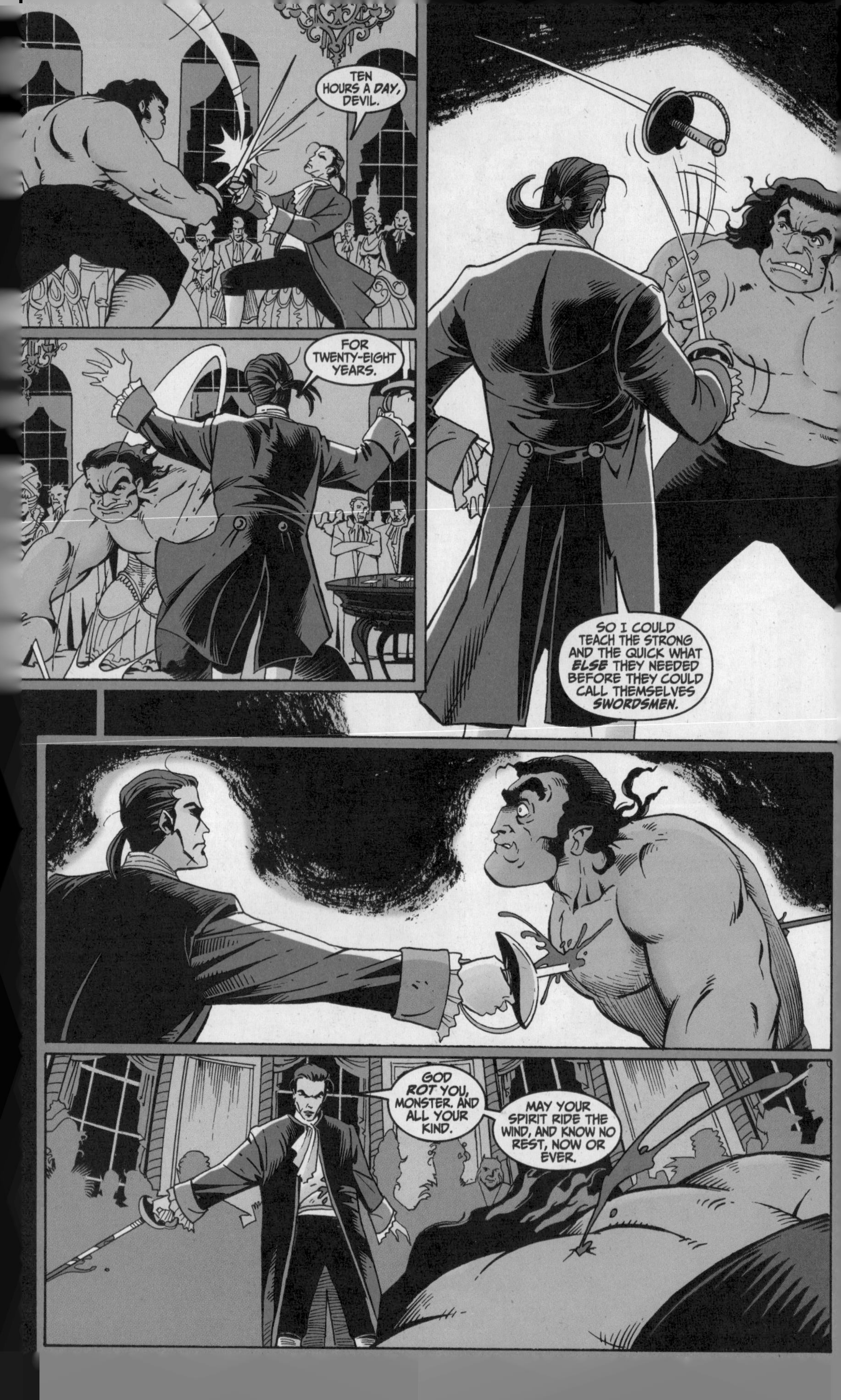
TEN HOURS A DAY, DEVIL.
FOR TWENTY-EIGHT YEARS.
SO I COULD TEACH THE STRONG AND THE QUICK WHAT ELSE THEY NEEDED BEFORE THEY COULD CALL THEMSELVES SWORDSMEN.
GOD ROT YOU, MONSTER. AND ALL YOUR KIND.
MAY YOUR SPIRIT RIDE THE WIND, AND KNOW NO REST, NOW OR EVER.

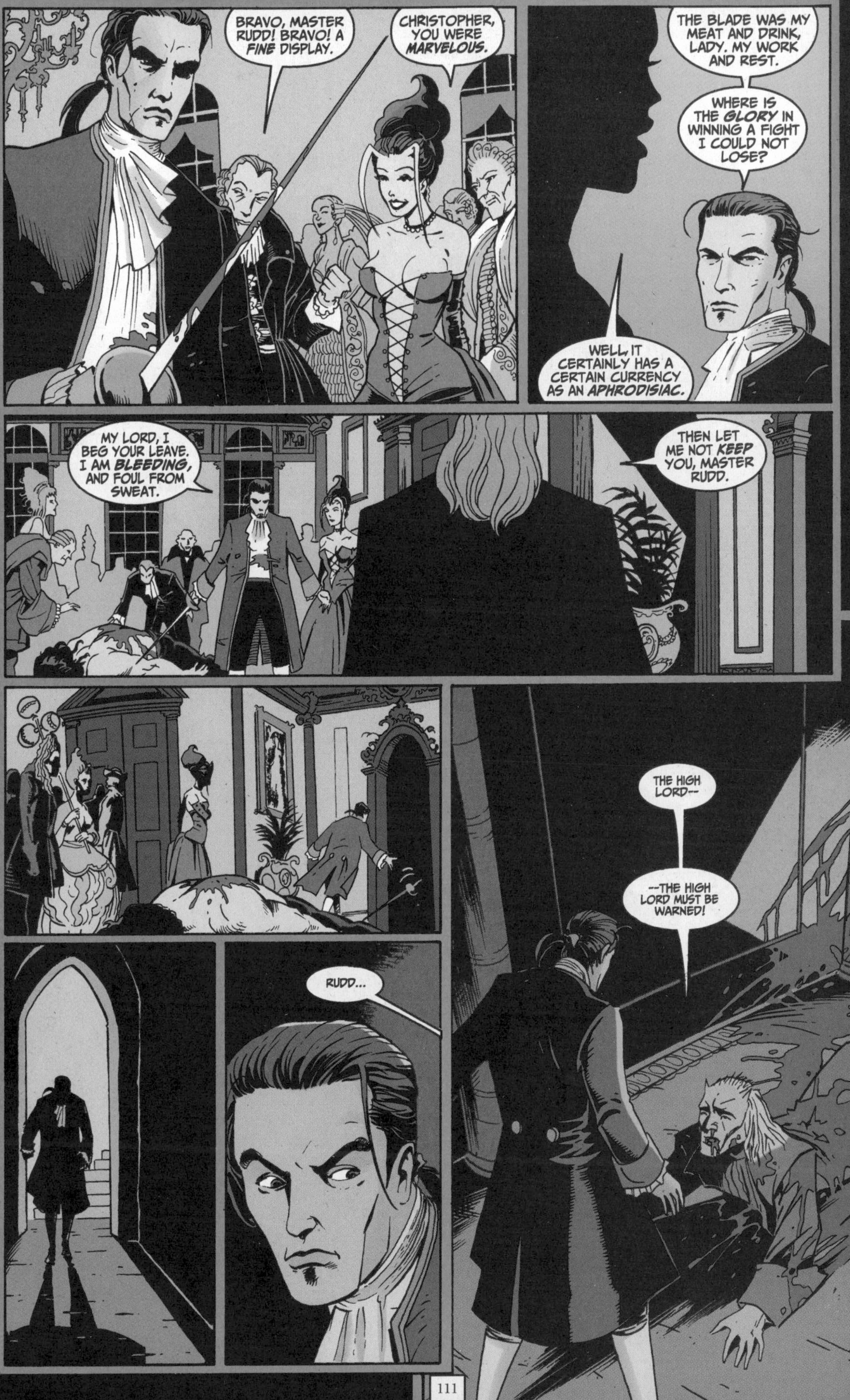
BRAVO, MASTER RUDD! BRAVO! A FINE DISPLAY.
CHRISTOPHER, YOU WERE MARVELOUS.
THE BLADE WAS MY MEAT AND DRINK, LADY. MY WORK AND REST.
WHERE IS THE GLORY IN WINNING A FIGHT I COULD NOT LOSE?
WELL, IT CERTAINLY HAS A CERTAIN CURRENCY AS AN APHRODISIAC.
MY LORD, I BEG YOUR LEAVE. I AM BLEEDING, AND FOUL FROM SWEAT.
THEN LET ME NOT KEEP YOU, MASTER RUDD.
RUDD...
THE HIGH LORD--
--THE HIGH LORD MUST BE WARNED!

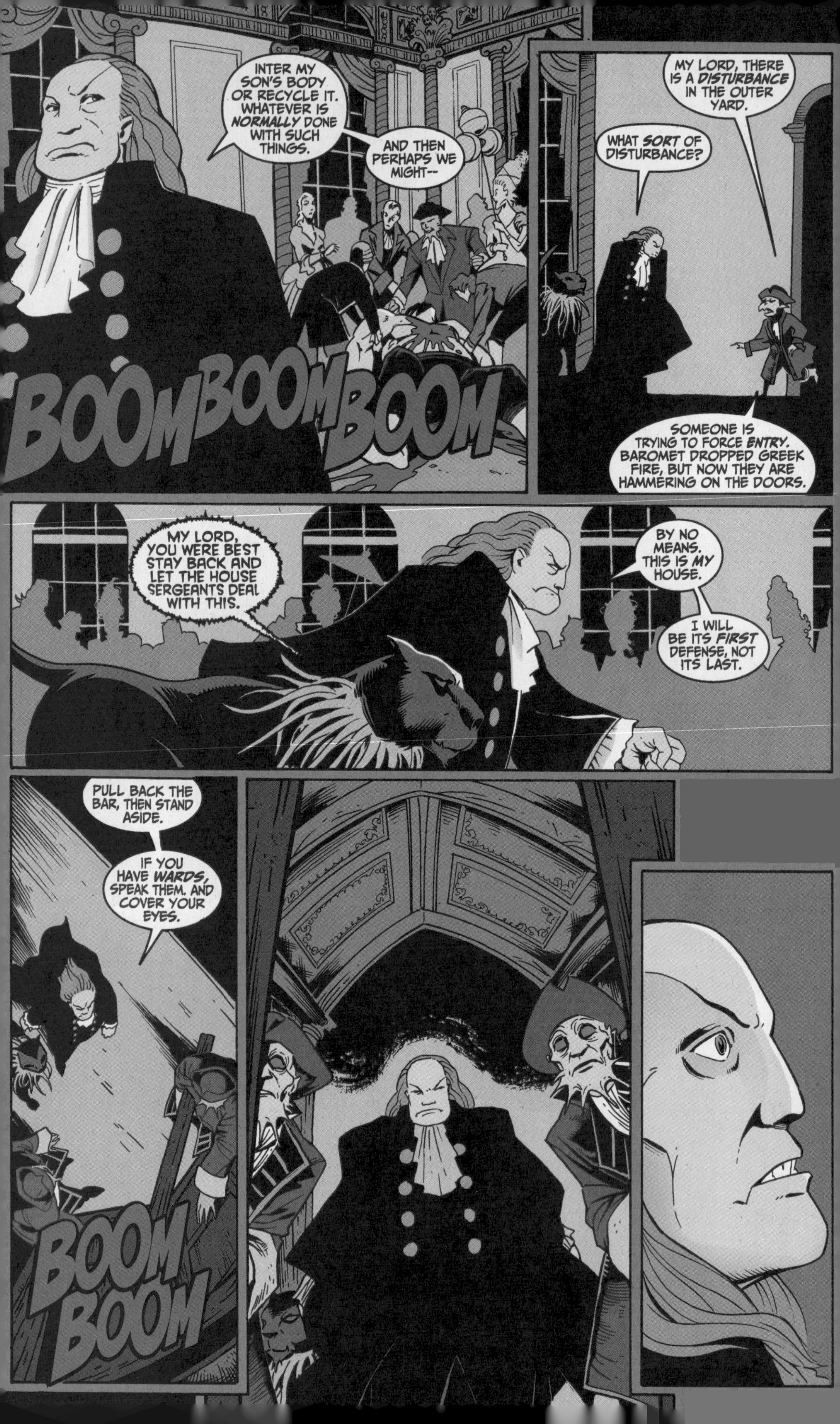
INTER MY SON'S BODY OR RECYCLE IT. WHATEVER IS NORMALLY DONE WITH SUCH THINGS.
AND THEN PERHAPS WE MIGHT--
BOOMBOOMBOOM
MY LORD, THERE IS A DISTURBANCE IN THE OUTER YARD.
WHAT SORT OF DISTURBANCE?
SOMEONE IS TRYING TO FORCE ENTRY. BAROMET DROPPED GREEK FIRE, BUT NOW THEY ARE HAMMERING ON THE DOORS.
MY LORD, YOU WERE BEST STAY BACK AND LET THE HOUSE SERGEANTS DEAL WITH THIS.
BY NO MEANS. THIS IS MY HOUSE.
I WILL BE ITS FIRST DEFENSE, NOT ITS LAST.
PULL BACK THE BAR, THEN STAND ASIDE.
IF YOU HAVE WARDS, SPEAK THEM. AND COVER YOUR EYES.
BOOM BOOM

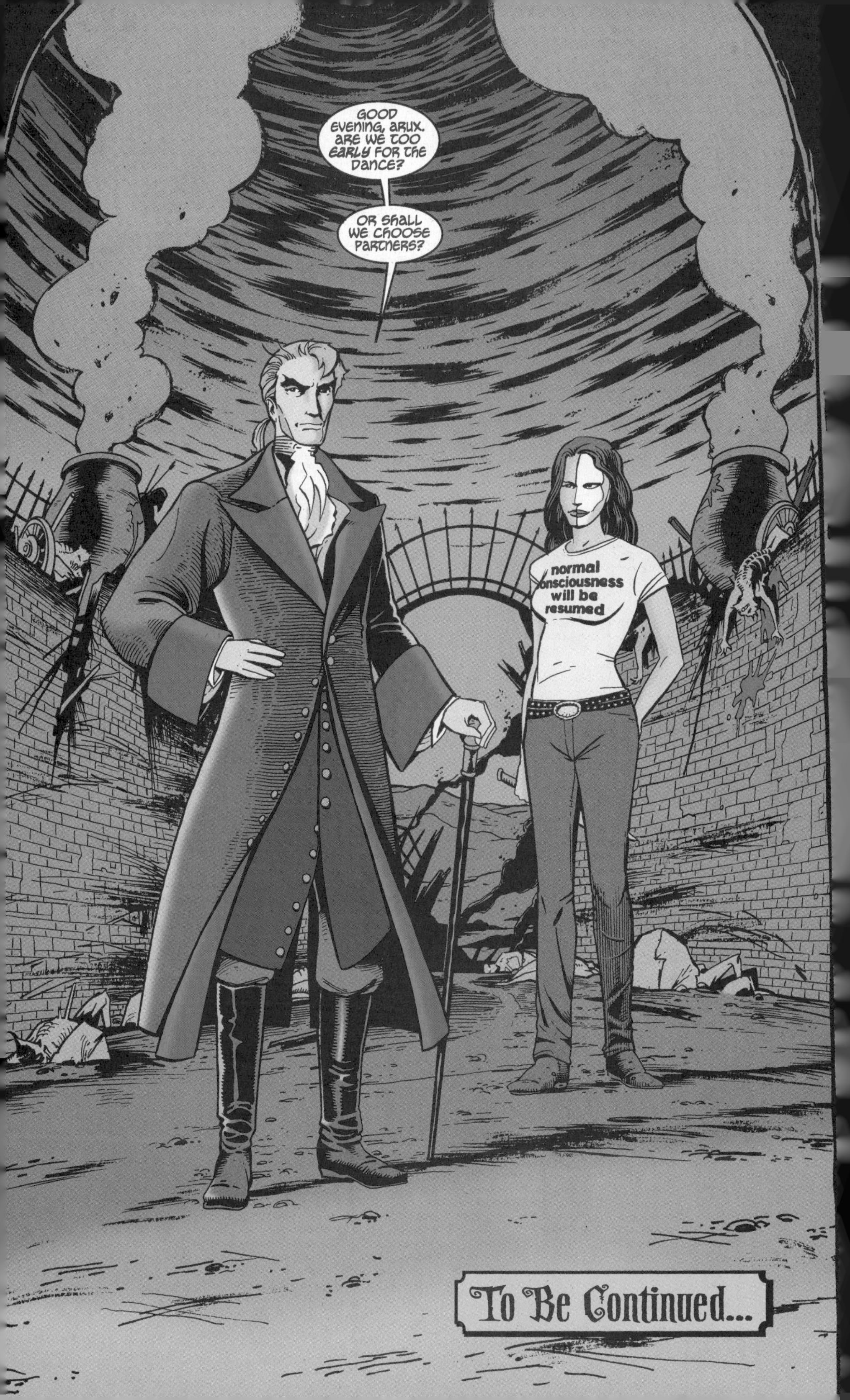
GOOD EVENING, ARUX. ARE WE TOO EARLY FOR THE DANCE?
OR SHALL WE CHOOSE PARTNERS?
normal onsciousness will be resumed
To Be Continued...

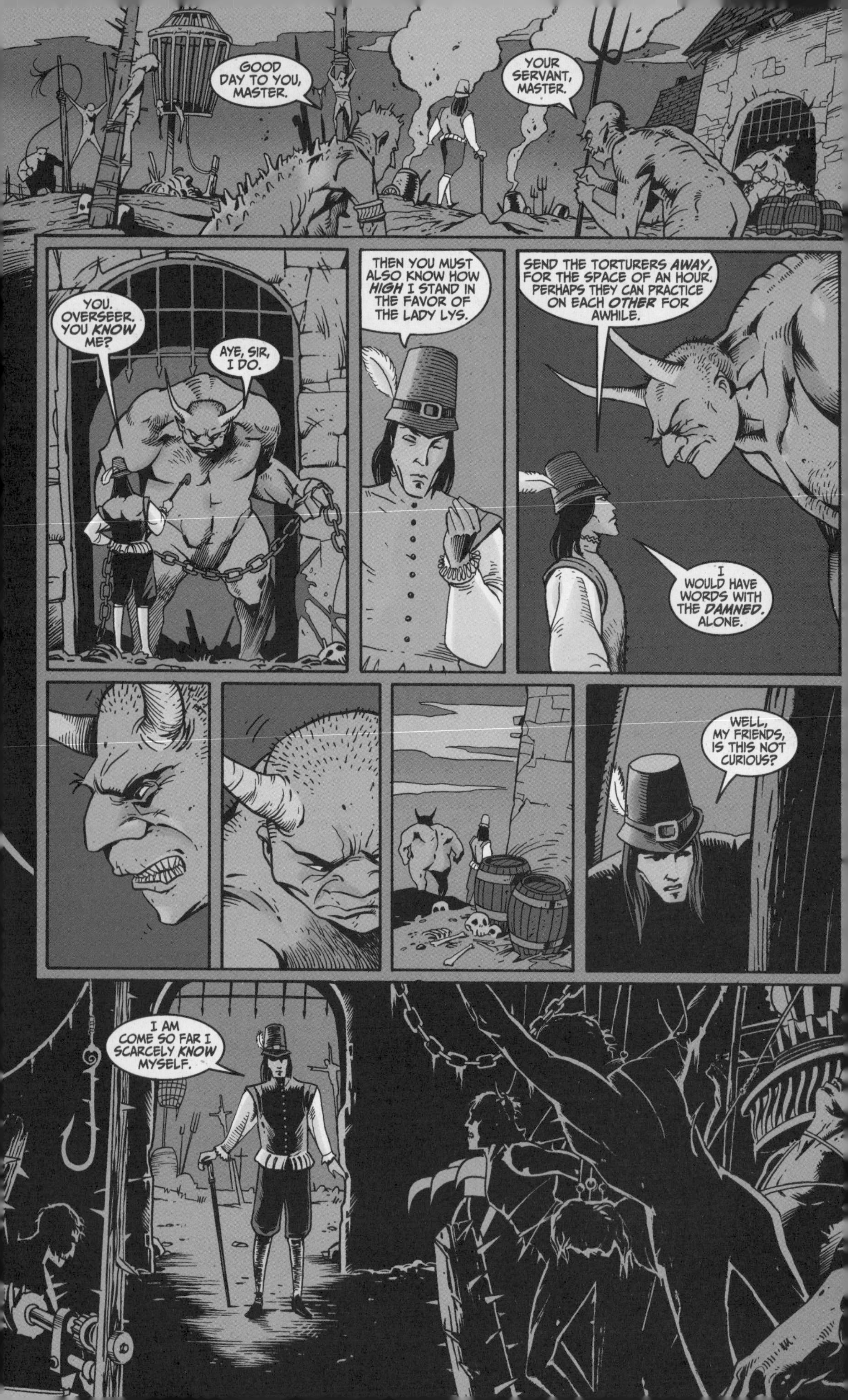
GOOD DAY TO YOU, MASTER.
YOUR SERVANT, MASTER.
YOU. OVERSEER. YOU KNOW ME?
AYE, SIR, I DO.
THEN YOU MUST ALSO KNOW HOW HIGH I STAND IN THE FAVOR OF THE LADY LYS.
SEND THE TORTURERS AWAY, FOR THE SPACE OF AN HOUR. PERHAPS THEY CAN PRACTICE ON EACH OTHER FOR AWHILE.
I WOULD HAVE WORDS WITH THE DAMNED. ALONE.
WELL, MY FRIENDS, IS THIS NOT CURIOUS?
I AM COME SO FAR I SCARCELY KNOW MYSELF.

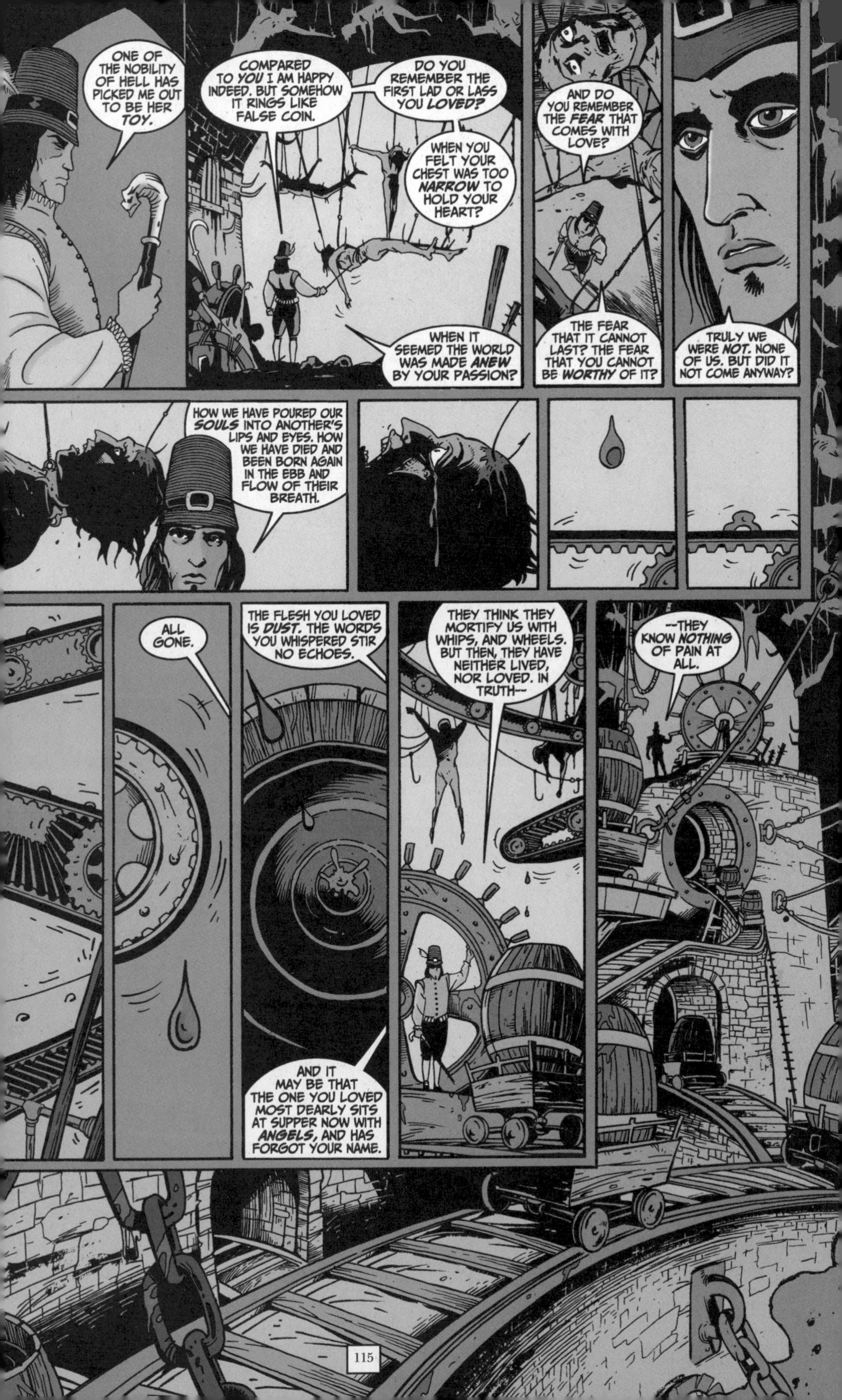
ONE OF THE NOBILITY OF HELL HAS PICKED ME OUT TO BE HER TOY.
COMPARED TO YOU I AM HAPPY INDEED. BUT SOMEHOW IT RINGS LIKE FALSE COIN.
DO YOU REMEMBER THE FIRST LAD OR LASS YOU LOVED?
WHEN YOU FELT YOUR CHEST WAS TOO NARROW TO HOLD YOUR HEART?
WHEN IT SEEMED THE WORLD WAS MADE ANEW BY YOUR PASSION?
AND DO YOU REMEMBER THE FEAR THAT COMES WITH LOVE?
THE FEAR THAT IT CANNOT LAST? THE FEAR THAT YOU CANNOT BE WORTHY OF IT?
TRULY WE WERE NOT. NONE OF US. BUT DID IT NOT COME ANYWAY?
HOW WE HAVE POURED OUR SOULS INTO ANOTHER'S LIPS AND EYES. HOW WE HAVE DIED AND BEEN BORN AGAIN IN THE EBB AND FLOW OF THEIR BREATH.
ALL GONE.
THE FLESH YOU LOVED IS DUST. THE WORDS YOU WHISPERED STIR NO ECHOES.
AND IT MAY BE THAT THE ONE YOU LOVED MOST DEARLY SITS AT SUPPER NOW WITH ANGELS, AND HAS FORGOT YOUR NAME.
THEY THINK THEY MORTIFY US WITH WHIPS, AND WHEELS. BUT THEN, THEY HAVE NEITHER LIVED, NOR LOVED. IN TRUTH--
--THEY KNOW NOTHING OF PAIN AT ALL.

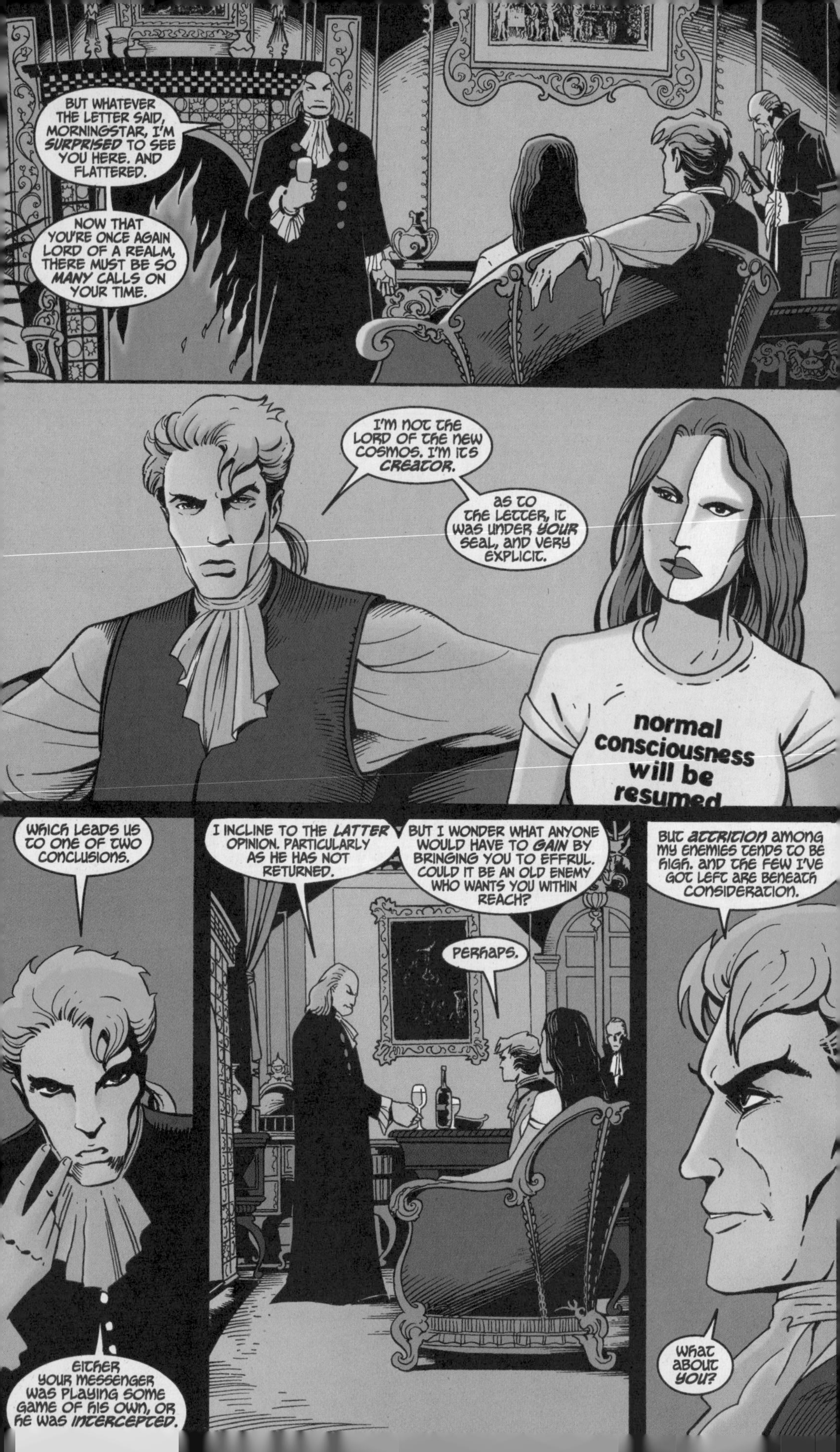
BUT WHATEVER THE LETTER SAID, MORNINGSTAR, I'M SURPRISED TO SEE YOU HERE. AND FLATTERED.
NOW THAT YOU'RE ONCE AGAIN LORD OF A REALM, THERE MUST BE SO MANY CALLS ON YOUR TIME.
I'M NOT THE LORD OF THE NEW COSMOS. I'M ITS CREATOR.
AS TO THE LETTER, IT WAS UNDER YOUR SEAL, AND VERY EXPLICIT.
normal consciousness will be resumed
WHICH LEADS US TO ONE OF TWO CONCLUSIONS.
EITHER YOUR MESSENGER WAS PLAYING SOME GAME OF HIS OWN, OR HE WAS INTERCEPTED.
I INCLINE TO THE LATTER OPINION. PARTICULARLY AS HE HAS NOT RETURNED.
BUT I WONDER WHAT ANYONE WOULD HAVE TO GAIN BY BRINGING YOU TO EFFRUL. COULD IT BE AN OLD ENEMY WHO WANTS YOU WITHIN REACH?
PERHAPS.
BUT ATTRITION AMONG MY ENEMIES TENDS TO BE HIGH. AND THE FEW I'VE GOT LEFT ARE BENEATH CONSIDERATION.
WHAT ABOUT YOU?

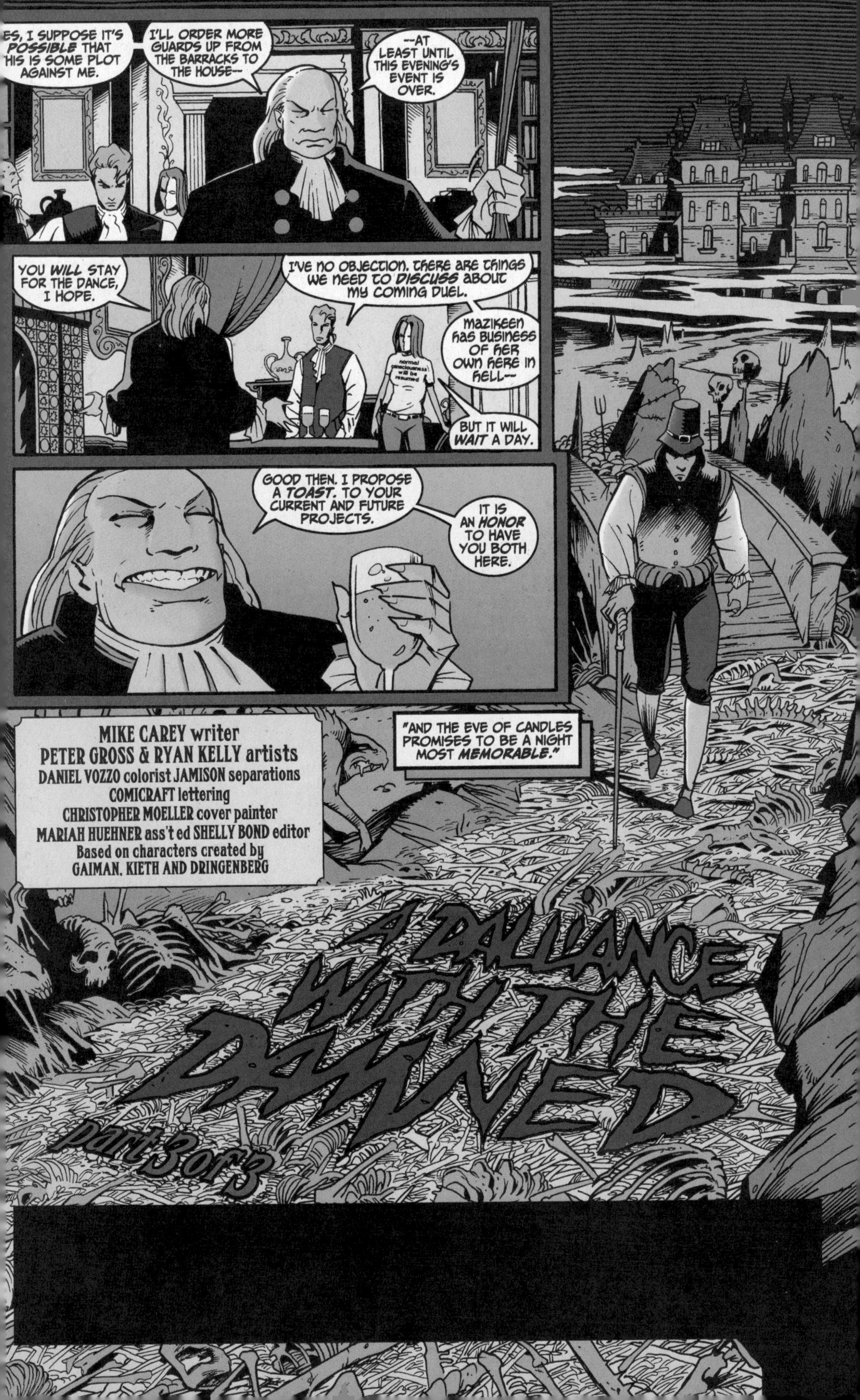
ES, I SUPPOSE IT'S POSSIBLE THAT HIS IS SOME PLOT AGAINST ME.
I'LL ORDER MORE GUARDS UP FROM THE BARRACKS TO THE HOUSE--
--AT LEAST UNTIL THIS EVENING'S EVENT IS OVER.
YOU WILL STAY FOR THE DANCE, I HOPE.
I'VE NO OBJECTION. THERE ARE THINGS WE NEED TO DISCUSS ABOUT MY COMING DUEL.
MAZIKEEN HAS BUSINESS OF HER OWN HERE IN HELL--
BUT IT WILL WAIT A DAY.
GOOD THEN. I PROPOSE A TOAST. TO YOUR CURRENT AND FUTURE PROJECTS.
IT IS AN HONOR TO HAVE YOU BOTH HERE.
MIKE CAREY writer
PETER GROSS & RYAN KELLY artists
DANIEL VOZZO colorist JAMISON separations
COMICRAFT lettering
CHRISTOPHER MOELLER cover painter
MARIAH HUEHNER ass't ed SHELLY BOND editor
Based on characters created by
GAIMAN, KIETH AND DRINGENBERG
"AND THE EVE OF CANDLES PROMISES TO BE A NIGHT MOST MEMORABLE."
A DALLIANCE WITH THE DAMNED
part 3 of 3
[redacted]

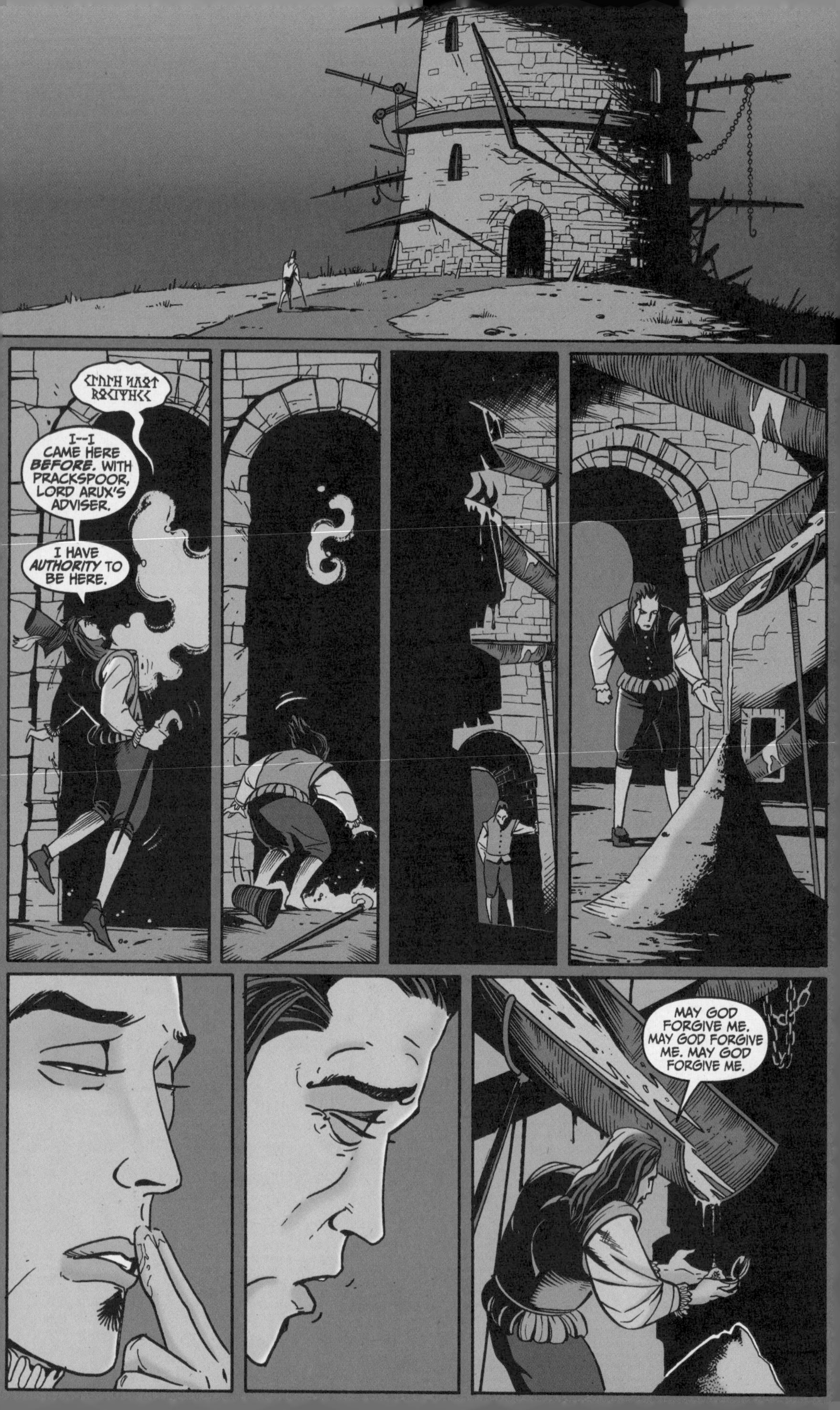

I--I CAME HERE BEFORE. WITH PRACKSPOOR, LORD ARUX'S ADVISER.
I HAVE AUTHORITY TO BE HERE.
MAY GOD FORGIVE ME. MAY GOD FORGIVE ME. MAY GOD FORGIVE ME.

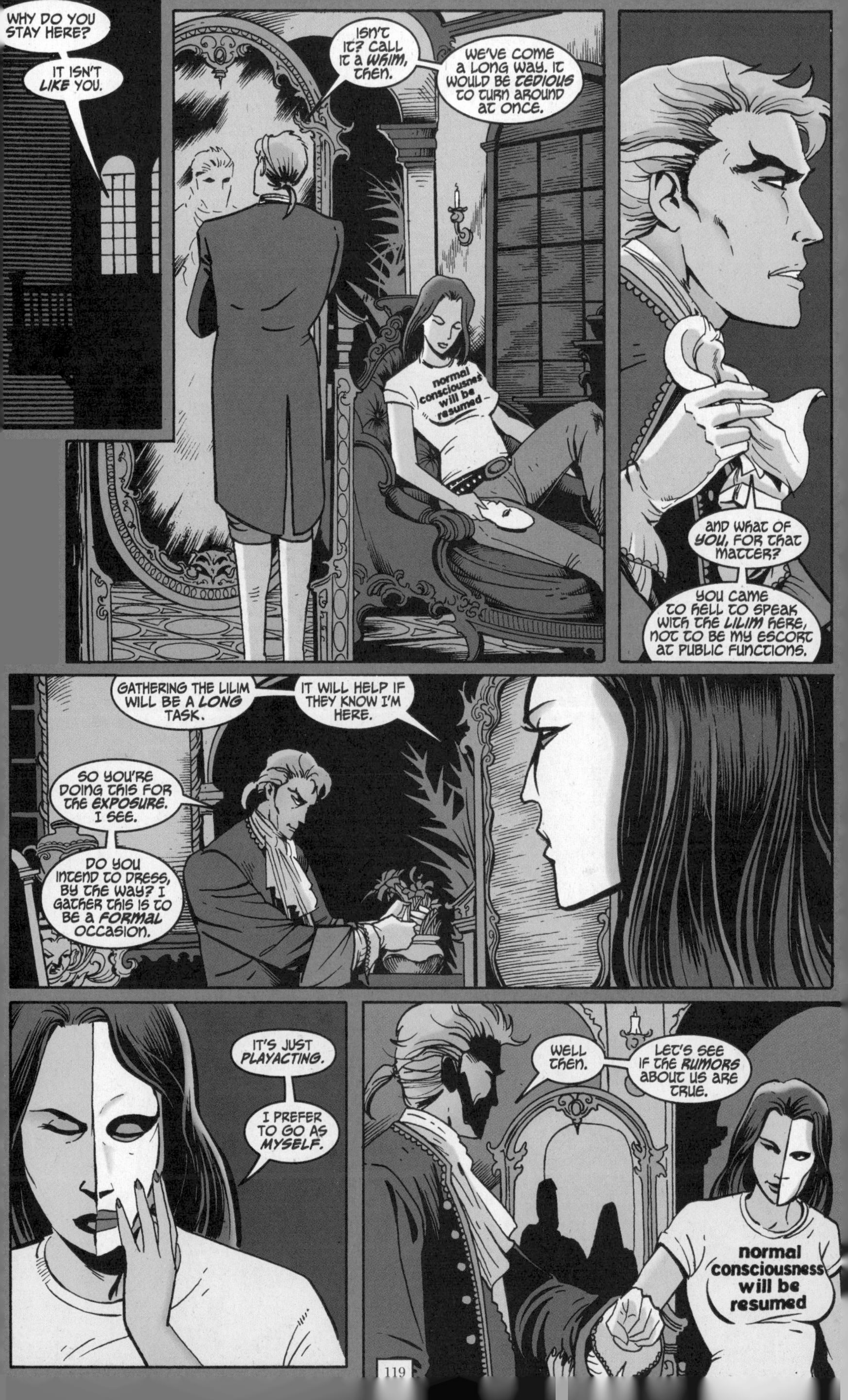

WHY DO YOU STAY HERE?
IT ISN'T LIKE YOU.
ISN'T IT? CALL IT A WHIM, THEN.
WE'VE COME A LONG WAY. IT WOULD BE TEDIOUS TO TURN AROUND AT ONCE.
normal consciousness will be resumed
AND WHAT OF YOU, FOR THAT MATTER?
YOU CAME TO HELL TO SPEAK WITH THE LILIM HERE, NOT TO BE MY ESCORT AT PUBLIC FUNCTIONS.
GATHERING THE LILIM WILL BE A LONG TASK.
IT WILL HELP IF THEY KNOW I'M HERE.
SO YOU'RE DOING THIS FOR THE EXPOSURE. I SEE.
DO YOU INTEND TO DRESS, BY THE WAY? I GATHER THIS IS TO BE A FORMAL OCCASION.
IT'S JUST PLAYACTING.
I PREFER TO GO AS MYSELF.
WELL THEN.
LET'S SEE IF THE RUMORS ABOUT US ARE TRUE.
normal consciousness will be resumed

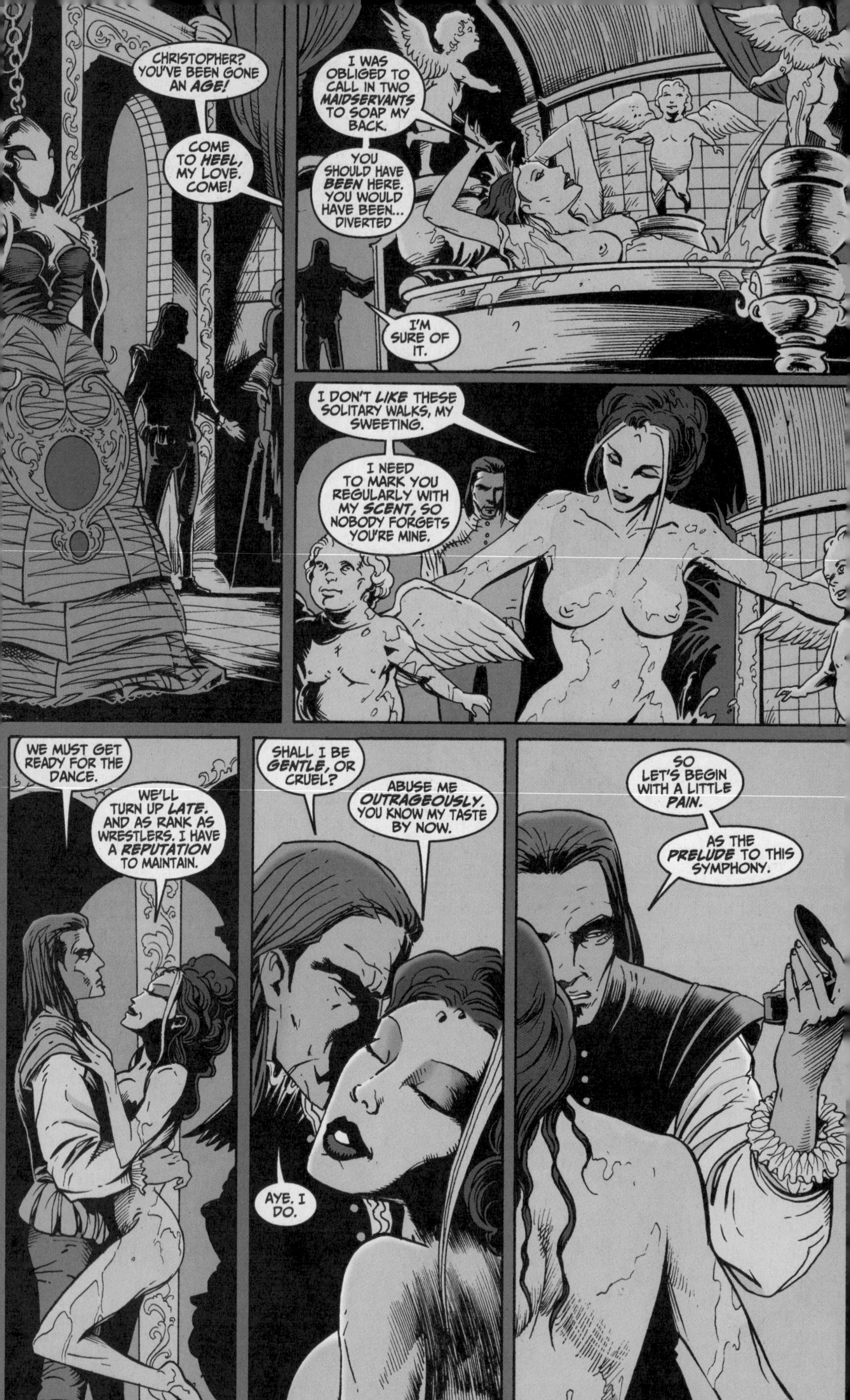
CHRISTOPHER? YOU'VE BEEN GONE AN AGE!
COME TO HEEL, MY LOVE. COME!
I WAS OBLIGED TO CALL IN TWO MAIDSERVANTS TO SOAP MY BACK.
YOU SHOULD HAVE BEEN HERE. YOU WOULD HAVE BEEN... DIVERTED
I'M SURE OF IT.
I DON'T LIKE THESE SOLITARY WALKS, MY SWEETING.
I NEED TO MARK YOU REGULARLY WITH MY SCENT, SO NOBODY FORGETS YOU'RE MINE.
WE MUST GET READY FOR THE DANCE.
WE'LL TURN UP LATE. AND AS RANK AS WRESTLERS. I HAVE A REPUTATION TO MAINTAIN.
SHALL I BE GENTLE, OR CRUEL?
ABUSE ME OUTRAGEOUSLY. YOU KNOW MY TASTE BY NOW.
AYE. I DO.
SO LET'S BEGIN WITH A LITTLE PAIN.
AS THE PRELUDE TO THIS SYMPHONY.

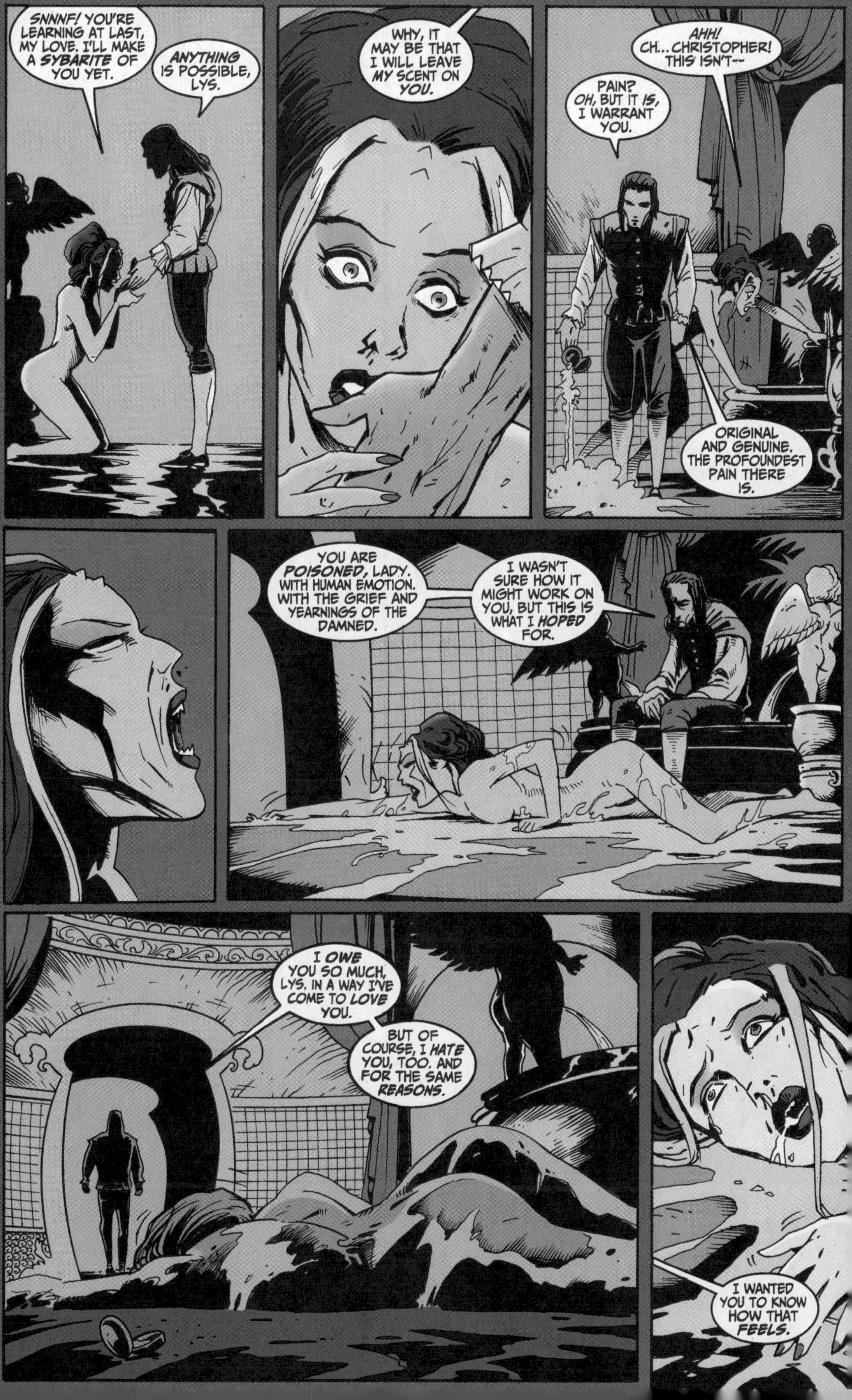

SNNNF! YOU'RE LEARNING AT LAST, MY LOVE. I'LL MAKE A SYBARITE OF YOU YET.
ANYTHING IS POSSIBLE, LYS.
WHY, IT MAY BE THAT I WILL LEAVE MY SCENT ON YOU.
AHH! CH... CHRISTOPHER! THIS ISN'T--
PAIN? OH, BUT IT IS, I WARRANT YOU.
ORIGINAL AND GENUINE. THE PROFOUNDEST PAIN THERE IS.
YOU ARE POISONED, LADY. WITH HUMAN EMOTION. WITH THE GRIEF AND YEARNINGS OF THE DAMNED.
I WASN'T SURE HOW IT MIGHT WORK ON YOU, BUT THIS IS WHAT I HOPED FOR.
I OWE YOU SO MUCH, LYS. IN A WAY I'VE COME TO LOVE YOU.
BUT OF COURSE, I HATE YOU, TOO. AND FOR THE SAME REASONS.
I WANTED YOU TO KNOW HOW THAT FEELS.

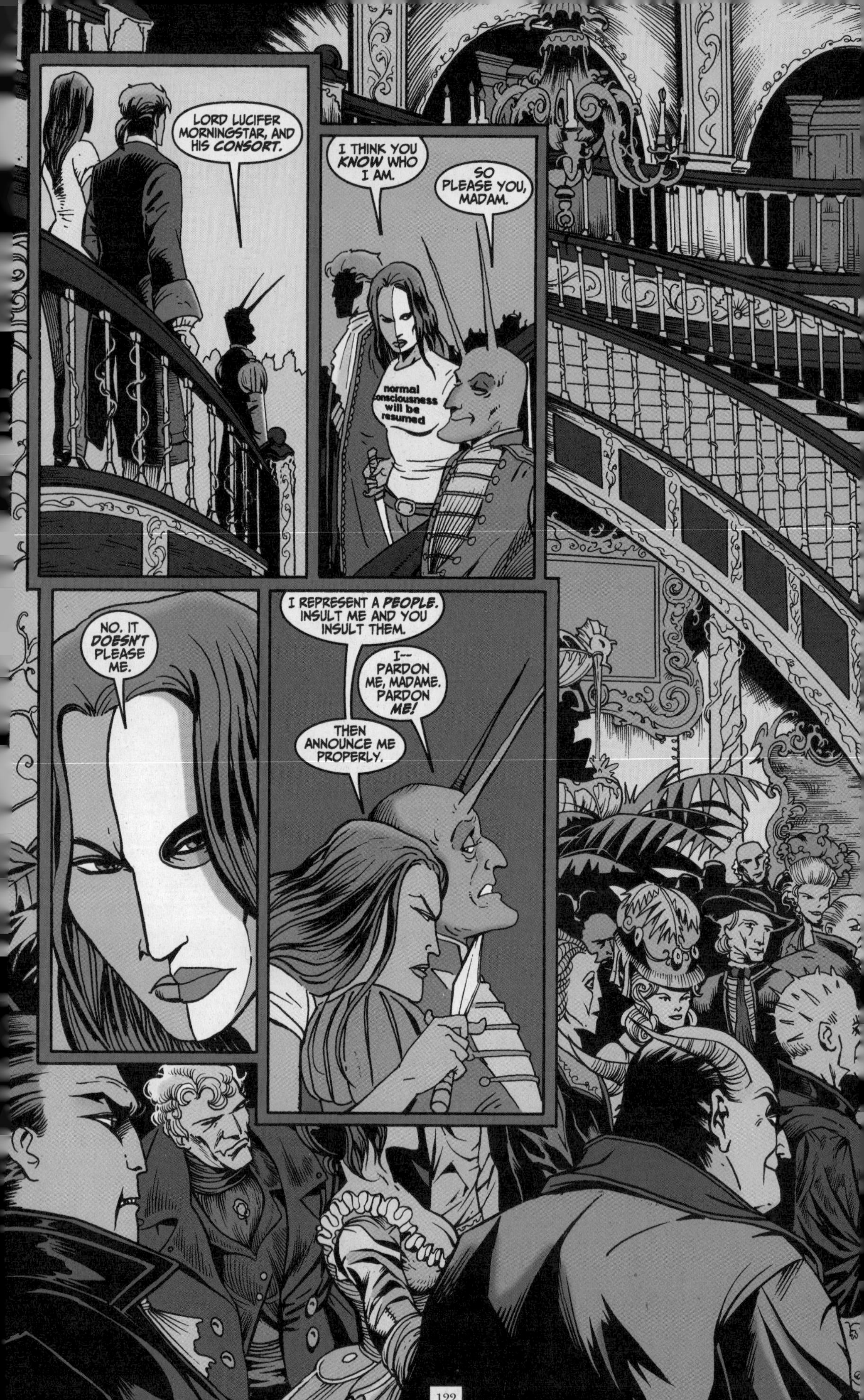
LORD LUCIFER MORNINGSTAR, AND HIS CONSORT.
I THINK YOU KNOW WHO I AM.
SO PLEASE YOU, MADAM.
normal consciousness will be resumed
NO. IT DOESN'T PLEASE ME.
I REPRESENT A PEOPLE. INSULT ME AND YOU INSULT THEM.
I-- PARDON ME, MADAME. PARDON ME!
THEN ANNOUNCE ME PROPERLY.

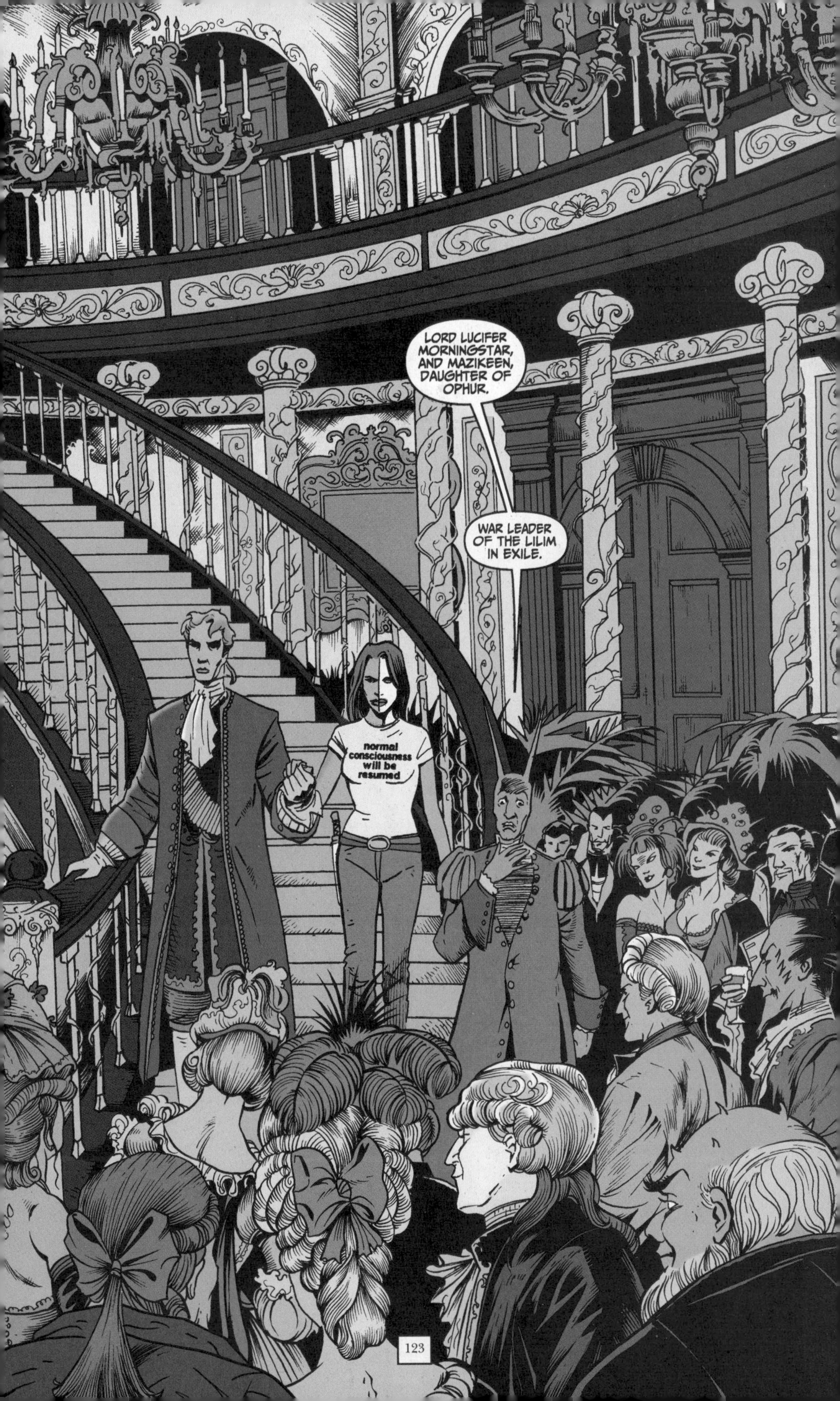
LORD LUCIFER MORNINGSTAR, AND MAZIKEEN, DAUGHTER OF OPHUR.
WAR LEADER OF THE LILIM IN EXILE.
normal consciousness will be resumed

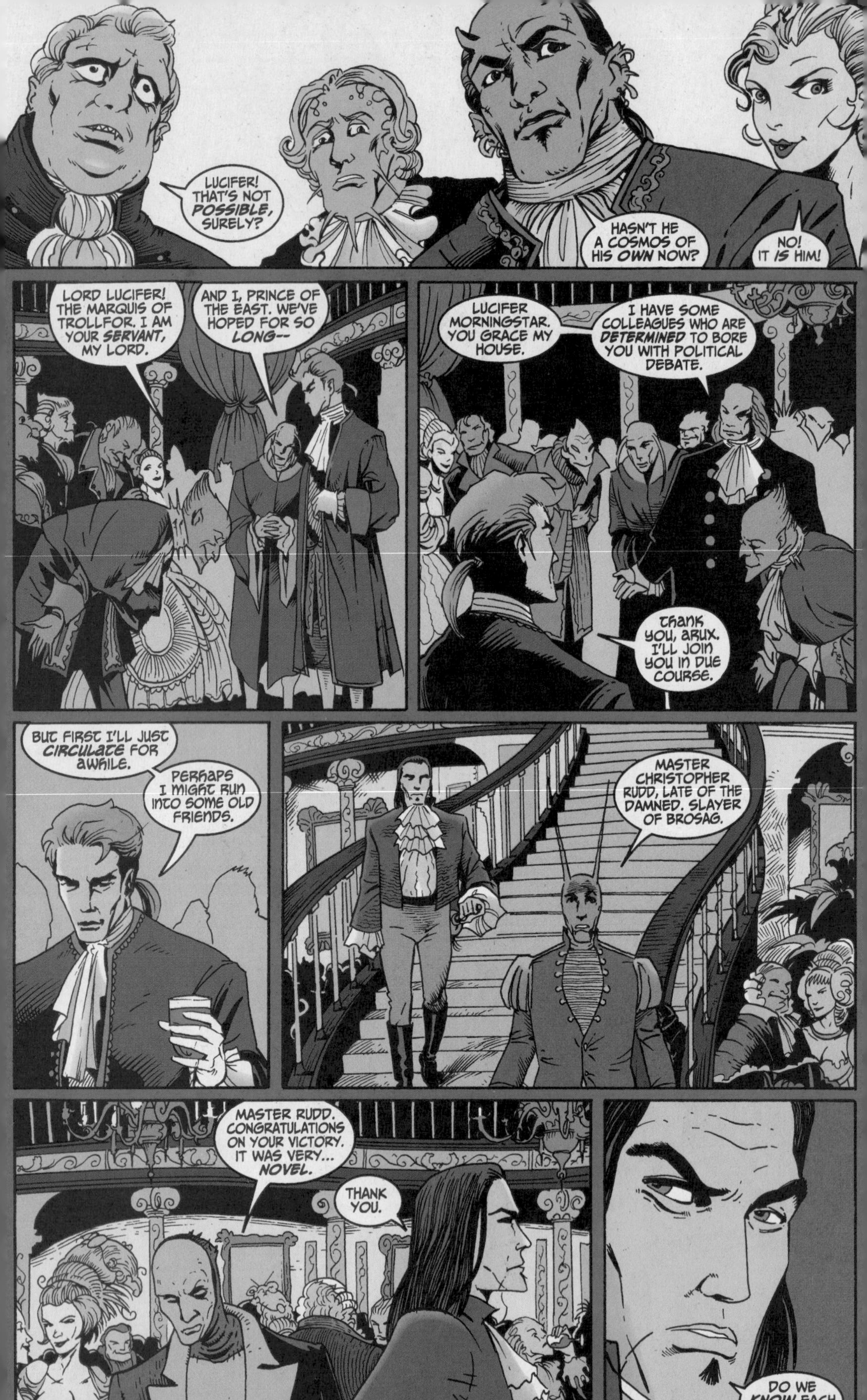
LUCIFER! THAT'S NOT POSSIBLE, SURELY?
HASN'T HE A COSMOS OF HIS OWN NOW?
NO! IT IS HIM!
LORD LUCIFER! THE MARQUIS OF TROLLFOR. I AM YOUR SERVANT, MY LORD.
AND I, PRINCE OF THE EAST. WE'VE HOPED FOR SO LONG--
LUCIFER MORNINGSTAR. YOU GRACE MY HOUSE.
I HAVE SOME COLLEAGUES WHO ARE DETERMINED TO BORE YOU WITH POLITICAL DEBATE.
THANK YOU, ARUX. I'LL JOIN YOU IN DUE COURSE.
BUT FIRST I'LL JUST CIRCULATE FOR AWHILE.
PERHAPS I MIGHT RUN INTO SOME OLD FRIENDS.
MASTER CHRISTOPHER RUDD, LATE OF THE DAMNED. SLAYER OF BROSAG.
MASTER RUDD. CONGRATULATIONS ON YOUR VICTORY. IT WAS VERY... NOVEL.
THANK YOU.
DO WE KNOW EACH OTHER?

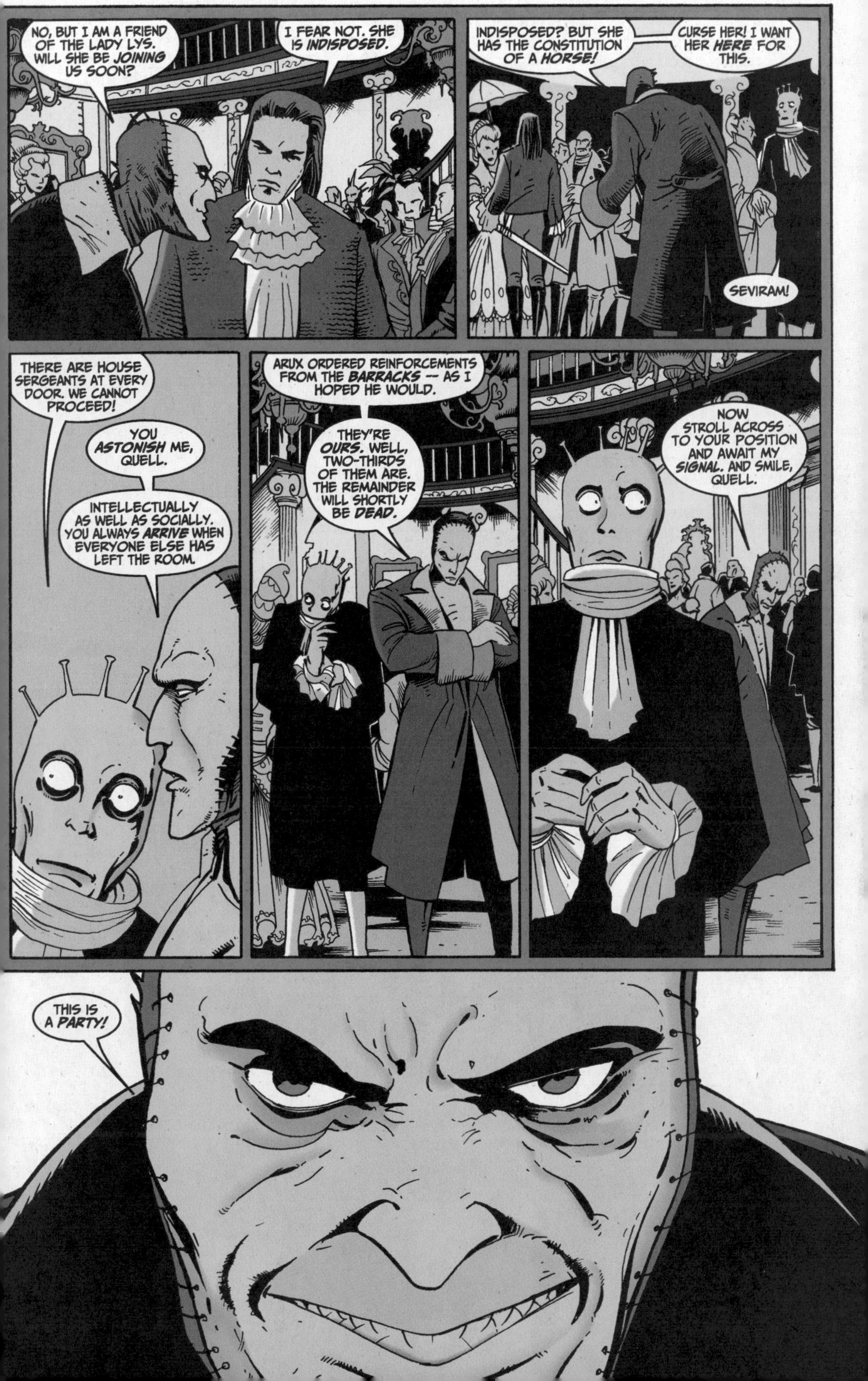
NO, BUT I AM A FRIEND OF THE LADY LYS. WILL SHE BE JOINING US SOON?
I FEAR NOT. SHE IS INDISPOSED.
INDISPOSED? BUT SHE HAS THE CONSTITUTION OF A HORSE!
CURSE HER! I WANT HER HERE FOR THIS.
SEVIRAM!
THERE ARE HOUSE SERGEANTS AT EVERY DOOR. WE CANNOT PROCEED!
YOU ASTONISH ME, QUELL.
INTELLECTUALLY AS WELL AS SOCIALLY. YOU ALWAYS ARRIVE WHEN EVERYONE ELSE HAS LEFT THE ROOM.
ARUX ORDERED REINFORCEMENTS FROM THE BARRACKS -- AS I HOPED HE WOULD.
THEY'RE OURS. WELL, TWO-THIRDS OF THEM ARE. THE REMAINDER WILL SHORTLY BE DEAD.
NOW STROLL ACROSS TO YOUR POSITION AND AWAIT MY SIGNAL. AND SMILE, QUELL.
THIS IS A PARTY!

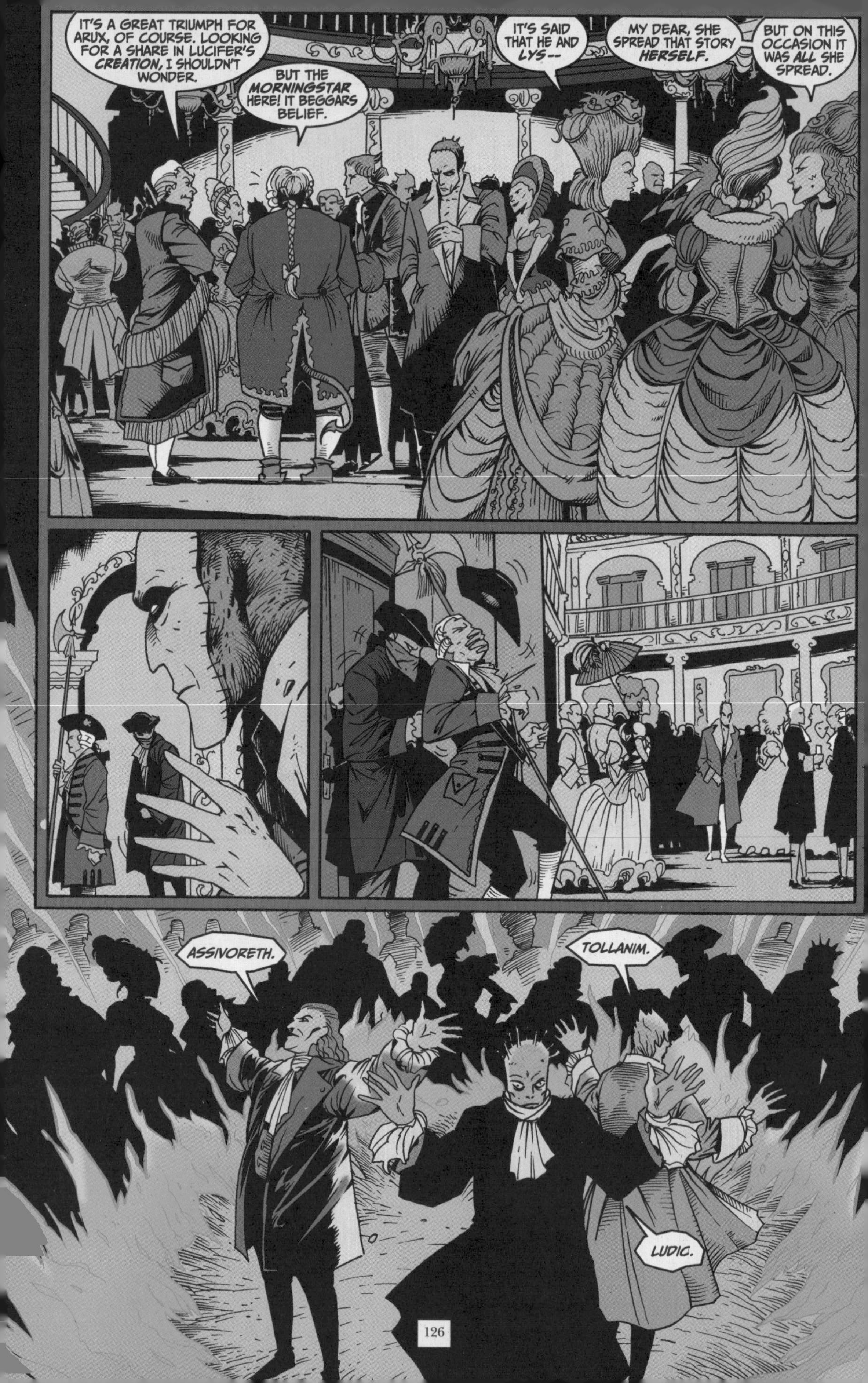
IT'S A GREAT TRIUMPH FOR ARUX, OF COURSE. LOOKING FOR A SHARE IN LUCIFER'S CREATION, I SHOULDN'T WONDER.
BUT THE MORNINGSTAR HERE! IT BEGGARS BELIEF.
IT'S SAID THAT HE AND LYS--
MY DEAR, SHE SPREAD THAT STORY HERSELF.
BUT ON THIS OCCASION IT WAS ALL SHE SPREAD.
ASSIVORETH.
TOLLANIM.
LUDIC.

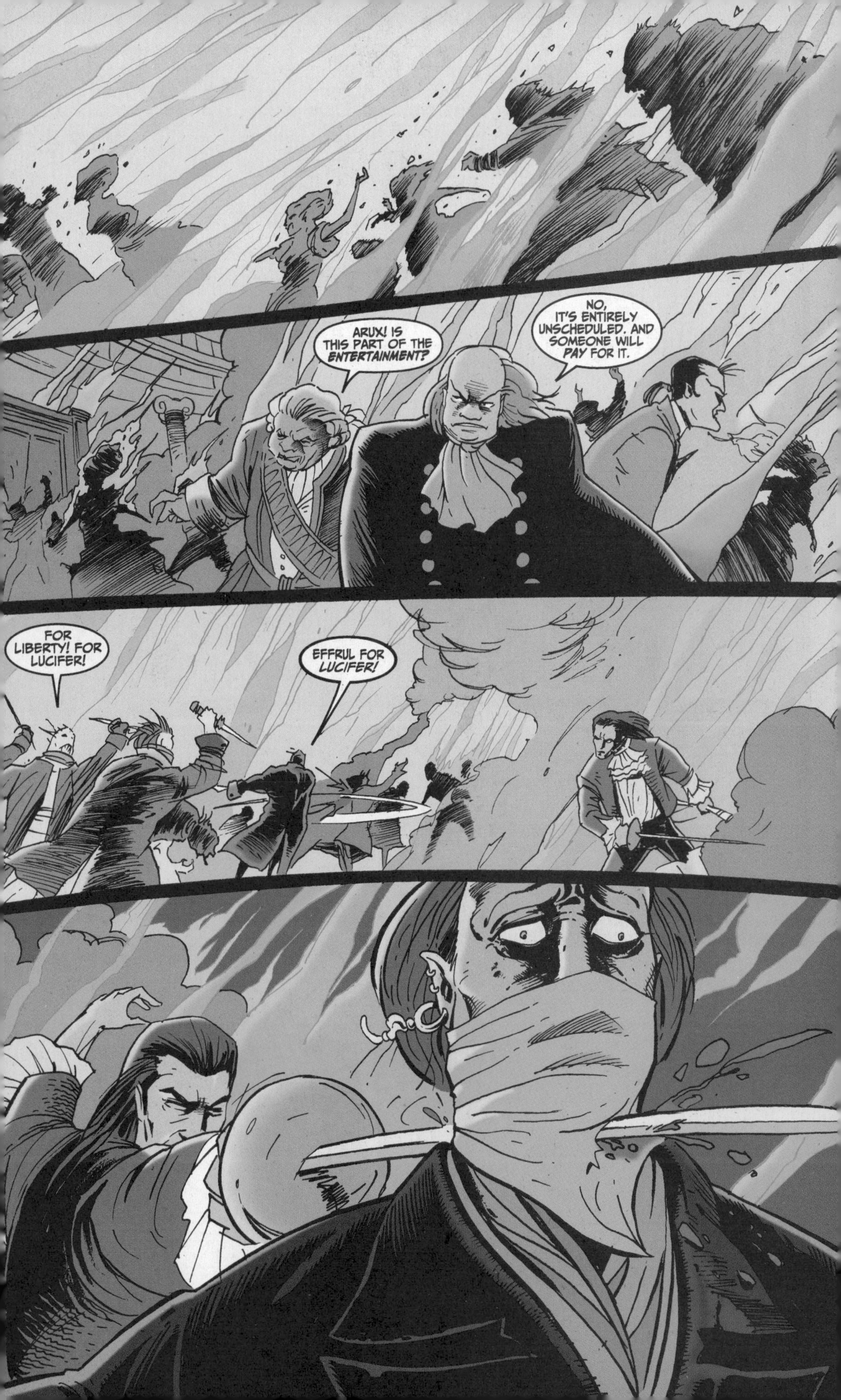
ARUX! IS THIS PART OF THE ENTERTAINMENT?
NO, IT'S ENTIRELY UNSCHEDULED. AND SOMEONE WILL PAY FOR IT.
FOR LIBERTY! FOR LUCIFER!
EFFRUL FOR LUCIFER!

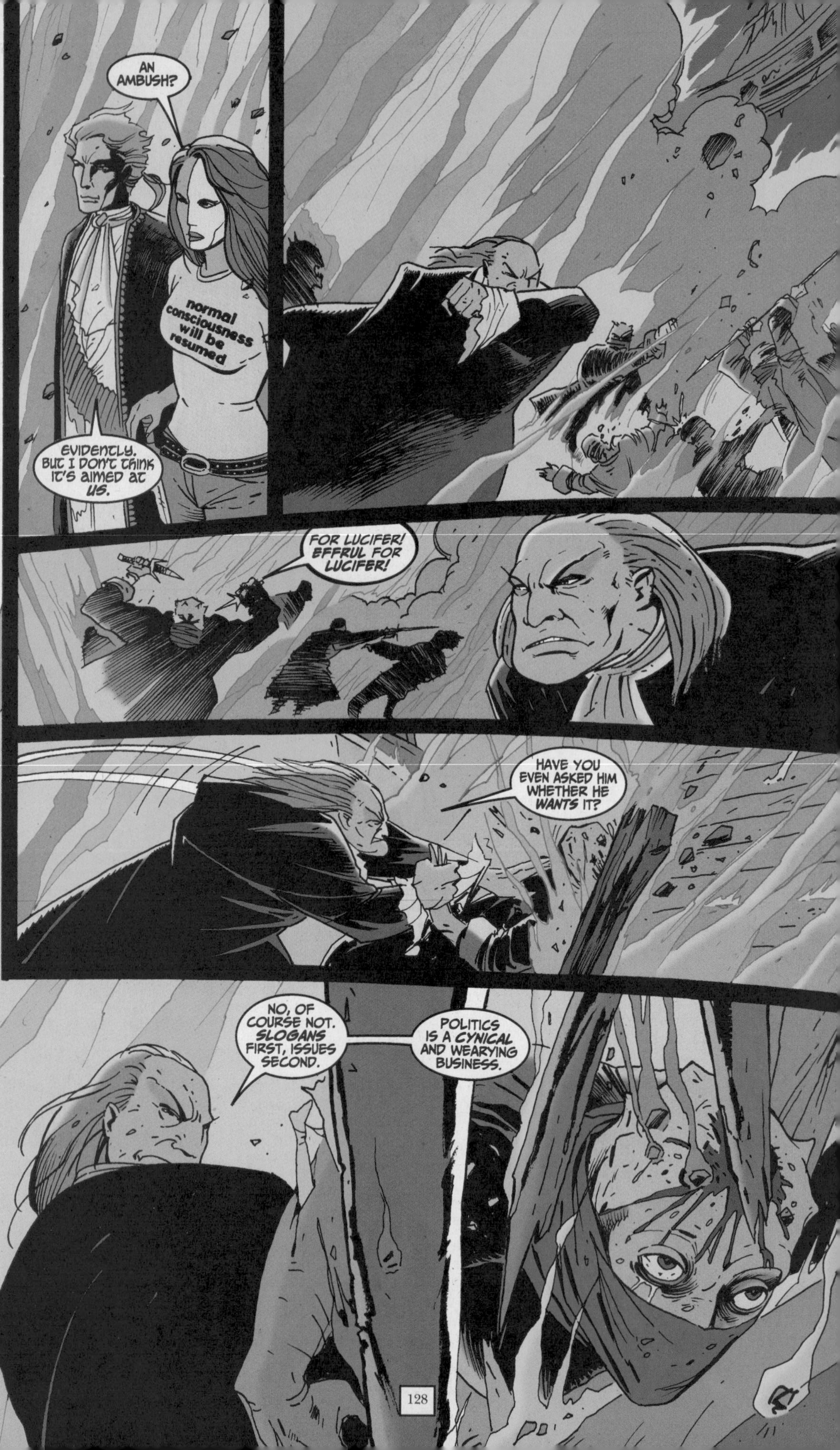

AN AMBUSH?
normal consciousness will be resumed
EVIDENTLY. BUT I DON'T THINK IT'S AIMED AT US.
FOR LUCIFER! EFFRUL FOR LUCIFER!
HAVE YOU EVEN ASKED HIM WHETHER HE WANTS IT?
NO, OF COURSE NOT. SLOGANS FIRST, ISSUES SECOND.
POLITICS IS A CYNICAL AND WEARYING BUSINESS.

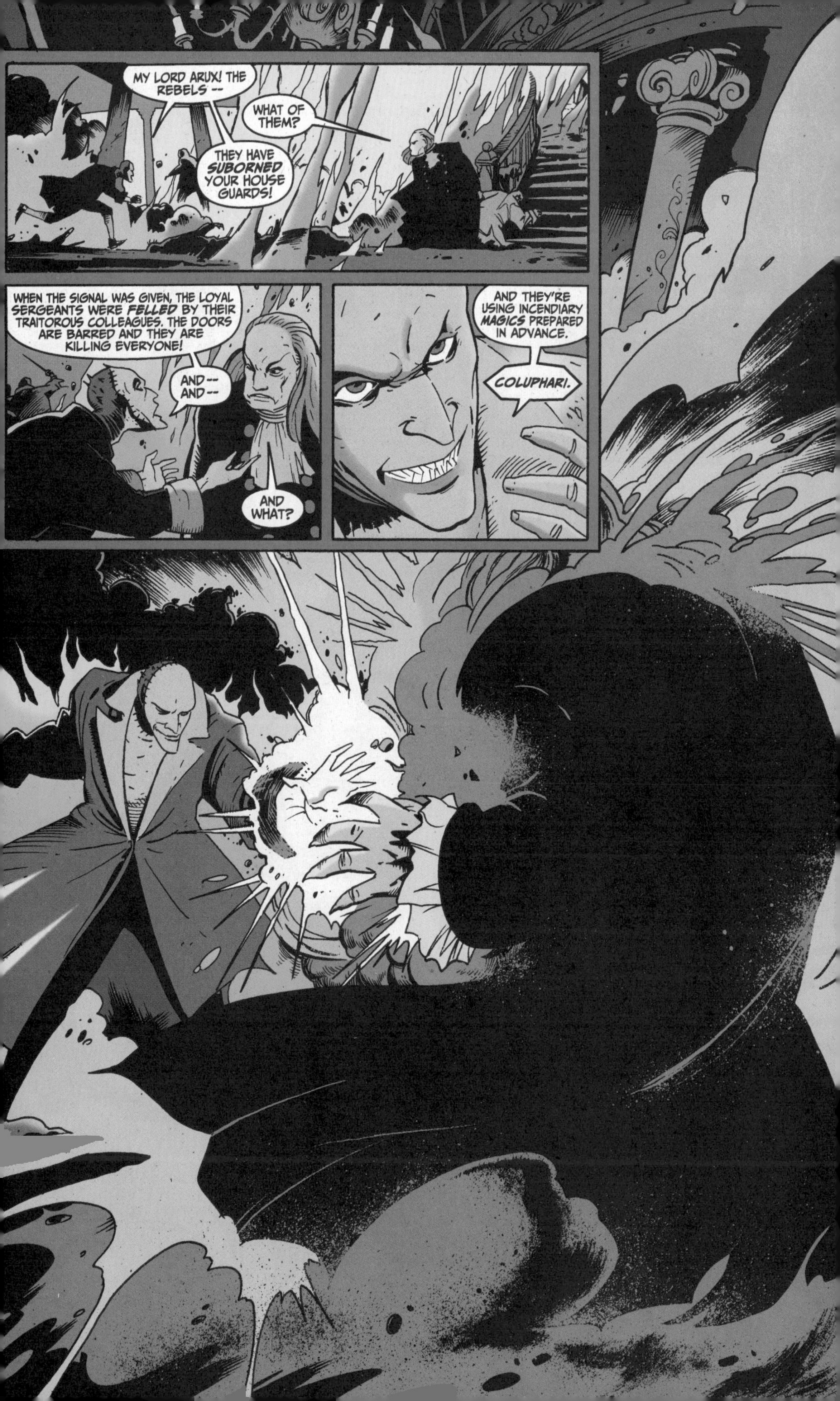
MY LORD ARUX! THE REBELS --
WHAT OF THEM?
THEY HAVE SUBORNED YOUR HOUSE GUARDS!
WHEN THE SIGNAL WAS GIVEN, THE LOYAL SERGEANTS WERE FELLED BY THEIR TRAITOROUS COLLEAGUES. THE DOORS ARE BARRED AND THEY ARE KILLING EVERYONE!
AND-- AND--
AND WHAT?
AND THEY'RE USING INCENDIARY MAGICS PREPARED IN ADVANCE.
COLUPHARI.

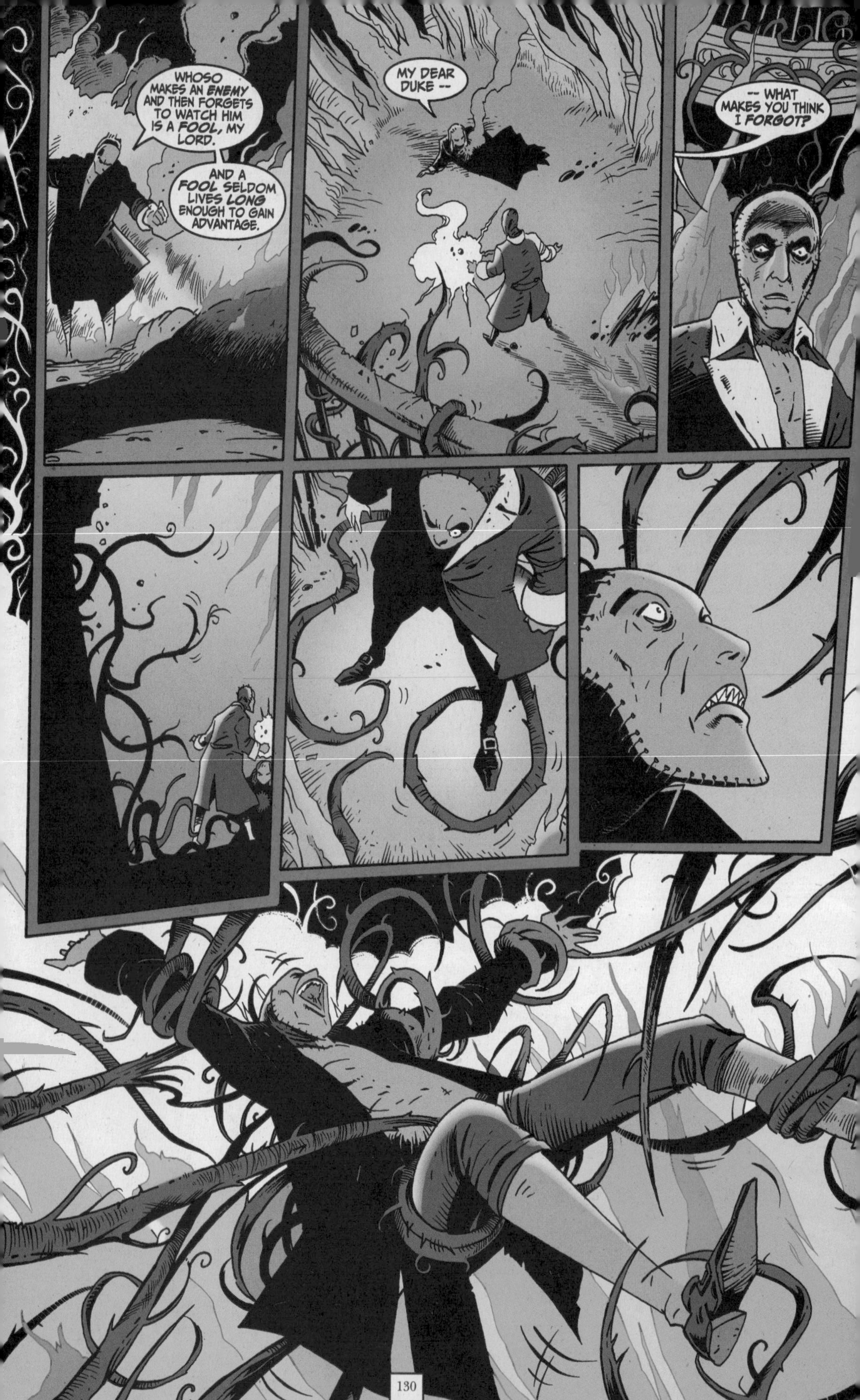
WHOSO MAKES AN ENEMY AND THEN FORGETS TO WATCH HIM IS A FOOL, MY LORD.
AND A FOOL SELDOM LIVES LONG ENOUGH TO GAIN ADVANTAGE.
MY DEAR DUKE --
-- WHAT MAKES YOU THINK I FORGOT?

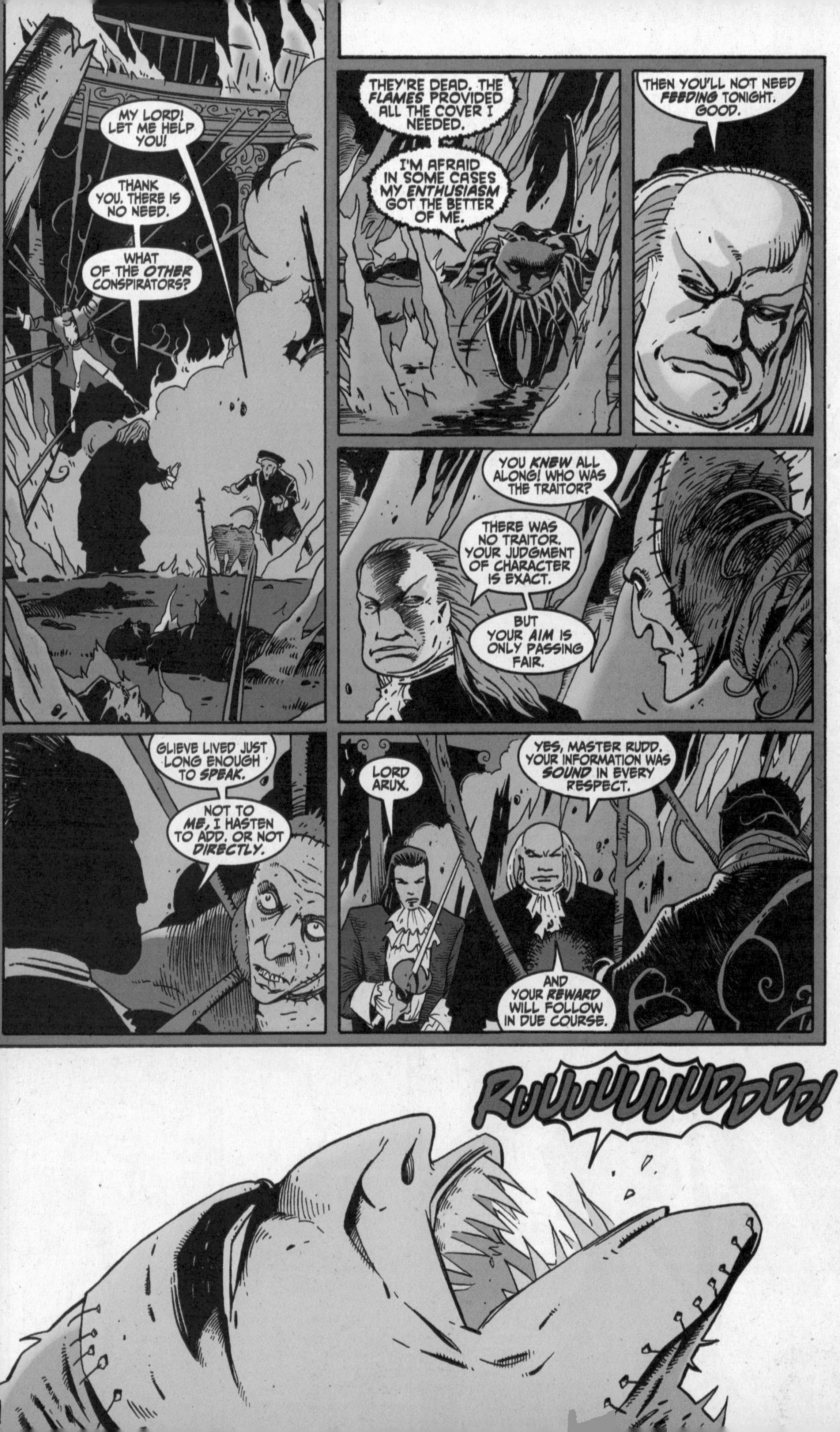
MY LORD! LET ME HELP YOU!
THANK YOU. THERE IS NO NEED.
WHAT OF THE OTHER CONSPIRATORS?
THEY'RE DEAD. THE FLAMES PROVIDED ALL THE COVER I NEEDED.
I'M AFRAID IN SOME CASES MY ENTHUSIASM GOT THE BETTER OF ME.
THEN YOU'LL NOT NEED FEEDING TONIGHT. GOOD.
YOU KNEW ALL ALONG! WHO WAS THE TRAITOR?
THERE WAS NO TRAITOR. YOUR JUDGMENT OF CHARACTER IS EXACT.
BUT YOUR AIM IS ONLY PASSING FAIR.
GLIEVE LIVED JUST LONG ENOUGH TO SPEAK.
NOT TO ME, I HASTEN TO ADD. OR NOT DIRECTLY.
LORD ARUX.
YES, MASTER RUDD. YOUR INFORMATION WAS SOUND IN EVERY RESPECT.
AND YOUR REWARD WILL FOLLOW IN DUE COURSE.
RUUUUUUUDDDD!

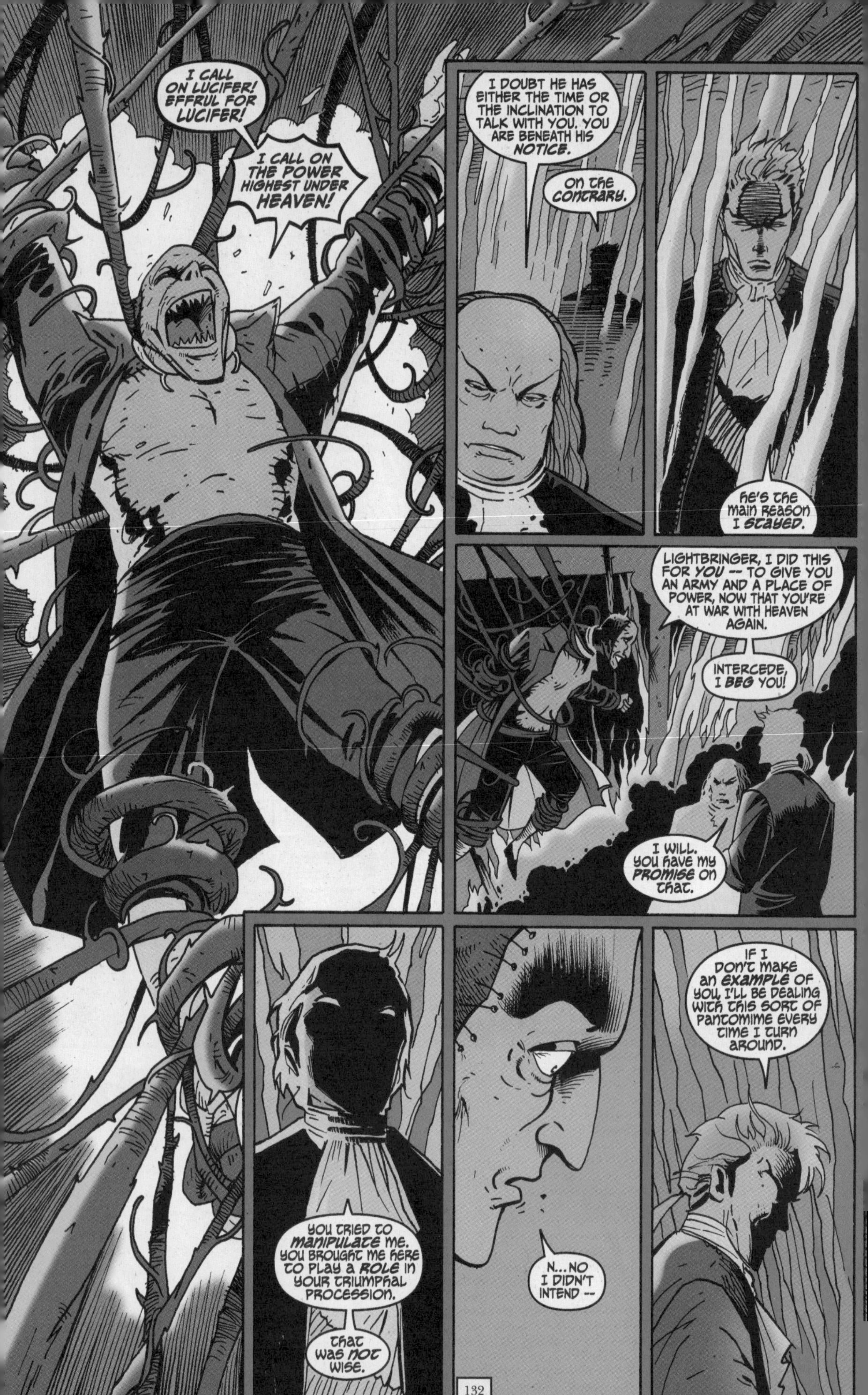
I CALL ON LUCIFER! EFFRUL FOR LUCIFER!
I CALL ON THE POWER HIGHEST UNDER HEAVEN!
I DOUBT HE HAS EITHER THE TIME OR THE INCLINATION TO TALK WITH YOU. YOU ARE BENEATH HIS NOTICE.
ON THE CONTRARY.
HE'S THE MAIN REASON I STAYED.
LIGHTBRINGER, I DID THIS FOR YOU -- TO GIVE YOU AN ARMY AND A PLACE OF POWER, NOW THAT YOU'RE AT WAR WITH HEAVEN AGAIN.
INTERCEDE, I BEG YOU!
I WILL. YOU HAVE MY PROMISE ON THAT.
YOU TRIED TO MANIPULATE ME. YOU BROUGHT ME HERE TO PLAY A ROLE IN YOUR TRIUMPHAL PROCESSION.
THAT WAS NOT WISE.
N... NO I DIDN'T INTEND --
IF I DON'T MAKE AN EXAMPLE OF YOU, I'LL BE DEALING WITH THIS SORT OF PANTOMIME EVERY TIME I TURN AROUND.

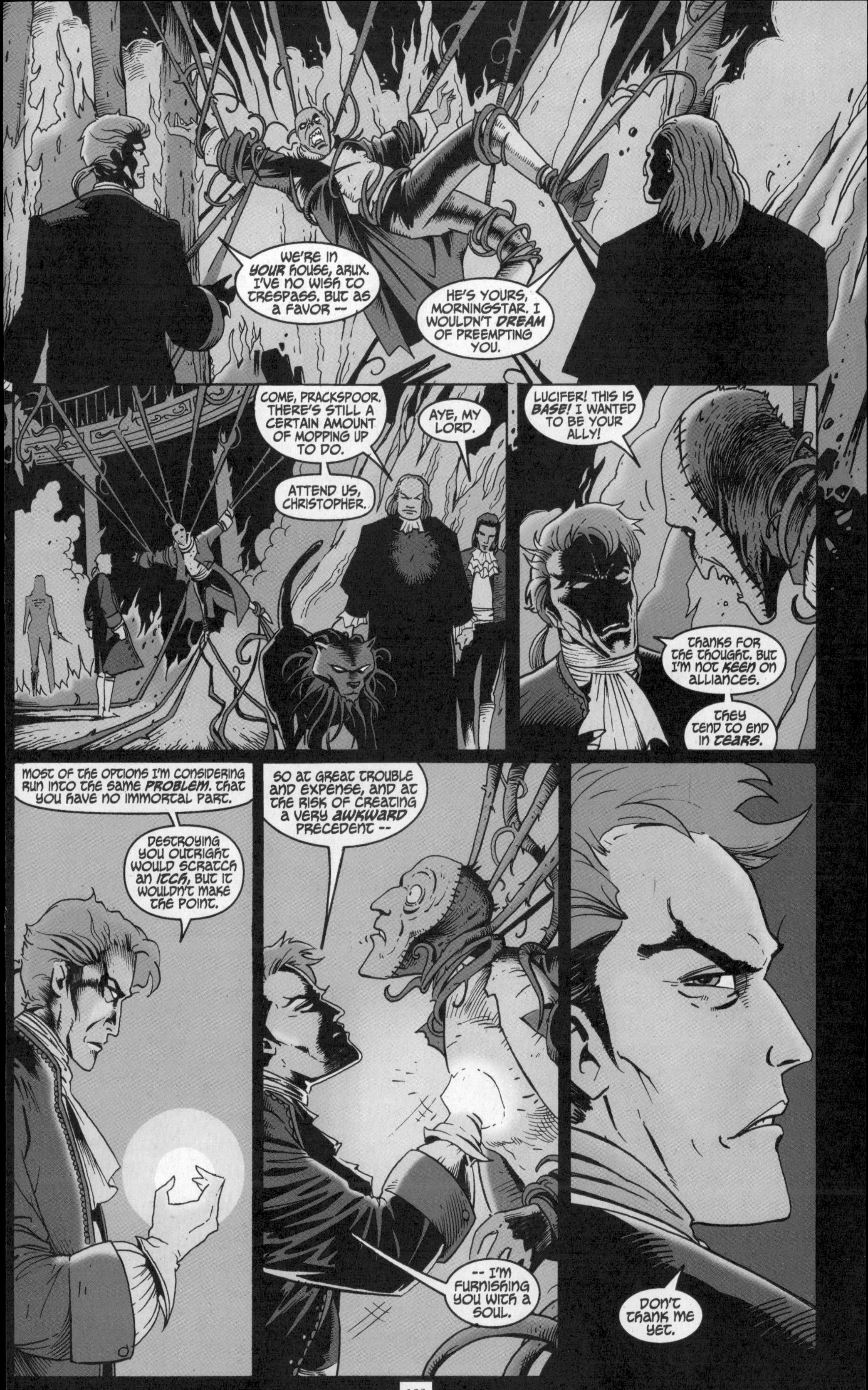
WE'RE IN YOUR HOUSE, ARUX. I'VE NO WISH TO TRESPASS. BUT AS A FAVOR --
HE'S YOURS, MORNINGSTAR. I WOULDN'T DREAM OF PREEMPTING YOU.
COME, PRACKSPOOR. THERE'S STILL A CERTAIN AMOUNT OF MOPPING UP TO DO.
AYE, MY LORD.
ATTEND US, CHRISTOPHER.
LUCIFER! THIS IS BASE! I WANTED TO BE YOUR ALLY!
THANKS FOR THE THOUGHT. BUT I'M NOT KEEN ON ALLIANCES.
THEY TEND TO END IN TEARS.
MOST OF THE OPTIONS I'M CONSIDERING RUN INTO THE SAME PROBLEM. THAT YOU HAVE NO IMMORTAL PART.
DESTROYING YOU OUTRIGHT WOULD SCRATCH AN ITCH, BUT IT WOULDN'T MAKE THE POINT.
SO AT GREAT TROUBLE AND EXPENSE, AND AT THE RISK OF CREATING A VERY AWKWARD PRECEDENT --
-- I'M FURNISHING YOU WITH A SOUL.
DON'T THANK ME YET.

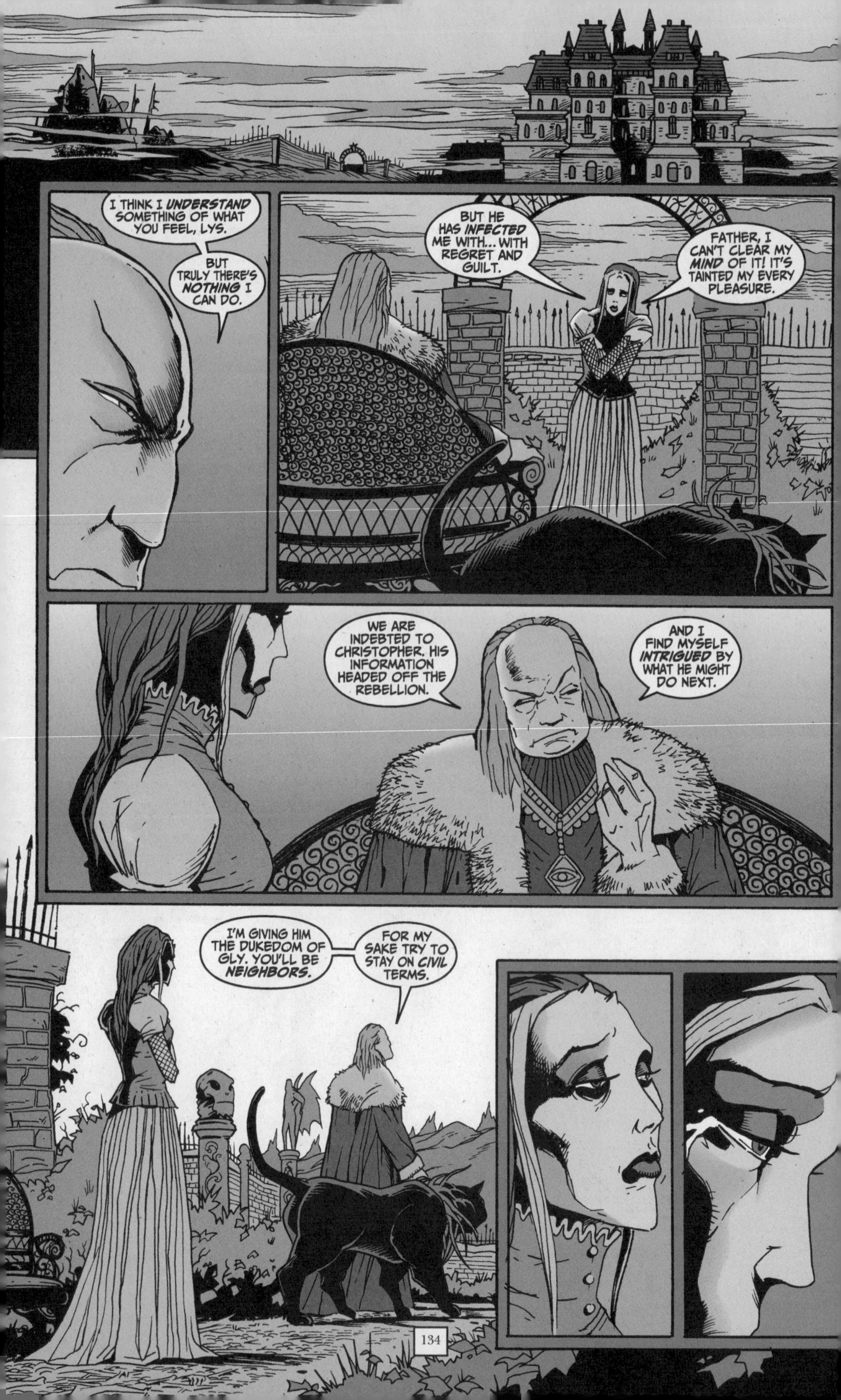
I THINK I UNDERSTAND SOMETHING OF WHAT YOU FEEL, LYS.
BUT TRULY THERE'S NOTHING I CAN DO.
BUT HE HAS INFECTED ME WITH... WITH REGRET AND GUILT.
FATHER, I CAN'T CLEAR MY MIND OF IT! IT'S TAINTED MY EVERY PLEASURE.
WE ARE INDEBTED TO CHRISTOPHER. HIS INFORMATION HEADED OFF THE REBELLION.
AND I FIND MYSELF INTRIGUED BY WHAT HE MIGHT DO NEXT.
I'M GIVING HIM THE DUKEDOM OF GLY. YOU'LL BE NEIGHBORS.
FOR MY SAKE TRY TO STAY ON CIVIL TERMS.

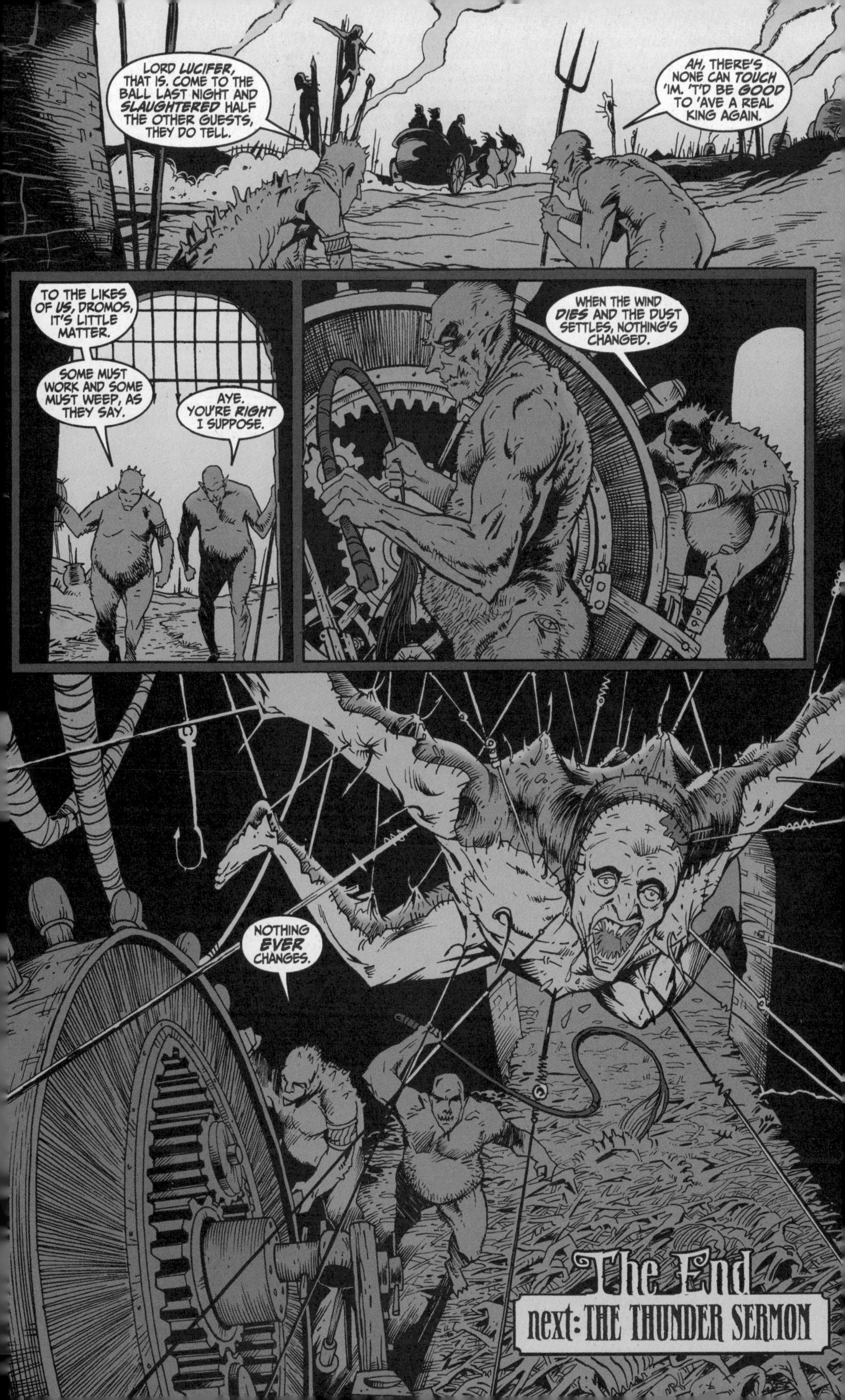
LORD LUCIFER, THAT IS. COME TO THE BALL LAST NIGHT AND SLAUGHTERED HALF THE OTHER GUESTS, THEY DO TELL.
AH, THERE'S NONE CAN TOUCH 'IM. 'T'D BE GOOD TO 'AVE A REAL KING AGAIN.
TO THE LIKES OF US, DROMOS, IT'S LITTLE MATTER.
SOME MUST WORK AND SOME MUST WEEP, AS THEY SAY.
AYE. YOU'RE RIGHT I SUPPOSE.
WHEN THE WIND DIES AND THE DUST SETTLES, NOTHING'S CHANGED.
NOTHING EVER CHANGES.
The End
next: THE THUNDER SERMON

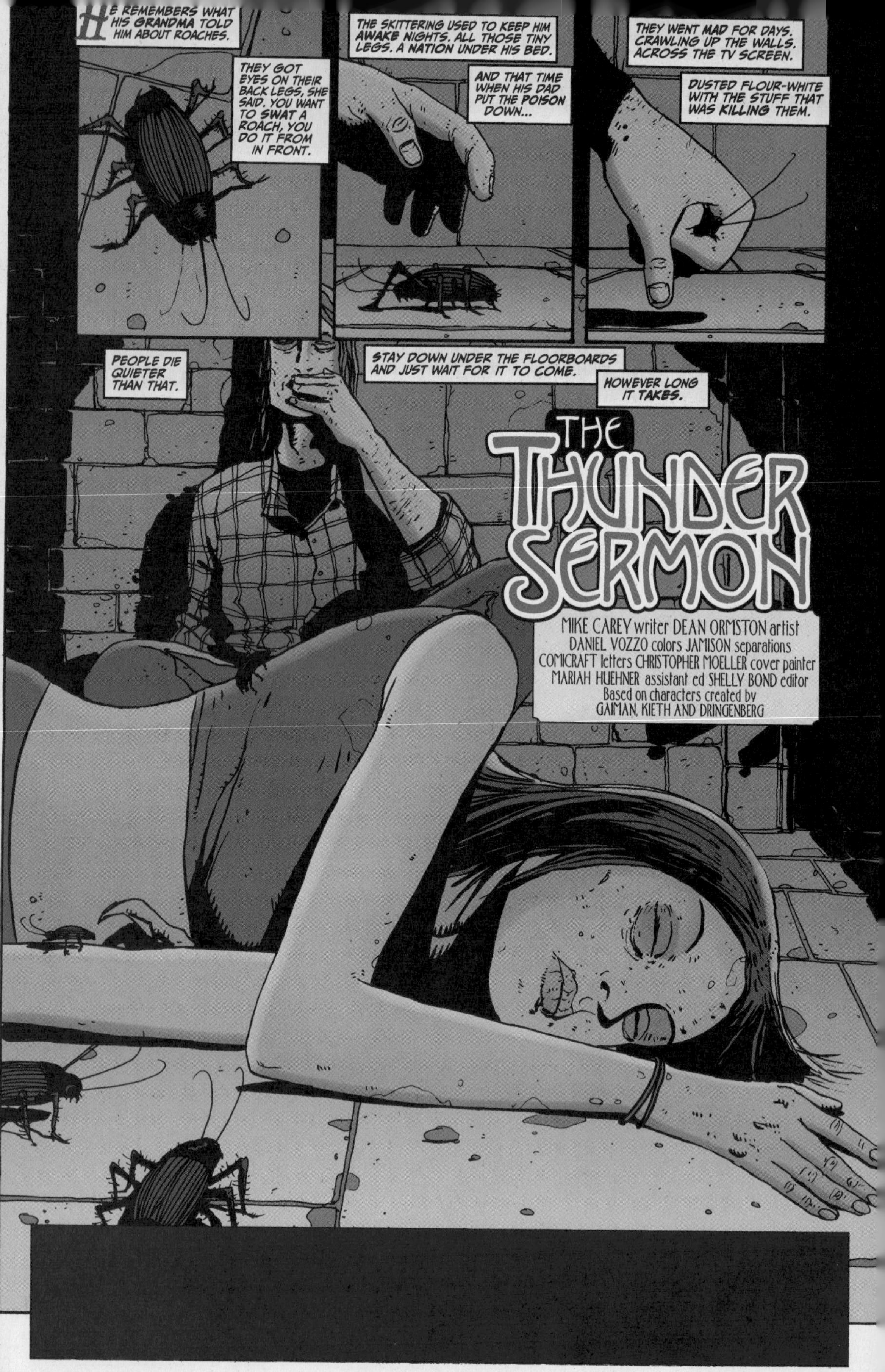
HE REMEMBERS WHAT HIS GRANDMA TOLD HIM ABOUT ROACHES.
THEY GOT EYES ON THEIR BACK LEGS, SHE SAID. YOU WANT TO SWAT A ROACH, YOU DO IT FROM IN FRONT.
THE SKITTERING USED TO KEEP HIM AWAKE NIGHTS. ALL THOSE TINY LEGS. A NATION UNDER HIS BED.
AND THAT TIME WHEN HIS DAD PUT THE POISON DOWN...
THEY WENT MAD FOR DAYS. CRAWLING UP THE WALLS. ACROSS THE TV SCREEN.
DUSTED FLOUR-WHITE WITH THE STUFF THAT WAS KILLING THEM.
PEOPLE DIE QUIETER THAN THAT.
STAY DOWN UNDER THE FLOORBOARDS AND JUST WAIT FOR IT TO COME.
HOWEVER LONG IT TAKES.
THE THUNDER SERMON
MIKE CAREY writer DEAN ORMSTON artist
DANIEL VOZZO colors JAMISON separations
COMICRAFT letters CHRISTOPHER MOELLER cover painter
MARIAH HUEHNER assistant ed SHELLY BOND editor
Based on characters created by
GAIMAN, KIETH AND DRINGENBERG

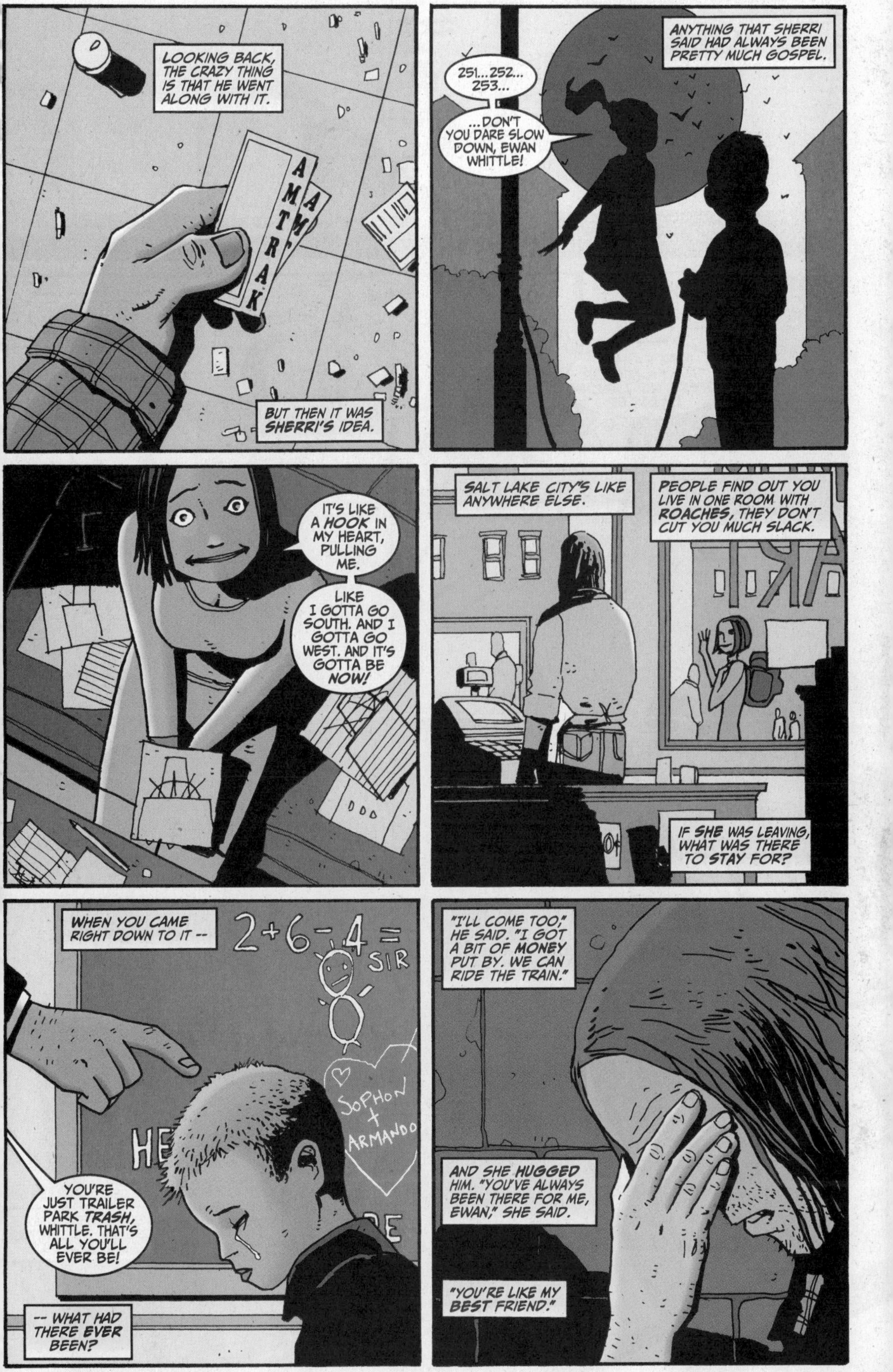
LOOKING BACK, THE CRAZY THING IS THAT HE WENT ALONG WITH IT.
AMTRAK
AMTRAK
BUT THEN IT WAS SHERRI'S IDEA.
ANYTHING THAT SHERRI SAID HAD ALWAYS BEEN PRETTY MUCH GOSPEL.
251...252... 253...
...DON'T YOU DARE SLOW DOWN, EWAN WHITTLE!
IT'S LIKE A HOOK IN MY HEART, PULLING ME.
LIKE I GOTTA GO SOUTH. AND I GOTTA GO WEST. AND IT'S GOTTA BE NOW!
SALT LAKE CITY'S LIKE ANYWHERE ELSE.
PEOPLE FIND OUT YOU LIVE IN ONE ROOM WITH ROACHES, THEY DON'T CUT YOU MUCH SLACK.
IF SHE WAS LEAVING, WHAT WAS THERE TO STAY FOR?
WHEN YOU CAME RIGHT DOWN TO IT --
2+6-4=
SIR
SOPHON + ARMANDO
YOU'RE JUST TRAILER PARK TRASH, WHITTLE. THAT'S ALL YOU'LL EVER BE!
-- WHAT HAD THERE EVER BEEN?
"I'LL COME TOO," HE SAID. "I GOT A BIT OF MONEY PUT BY. WE CAN RIDE THE TRAIN."
AND SHE HUGGED HIM. "YOU'VE ALWAYS BEEN THERE FOR ME, EWAN," SHE SAID.
"YOU'RE LIKE MY BEST FRIEND."

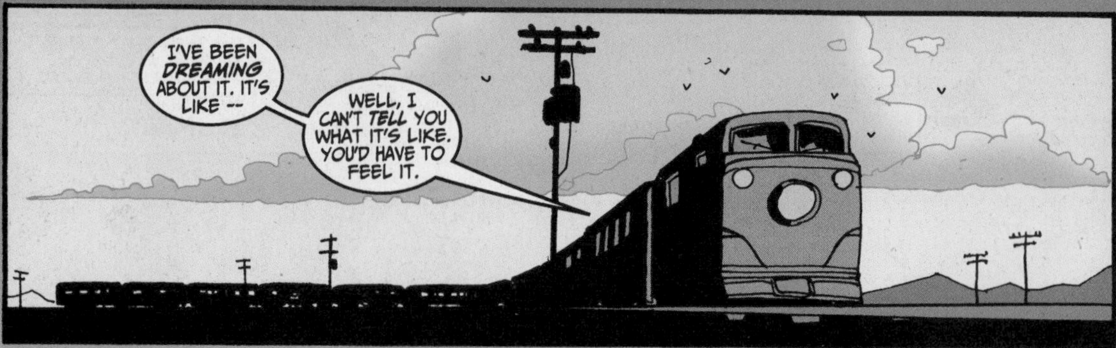
I'VE BEEN DREAMING ABOUT IT. IT'S LIKE --
WELL, I CAN'T TELL YOU WHAT IT'S LIKE. YOU'D HAVE TO FEEL IT.

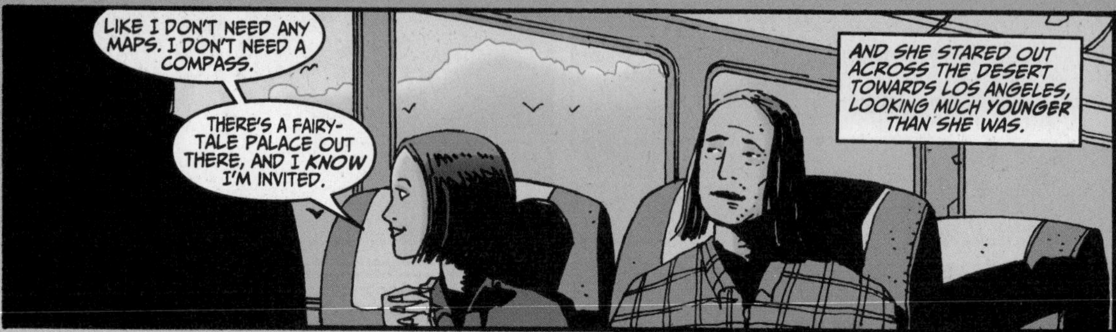
LIKE I DON'T NEED ANY MAPS. I DON'T NEED A COMPASS.
THERE'S A FAIRY-TALE PALACE OUT THERE, AND I KNOW I'M INVITED.
AND SHE STARED OUT ACROSS THE DESERT TOWARDS LOS ANGELES, LOOKING MUCH YOUNGER THAN SHE WAS.

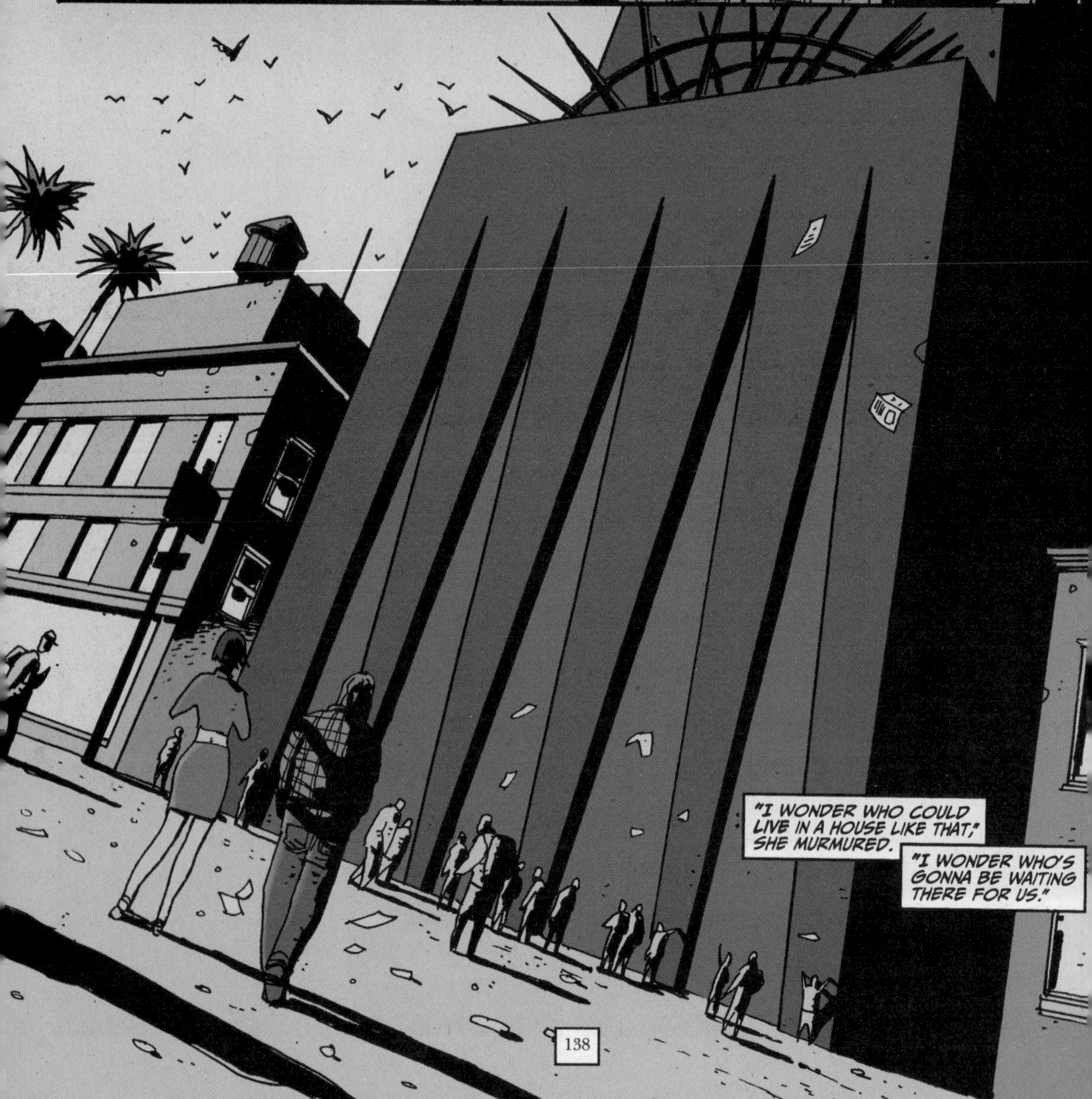
"I WONDER WHO COULD LIVE IN A HOUSE LIKE THAT," SHE MURMURED.
"I WONDER WHO'S GONNA BE WAITING THERE FOR US."

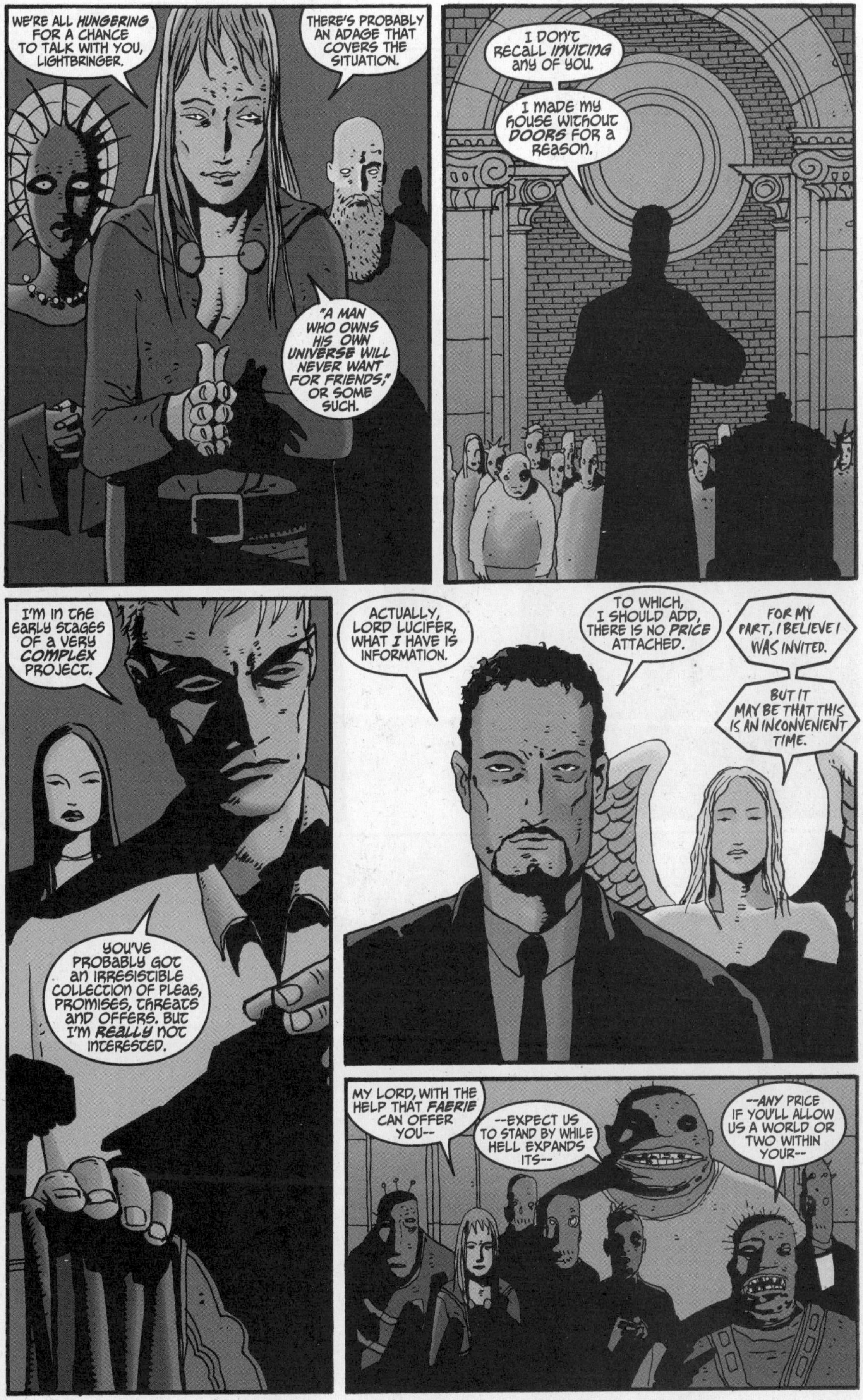
WE'RE ALL HUNGERING FOR A CHANCE TO TALK WITH YOU, LIGHTBRINGER.
THERE'S PROBABLY AN ADAGE THAT COVERS THE SITUATION.
"A MAN WHO OWNS HIS OWN UNIVERSE WILL NEVER WANT FOR FRIENDS," OR SOME SUCH.
I DON'T RECALL INVITING ANY OF YOU.
I MADE MY HOUSE WITHOUT DOORS FOR A REASON.
I'M IN THE EARLY STAGES OF A VERY COMPLEX PROJECT.
YOU'VE PROBABLY GOT AN IRRESISTIBLE COLLECTION OF PLEAS, PROMISES, THREATS AND OFFERS. BUT I'M REALLY NOT INTERESTED.
ACTUALLY, LORD LUCIFER, WHAT I HAVE IS INFORMATION.
TO WHICH, I SHOULD ADD, THERE IS NO PRICE ATTACHED.
FOR MY PART, I BELIEVE I WAS INVITED.
BUT IT MAY BE THAT THIS IS AN INCONVENIENT TIME.
MY LORD, WITH THE HELP THAT FAERIE CAN OFFER YOU--
--EXPECT US TO STAND BY WHILE HELL EXPANDS ITS--
--ANY PRICE IF YOU'LL ALLOW US A WORLD OR TWO WITHIN YOUR--

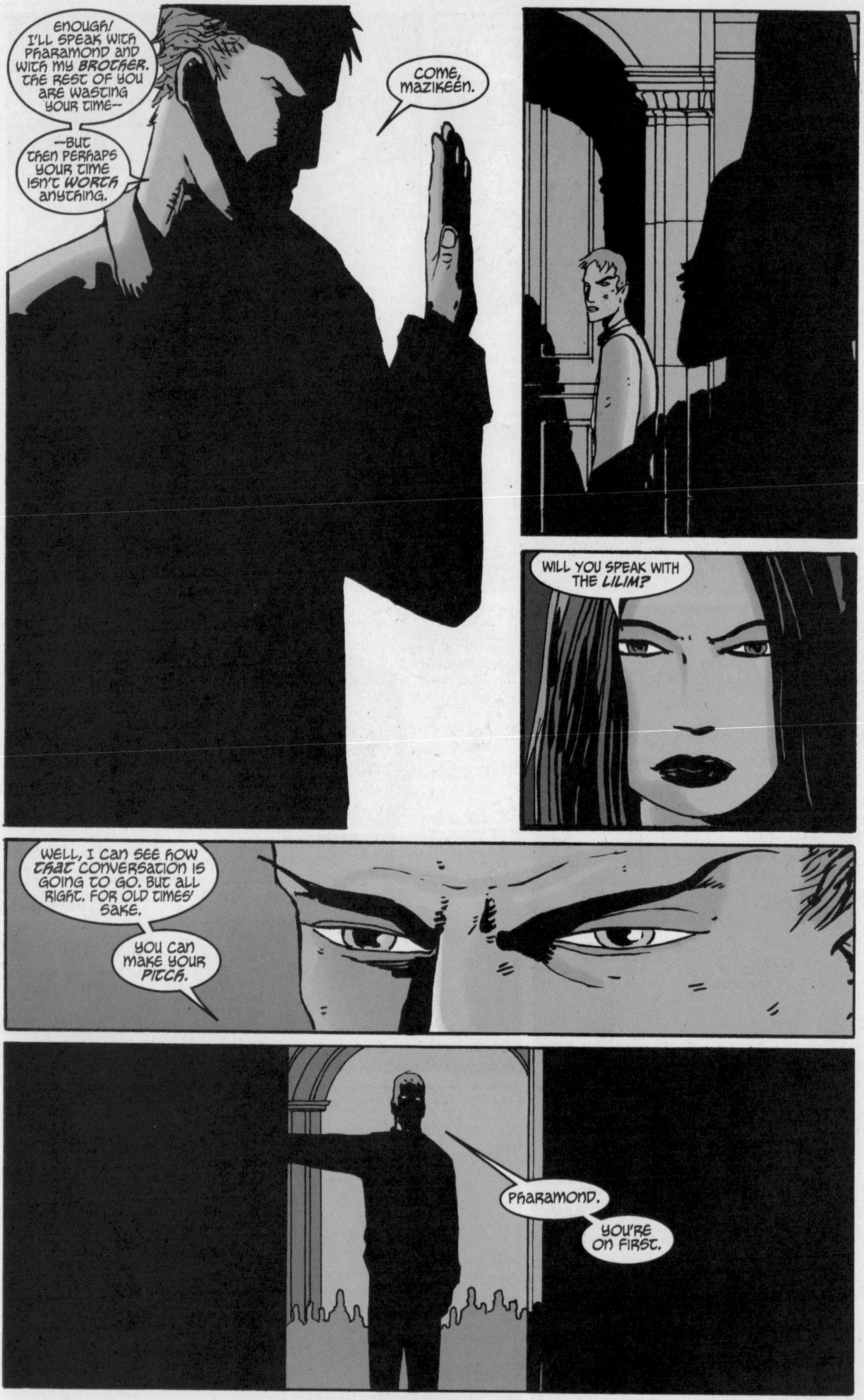
ENOUGH! I'LL SPEAK WITH PHARAMOND AND WITH MY BROTHER. THE REST OF YOU ARE WASTING YOUR TIME--
--BUT THEN PERHAPS YOUR TIME ISN'T WORTH ANYTHING.
COME, MAZIKEEN.
WILL YOU SPEAK WITH THE LILIM?
WELL, I CAN SEE HOW THAT CONVERSATION IS GOING TO GO. BUT ALL RIGHT. FOR OLD TIMES' SAKE.
YOU CAN MAKE YOUR PITCH.
PHARAMOND.
YOU'RE ON FIRST.

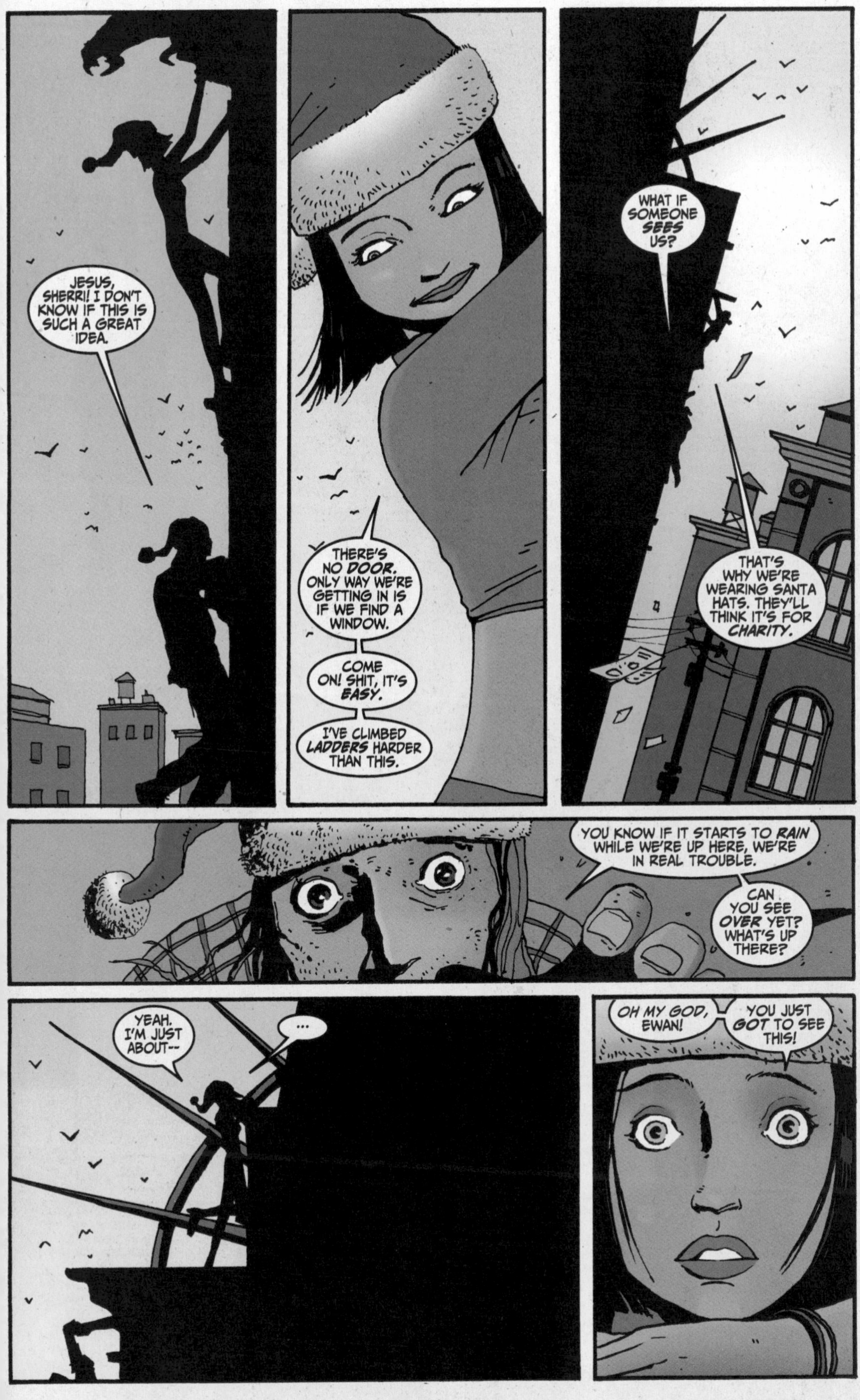
JESUS, SHERRI! I DON'T KNOW IF THIS IS SUCH A GREAT IDEA.
THERE'S NO DOOR. ONLY WAY WE'RE GETTING IN IS IF WE FIND A WINDOW.
COME ON! SHIT, IT'S EASY.
I'VE CLIMBED LADDERS HARDER THAN THIS.
WHAT IF SOMEONE SEES US?
THAT'S WHY WE'RE WEARING SANTA HATS. THEY'LL THINK IT'S FOR CHARITY.
YOU KNOW IF IT STARTS TO RAIN WHILE WE'RE UP HERE, WE'RE IN REAL TROUBLE.
CAN YOU SEE OVER YET? WHAT'S UP THERE?
YEAH. I'M JUST ABOUT--
...
OH MY GOD, EWAN!
YOU JUST GOT TO SEE THIS!

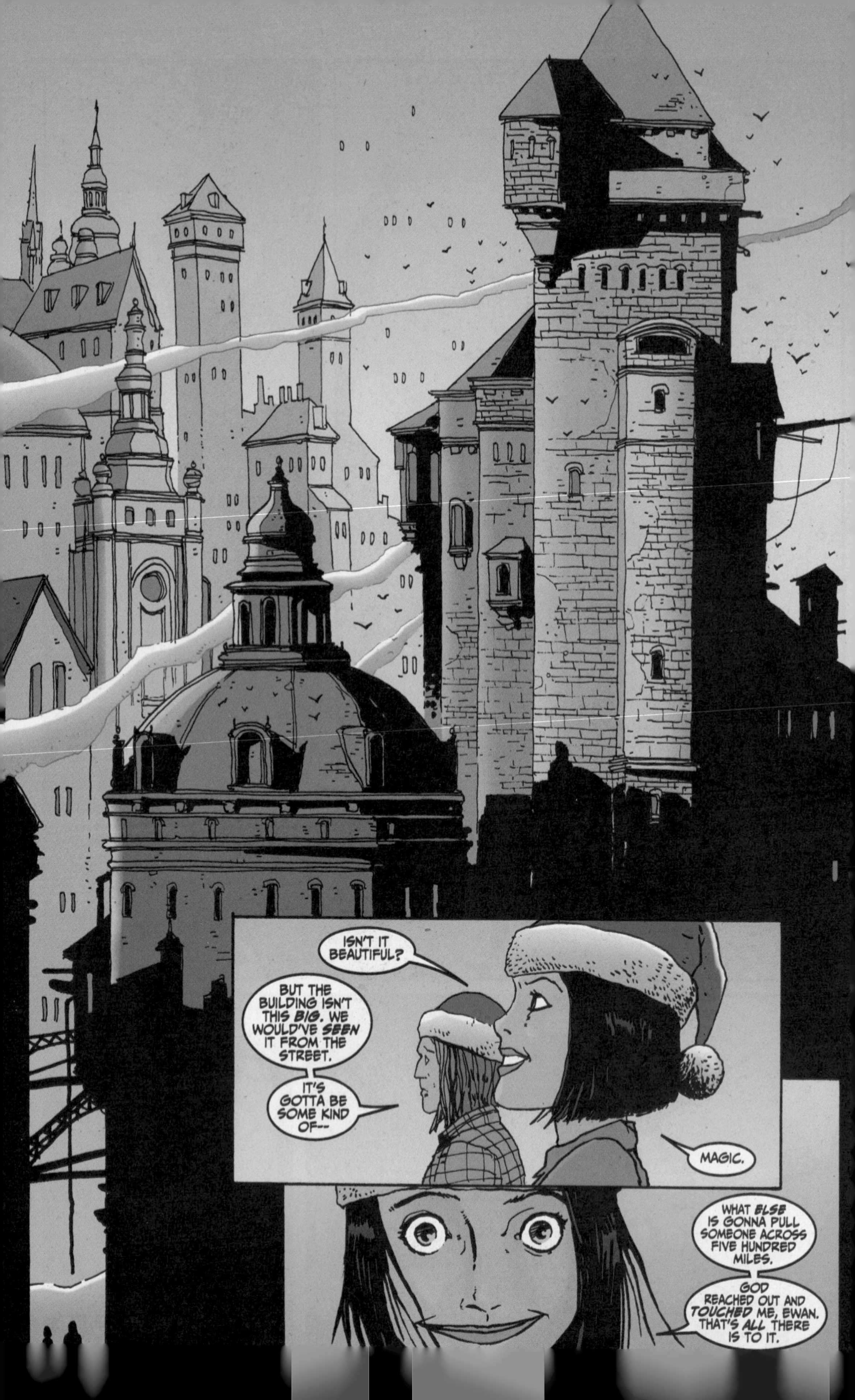
ISN'T IT BEAUTIFUL?
BUT THE BUILDING ISN'T THIS BIG. WE WOULD'VE SEEN IT FROM THE STREET.
IT'S GOTTA BE SOME KIND OF--
MAGIC.
WHAT ELSE IS GONNA PULL SOMEONE ACROSS FIVE HUNDRED MILES.
GOD REACHED OUT AND TOUCHED ME, EWAN. THAT'S ALL THERE IS TO IT.

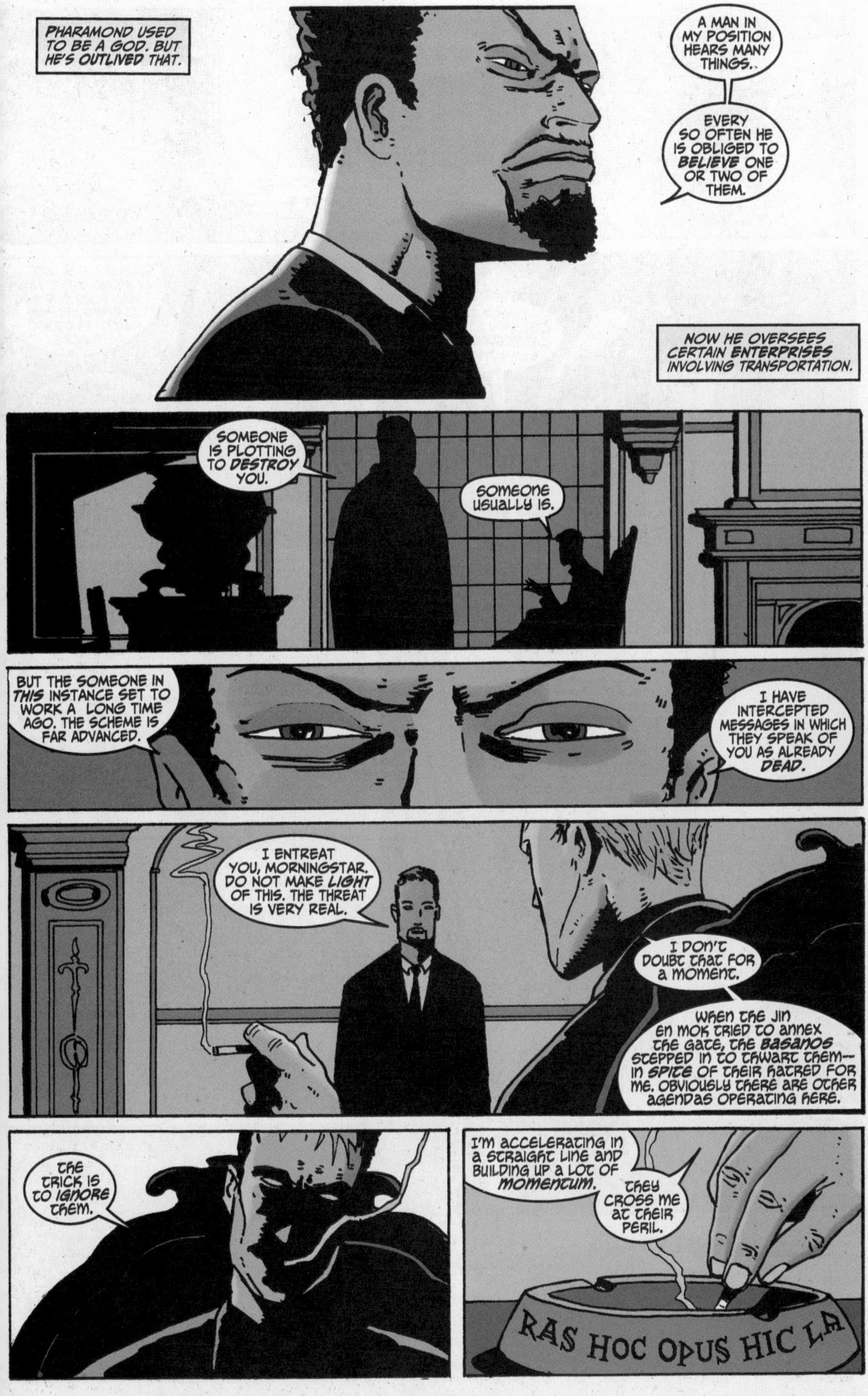
PHARAMOND USED TO BE A GOD. BUT HE'S OUTLIVED THAT.
A MAN IN MY POSITION HEARS MANY THINGS..
EVERY SO OFTEN HE IS OBLIGED TO BELIEVE ONE OR TWO OF THEM.
NOW HE OVERSEES CERTAIN ENTERPRISES INVOLVING TRANSPORTATION.
SOMEONE IS PLOTTING TO DESTROY YOU.
SOMEONE USUALLY IS.
BUT THE SOMEONE IN THIS INSTANCE SET TO WORK A LONG TIME AGO. THE SCHEME IS FAR ADVANCED.
I HAVE INTERCEPTED MESSAGES IN WHICH THEY SPEAK OF YOU AS ALREADY DEAD.
I ENTREAT YOU, MORNINGSTAR. DO NOT MAKE LIGHT OF THIS. THE THREAT IS VERY REAL.
I DON'T DOUBT THAT FOR A MOMENT.
WHEN THE JIN EN MOK TRIED TO ANNEX THE GATE, THE BASANOS STEPPED IN TO THWART THEM-- IN SPITE OF THEIR HATRED FOR ME. OBVIOUSLY THERE ARE OTHER AGENDAS OPERATING HERE.
THE TRICK IS TO IGNORE THEM.
I'M ACCELERATING IN A STRAIGHT LINE AND BUILDING UP A LOT OF MOMENTUM.
THEY CROSS ME AT THEIR PERIL.
RAS HOC OPUS HIC LA

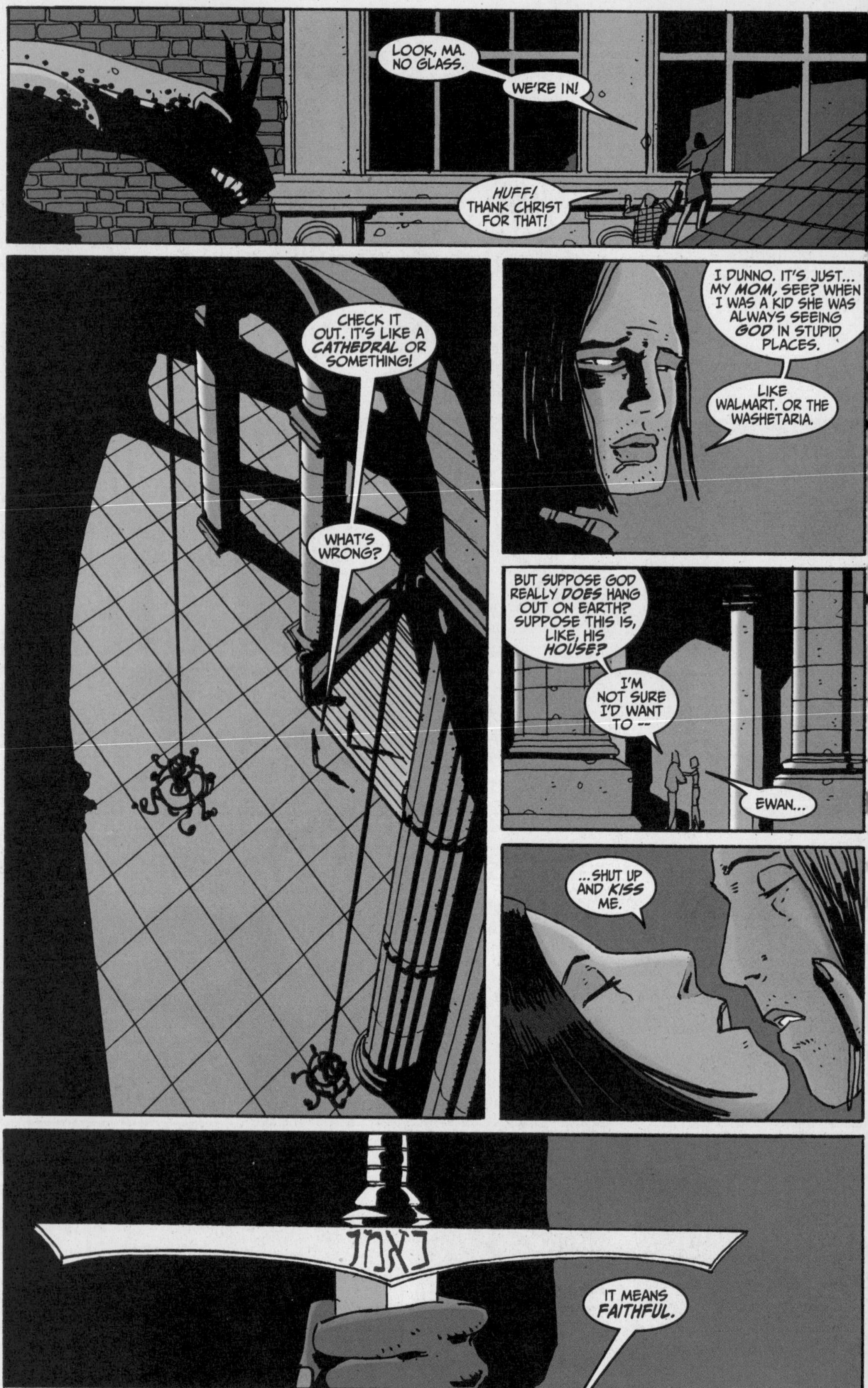
LOOK, MA. NO GLASS.
WE'RE IN!
HUFF! THANK CHRIST FOR THAT!
CHECK IT OUT. IT'S LIKE A CATHEDRAL OR SOMETHING!
WHAT'S WRONG?
I DUNNO. IT'S JUST... MY MOM, SEE? WHEN I WAS A KID SHE WAS ALWAYS SEEING GOD IN STUPID PLACES.
LIKE WALMART. OR THE WASHETARIA.
BUT SUPPOSE GOD REALLY DOES HANG OUT ON EARTH? SUPPOSE THIS IS, LIKE, HIS HOUSE?
I'M NOT SURE I'D WANT TO --
EWAN...
...SHUT UP AND KISS ME.
נאמן
IT MEANS FAITHFUL.

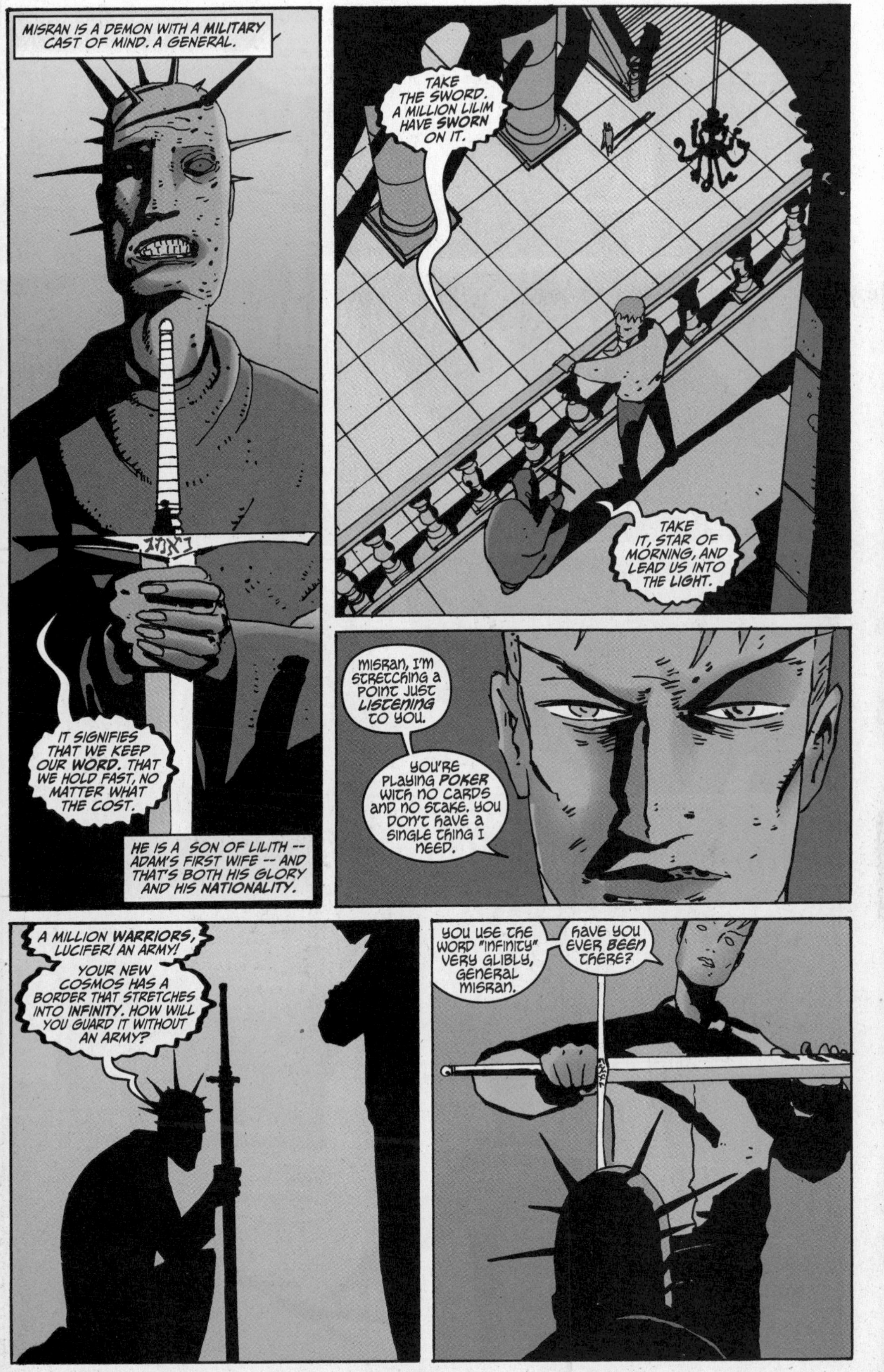
MISRAN IS A DEMON WITH A MILITARY CAST OF MIND. A GENERAL.
IT SIGNIFIES THAT WE KEEP OUR WORD. THAT WE HOLD FAST, NO MATTER WHAT THE COST.
HE IS A SON OF LILITH -- ADAM'S FIRST WIFE -- AND THAT'S BOTH HIS GLORY AND HIS NATIONALITY.
TAKE THE SWORD. A MILLION LILIM HAVE SWORN ON IT.
TAKE IT, STAR OF MORNING, AND LEAD US INTO THE LIGHT.
MISRAN, I'M STRETCHING A POINT JUST LISTENING TO YOU.
YOU'RE PLAYING POKER WITH NO CARDS AND NO STAKE. YOU DON'T HAVE A SINGLE THING I NEED.
A MILLION WARRIORS, LUCIFER! AN ARMY!
YOUR NEW COSMOS HAS A BORDER THAT STRETCHES INTO INFINITY. HOW WILL YOU GUARD IT WITHOUT AN ARMY?
YOU USE THE WORD "INFINITY" VERY GLIBLY, GENERAL MISRAN.
HAVE YOU EVER BEEN THERE?

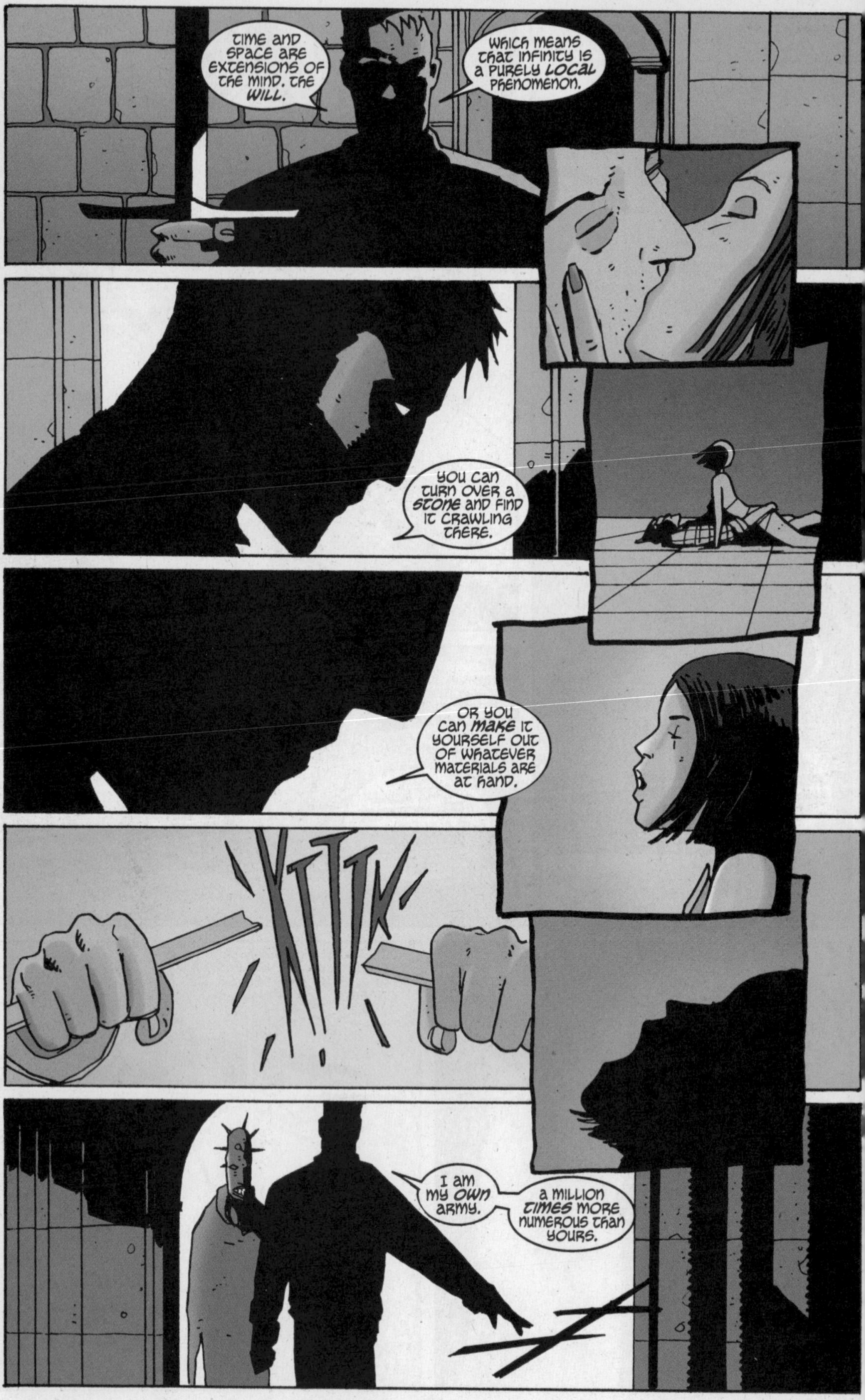
TIME AND SPACE ARE EXTENSIONS OF THE MIND. THE WILL.
WHICH MEANS THAT INFINITY IS A PURELY LOCAL PHENOMENON.
YOU CAN TURN OVER A STONE AND FIND IT CRAWLING THERE.
OR YOU CAN MAKE IT YOURSELF OUT OF WHATEVER MATERIALS ARE AT HAND.
KTTTK
I AM MY OWN ARMY.
A MILLION TIMES MORE NUMEROUS THAN YOURS.

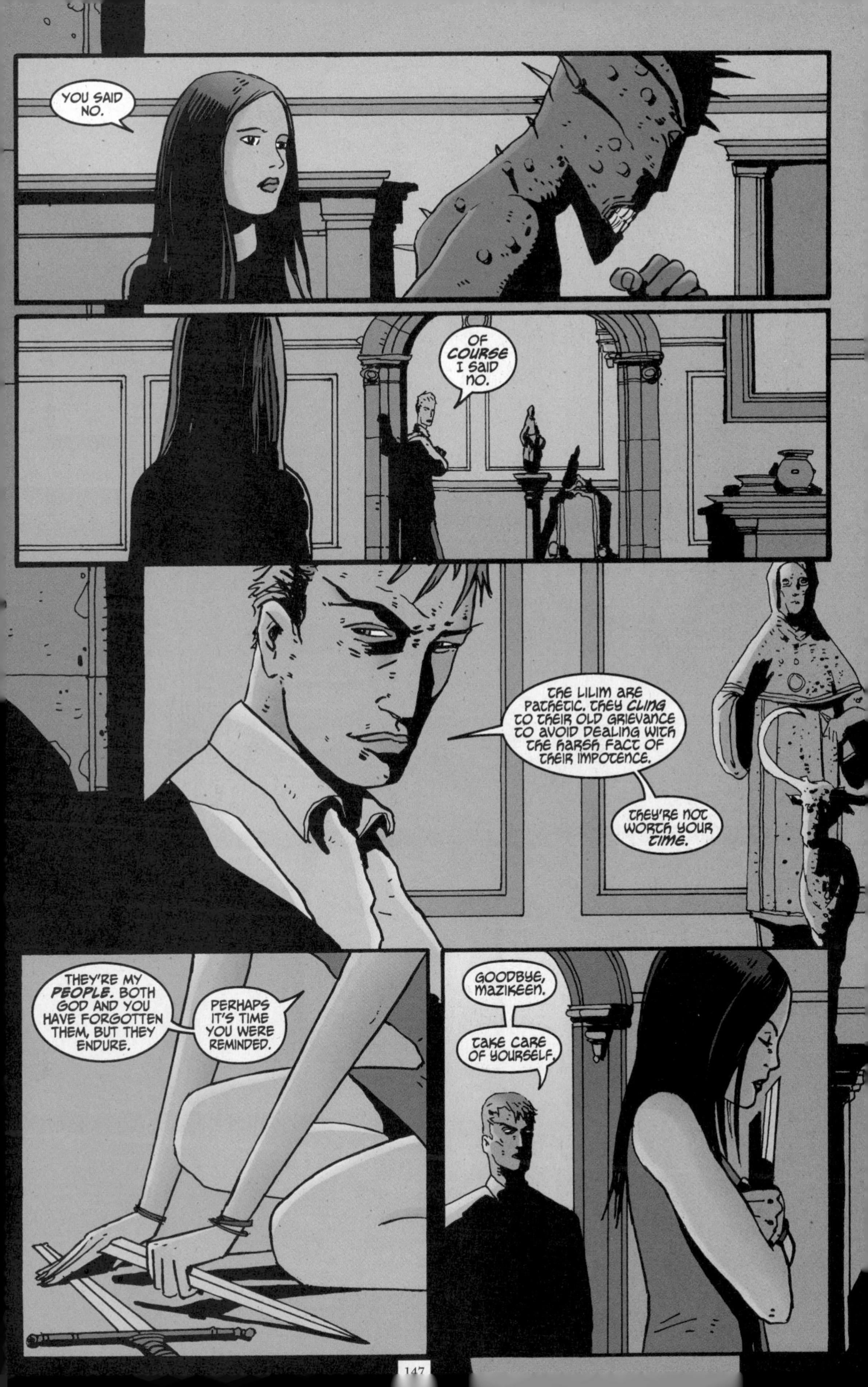
YOU SAID NO.
OF COURSE I SAID NO.
THE LILIM ARE PATHETIC. THEY CLING TO THEIR OLD GRIEVANCE TO AVOID DEALING WITH THE HARSH FACT OF THEIR IMPOTENCE.
THEY'RE NOT WORTH YOUR TIME.
THEY'RE MY PEOPLE. BOTH GOD AND YOU HAVE FORGOTTEN THEM, BUT THEY ENDURE.
PERHAPS IT'S TIME YOU WERE REMINDED.
GOODBYE, MAZIKEEN.
TAKE CARE OF YOURSELF.

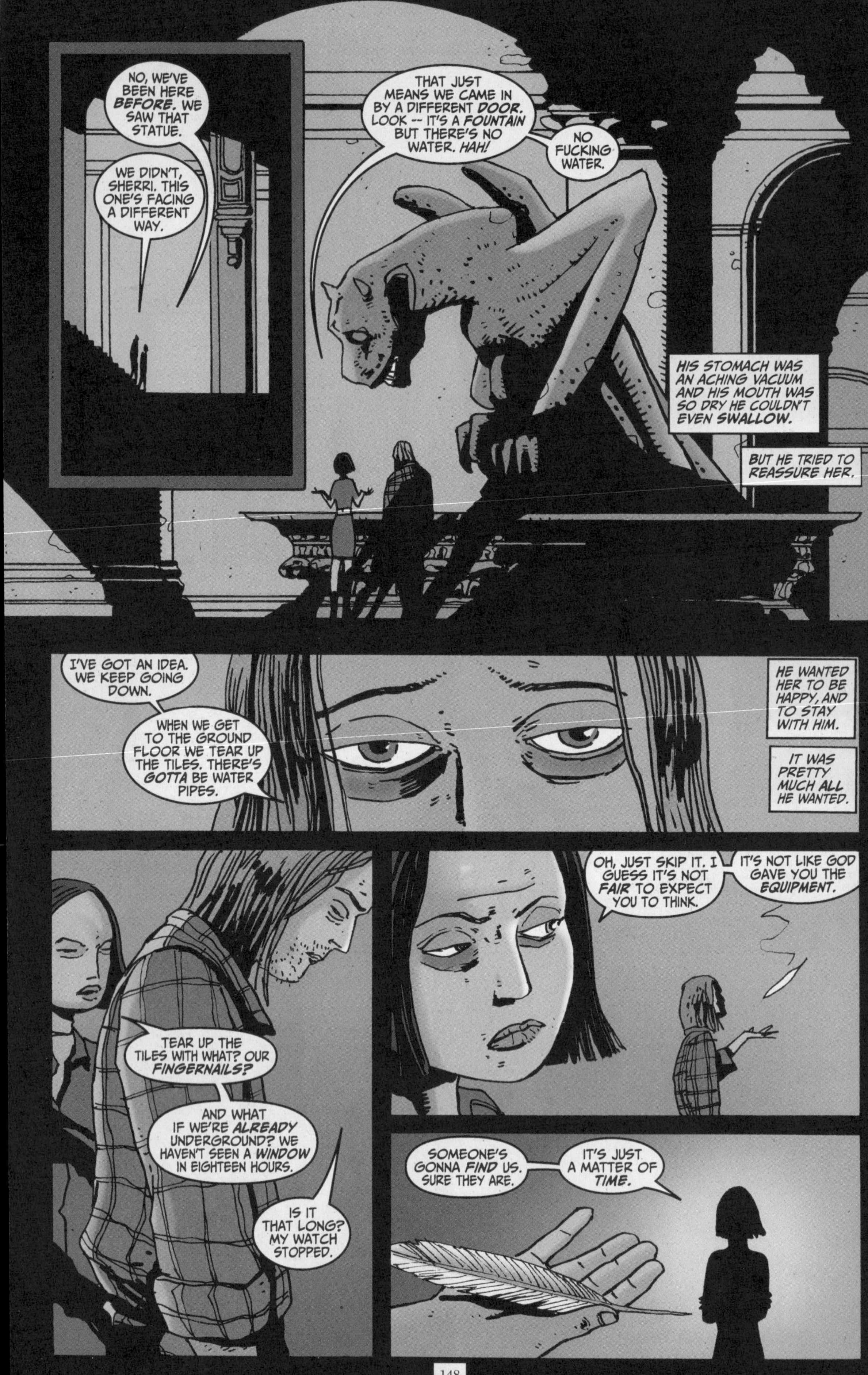
NO, WE'VE BEEN HERE BEFORE. WE SAW THAT STATUE.
WE DIDN'T, SHERRI. THIS ONE'S FACING A DIFFERENT WAY.
THAT JUST MEANS WE CAME IN BY A DIFFERENT DOOR. LOOK -- IT'S A FOUNTAIN BUT THERE'S NO WATER. HAH!
NO FUCKING WATER.
HIS STOMACH WAS AN ACHING VACUUM AND HIS MOUTH WAS SO DRY HE COULDN'T EVEN SWALLOW.
BUT HE TRIED TO REASSURE HER.
I'VE GOT AN IDEA. WE KEEP GOING DOWN.
WHEN WE GET TO THE GROUND FLOOR WE TEAR UP THE TILES. THERE'S GOTTA BE WATER PIPES.
HE WANTED HER TO BE HAPPY, AND TO STAY WITH HIM.
IT WAS PRETTY MUCH ALL HE WANTED.
TEAR UP THE TILES WITH WHAT? OUR FINGERNAILS?
AND WHAT IF WE'RE ALREADY UNDERGROUND? WE HAVEN'T SEEN A WINDOW IN EIGHTEEN HOURS.
IS IT THAT LONG? MY WATCH STOPPED.
OH, JUST SKIP IT. I GUESS IT'S NOT FAIR TO EXPECT YOU TO THINK.
IT'S NOT LIKE GOD GAVE YOU THE EQUIPMENT.
SOMEONE'S GONNA FIND US. SURE THEY ARE.
IT'S JUST A MATTER OF TIME.

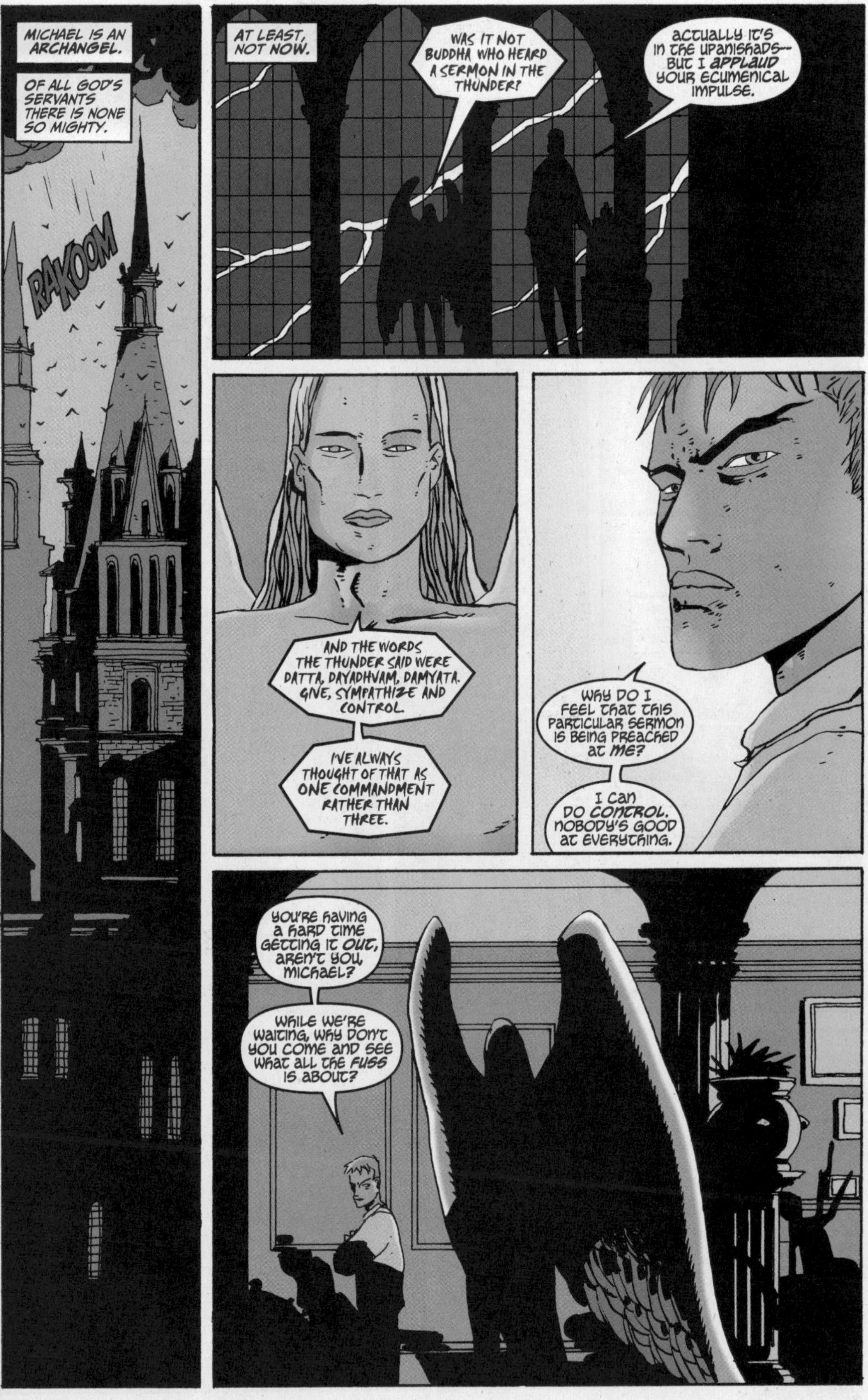

MICHAEL IS AN ARCHANGEL.
OF ALL GOD'S SERVANTS THERE IS NONE SO MIGHTY.
RAKOOM
AT LEAST, NOT NOW.
WAS IT NOT BUDDHA WHO HEARD A SERMON IN THE THUNDER?
ACTUALLY IT'S IN THE UPANISHADS--BUT I APPLAUD YOUR ECUMENICAL IMPULSE.
AND THE WORDS THE THUNDER SAID WERE DATTA, DAYADHVAM, DAMYATA. GIVE, SYMPATHIZE AND CONTROL.
I'VE ALWAYS THOUGHT OF THAT AS ONE COMMANDMENT RATHER THAN THREE.
WHY DO I FEEL THAT THIS PARTICULAR SERMON IS BEING PREACHED AT ME?
I CAN DO CONTROL. NOBODY'S GOOD AT EVERYTHING.
YOU'RE HAVING A HARD TIME GETTING IT OUT, AREN'T YOU, MICHAEL?
WHILE WE'RE WAITING, WHY DON'T YOU COME AND SEE WHAT ALL THE FUSS IS ABOUT?

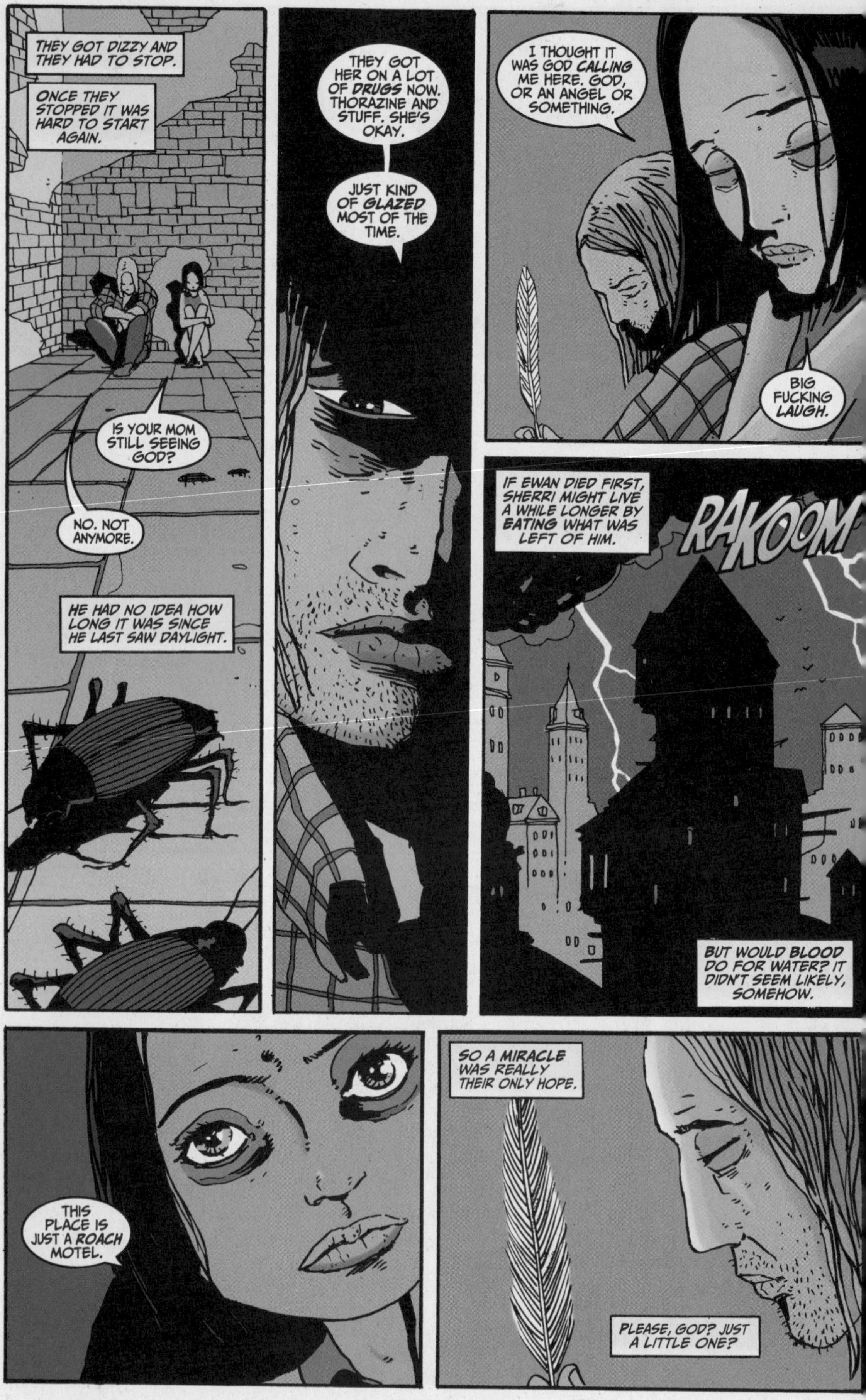
THEY GOT DIZZY AND THEY HAD TO STOP.
ONCE THEY STOPPED IT WAS HARD TO START AGAIN.
IS YOUR MOM STILL SEEING GOD?
NO. NOT ANYMORE.
HE HAD NO IDEA HOW LONG IT WAS SINCE HE LAST SAW DAYLIGHT.
THEY GOT HER ON A LOT OF DRUGS NOW. THORAZINE AND STUFF. SHE'S OKAY.
JUST KIND OF GLAZED MOST OF THE TIME.
I THOUGHT IT WAS GOD CALLING ME HERE. GOD, OR AN ANGEL OR SOMETHING.
BIG FUCKING LAUGH.
IF EWAN DIED FIRST, SHERRI MIGHT LIVE A WHILE LONGER BY EATING WHAT WAS LEFT OF HIM.
RAKOOM
BUT WOULD BLOOD DO FOR WATER? IT DIDN'T SEEM LIKELY, SOMEHOW.
THIS PLACE IS JUST A ROACH MOTEL.
SO A MIRACLE WAS REALLY THEIR ONLY HOPE.
PLEASE, GOD? JUST A LITTLE ONE?

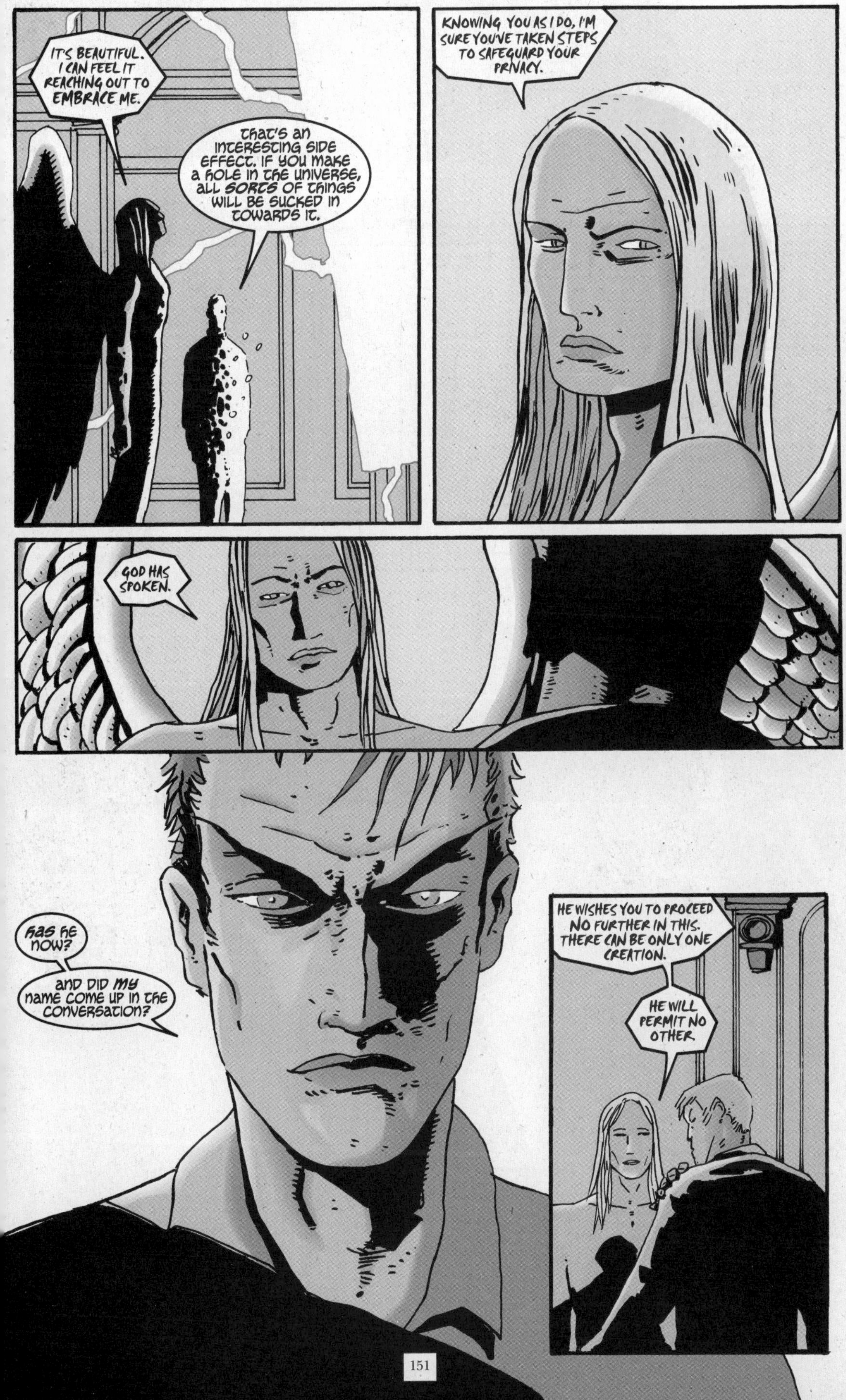
IT'S BEAUTIFUL. I CAN FEEL IT REACHING OUT TO EMBRACE ME.
THAT'S AN INTERESTING SIDE EFFECT. IF YOU MAKE A HOLE IN THE UNIVERSE, ALL SORTS OF THINGS WILL BE SUCKED IN TOWARDS IT.
KNOWING YOU AS I DO, I'M SURE YOU'VE TAKEN STEPS TO SAFEGUARD YOUR PRIVACY.
GOD HAS SPOKEN.
HAS HE NOW?
AND DID MY NAME COME UP IN THE CONVERSATION?
HE WISHES YOU TO PROCEED NO FURTHER IN THIS. THERE CAN BE ONLY ONE CREATION.
HE WILL PERMIT NO OTHER.

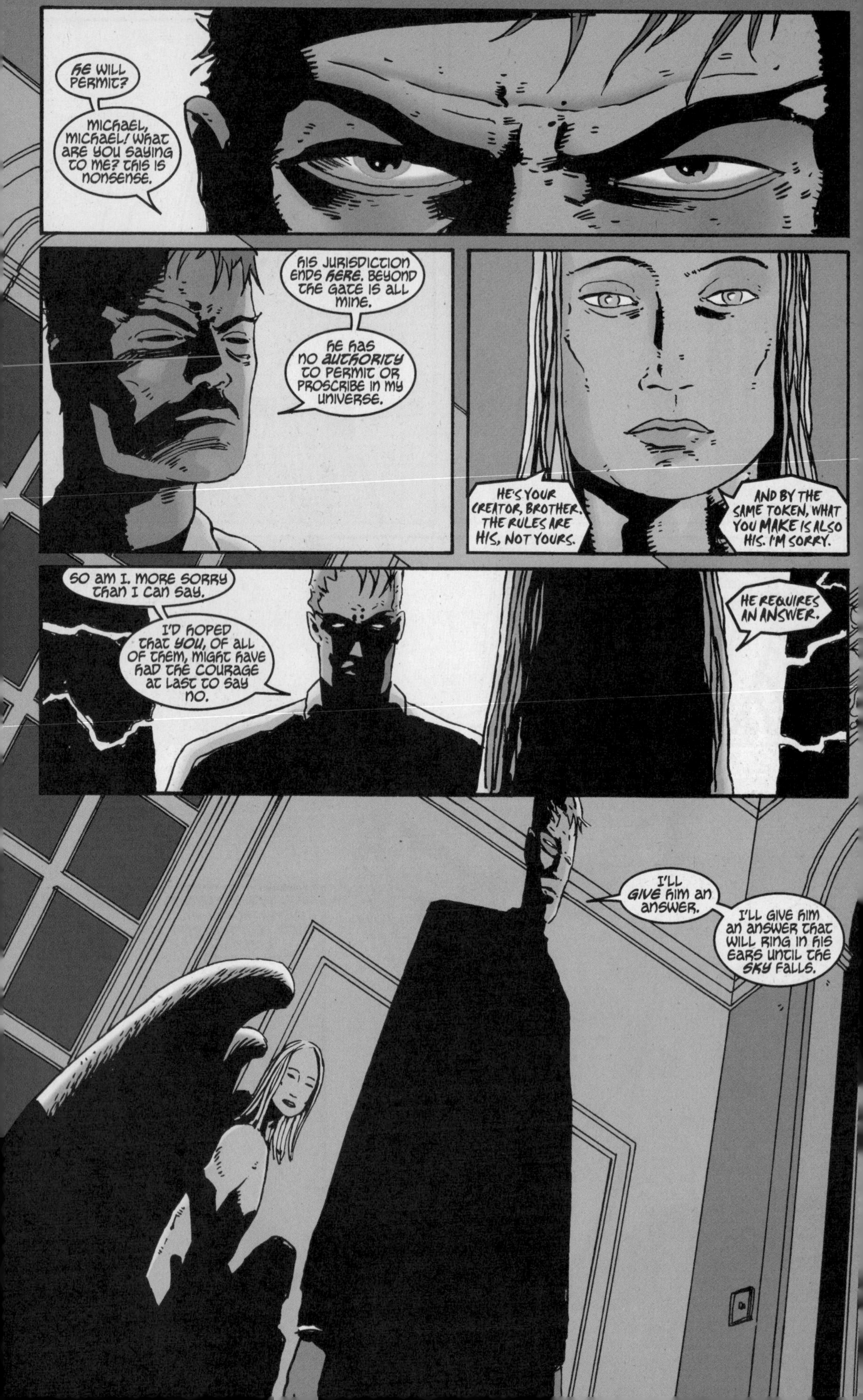

HE WILL PERMIT?
MICHAEL, MICHAEL! WHAT ARE YOU SAYING TO ME? THIS IS NONSENSE.
HIS JURISDICTION ENDS HERE. BEYOND THE GATE IS ALL MINE.
HE HAS NO AUTHORITY TO PERMIT OR PROSCRIBE IN MY UNIVERSE.
HE'S YOUR CREATOR, BROTHER. THE RULES ARE HIS, NOT YOURS.
AND BY THE SAME TOKEN, WHAT YOU MAKE IS ALSO HIS. I'M SORRY.
SO AM I. MORE SORRY THAN I CAN SAY.
I'D HOPED THAT YOU, OF ALL OF THEM, MIGHT HAVE HAD THE COURAGE AT LAST TO SAY NO.
HE REQUIRES AN ANSWER.
I'LL GIVE HIM AN ANSWER.
I'LL GIVE HIM AN ANSWER THAT WILL RING IN HIS EARS UNTIL THE SKY FALLS.

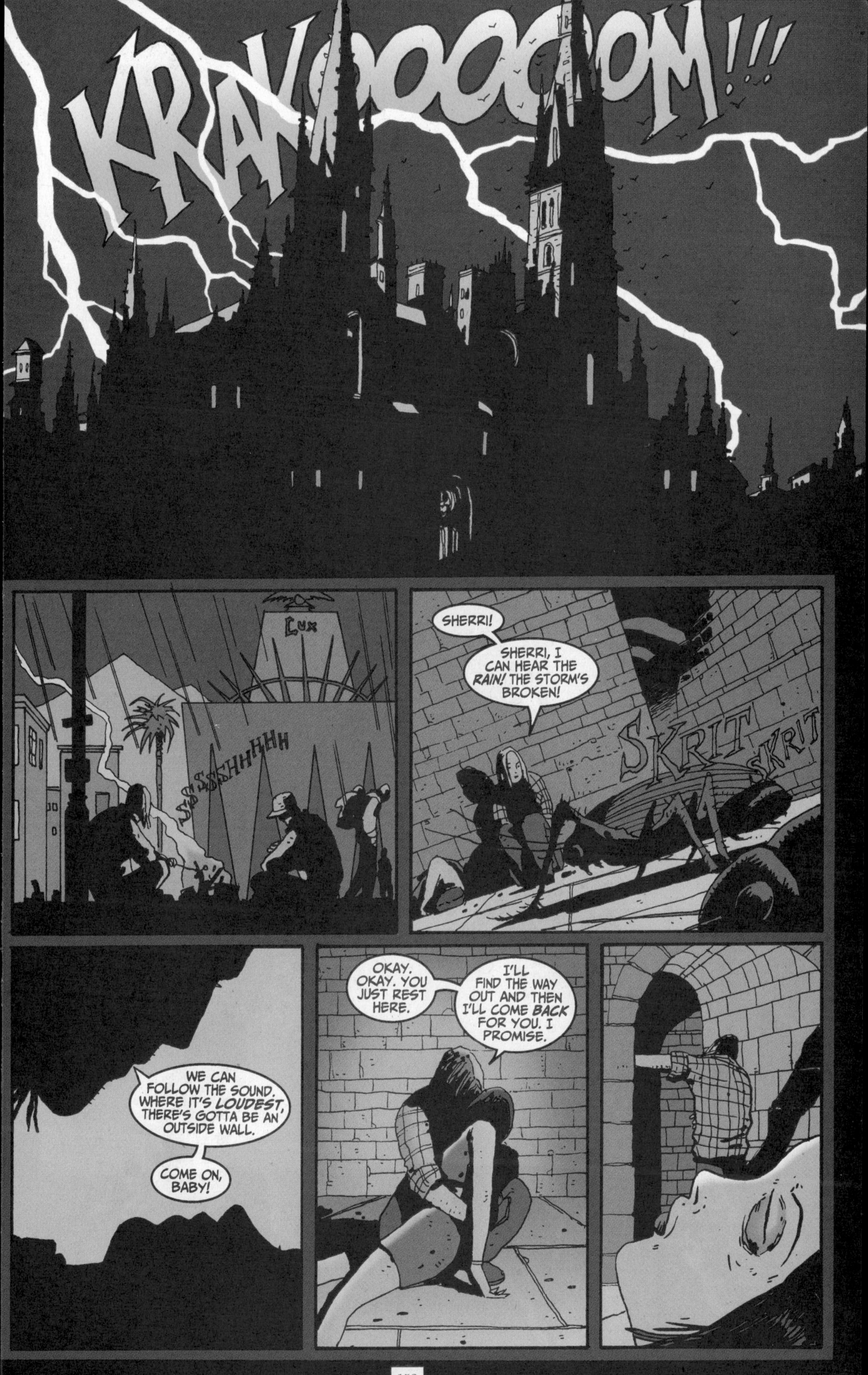
KRAKOOOOOM!!!
LUX
SSSSHHHHHH
SHERRI!
SHERRI, I CAN HEAR THE RAIN! THE STORM'S BROKEN!
SKRIT
SKRIT
WE CAN FOLLOW THE SOUND. WHERE IT'S LOUDEST, THERE'S GOTTA BE AN OUTSIDE WALL.
COME ON, BABY!
OKAY. OKAY. YOU JUST REST HERE.
I'LL FIND THE WAY OUT AND THEN I'LL COME BACK FOR YOU. I PROMISE.

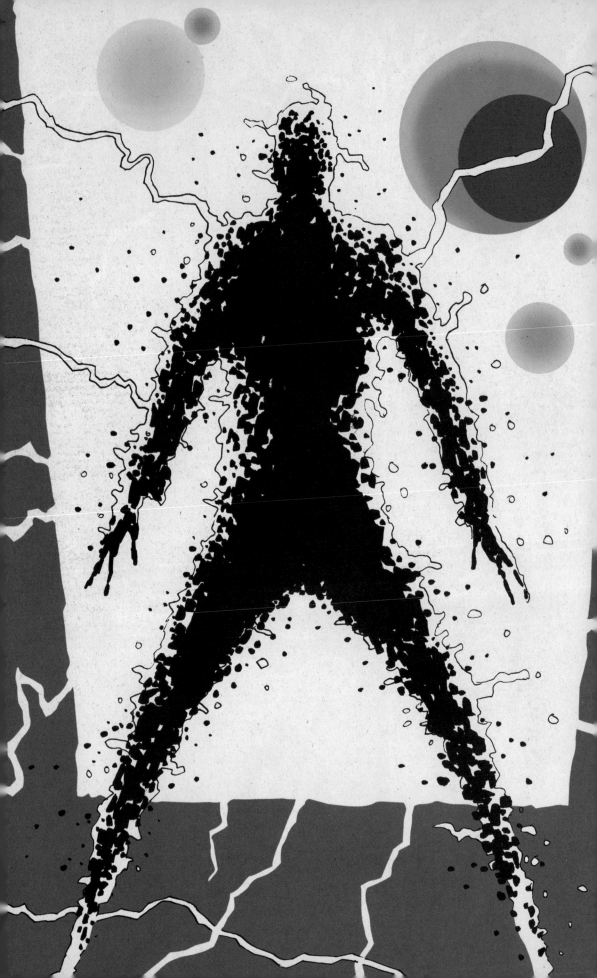

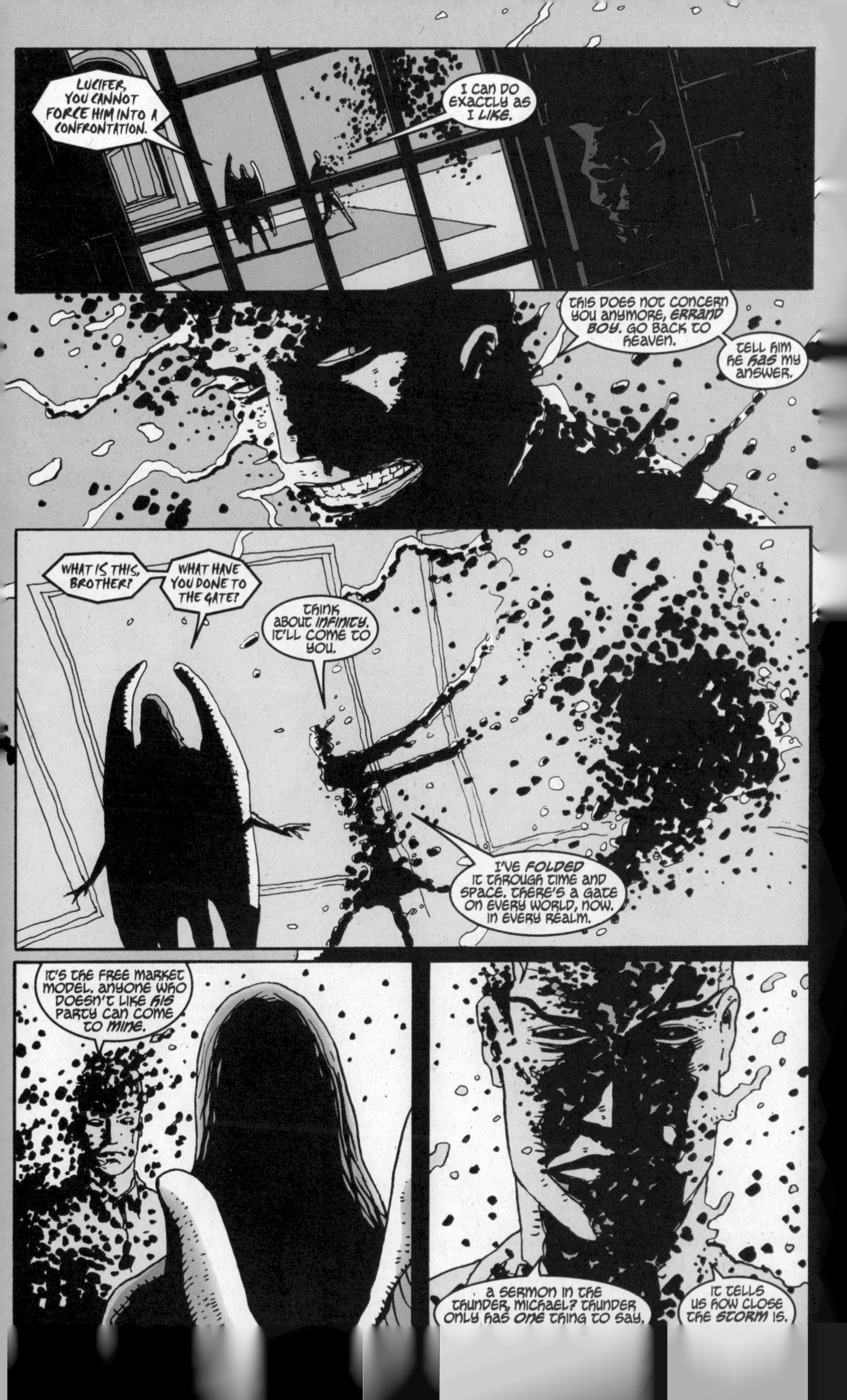
LUCIFER, YOU CANNOT FORCE HIM INTO A CONFRONTATION.
I CAN DO EXACTLY AS I LIKE.
THIS DOES NOT CONCERN YOU ANYMORE, ERRAND BOY. GO BACK TO HEAVEN.
TELL HIM HE HAS MY ANSWER.
WHAT IS THIS, BROTHER?
WHAT HAVE YOU DONE TO THE GATE?
THINK ABOUT INFINITY. IT'LL COME TO YOU.
I'VE FOLDED IT THROUGH TIME AND SPACE. THERE'S A GATE ON EVERY WORLD, NOW. IN EVERY REALM.
IT'S THE FREE MARKET MODEL. ANYONE WHO DOESN'T LIKE HIS PARTY CAN COME TO MINE.
A SERMON IN THE THUNDER, MICHAEL? THUNDER ONLY HAS ONE THING TO SAY.
IT TELLS US HOW CLOSE THE STORM IS.

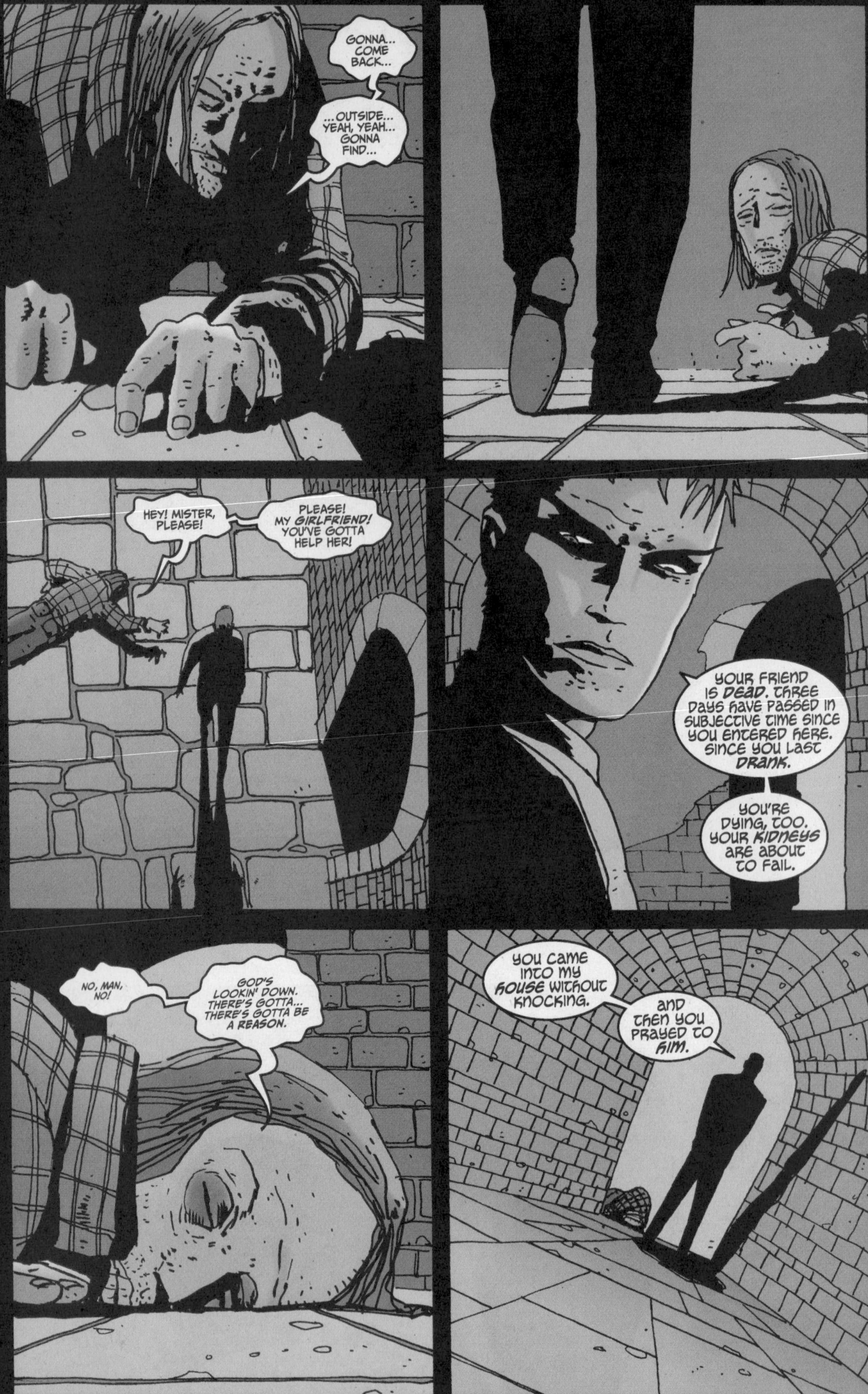
GONNA... COME BACK...
...OUTSIDE... YEAH, YEAH... GONNA FIND...
HEY! MISTER, PLEASE!
PLEASE! MY GIRLFRIEND! YOU'VE GOTTA HELP HER!
YOUR FRIEND IS DEAD. THREE DAYS HAVE PASSED IN SUBJECTIVE TIME SINCE YOU ENTERED HERE. SINCE YOU LAST DRANK.
YOU'RE DYING, TOO. YOUR KIDNEYS ARE ABOUT TO FAIL.
NO, MAN, NO!
GOD'S LOOKIN' DOWN. THERE'S GOTTA... THERE'S GOTTA BE A REASON.
YOU CAME INTO MY HOUSE WITHOUT KNOCKING.
AND THEN YOU PRAYED TO HIM.

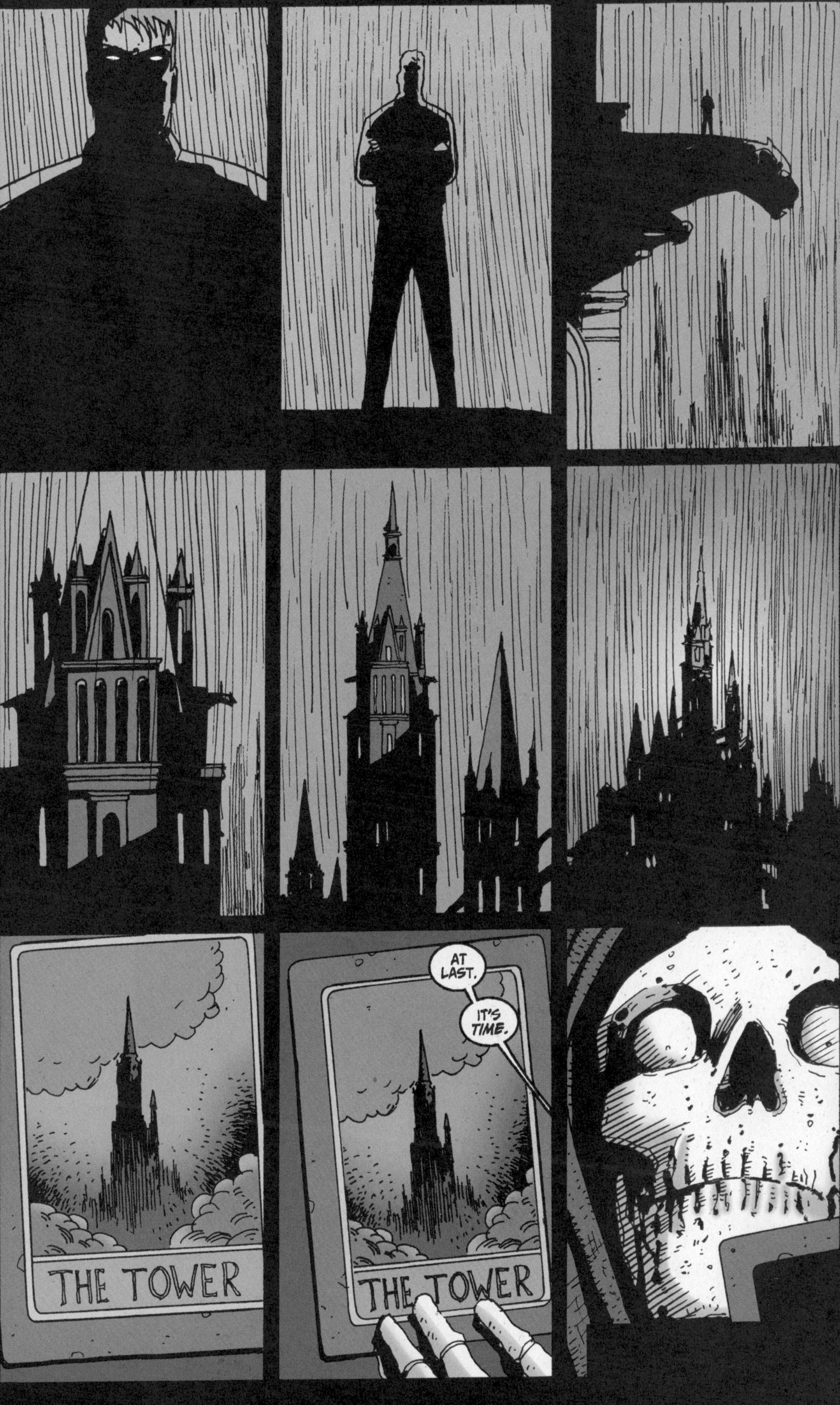
THE TOWER
AT LAST.
IT'S TIME.
THE TOWER

Cover by Duncan Fegredo

Cover by John Van Fleet

Covers by Christopher Moeller

Look for these other Vertigo books:

All Vertigo titles are Suggested for Mature Readers

To find more collected editions and monthly comic books from DC Comics,
call 1-888-COMIC BOOK for the nearest comics shop or go to your local book store.

Visit us at www.dccomics.com